D0593162

RAW MATERIALS
A Study of American Policy

SOME PUBLICATIONS OF THE

COUNCIL ON FOREIGN RELATIONS

FOREIGN AFFAIRS (quarterly), edited by Hamilton Fish Armstrong.

THE UNITED STATES IN WORLD AFFAIRS (annual). Volumes for 1931, 1932, and 1933, by Walter Lippmann and William O. Scroggs; for 1934–1935, 1936, 1937, 1938, 1939 and 1940, by Whitney H. Shepardson and William O. Scroggs; for 1945–1947, 1947–1948 and 1948–1949, by John C. Campbell; for 1949, 1950, 1951, 1952, 1953 and 1954, by Richard P. Stebbins; for 1955, by Hollis W. Barber; for 1956 and 1957, by Richard P. Stebbins.

DOCUMENTS ON AMERICAN FOREIGN RELATIONS (annual). Volume for 1952 edited by Clarence W. Baier and Richard P. Stebbins; for 1953 and 1954, edited by Peter V. Curl; for 1955, 1956 and 1957, edited by Paul E. Zinner.

POLITICAL HANDBOOK OF THE WORLD (annual), edited by Walter H. Mallory.

FOREIGN POLICY: THE NEXT PHASE, by Thomas K. Finletter.

NATO AND THE FUTURE OF EUROPE, by Ben T. Moore.

AFRICAN ECONOMIC DEVELOPMENT, by William A. Hance.

DEFENSE OF THE MIDDLE EAST: Problems of American Policy, by John C. Campbell.

INDIA AND AMERICA: A Study of Their Relations, by Phillips Talbot and S. L. Poplai.

JAPAN BETWEEN EAST AND WEST, by Hugh Borton, Jerome B. Cohen, William J. Jorden, Donald Keene, Paul F. Langer and C. Martin Wilbur.

NUCLEAR WEAPONS AND FOREIGN POLICY, by Henry A. Kissinger.

MOSCOW-PEKING AXIS: Strengths and Strains, by Howard L. Boorman, Alexander Eckstein, Philip E. Mosely and Benjamin Schwartz.

CLIMATE AND ECONOMIC DEVELOPMENT IN THE TROPICS, by Douglas H. K. Lee.

WHAT THE TARIFF MEANS TO AMERICAN INDUSTRIES, by Percy W. Bidwell.

UNITED STATES SHIPPING POLICY, by Wytze Gorter.

RUSSIA AND AMERICA: Dangers and Prospects, by Henry L. Roberts.

STERLING: Its Meaning in World Finance, by Judd Polk.

KOREA: A Study of U. S. Policy in the United Nations, by Leland M. Goodrich.

FOREIGN AFFAIRS BIBLIOGRAPHY, 1942–1952, by Henry L. Roberts.

AMERICAN AGENCIES INTERESTED IN INTERNATIONAL AFFAIRS, compiled by Ruth Savord and Donald Wasson.

JAPANESE AND AMERICANS: A Century of Cultural Relations, by Robert S. Schwantes.

THE FUTURE OF UNDERDEVELOPED COUNTRIES: Political Implications of Economic Development, by Eugene Staley.

THE UNDECLARED WAR, 1940–1941, by William L. Langer and S. Everett Gleason.

THE CHALLENGE TO ISOLATION, 1937–1940, by William L. Langer and S. Everett Gleason.

MIDDLE EAST DILEMMAS: The Background of United States Policy, by J. C. Hurewitz.

BRITAIN AND THE UNITED STATES: Problems in Cooperation, a joint report prepared by Henry L. Roberts and Paul A. Wilson.

TRADE AND PAYMENTS IN WESTERN EUROPE: A Study in Economic Cooperation, 1947–1951, by William Diebold, Jr.

PUBLIC OPINION AND FOREIGN POLICY, by Lester Markel and Others.

THE FOREIGN AFFAIRS READER, edited by Hamilton Fish Armstrong.

THE STUDY OF INTERNATIONAL RELATIONS IN AMERICAN COLLEGES AND UNIVERSITIES, by Grayson Kirk.

SURVEY OF AMERICAN FOREIGN RELATIONS (in four volumes, 1928–1931), prepared under the direction of Charles P. Howland.

RAW MATERIALS

A Study of American Policy

by

PERCY W. BIDWELL

Published for the
COUNCIL ON FOREIGN RELATIONS
by
HARPER & BROTHERS
New York
1958

The Council on Foreign Relations is a non-profit institution devoted to study of the international aspects of American political, economic and strategic problems. It takes no stand, expressed or implied, on American policy.

The authors of books published under the auspices of the Council are responsible for their statements of fact and expressions of opinion. The Council is responsible only for determining that they should be presented to the public.

RAW MATERIALS: A STUDY OF AMERICAN POLICY

For information, address Council on Foreign Relations, 58 East 68th Street, New York 21

FIRST EDITION

The Colonial Press Inc., Clinton, Mass.

Library of Congress catalog card number: LC 58-11388

Published in Great Britain and the British Commonwealth, excluding Canada, by London: Oxford University Press

COUNCIL ON FOREIGN RELATIONS

PREFACE

THE PURPOSES of this book are to examine the more important measures of United States policy which affect the supply of materials for American industries and to suggest changes in national policies which will make them better adapted to the technological advances and changes in international relations which may be expected in the immediate future.

The first chapter discusses the objectives of national policy. Chapters 2 and 3 describe the principal legislative and executive measures affecting industrial materials, with particular attention to developments since the end of World War II. A series of case studies, Chapters 4 to 10, show the specific application of policy to a number of raw materials. In the concluding chapter, I have summarized the accomplishments and failures of national policy and suggested measures of reform.

During the course of the research on which the book is based, the author derived much profit from his association with a study group of Council members who read various chapters in draft form and discussed them in a series of meetings, October 1956 to May 1957. The members of the group were:

LANGBOURNE M. WILLIAMS, *Chairman*—Freeport Sulphur Company
CHARLES H. BEHRE, JR.—Columbia University
ARTHUR H. BUNKER—American Metal Climax, Inc.
WILLIAM A. M. BURDEN—William A. M. Burden Company
IMRIE DE VEGH—de Vegh & Company
WILLIAM DIEBOLD, JR.—Council on Foreign Relations
MANLY FLEISCHMANN—Fleischmann, Jaeckle, Stokes & Hitchcock
ISAIAH FRANK—U. S. Department of State

HEMAN GREENWOOD—Carrier International, Ltd.
WILLEM HOLST—Standard Vacuum Oil Company
DEXTER M. KEEZER—McGraw-Hill Publishing Company, Inc.
CHARLES H. KENDALL—Office of Defense Mobilization
CHARLES P. KINDLEBERGER—Massachusetts Institute of Technology
WALTER J. LEVY—Economist
K. C. LI—Wah Chang Corporation
SHAW LIVERMORE—Economist
ISADOR LUBIN—Department of Labor, State of New York
J. MORDEN MURPHY—Bankers Trust Company
A. L. NICKERSON—Socony Mobil Oil Company, Inc.
HOWARD S. PIQUET—U. S. Library of Congress
JUDD POLK—California Texas Oil Company, Ltd.
MORRIS S. ROSENTHAL—Foreign trade consultant
NATHANIEL SAMUELS—Kuhn, Loeb & Company
WILLARD L. THORP—Amherst College
RAYMOND VERNON—Regional Plan Association
JEAN VUILLEQUEZ—American Metal Climax, Inc.
FELIX E. WORMSER—U. S. Department of the Interior

In addition, a number of persons particularly conversant with the subject matter were invited to attend the meetings. Their contributions of expert knowledge and opinion were extremely valuable.

Field work was undertaken in April and May 1957. During these months the author discussed the subject matter of the book with Committees on Foreign Relations, groups affiliated with the Council, in Wichita, Boise, Salt Lake City, Denver, Tulsa and Little Rock. Introductions supplied by Committee members made possible also many helpful interviews with oil producers and oil geologists, producers of nonferrous metals and sheep ranchers.

In the Appendix I have listed the persons who were particularly helpful to me in the field, as well as those who came to the meetings of the study group in New York. To all I extend my sincere thanks for their generous assistance. It should be understood that neither they nor the members of the study group are in any way responsible for the accuracy of the facts presented in the book or for the opinions and judgments expressed by the author.

I am deeply indebted to the Council's Committee on Studies for entrusting this research project to my direction. Thanks are due also to Walter H. Mallory, George S. Franklin, Jr., Philip E. Mosely, William Diebold, Jr., John C. Campbell, and other members of the Council's administrative and research staff for helpful comment and expert advice. I am grateful to Ruth Savord, the Council's librarian, and to members of her staff for help in obtaining information and in locating published material. William D. Schlutow drew the charts. Bernice Tell and Aaron Cohen typed the manuscript, and Mrs. Tell also assisted in research. In this field Helena Stalson had major responsibility; to her I am indebted for invaluable help throughout the course of the project.

To my wife I owe more than can easily be expressed for her encouragement and for her confidence in the success of the enterprise.

PERCY W. BIDWELL

New York
June 1958

CONTENTS

Tables

CHARTS

RAW MATERIALS

A Study of American Policy

Chapter 1

PROBLEMS OF NATIONAL POLICY

THE DOMINANT fact which emerges from all discussions of the raw materials position of the United States is the nation's increasing dependence on foreign sources of supply. Less than 50 years ago this country produced within its own borders practically all of the basic materials required by its industries and in addition had some surpluses for export. The transition from a position of relative self-sufficiency in industrial materials[1] to that of the world's greatest importing nation deserves to be regarded as a major event in modern economic history. It marks the transformation of the United States from an underdeveloped to a highly developed industrial economy. Today, for the seemingly insatiable demands of our manufacturing industries, we use between 35 and 40 percent of the Free World's output of basic materials. Our purchases from abroad each year put at the disposal of foreign countries, most of them in the category known as "underdeveloped," about $6 billion. Their exports to this country furnish in many cases a substantial share of government revenues and of dollar exchange. Thus we have become involved with them in a condition of interdependence which, while it raises difficult questions of policy, is fraught with great potential benefits both to us and to them.

In the decade 1901-1910, foreign trade in crude materials and semimanufactured products showed an *export* balance of $100 million in total export and import transactions in these commodities of $1,300 million. Forty years later, the 5-year average 1951-1955 showed an *import* balance of

[1] The phrases, raw materials, industrial materials, basic materials, and primary commodities, used synonymously in this study refer to the Department of Commerce classifications, crude materials and semimanufactures. They do not include foodstuffs.

$1,650 million in total trade of $9,100 million. (See Table 1 and Chart A.)

Table 1

U. S. TRADE IN CRUDE MATERIALS AND SEMIMANUFACTURES

(in millions of dollars)

	1901–1910	1926–1930	1936–1940	1951–1955	1956
		(annual averages)			
Crude materials					
Exports	493	1,144	603	1,977	2,511
Imports	395	1,484	807	2,835	3,075
Balance[a]	+98	−340	−204	−858	−564
Semimanufactures					
Exports	205	663	611	1,767	2,758
Imports	201	762	511	2,558	3,002
Balance[a]	+4	−99	+100	−791	−244
Total, both groups					
Exports	698	1,807	1,214	3,744	5,269
Imports	596	2,246	1,318	5,393	6,077
Balance[a]	+102	−439	−104	−1,649	−808

[a] (+) = export balance; (−) = import balance.
Source: U. S. Bureau of the Census

In the late 1930's, just before World War II began in Europe, we were still, on the average, exporting more crude petroleum and copper than we imported. But already we were buying from abroad about a fifth of our total supply of clothing wool, between two and three percent of our iron ore, six percent of our zinc and 13 percent of fluorspar, 40 percent of tungsten, more than half of our bauxite. All of our natural rubber and nickel and practically all of our manganese came from abroad. (See Table 2 and Chart B.)

The Drift Away from Self-Sufficiency

The causes of the revolutionary change in our raw materials position are not far to seek. The rapid industrial expansion of the country after 1900 drained our natural mineral resources at an extraordinary rate. It has been estimated that the consumption of all basic materials in the 50 years 1900-1950 was equal to the accumulated con-

CHART A

U. S. TRADE IN CRUDE MATERIALS AND SEMIMANUFACTURES
(in millions of dollars)

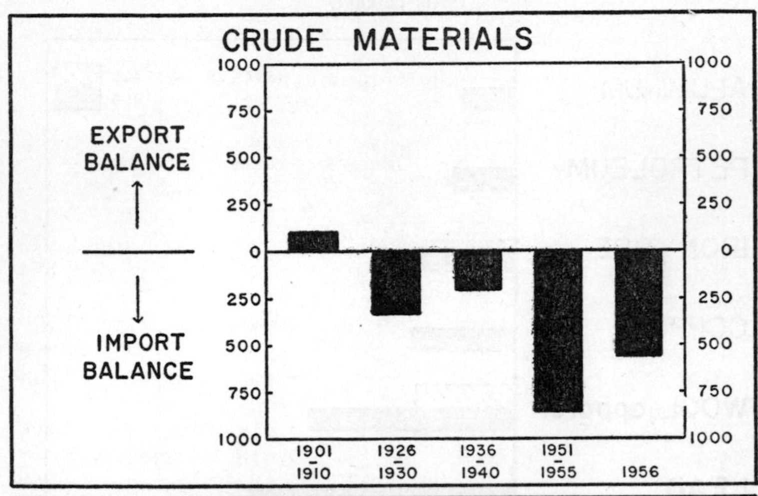

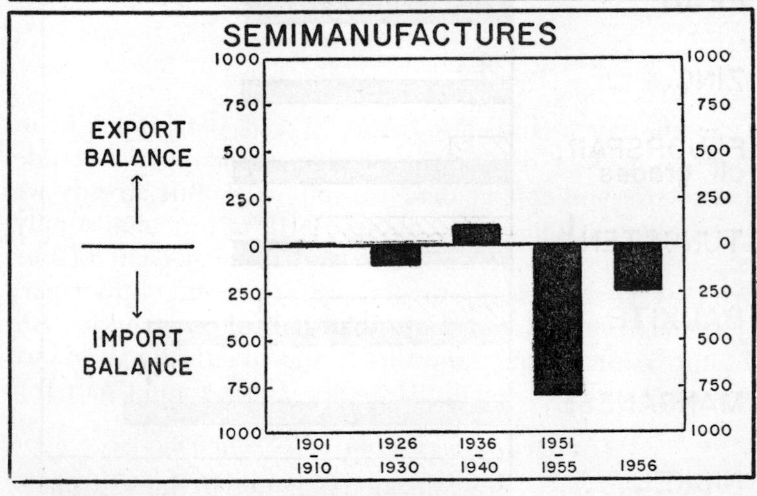

Source: Table 1

CHART B

CERTAIN INDUSTRIAL MATERIALS: RATIO OF NET IMPORTS TO U. S. SUPPLY,[a] 1937-39, 1956
(in percent)

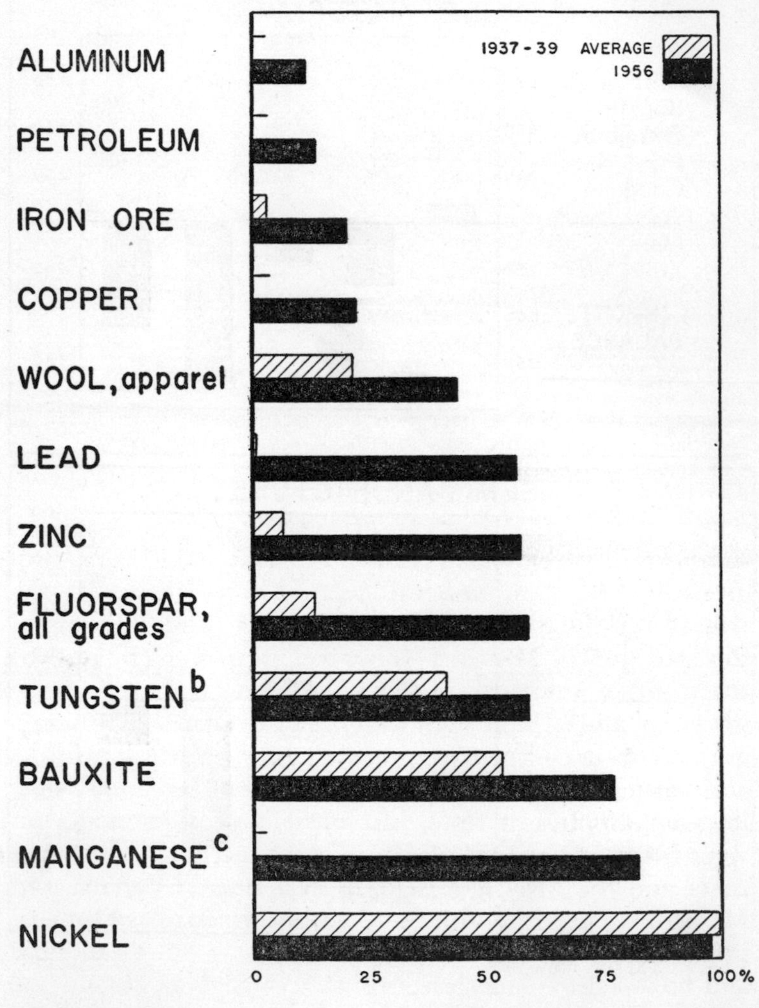

[a] Supply = Production + Imports — Exports. Scrap and other reclaimed material have been omitted.
[b] Excluding ferrotungsten.
[c] Excluding ferromanganese.
Source: Table 2

Table 2

CERTAIN INDUSTRIAL MATERIALS: RATIO OF NET IMPORTS TO U. S. SUPPLY,[a] 1937-39, 1956

(in percent)

	1937–39 (average)	*1956*
Aluminum	0	11.3
Bauxite	53.0	78.1
Petroleum	0	13.5
Iron ore	2.6	20.3
Copper	0	22.4
Wool, apparel	21.9	43.9
Lead	0.2	56.5
Zinc	6.3	57.8
Fluorspar, all grades	13.4	59.5
Tungsten[b]	41.8	59.7
Manganese[c]	n.a.	82.7
Nickel	99.2	95.5

[a] Supply = Production + Imports − Exports. Scrap and other reclaimed material have been omitted.
[b] Excluding ferrotungsten.
[c] Excluding ferromanganese.
Source: U. S. Bureau of Mines, U. S. Bureau of the Census

sumption of all previous years of our national history. Progressively, the best mineral deposits were depleted: the iron ore of the Mesabi range, the copper of Michigan and the lead ores of Missouri. Moreover, as settlement pushed the frontier westward, primary industries had to compete for labor and capital with other employments. The sheep grazers had to compete for grazing land with wheat growers and cattlemen. While this was happening at home, new low-cost supplies of wool, oil, metals and other materials were becoming available in foreign countries: oil in Venezuela and the Middle East, lead and zinc in Canada and Mexico, copper in South America and in Africa. Much of the development abroad was undertaken by American firms and financed by American capital. World War II, and the rearmament boom which began in 1949, accelerated the rising demand for industrial materials throughout the Free World. Long-term contracts made by the U. S. government with both domestic and foreign suppliers promoted the expansion of production at home and abroad. For a number of years large government purchases for stockpiling accelerated imports of strategic materials.

A Department of Commerce study has classified 97 raw materials and semimanufactured commodities imported in 1956 according to the "degree of dependency," i.e., according to the percentage ratio of imports to new supply. The results are shown below.

Class	*Ratio of imports to new supply on a quantity basis* (percent)	*Number of commodities*	*Value of imports, 1956* (million $)
A	80 to 100	39	1,944.8
B	50 to 79	15	1,172.7
C	10 to 49	20	2,743.3
D	Less than 10	23	708.4
	Total	97	6,569.2

Source: U. S. Bureau of Foreign Commerce, *Contribution of Imports to U. S. Raw Material Supplies, 1956,* by Muriel S. Moore, World Trade Information Service, pt. 3, no. 57-50 (Washington: GPO, 1957). Only commodities imported to the value of $5 million or more were included.

In the top classification were tin, nickel, manganese, chrome, natural rubber, cork, coconut oil and other vegetable oils, tanning materials, jute and burlap, carpet wool, raw silk, industrial diamonds. Group B included newsprint, bauxite, fluorspar, lead, mercury, tungsten and zinc. Our dependency was less than 50 percent for apparel wool, iron ore, leather, lumber, petroleum.

The principal industrial materials purchased abroad in 1956 are shown in Table 3. Taken together, the commodities listed made up over 80 percent by value of all imports of crude materials and semimanufactures. The outstanding importance of minerals and metals is obvious. In total value they accounted for more than half of all imported crude and semimanufactured materials.

Sources of Imports

Analysis of imports according to the sources of supply discloses great reliance on countries in the Western Hemisphere, and particularly on Canada and Mexico. In addi-

Table 3

U. S. IMPORTS OF INDUSTRIAL MATERIALS, 1956: COMMODITIES VALUED AT MORE THAN $50 MILLION

(in millions of dollars)

Commodity	Value
Petroleum and nonmetallic minerals:	
Crude petroleum	829
Petroleum products	387
Diamonds	235
Asbestos	62
Nonferrous ores and metals:	
Copper	450
Nickel	188
Tin	178
Bauxite and aluminum	176
Lead	141
Zinc	118
Platinum group metals	58
Ferrous and ferroalloying ores and metals:	
Iron ore and concentrates	250
Manganese ore and alloys	101
Chrome ore and alloys	61
Tungsten ore and metal	60
Crude rubber:	399
Wood and paper:	
Newsprint	688
Lumber and logs	335
Woodpulp and pulpwood	334
Plywood and veneers	72
Fibers and semimanufactures:	
Raw wool and semimanufactures	293
Raw jute, burlaps and semimanufactures	111
Hides and furs:	
Furs	81
Hides and skins	66
Fertilizer materials:	102
Total of items listed:	5,773
Total imports of industrial materials[a]*:*	6,918

[a] Including the Department of Commerce classifications, crude materials and semimanufactures and, in addition, three items which the Department classifies as finished manufactures, viz., jute burlaps, newsprint and plywood and veneers.
Source: U. S. Bureau of the Census

tion to the metals which came to the United States directly from the producing countries, there were large imports of metals refined in Western Europe from ores and concentrates produced elsewhere. These included antimony, bismuth, cadmium, cobalt, columbium, mercury and the platinum group of metals. (See Table A in the Appendix.)

The Western Hemisphere in 1956 furnished *directly* more than 80 percent of all imports of

- aluminum
- bauxite
- copper
- iron ore
- nickel
- vanadium
- zinc

In addition the Hemisphere supplied more than half of the imports of

fluorspar	antimony
lead	bismuth
petroleum	cadmium
tungsten	titanium ore (ilmenite)

Imports from Canada supplied, in round numbers, the following proportions of the materials listed:

	Percent of total imports, 1956		*Percent of total imports, 1956*
Aluminum	85	Zinc	36
Nickel	80	Copper	20
Titanium ore (ilmenite)	55	Petroleum	12
Iron	45	Lead	10
		Tungsten	8

Mexico's contribution to the United States supply of minerals and metals was:

	Percent of total imports, 1956		*Percent of total imports, 1956*
Fluorspar	65	Lead	18
Antimony	34	Bismuth	14
Cadmium	31	Copper	10
Zinc	30	Manganese	8
Mercury	24		

In the Eastern Hemisphere, the continent of Africa was the leading source of supply for metals, particularly the newer metals which are of critical importance in electronics and in alloys capable of withstanding high temperatures. From the African continent the United States imported:

	Percent of total imports, 1956		*Percent of total imports, 1956*
Tantalum	79	Manganese	42
Columbium	78	Chrome	40
Cobalt	76	Beryl	31

Australia contributed almost our entire supply from foreign sources of zirconium and rutile, 40 percent of apparel wool, and 25 percent of lead. Southeast Asia was important as a source of tin, chrome and natural rubber. India supplied beryl, ilmenite ore and manganese. Our principal imports from the Middle East were petroleum, 30 percent of our total imports; chrome, 27 percent; and carpet wool, 12 percent.

Sources of supply outside the Western Hemisphere have attained increasing importance in postwar years. The rare metals, columbium and tantalum, used in the production of jet engines and gas turbines, come principally from the African continent. Yugoslavia and Australia supply substantial amounts of lead. Southeast Asia furnishes wool, tungsten and rubber.

The U. S. Market for Industrial Materials

Our dependence on foreign countries for supplies is matched by their dependence on our markets. Canada in 1955 found in the United States a market for all of its exports of crude petroleum, more than 75 percent of all exports of newsprint, wood pulp and iron ore, and between 50 and 75 percent of nickel, asbestos and zinc exports.

The United States uses about 80 percent of the copper output of all the Latin American republics, 70 percent of their lead and zinc and 17 percent of their crude oil. More than one-third of Argentina's wool exports were sold in the United States, 93 percent of Brazil's manganese exports and 42 percent of its iron ore. Bolivia in 1955 sent to the United States 40 percent of its tin and more than 90 percent of its exports of lead, zinc, copper and antimony ores. Chile in 1954 shipped to U. S. markets 44 percent of its exports of copper, 43 percent of its nitrates and 93 percent of its iron ore. The United States furnishes a market for 85 percent of Mexico's oil exports and 81 percent of its exports of copper. Peru sent more than 50 percent of all its exports of lead, copper, zinc, iron ore and alpaca wool. Uruguay markets about one-fourth of all its wool exports in the United States, and Venezuela over one-third of its oil.

In the Eastern Hemisphere, India finds a market in the United States for about half its exports of jute burlaps and approximately 40 percent of its manganese, mica and wool. Indonesia marketed in the United States, in 1955, 28 percent of its rubber, and Malaya, 18 percent. (See Table B in the Appendix.)

Problems of National Policy

The preceding pages have presented a background of fact showing this country's great and increasing dependence on foreign countries for its supplies of industrial materials. We turn now to the consideration of the significance of these facts in terms of national policy. The over-all objective of a national materials policy for the United States, according to the Paley Commission, should be *"to insure an adequate and dependable flow of materials at the lowest cost consistent with national security and with the welfare of friendly nations."*[2] This terse statement bristles with conflicts. Take oil, for example. The flow of oil from Venezuela and the Middle East into the United States might be adequate, but can it be called dependable, in view of the possible activity of hostile submarines? Again, the domestic oil supply over the next 20 or 25 years, as far as we can see now, will be dependable, and production might be stepped up so that, in physical terms, it would be adequate. But it will cost more per barrel than oil from more productive foreign wells. Hence exclusive reliance on domestic supplies would violate the principle of minimum real cost.

Or, take the requirement that in our national materials policy we take account of the welfare of friendly nations. We should like to be able to count the Middle Eastern oil-supplying countries, Iraq, Saudi Arabia and others, in that category. They are among the underdeveloped countries to which we have pledged our economic aid. It seems logical, therefore, that we should continue, and expand, our purchases of their oil. But military authorities warn that too great dependence on an overseas source of an essential fuel might endanger national security. Furthermore, any attempt to expand imports of oil would run headlong against the opposition of domestic oil producers.

[2] President's Materials Policy Commission, *Resources for Freedom* (Washington: GPO, 1952), v. 1, *Foundations for Growth and Security*, p. 3.

People will disagree about the reasons for our concern, as a nation, for "the welfare of friendly nations." Are our motives only self-seeking? Are we interested in raising standards of living in the underdeveloped countries merely as a way of building a bulwark against Russian penetration and thus safeguarding our own security? Or have we their welfare at heart regardless of possible benefits to ourselves? When materials are in short supply, should we take account, also, of the interests of industrial nations, for example, in Western Europe? Should we restrict our imports of materials in order that their industries may not have to shut down? Again, shall we take such action only if we think our own interests are endangered?

Raw Materials and Defense

Our increasing reliance on foreign sources of supply for strategic materials raises questions of national security. The over-all consumption in wartime is not, contrary to popular belief, much larger than the amounts which would be consumed in peacetime "at equivalent levels of employment and production." But the war effort involves much larger requirements for particular materials. The consumption in World War II of copper, lead and zinc reached levels higher than in any earlier year.

Now the jet engine, the gas turbine and the nuclear reactors are changing the character of military demand. Copper, lead and zinc will become relatively less important, and the newer high-temperature metals, nickel, columbium, tungsten, cobalt and chromium, more so.

The advent of the gas turbine and jets for fighter aircraft, and the possible development for commercial flying and later for automobiles, has accentuated the need for materials to withstand high temperature and stress. One reason why it has taken so long to develop the gas turbine commercially is that there were no materials that could withstand red heat and at the same time take the stress of the centrifugal forces generated by 20,000 revolutions per minute. Since in the gas turbine the higher the temperature, the greater the efficiency, there is urgent need for metals, ceramics, or other substances that can operate under stress in the range above 2,000 degrees Fahrenheit.

There are also requirements for materials for carrying out

nuclear reactions, many of which occur at high temperatures. Some of these materials must have a low capacity for neutron absorption as well. Thus, the need for higher and even higher temperature resistance becomes one of our most critical problems.[3]

Defense authorities have designated some 60-odd[4] industrial materials as strategic and critical. Taken together, the 1955 imports of these materials were valued at $2,320 million, which was 41 percent of imports of all industrial materials in that year. A classification of strategic materials according to the degree of dependency on imports is shown below:

Ratio of imports to new supply (quantity basis) (percent)	*Number of materials*	*Value of imports, 1955* (million $)
80–100	38	$1,352
60–79	6	54
40–59	8	401
20–39	3	417
Less than 20	7	95
		$2,320

Source: U. S. Bureau of the Census, U. S. Bureau of Mines

Imports of strategic materials raise vital questions of national policy. Is it wise, where a choice exists, to depend on sources of supply outside the country, in regions beyond our political jurisdiction? If such dependence is unwise, should not our policy aim to expand domestic production of these materials so as to provide a greater degree of na-

[3] *Resources for Freedom,* cited, v. 4, *The Promise of Technology,* p. 11.

A modern jet engine uses the following amounts of critical materials:

	Pounds
Tungsten	80–100
Columbium	10–12
Nickel	1,300–1,600
Chromium	2,500–2,800
Molybdenum	90–100
Cobalt	30–40
Total critical materials	4,000–4,700

[4] The count of items depends on whether or not several varieties of the same material, e.g., mica, are combined or enumerated separately. In this classification certain items have been put together which were stated separately in official lists. This treatment has not affected the values of the imports in the various groups or the total value.

tional self-sufficiency? Or, should we encourage imports in peacetime so as to conserve our own supplies for use in emergencies?

The provision in advance of supplies of industrial materials adequate for a possible future war would not be so difficult if we knew what kind of war it would be. The bomb that dropped on Hiroshima jolted our strategic planning, so that military experts are unable to tell us whether we are to expect (1) an all-out struggle which the use of thermonuclear weapons would bring to an end within a few days, or at most a few weeks, or (2) a long, drawn-out conflict fought with conventional weapons, a stepped-up version of World War II. A third possibility is an indefinite prolongation of the present state of international tension, interrupted at times by brush-fire wars.

To be fully prepared for atomic warfare, the Defense Department and the Atomic Energy Commission have set in motion programs leading to the discovery and development of uranium deposits in this country. By long-term purchase contracts the government has promoted the expansion of uranium mining in Canada. Our stockpiling program, on the other hand, with its accumulation of millions of tons of copper, lead and zinc, nickel and other ferroalloys, rubber and wool, is designed to provide for a 3-year war requiring full-scale conversion of American industries to war production. Is this kind of stockpiling a wise expenditure of public money? Should we not rather turn our attention to the accumulation of emergency food rations, antibiotics, surgical instruments and dressings and other commodities necessary to relieve victims of bombing?

Materials for the Peacetime Economy

The provision of an adequate supply of strategic and critical materials for the use of defense industries in wartime is only part of the raw materials problem. The continuous supply of materials, at minimum costs, is an essential condition for the peacetime expansion of manufacturing industries and for the continued growth of the American economy. Failure to obtain supplies would threaten the maintenance of our standard of living. Our democratic social and political institutions, which have been developed in an expanding economy, might also be endangered.

Wars and the threat of wars have been responsible for spasmodic shortages of materials, as for example in the years 1950-1951. But what about the secular trend? If the present state of tension in international relations should be replaced by peace and security, would the Free World's resources of fuels and metals be adequate for the expanding needs of the United States and other industrially developed nations? Will depletion of the Free World's richest and most accessible supplies bring burdensome increases in real costs, or can we rely on the counteracting forces of new discoveries and improved technology to free us from this impending danger?

Instability of Prices

Supplies of raw materials are notoriously inflexible, for producers are unable to adjust their operations rapidly to changes in demand. To bring a newly planted grove of rubber trees into full bearing requires 5 to 7 years. The development of new mineral output, if we count from the beginnings of exploration and discovery, is often more time-consuming. Even after a promising ore deposit has been located, large investments will be needed in opening shafts, setting up milling and concentrating plants and perhaps refineries as well. If the location is in a remote area, as for example the new nickel mines in Manitoba, copper mines in Peru and iron mines in Labrador, it may be necessary to construct railways and even to build new towns to house workers before the first shipments can be made. By the time the increased output can be marketed, demand may have slackened, but, because of the large capital investments and high ratio of fixed to total costs in mining and other primary production, supply does not readily contract. Hence production of basic materials is peculiarly vulnerable to declining business activity in industrialized countries. Moreover, the great durability of the products into which metals are fabricated means that demand fluctuates rather violently with the business cycle.

The resulting instability of prices of raw materials raises questions of national policy and of international relations. During periods of depression exporting countries have attempted to raise prices and to maintain their output at profitable levels by means of international control of production and exports. Should the United States lend its aid to such schemes, or should it oppose them as contrary to national policy and national interest? Thus far this country has steadily opposed agreements by private firms to control production. Should the same objective apply to intergovernmental agreements?

High- and Low-Cost Producers

In domestic policy, the most troublesome question is that presented by commodities such as wool, copper, lead, zinc and oil, the supply of which is provided partly by imports and partly by domestic producers. In some cases this division of the supply reflects cost differences. A limited quantity of the product in question can usually be supplied from domestic sources at costs which can meet foreign competition. Some domestic producers, moreover, survive because of their nearness to the principal United States markets. But tariff protection and other measures of government aid have extended domestic production into areas where costs are much higher than in friendly foreign countries.

What now should be our policy? Should we continue to disregard the minimum-cost objective, or should we eliminate tariff protection and other measures of assistance, permitting cost differences to determine the shares supplied from domestic and foreign sources? Will the gain accruing to the nation as a whole from cheaper raw materials, and from the expansion of foreign trade, overbalance the losses sustained by local and special interests? If we are persuaded that this is true, what programs of assistance, if any, should government undertake to enable displaced domestic labor and capital to shift into industries and occupations requiring no protection from foreign competition?

When we say that national policy should provide adequate supplies of materials for industry, what time period should we have in mind? Should we be concerned for this generation only or should we restrict present consumption so as to conserve our soil, our forests, our oil and our metals for the use of generations to come?

The Problem of Free Access

Even if the physical and economic limitations on raw materials supplies can be overcome, as many believe, obstacles of a political nature may hamper the free flow of industrial materials in international trade. Most of the world's supply of these materials is produced by countries which are underdeveloped industrially. Before World War II, many of them were either colonies or in some condition of dependence on Western European powers. India obtained its independence in 1947, and Indonesia in 1949-1950. By that time French control in Indochina had practically disappeared. Altogether in the decade 1946-1956 some 20 countries which supply raw materials to the United States acquired political independence. They are now free to regulate production and foreign trade, and to deal with foreign plantation owners, and holders of oil and mining concessions, according to their views of national interest. Their economic policies, and those of underdeveloped countries in Latin America which obtained political freedom in the early 19th century, aim at rapid industrialization. They want to establish new manufacturing enterprises which they will staff as far as possible with native workers and technicians. They want to get rid of foreign owners and managers. Will the new industrialization programs check the development of production and exports of basic materials, or will the new manufacturing and the older extractive industries flourish together?

Problems of Export Policy

Thus far our discussion of materials policy has referred only to imports. But the United States, although *on balance* an importing nation, still exports each year $4 to $5 billion worth of crude materials and semimanufactures.[5] For the most part, these exports consist of commodities, such as coal, produced in this country at lower costs than those in the countries to which they are sold. Low costs, also, for many years explained the great exports of American cotton, but since the 1930's the United States government has subsidized these exports as an integral part of its farm program. This policy has caused other cotton-exporting countries, Mexico, India, Egypt, Brazil, to complain of unfair competition. These are "friendly" countries. Does our export policy give due consideration to their welfare?

The United States now restricts, on grounds of national security, exports of certain industrial materials to the U.S.S.R. and to its satellites, as well as to Communist China under the general embargo on exports to that country. In addition, the Congress has authorized the Department of Commerce to restrict, on economic grounds, exports to any destination. Does the national interest require that the Department should retain this power; if so, could its administration be improved?

* * * *

In the following chapters I shall not attempt to arrange systematically all the bits and pieces of legislation and administrative regulations affecting industrial materials, so as to construct artificially a nonexistent, comprehensive and logically consistent national policy. Instead, I shall describe only the principal features of policy as it exists today, giving a brief account of their development. Chapter 2 will be devoted to three types of policy initiated before World War II in an era characterized by peace and self-sufficiency. All three, land laws, tariff protection and tax incentives, were designed to encourage production of oil, metals and other industrial materials at home, with little

[5] The values, in millions of dollars, of the principal crude materials and semimanufactures exported in 1956 were coal, $732.1; raw cotton, $718.1; iron ore, pig iron and semimanufactured iron and steel products, $589.7; crude petroleum and semimanufactured petroleum products, $334.5; tobacco, unmanufactured, $333.5; iron and steel scrap, $291.2; fertilizers and fertilizer materials, $115.4; and lumber and semimanufactured wood products, $109.0.

or no regard to the needs of national defense or to the possible effects on international relations. Chapter 3 describes and evaluates measures undertaken during World War II and in the Korean struggle to provide adequate supplies of industrial materials for defense production and for civilian use, and considers their legacy of postwar problems. This chapter also deals with modifications of trade policy brought about by war and postwar conditions.

Chapter 2

NATIONAL POLICY IN AN ERA OF PEACE AND SELF-SUFFICIENCY

IT WOULD BE a mistake to describe either land legislation or tariff protection or tax policy as integral parts of a consciously adopted national policy on raw materials. These policies were shaped in response to the demands of individuals and corporations who had a stake in farming, cattle and sheep raising, mining, lumbering and oil production. The rest of the community accepted the legislation in the belief that expansion of production of all kinds was desirable. In the first hundred years of their existence as a nation, Americans showed little concern for the depletion of the country's natural resources. They seem to have been equally indifferent to the country's increasing dependence on foreign sources of supply. Peace, even after World War I, was assumed to be the normal state of international relations, and hence little thought was devoted to providing an emergency supply of industrial materials. These attitudes, despite radical changes in political and economic conditions, strongly influence policy today.

Public Land Policy

Public land policy was at first directed toward providing revenue for the new government. But after 1820 a second objective became progressively more important, to promote the settlement and development of the country. Prices were reduced, and the land was made more easily available to actual settlers. Large grants were made, also, to aid in the construction of canals and railroads. With the passage of the Homestead Act in 1862, the fiscal motive disappeared entirely from land policy.

At first, forest land and mineral-bearing lands were not

segregated from land suitable for agriculture. The easy terms on which land of all kinds could be acquired resulted in wasteful practices in agriculture, forestry and mining, but it was not until the end of the 19th century that Congress recognized the need for reform in land laws so as to promote more economical use of what remained of the public domain. Conservation of natural resources appeared as a new objective in a land reform act of 1891. Under that act and subsequent legislation, the government retains ownership of forests and grazing land and also of lands overlying reserves of oil and coal. The development and use of these lands by private enterprise are permitted, but only under conditions established by public authority.

Mining laws affecting the exploitation of lead, copper, zinc and other metal deposits are still reminiscent of an era when free gifts characterized federal land policy. Anyone who discovers a mineral deposit on public land can obtain legal possession by staking out a claim. Then he can develop the mine or not, as he wishes. But as long as he spends $100 a year on labor or improvements, he cannot be dispossessed by another claimant. If he wishes to acquire full title, he can obtain a patent giving complete rights to the mineral deposits and surface uses, by establishing proof of discovery of minerals, by the expenditure of $500 in improving the property and by the payment of nominal acreage fees.

The liberal provisions of laws relating to public lands have been much abused by persons who have obtained valuable timber and water rights without ever developing the mineral resources underlying their claims. Legislation, also, has not kept pace with technology. New and expensive methods of exploration cannot be profitably employed except over a large area. But under present laws the prospector cannot acquire exclusive temporary rights to explore areas not included in his claim. Mining laws in their present form also discourage expensive subsurface operations which may be necessary to protect the miner's rights. In order to encourage exploration and discovery of new mineral deposits, the Paley Commission recommended that, for mineral deposits with no surface manifestation, a concession-leasing system should be introduced. By providing exclusive rights of exploration over large areas and rights of exploitation of discovered deposits, this change would give inducement for the use of advanced techniques.

Tax Policy

Two devices in federal income tax legislation are designed to provide special incentives for the development of domestic mineral industries. They are (1) "percentage depletion" and (2) the "expensing" of certain costs of exploring, discovering and developing mineral properties, i.e., charging to current expenses costs which otherwise would be considered capital outlays.

Tax-free recovery of capital assets is a well-established principle in the federal income tax which has regularly permitted the taxpayer to deduct from taxable income an allowance for the depletion of mineral reserves. An act of 1926 provided that owners of oil and gas wells might calculate their deductions by either of two methods, cost depletion or percentage depletion. In the Revenue Act of 1951 these methods of computing depletion were extended to all metals and to some 50 nonmetallic minerals.

By the method of *cost depletion* the taxpayer recovers the investment in a mine, tax-free, over a series of years.[1] When the sum of all depletion deductions equals the amount of the investment, no further deduction can be taken. If, on the other hand, the owner of an oil well or a mine chooses *percentage depletion,* he may deduct a

[1] In making out his first year's return, he divides the cost of the property (or, if larger than the cost, the 1913 fair market value) by the estimated tons of recoverable minerals or metals. The quotient is the depletion allowance per ton. His depletion deduction is the product of the unit allowance times the number of tons produced and sold in the taxable period. In the second and later years, the unrecovered cost, the original investment less the depletion already deducted, divided by the tonnage of remaining reserves, is the basis for computing the unit depletion allowance. If, as often happens, the reserves of ore in a mine prove, without additional investment, larger than the original estimate, the unit depletion allowance will fall, and vice versa.

specified percentage[2] of the *gross income* from the property. The amount of the deduction, however, is limited to 50 percent of the taxable income from the property, excluding allowance for depletion. Unlike cost depletion, percentage depletion may be deducted as long as the mine yields any net operating income, although the owner may have already recovered, tax free, his entire original investment. The owner of a mining property which yields no net income cannot charge off any depletion by the percentage method. He may, however, deduct an allowance by the alternative method of cost depletion. Percentage depletion, since it is calculated on gross income within the limits of 50 percent of net operating income, tends to rise when product prices are rising. The amounts which can be deducted by the cost depletion method are unaffected by changes in current market prices.

Total depletion deductions claimed by corporations and individuals on mineral properties in 1948 were estimated at $1.9 billion. Of this amount, between 75 and 80 percent was claimed by producers of oil and gas and 10 percent by owners of metal-mining properties. The Treasury calculated that the tax advantage accruing to 260 corporations from the "depletion differential," the additional tax-free return imputed to the use of the percentage depletion device, amounted in 1948 to $1,214 million and in 1949 to $1,059 million. Producers of lead and zinc gained $13 million thereby in 1948 and $9 million in 1949. The subsequent rise in the corporate tax rates, from 38 to 52 percent, and the addition of an excess profits tax have increased the advantage of calculating depletion by the percentage method. Rising prices of oil and minerals, so far as they have increased gross sales, have had a similar effect.

The preferential treatment which the percentage depletion method accords to owners of mineral properties arises principally from its use in connection with a second tax incentive, viz., the privilege of charging to current

[2] The rates on minerals very from 5 percent on sand and gravel to 27½ percent on oil and gas.

expense outlays for exploration and development, instead of writing them off as capital outlays over a period of years. (Owners of oil and gas wells may treat all intangible drilling and development costs as current expense. In the mining industries only $75,000 of exploration costs are expensible in each of four taxable years and only a cumulative limit of $300,000 by any taxpayer.)

An official of the U. S. Treasury has explained how the combination of the expensing of capital costs with percentage depletion permits the owners of gas and oil wells and mines to take a double deduction from their taxable incomes.

> If this arrangement for recouping development costs out of current receipts were coupled with the general tax rule for recovery of capital, the result would be merely a speeding-up of recoupment. To the extent that development costs were offset by net receipts in the development period, the costs basis of the depletable asset would be reduced, and future depletion deductions would be correspondingly less. In effect, the taxpayer would enjoy an interest-free loan from the government; net income after taxes would be larger in the early years and less in later years.
>
> Percentage depletion, however, is unaffected by the amount of development costs already recovered since it is computed without regard to the unamortized cost basis. Instead of merely changing the timing of the same aggregate deductions for capital recovery, percentage depletion commonly permits a double deduction. The taxpayer may, to the extent that he has receipts, deduct development costs of depletable assets during the development stage and then take full percentage depletion throughout the life of the asset.[3]

Spokesmen for the American mining industry insist that percentage depletion and other tax incentives must be continued in order to sustain domestic production of metals and minerals on a profitable basis. The growth of the national economy, they urge, demands expanding

[3] Douglas H. Eldridge, "Tax Incentives for Mineral Enterprises," *Journal of Political Economy,* v. 58, no. 3 (June 1950), pp. 225-226. See also "Incentives for Minerals Industries" by Eugene E. Oakes, Report 3 in President's Materials Policy Commission, *Resources for Freedom* (Washington: GPO, 1952), v. 5, *Selected Reports to the Commission,* pp. 10-25.

supplies of these materials, and national security requires that a substantial part of the supplies be derived from domestic mines. The domestic mining industry must be maintained in a strong and vigorous condition so as to provide an "adequate mobilization base." Since mining enterprises, they say, are peculiarly hazardous, the new investment necessary to enlarge, or even to maintain, the present level of mine output in the United States will not be forthcoming without government assistance. A spokesman for the mining industry has said:

> Most mineral deposits found, even most of those developed to a production stage, never yield profits and never repay the expenditures for them. To furnish incentive for trying to find, develop, and bring into production mineral properties, there must be the hope of finding a successful property whose profits, after taxes, will be adequate to cover the costs for it and the losses on unsuccessful ventures, and yield a net overall gain, commensurate with the expenditures, effort, and risk involved. Taxation at high rates should take this into account if incentives for mineral production are to be maintained.[4]

The mining industries, it is said, require special tax treatment because they are engaged in exhausting ore deposits which are not replaceable. "Other deposits may perhaps be found, with much uncertainty and risk.... Even when mineral is found, there may be great variations in its character and quality, in costs of production and in market prices from year to year.... If the mineral venture is not successful, expenditures for the deposit and its plant and equipment cannot readily be shifted to other uses."[5]

Critics of percentage depletion question whether the extraordinary and unavoidable hazards in mineral enterprises are actually much different from those in manufacturing or other types of investment. The mine owner, when he has exhausted his ore reserves in one location,

[4] Henry B. Fernald, "Distinctive Tax Treatment of Income from Mineral Extraction," in papers submitted to the Joint Committee on the Economic Report, *Federal Tax Policy for Economic Growth and Stability*, 84th Cong., 1st sess. (Washington: GPO, 1956), p. 419.

[5] Same.

may turn to other deposits, and by diversifying his investments he can reduce the risk of loss in a single venture. Individual owners of mines and oil wells can divide the risk with landowners, geologists, lawyers and engineers through royalty agreements and other arrangements. It seems, therefore, that the exhaustion of capital resources which takes place in mining is significant principally from the point of view of the national interest rather than from that of private business enterprise. But, from the national point of view, conservationists have opposed tax incentives to mining as unduly hastening the exhaustion of a valuable natural resource.

The U. S. Treasury has opposed exceptional depletion allowances on the grounds that they conflict with principles of uniformity and equity in taxation. Economists object that tax incentives to mineral industries, like other species of preferential treatment of particular industries, divert into mining and oil production capital which would have been more productive in other enterprises. If supply could be readily expanded without raising unit costs, the increased investment would serve to expand production and drive down prices. The mine owner's profit, consequently, would not be much greater than under "neutral" tax treatment. If, however, additional supplies cannot be produced except at increasing unit costs, as seems to be the case with oil, lead and zinc and perhaps other metals, the effect of tax incentives is to raise profits and increase the value of mineral properties.[6]

The Paley Commission recognized that the proper adjustment of rates to the various branches of the mineral industries was a task of extreme difficulty. It pointed out also "the strong tendency of special tax incentive devices to spread far beyond the area of original intent and justification, particularly where there is difficulty in assessing the precise economic needs and consequences."[7] The Com-

[6] See Arnold C. Harberger, "The Taxation of Mineral Industries," in *Federal Tax Policy for Economic Growth and Stability,* cited, p. 444.
[7] *Resources for Freedom* cited, v. 1, *Foundations for Growth and Security,* p. 35.

mission, therefore, protested against the indiscriminate and excessive application of percentage depletion in the Revenue Act of 1951. Nevertheless, the Commission was strongly convinced that private enterprise could not be relied upon adequately to develop production of oil and other critical minerals without some kind of government assistance. It therefore recommended that, with all its faults, percentage depletion should be retained.

But the conclusion did not follow necessarily from the premises. Considerations of national security may require that government afford special assistance to certain producers of raw materials in order to keep in being industries of minimum dimensions. But it is not at all clear that tax incentives provide the most effective means.

The Joint Committee on the Economic Report condemned preferential tax provisions on the grounds that they interfered with the most economical use of the nation's resources and consequently restricted growth of productive capacity. "It should be recognized," the Committee said, "that the use of the Federal tax system as a means of stimulating the growth of any particular industry necessarily means willingness to deter the growth of others not equally favored.... A prime objective of Federal tax policy should be to strive for neutrality in the application of our revenue laws. This neutrality in impact will be closely approximated by providing uniform tax treatment for all taxpayers with equal taxpaying ability, without reference to the particular circumstances out of which the taxpaying ability arises."[8]

Preferential taxes, such as the percentage depletion device, constitute a concealed subsidy to the favored industries. In the national interest the subsidy may be necessary, but must it necessarily be concealed? Percentage depletion is a complex affair. Few laymen will take the trouble to unravel its intricacies, and even the tax experts are hard put to it to explain them. But in a democracy, one

[8] *Federal Tax Policy for Economic Growth and Stability,* Report no. 1310 of the Joint Committee on the Economic Report, 84th Cong., 2d sess. (Washington: GPO, 1956), pp. 8, 9.

of the prime requisites of policy is that the electorate should understand its costs as well as its benefits. For this reason subsidies, paid directly from the Treasury, in the writer's opinion, are preferable to indirect means of assistance, such as tax incentives and tariffs.[9] If the national interest requires that an industry be established, or continued, or enlarged, the taxpayers should be willing to foot the bill, but they are entitled to know its amount. That they can never find out unless the payment figures in the national budget.

Incentives to Foreign Investment

Certain features of federal tax laws designed to stimulate investment of U. S. capital abroad tend to promote the expansion of production of oil, metals and other basic materials in friendly foreign countries. For example, taxpayers are allowed to deduct depletion by the percentage method (discussed above) on income derived from investments in foreign oil wells and mines. Certain other provisions of the tax laws, however, act as a handicap to foreign investment.[10]

Under the tax laws of the United States, income derived from foreign as well as from domestic investments is taxable. But foreign countries, also, levy taxes on the income derived from sources within their jurisdiction. Hence, in order to reduce the burden of multiple taxation, the American taxpayer is allowed a credit on his U. S. tax to compensate for *income* taxes paid to foreign governments. To prevent the taxpayer from escaping completely his obligations to the U. S. Treasury, by offsetting against them the taxes paid abroad, the allowable credit is restricted.

Foreign investment is favored also by special exemptions

[9] Subsidies can be made selective, i.e., they can be apportioned according to the production costs of the recipients, with the largest payments going to the marginal firms. Administratively it would be more difficult to practice this sort of discrimination in granting depletion allowances, and impossible in the collection of import duties.

[10] A thorough discussion of the taxation of foreign investments is beyond the scope of the present study. In what follows only a few of the pertinent features will be considered.

in the tax laws for income derived from investments in the possessions of the United States and in the Western Hemisphere, an area which contributes largely to the U. S. supply of raw materials. Any corporation deriving 90 percent of its gross income from active trade or business, which conducts all of its business in Western Hemisphere countries, and which derives 95 percent of its income from sources outside the United States, is granted a reduction in its normal tax and surtax equal to approximately 14 percent of its taxable income.

However, because of administrative restrictions the principal effect of the legislation has been to encourage export trade rather than foreign investment.[11] In fact, the influence of tax policies on foreign investment has perhaps been overemphasized. Two investigators who studied the subject in 1954 came to the conclusion that United States tax laws had played only a minor role in determining the attitudes and policies of business firms toward foreign investment and that changes in taxes "cannot alone be expected to have a significant effect upon the attitudes of the executives responsible for investment decisions."[12]

The Tariff

The encouragement of manufacturing was the predominant purpose of the American tariff, as viewed by Alexander Hamilton and other early advocates of protectionism. They intended, however, that indirectly, through the establishment of a home market for food and basic materials, farmers, miners and lumbermen would benefit. But Congress, in early tariff acts, soon made them direct beneficiaries, including among the commodities subject to import duties iron ore, coal, copper, lead, wool and hides. Before World War I, this type of protection was applied

[11] See *Staff Papers* presented to the Commission on Foreign Economic Policy (Washington: GPO, 1954), pp. 110-112.

[12] E. R. Barlow and Ira T. Wender, *United States Tax Incentives to Direct Foreign Investment* (Cambridge, Mass.: Harvard Law School, 1954), (mimeographed), p. 4.

only sporadically and, since the United States was on balance an exporter of raw materials, the duties for the most part were not effective in raising prices in the domestic market. To this rule, wool and copper constituted the principal exceptions. Beginning in 1816 duties on imports of foreign wools were levied in practically every tariff act and, because imports were substantial, the duties actually raised the prices received by domestic growers. Copper was first made dutiable in 1869, and effective protection was maintained for 20 years thereafter.

The collapse of prices of primary products after World War I led to demands for restriction of imports. The war had intensified the feeling for national self-sufficiency and had emphasized the need for greater preparedness. Many industries which had enlarged their productive capacity in order to fill wartime demands now were overexpanded. The response of Congress to this situation was the Fordney-McCumber Act of 1922 which rigorously applied high protective duties to metals as well as to agricultural products and finished manufactures. Materials which under the Act of 1913 had entered free were restored to the dutiable list. Additional materials were made dutiable. But the remedy did not prove effective. During the twenties, when manufacturers were enjoying great prosperity, wool growers, miners and others engaged in extractive industries suffered from overproduction and low prices. A stronger dose of protectionism was applied in the Hawley-Smoot Tariff (Act of 1930), which raised import duties on both manufactures and primary products to the highest levels ever attained. In 1931 the duties on clothing wool averaged 79 percent and on combing wool 90 percent of the foreign value of the imports. Ad valorem equivalents of the duties on other important raw materials in 1931 are shown below:

	Equivalent ad valorem (in percent)
Lead:	
Ore	27
Refined metal	66

	Equivalent ad valorem (in percent)
Zinc:	
Ore	55
Refined metal	65
Tungsten:	
Ore	173
Refined metal	153
Manganese ore:	101
Fluorspar:	
Over 97% calcium fluoride	38
Not over 97% calcium fluoride	91

The collapse of prices in the 1930's, the rise of unemployment and the stagnation of business weakened belief in the tariff as a prosperity policy. In 1932 the Democratic party, traditionally committed to low tariffs, came into power, but producers of three basic materials, coal, copper and oil, were able to mobilize enough support in Congress to get tariff protection on these commodities, not dutiable in the Tariff Acts of 1922 and 1930. The imposition of an import *tax* instead of an import *duty* was a transparent device to avoid transferring the articles from the Free to the Dutiable List, an action which might have established an undesirable precedent.[13]

The Trade Agreements Act of 1934 reversed the protectionist trend of the two preceding tariff acts, and since that time the tariff, except in a few cases, has become one of the minor factors affecting the supply of industrial materials. Between 1936 and 1956, a succession of bilateral and multilateral agreements reduced duties on crude materials and semimanufactures, as well as on finished commodities. Examination of 109 crude and semimanufactured products[14] shows that in the Act of 1930 nearly half had entered free of duty and 58 of them had been subject to duties. The trade agreements reduced the duties on 56. In 29 cases the reduction brought the duty down to less than half the 1930 rate. In 19 cases the duties were cut in half,

[13] See Roy G. and Gladys C. Blakey, "Revenue Act of 1932," *American Economic Review,* v. 22, no. 4 (December 1932), p. 637.

[14] The commodities selected were those imported to a value of $5 million or more in 1955.

and in only 8 was the reduction less than 50 percent. On 2 products, tungsten ore and cut diamonds, no reduction was made.

Actually, the effectiveness of tariff protection on raw materials was lessened in the 20-year period far more than is indicated by changes in rates of duty. The explanation is found in the upward trend in prices which began in the middle 1930's. On most raw materials and semimanufactured products the Tariff Act of 1930 and earlier acts levied duties on a "specific" basis, e.g., so many cents per pound. With the rise in commodity prices, the effective rates, the equivalent percentages of foreign value, dropped. For example, take the principal grade of wool on which the 1930 Act imposed a duty of 34 cents a pound, clean content. At the current foreign value of 38 cents a pound, the duty was equivalent to 89 percent of the foreign value. In 1956 the foreign price of the principal grade of imported apparel wool was $1.14. Had there been no change in the specific rate, the duty still would have fallen to 30 percent, merely because of the price change.

Continuation of this account of trade policy will be found on pages 59-60 of the following chapter which deals with national policies on raw materials during World War II and in postwar years.

Chapter 3

POLICIES FOR NATIONAL SECURITY

In both World Wars and again in the Korean conflict the provision of adequate supplies of basic materials was one of the prime objectives of national policy. Each emergency found the nation unprepared. In 1917, months before Congress declared war, political and business leaders were stressing the need for "preparedness," but neither in the War Department nor elsewhere in government was there any definite plan for economic mobilization. The initial impulse for planning the effective use of manpower and resources came from men in private life. At first, the government tried to introduce economic controls through persuasion, relying on the voluntary cooperation of the business community. It was not until six months after the declaration of war that compulsory control of exports and imports of raw materials was set up, and almost a year before the control of priorities and price fixing was concentrated in the War Industries Board.[1]

The Procurement of Strategic Materials

In the interval between the two wars the U. S. War Department devoted much labor to the preparation of plans (four in all) for industrial mobilization. As part of these plans, the Army and Navy Munitions Board drew

[1] A detailed discussion of raw materials policies in the years preceding the two World Wars, and during those conflicts, lies outside the scope of this book. In the following pages the subject will be sketched only in broadest outlines. For more detailed information, the reader may turn to *The History of Basic Metals: Price Control in World War II,* by Robert F. Campbell (New York: Columbia University Press, 1948), and *North American Supply,* by H. Duncan Hall (London: HMSO, 1955). Also Harold J. Tobin and Percy W. Bidwell, *Mobilizing Civilian America* (New York: Council on Foreign Relations, 1940).

up lists of critical and strategic commodities.[2] In June 1939, when a European war seemed imminent, Congress appropriated $100 million to build up stockpiles of these materials, giving the program a protectionist slant by the requirement that the money be spent in accordance with the Buy American Act (see note 13, p. 40). To acquire reserve supplies of critical and strategic materials, Congress created two corporations. The Rubber Reserve Company bought large quantities of raw rubber in Southeast Asia and contracted for all the exportable rubber of Liberia and Nicaragua. The Metals Reserve Company contracted to purchase iron ore from Brazil, copper from Chile, nickel from Cuba, lead and zinc from foreign and domestic mines. It financed, also, the expansion of producing facilities at home and abroad.

During the early years of World War II, government purchases of foreign materials had two objectives: to add to domestic supplies and to prevent the Axis powers from obtaining metals and other materials which they required for war production. In pre-emptive contracts, the government bought the entire Mexican exportable surpluses of antimony, cobalt, graphite, copper, lead and mercury, and made similar contracts with Bolivia, Brazil and Argentina. Contracts were made for the purchase of tungsten from eight foreign countries, principally from China.

[2] Strategic commodities were those "essential to national defense, for the supply of which in war dependence must be placed in whole, or in substantial part, on sources outside the continental limits of the United States; and for which strict conservation and distribution control measures will be necessary." Critical materials were defined as "those essential to national defense, the procurement problems of which in war would be less difficult than those of strategic materials either because they have a lesser degree of essentiality or are obtainable in more adequate quantities from domestic sources; and for which some degree of conservation and distribution control will be necessary." Army and Navy Munitions Board, *The Strategic and Critical Materials* (Washington: Author, 1940), p. 3.

The distinction has now been abandoned and the term "strategic and critical" is used to describe both categories. A new definition adopted by the Army and Navy Munitions Board in 1944 reads: "Strategic and critical materials are those materials required for essential uses in a war emergency, the procurement of which in adequate quantities, quality, and time is sufficiently uncertain for any reason to require prior provision for the supply thereof."

Measures to Increase Domestic Supplies

The Premium Price Plan, a combination of differential pricing techniques with subsidy payments, was an effective means for stimulating domestic output of copper, lead and zinc, and at the same time keeping prices under control. For each producing mine a quota was established, representing the output that could reasonably be expected at the ceiling price. For over-quota production, premiums were paid, representing estimates of the additional costs of mining the marginal output. As costs increased it was found necessary to decrease quotas and to raise premium payments. In general, however, as a result of the plan, the prices of metals remained remarkably stable from 1942 until the end of the war.[3]

Domestic industries were reluctant to expand their production facilities. Some businessmen found it difficult to grasp the dimensions of the war effort, and many feared that a shrunken postwar demand would not furnish an adequate market for vastly increased productive capacity and that cutthroat competition would result. In the majority of cases the bulk of the additional supplies of materials came from imports. Important exceptions were iron ore, petroleum and bauxite.[4]

In order to supplement primary supplies, campaigns were instituted to increase salvage of secondary or scrap metals—iron and steel, copper, lead and zinc. Restrictions on the use of scarce materials, so as to channel consumption into essential uses, were brought about by the Controlled Materials Plan. "This was a complete and detailed allocation scheme for steel, copper, aluminum and their alloys. Allocations of many other materials were indirectly affected by provisions that keyed them to the allotments of these three basic materials."[5] Price controls helped to

[3] Robert F. Campbell, *The History of Basic Metals . . .*, cited, pp. 82-84, 101-103, 171-212.

[4] The greatest expansion in domestic production of basic metals, except for aluminum, took place before the United States entered the war. Before the close of 1943 the expansion had ended.

[5] Donald H. Wallace, *Economic Controls and Defense* (New York: Twentieth Century Fund, 1953), p. 118.

make the allocations effective by diminishing the tendency to hoard. To increase supplies of nickel, the government took the unusual step of investing $33 million in a plant in Cuba for the production of nickel oxide. It supplemented the dwindling imports of natural rubber by building up, at a cost of $700 million, an entirely new synthetic rubber industry. These wartime excursions into fields formerly reserved for private enterprise, I have described in Chapter 6, pp. 148-151, 162-163, and Chapter 9, pp. 246-248.

The Combined Raw Materials Board

The Roosevelt administration, as early as 1939, was actively cooperating with the United Kingdom in the control of supplies of raw materials, especially ferroalloys. An English author has written: "Neutral America and belligerent Britain had a common interest on grounds of public policy in denying supplies to aggressor countries. They had also a second interest in common—that of securing for the United States and the Allies supplies of the scarcer strategic raw materials and strategic manufactures such as machine tools." [6] One feature of the informal collaboration was the unsuccessful attempt of the U. S. State Department to control exports of strategic commodities to dangerous destinations through "moral embargoes."[7]

After Pearl Harbor, the United States and the United Kingdom set up the Combined Raw Materials Board to coordinate their policies in purchasing and allocating raw materials. The Board eventually regulated supply and demand of nickel, molybdenum, zinc, manganese, tungsten, chromite, tin, lead, rubber and copper for all the United Nations. It endeavored to increase supplies as well as to allocate them, to stabilize prices and to introduce economies in use. Among these functions, allocation—the elimination of competitive trading and the transfer of supplies from one consuming country to another—was of primary importance. There was no common pool.

[6] H. Duncan Hall, *North American Supply,* cited, pp. 80-81.
[7] See Tobin and Bidwell, cited, pp. 220-222.

Instead, the Board recommended actions which were implemented by national authorities.

The Challenge of Korea

Before both World Wars, the United States had time for preparation, but the Korean conflict gave no warning. Except for laws authorizing stockpiling and restriction of exports, the emergency legislation enacted during World War II had been repealed in the economic demobilization which took place soon after V-J Day.[8] Moreover, in the years preceding World War II the country was emerging from the Great Depression. Labor still was not fully employed and no shortages of materials were evident. But in June 1950 the situation was quite different. The expected postwar depression had not developed. Except for 1949, the country had been experiencing several years of unexampled prosperity.

Less than three months after the United States forces were sent into Korea, Congress enacted the Defense Production Act of 1950 which, with subsequent amendments, provided authority for purchasing strategic materials, for stimulating production at home and abroad, for price control and allocation and other measures of economic mobilization. Some of the powers delegated by the original Act were to expire in June 1951, the remaining powers a year later. But when the Korean conflict was prolonged, and a new rearmament program was undertaken, the Act was repeatedly extended. In 1956 its termination was fixed for June 1958.[9]

Under DPA authority, price control was introduced, somewhat belatedly in January 1951, after prices of raw materials had already made large advances. In July the government reintroduced the Controlled Materials Plan

[8] The National Security Resources Board, established in 1947, had prepared drafts of emergency powers legislation. Much of its proposed program was incorporated in the Defense Production Act of 1950.

[9] Except for a part of Section 303 of the Act, dealing with the procurement of strategic materials, which was extended to June 1965.

which governed completely the flow of steel, copper and aluminum. Restrictions on uses of other metals varied from the almost complete diversion of nickel to military uses to 10-percent diversion of sulphur. The consumption of rubber, owing to the government's success in building up a synthetic rubber industry, was left practically free.

Accelerated Depreciation

To stimulate the expansion of productive facilities in industries essential to national defense, government legislation provided that the owners might depreciate them over a period of 5 years, instead of 20 years. The law provided that accelerated depreciation might be computed on the total cost of strategic facilities, but in practice the average amount certified for tax reduction was 60 percent. Fast tax write-offs did not increase the total amount of allowable depreciation but permitted only a more rapid recovery of capital investment. Incidentally, the tax favor helped firms to obtain bank loans by assuring that a larger percentage of gross income would be promptly available for interest payments. As of January 1957, the cumulative amount of investment eligible for rapid depreciation of facilities producing strategic materials was $22.3 billion.

At first the primary emphasis in the program was on industries producing and fabricating basic materials, especially taconite, nonferrous ores, bauxite and aluminum concentrates, and radioactive ores. Later, the bulk of the certificates were issued to promote development of aircraft production, railroad transportation, electric-power production and transmission, and petroleum refining, pipeline and storage facilities. The ODM set up production goals in more than 228 fields and, as the planned expansion in each field was completed, closed them out. Of the original goals only 28 remained open in January 1957. They included nickel, mercury, manganese and chromite.

The program was criticized by Secretary of the Treasury Humphrey who complained of the immediate loss of revenue. He said that the program cost $880 million during the fiscal year 1956. The program was attacked also in a report of the Joint Congressional Committee on Internal Revenue Taxation on the grounds that a tax program which has originated during a war emergency might not be well adapted for a semimobilization period which might continue many years. In response to these and other criticisms, the ODM in December 1956 announced that tax amortization would be granted only on applications directly involving procurement by the Department of Defense and the Atomic Energy Commission, or in cases where it could be clearly shown that under full mobilization the military and war-supporting requirements, plus the requirements of a rock-bottom civilian economy, would exceed the supplies available.

Stockpiling

In the 10 years following World War II, particularly in 1950-1956, the American stockpile program was the center of national policy on raw materials. Government purchases of strategic and critical materials spread their effects throughout the world's markets. Long-term contracts for delivery of copper, lead, nickel and zinc promoted development of new resources at home and in Canada and Mexico, in Brazil, Chile and elsewhere in South America, and in Africa. The vast program seemingly developed an inertia of its own for, even after its goals had been substantially achieved, the accumulation of materials still continued. Meanwhile, changes in the art of warfare had raised the question whether stockpiling of raw materials wasn't outdated. If so, what kinds of commodities, in an atomic age, should be hoarded? Finally, how could the government dispose of its accumulation of raw materials without upsetting world markets? To find answers to these questions was the task entrusted in October 1957 to a special advisory committee of 12 knowledgeable and well-informed citizens. A discussion of the committee's report will be found on pages 50-54.

The present stockpiling program had its origin in the

Strategic Materials Act of 1939,[10] which authorized the expenditure of $100 million over a four-year period for the purchase of strategic materials. As American participation in the European war seemed imminent, larger appropriations were added, so that even before Pearl Harbor the government's commitments to acquire minerals and metals were close to $1 billion. After Pearl Harbor, the United States joined with its allies in a concerted attack on the raw materials problem. As the result of the operations of the Combined Raw Materials Board, the United States and other members of the United Nations emerged from the war without having suffered "any really serious shortage of the raw materials essential for war purposes."[11] In fact, the end of the war found in U. S. stockpiles strategic and critical materials worth over $500 million.

Purposes of the Act of 1946

The Strategic and Critical Materials Stock Piling Act of 1946, an amended version of the 1939 Act, provided basic legislation for postwar activities in this field. Its preamble reads as follows:

> That the natural resources of the United States in certain strategic and critical materials being deficient or insufficiently developed to supply the industrial, military, and naval needs of the country for common defense, it is the policy of the Congress and the purpose and intent of this Act to provide for the acquisition and retention of stocks of these materials and to encourage the conservation and development of sources of these materials within the United States, and thereby decrease and prevent wherever possible a dangerous and costly dependence of the United States upon foreign nations for supplies of these materials in times of national emergency.[12]

[10] As early as 1921 officers in the Departments of War and of the Navy had discussed the need of a national stockpiling program for strategic materials. But Congress made no funds available for this purpose until 1937. In the Naval Appropriations Acts of that year and of 1939 and 1940, it authorized total expenditures of $4.5 million.

[11] Hall, *North American Supply,* cited, p. 369.

[12] *Public Law* no. 520, 79th Cong., 2d sess. (July 23, 1946). "Strategic and Critical Materials Stock Piling Act."

The framers of the Act obviously did not intend to provide simply for the accumulation of stocks of materials. Debates in Congress, as well as the language of the preamble, indicate that they had in mind also using stockpile purchases to build up domestic production. To make their purpose clear beyond a doubt, they ordered that purchasing agents should give preference to domestic suppliers, in accordance with the provisions of the Buy American Act.[13] In a further attempt to safeguard domestic interests, Congress at first refused to exempt government purchases of foreign materials from the payment of import duties, but subsequently an act of 1949 (*Public Law* no. 152) provided for free entry of materials acquired either for the strategic stockpile or the supplemental stockpile.

The 1946 program called for the accumulation of about $2 billion of materials over a five-year period. Commodities were to be selected for stockpiling only after an exhaustive review had indicated (1) that they were essential for defense, (2) that in wartime a serious deficit would exist between supply and requirements, and (3) that stockpiling was the most practical and efficient means of meeting the deficit.

At first the stockpile grew so slowly that in January 1949 the Hoover Commission reported its condition to be

[13] Title III, Act of March 3, 1933 (47 Stat. 1520). The Act lays down the general principle that only goods produced in the United States shall be acquired for public use. Goods of foreign origin may be purchased if supplies are not produced in the United States at "reasonable" costs. For a discussion of the history and administration of this Act, see the author's *What the Tariff Means to American Industries* (New York: Council on Foreign Relations, 1956), pp. 244-252. In purchasing strategic materials after World War II, procurement officers seem at first to have interpreted the Buy American provisions liberally. They awarded contracts to domestic bidders only if their bids were equal to or lower than the foreign bids. The Defense Production Act of 1950 authorized the President to temporarily suspend Buy American requirements, but it is not clear how far he made use of this permission in stockpile purchasing. After 1954 the choice between domestic and foreign materials seems to have been limited to purchases for the minimum stockpile, since the major purpose in setting up the long-range stockpile, viz., to relieve depressed conditions in domestic mining industries, could be accomplished only by buying materials of domestic origin. Only strategic materials of foreign origin were acquired for the supplemental stockpile.

"deplorable." An "obvious, basic reason" for the situation, the Commission found, was the lack of single centralized responsibility for framing and executing stockpile policies. Instead, responsibility was diffused among the National Security Resources Board, the Munitions Board, the Treasury and various other executive departments.[14] The Munitions Board had proceeded cautiously for fear of depriving civilian industries of the materials needed for postwar reconversion. Congress, furthermore, had been reluctant to appropriate funds. Between 1946 and 1950 it made available only one-half of the money needed for the five-year program. But under the Defense Production Act of 1950, enacted a few months after the outbreak of the war in Korea, it gave a new impetus to the accumulation of strategic materials by making available in the 18 months, July 1950 to December 1951, $3.8 billion in new money.

Congressional Criticism

The signing of the 1953 armistice brought to an end the fighting in Korea, but it did not bring a settled peace. Instead, there ensued a period of great tension in relations between the United States and the U.S.S.R., punctuated by incidents which threatened at any time to explode a third world war. The nation was keenly aware of the need for adequate preparedness in all fields, includ-

[14] The Committee on the National Security Organization, "Task Force Report on National Security Organization (Appendix G)," prepared for the Commission on the Organization of the Executive Branch of the Government (Washington: GPO, 1949), p. 92.

One of the "other" agencies to which Congress gave stockpiling responsibilities was the Economic Cooperation Administration. In 1948 this organization was authorized to use 5 percent of counterpart funds for the purchase of strategic materials. Acting on this authority the Administration made such inroads into the available Free World supplies as to arouse bitter complaints from European countries in the throes of economic recovery and reconstruction. The same lack of concentrated responsibility which the Hoover Commission had noted hampered the purchasing activities of the ECA. Outspoken criticism is to be found in *Strategic Materials Program of the Economic Cooperation Administration,* Report of a Special Senate Subcommittee on Foreign Economic Cooperation, 82d Cong., 2d sess. (Washington: GPO, 1952).

ing supplies of strategic materials. Western mining interests, suffering from the post-Korean slump in prices, demanded that Congress increase its appropriations for stockpiling, which for several years had been inconsiderable. The result was the 1953-1954 Congressional investigation of the situation of the United States with respect to its supplies of strategic and critical materials.[15] Under the chairmanship of Senator Malone of Nevada, the Committee turned in a report of a strongly isolationist trend, advocating increased government assistance to domestic raw materials production so as to attain a higher degree of national self-sufficiency. Among the remedies it recommended were increased depletion allowances and acceleration of the stockpiling program. It denounced the activities of the State Department in reducing tariffs, under the Trade Agreements program, and condemned United States participation, without Congressional sanction, in the International Materials Conference.

The Committee expressed in plain terms its dissatisfaction with the stockpiling program. It found almost incredible confusion in its administration. Some 54 different boards and agencies of the Executive Department all "had a finger" in it, either in framing or implementing policies. In addition, 5 major interdepartmental committees, 9 legislative committees, and 10 international groups were concerned with stockpiling operations. The Committee was particularly displeased by the failure of the administrative agencies to employ stockpile purchases as a means of encouraging the expansion and development of native sources of strategic and critical raw materials. The Buy American provision, they charged, had been circumvented, with the result that 80 percent of the materials purchased for the stockpile were of foreign origin. In the awarding of contracts for the expansion of minerals production, the Committee reported, in the period July 1950 through

[15] U.S. Senate, Minerals, Materials and Fuels Economic Subcommittee of the Interior and Insular Affairs Committee, *Stockpile and Accessibility of Strategic and Critical Materials to the United States in Time of War*, Hearings, 83rd Cong., 1st and 2d sess., pursuant to S. Res. 143 (Washington: GPO, 1953, 1954).

March 1, 1953, $594,126,000 had been spent on foreign programs, which was $66,000,000 more than the expenditures in encouraging domestic production.

New Long-range Objectives

While the Malone Committee's investigations were in progress, the Executive undertook a study in the same field. In October 1953, President Eisenhower appointed a Cabinet Committee on Minerals Policy to study the problems relating to the production and utilization of metals and minerals and to make recommendations for national policies in this field. The President referred to depressed conditions in segments of the mining industry, mentioning specifically the situation of the producers of lead and zinc. The Committee, consequently, gave particular attention to the lead-zinc industry as a "representative test case."

The Committee's preliminary report, submitted in March 1954,[16] laid the basis for a new "long-term" stockpiling program for metals and minerals, which the President at once initiated. Under this program, he estimated that the government would acquire additional supplies of 35 to 40 metals and minerals, wherever possible from domestic producers. Purchasers were to be timed to help "to reactivate productive capacity and in other ways to alleviate distressed conditions in connection with domestic mineral industries that are an important element of the nation's mobilization base."[17]

Stockpiling acquisitions had previously been determined by what the Cabinet Committee's report described as "minimum objectives," fixed on the assumption that imports would provide substantial supplies of needed materials. Under these conditions, the purpose of stockpiling was "to make up for anticipated loss of, or serious inter-

16 The Committee's report was not submitted until June 1954. U. S. Senate, Committee on Interior and Insular Affairs, Minerals, Materials and Fuels Economic Subcommittee, *Accessibility of Strategic and Critical Materials to the United States in Time of War and for Our Expanding Economy,* Report no. 1627, 83rd Cong., 2d sess. (Washington: GPO, 1954).
17 White House press release, March 26, 1954.

ference with, foreign sources of strategic materials in a five-year war period." [18] Long-term objectives, the new concept introduced by the Cabinet Committee, went further in the direction of self-sufficiency. They were calculated "to reduce dangerous and costly dependence on sources of minerals outside of the United States and accessible areas as defined by the National Security Council as well as to eliminate in wartime production programs the necessity for conservation measures so stringent as to jeopardize essential war-supporting activities." [19]

The Cabinet Committee recognized the need for a strong domestic mineral industry; it found that domestic production was inadequate to meet defense needs. It recommended that the levels of efficient domestic production requisite for an "adequate component of mobilization base" should be established by a case-by-case study. If the study should show that production of any mineral was inadequate, assistance of all existing authorities of government should be employed to bring production up to a safe level. Among the measures of assistance recommended were tax incentives and strengthened financial assistance. The Department of the Interior was urged to accelerate geological mapping and research and to expand its activities in exploration and discovery, but only when clearly in the national interest, and when it was reasonably certain that the work would not be done by private industry.

The Supplemental Stockpile—Barter Transactions

The disposal of farm surpluses was the new objective which Congress attached to the stockpile program in *Public Law* no. 85 of the 81st Congress (June 1949). The Act authorized the Commodity Credit Corporation to barter surplus agricultural commodities for strategic and critical materials of foreign origin. In the 1954 Agricultural Trade Development and Assistance Act, the plan

[18] *Report of the President's Cabinet Committee on Minerals Policy* (Washington: Author, November 30, 1954), p. 5.
[19] Same, p. 7.

was modified and enlarged so as to permit the use of foreign currencies received from the sale of surplus agricultural commodities to purchase strategic and critical materials, *either in the countries where they were produced or in third countries.* Thus facilitated, barter transactions increased until in 1956 they had become the largest single source of strategic materials. In the fiscal year 1956 the total value of all strategic materials acquired by barter for the supplemental stockpile was $104,900,000. The principal items were:

	Millions
Ferromanganese	$46.1
Diamonds, industrial	26.2
Fluorspar	11.8
Ferrochrome-silicon	10.0
Cadmium	5.1
Other metals and rare earths (including palladium, bismuth, manganese ore, mica)	5.7

As of June 1957 the cumulative value of the CCC contracts had reached $975 million, with lead and zinc making up $112 million.

The President directed the ODM to designate the materials to be acquired by barter.[20] Nevertheless, purchases often were influenced not so much by the needs of national defense as by the exigencies of the farm program.

During 1957, barter transactions were considerably restricted. Congress had reduced the funds available for the purchase of strategic materials,[21] and opposition to

[20] In July 1957, the ODM listed the following materials as eligible to be exchanged for farm surplus commodities:

aluminum	lead
antimony	manganese
asbestos	mica
bauxite	palladium
chromite	selenium
copper	silicon carbide (crude)
fluorspar	zinc

See ODM press release no. 601, July 24, 1957.

[21] Some of the minerals acquired by the CCC through barter transactions are purchased by the ODM for the strategic stockpile. For the balance, which go into the supplemental stockpile, the CCC must obtain repayment from Congress.

the program had developed in the Department of Agriculture and among farm leaders. Their original enthusiasm for the new method of getting rid of farm surpluses had cooled when they began to suspect that barter deals were taking the place of cash sales at better prices.

To meet rising criticism, the Department of Agriculture announced in May 1957 certain restrictions on bartering which ruled out proposed trades in cotton, wheat and feed grains with a large number of countries, unless the barter contractors could present satisfactory evidence that these countries were unable to pay cash. Another ruling required that all strategic materials acquired by barter must have been processed, as well as produced, abroad. This eliminated imports of ores for smelting in this country. Congress, however, did not intend to eliminate barter altogether. In extending, in July 1957, the 1954 Agricultural Trade Development and Assistance Act for another year, it authorized the expenditure of an additional $1.3 billion in disposing of surplus commodities to friendly nations. An amendment broadened the definition of "friendly" to include Poland and other European satellites of the U.S.S.R., but it specifically prohibited barter with Russia, Red China and all areas controlled by the Chinese Communists.

The Costs of Stockpiling

The government's investment in a vast hoard of metals, wool, rubber and other strategic materials has been condemned as a wasteful use of public funds.[22] The annual expenses of maintenance and administration amount to about $40 million. If, in addition, an allowance is made for interest on the investment at the government's borrowing rate, say 3 percent on long-term loans, the total annual cost rises to about $250 million. Also chargeable to stockpiling operations are certain intangible costs. Purchases

[22] On December 31, 1956, the nation's strategic stockpile contained 24½ million tons of 75 materials, valued at $6.5 billion. In early 1958 because of a decline in prices of materials stockpiled, the value was reported as $6.2 billion.

of materials, even if carefully managed, disturb world markets, both when they begin and when they end. Once in the stockpile, materials cannot be released, except under conditions prescribed by Congress. Nevertheless, the mere existence of the stocks, amounting in some cases to a substantial proportion of the Free World's annual output, and the possibility that they eventually will be liquidated may at times exert a depressing influence on world markets.

It has been argued that even if all the costs are taken into account, stockpiling probably is less expensive than alternative methods of providing emergency supplies of basic materials.[23] Purchasing and storing a 3-year or a 5-year supply of lead and zinc, for example, is far cheaper than supporting, by tariffs or subsidies, marginal mines in Missouri, in Idaho and in other Western states. The comparison is valid if stockpiling is regarded as a device merely for the accumulation of a store of strategic materials. But the American postwar program has had an additional purpose, and effect. By long-term contracts it actually stimulated domestic production of manganese, tungsten and other metals. Nevertheless, it should be recognized that stockpiling, because of its essentially temporary character, is not an effective means for building a mobilization base in domestic production. Accumulation of materials cannot go on forever. Eventually the "goals" of stockpiling, even the highest, are attained; old purchase contracts are completed, and no further commitments are made.

A writer in a well-known financial weekly[24] has denounced the stockpiling program as "a vast grab bag." He charged that it was run less with an eye to defense than to the demands of domestic mining interests. Apparent justification for this criticism can be found in President Eisenhower's use, in early 1954, of stockpile

[23] See "Stockpiling Materials for Security," Report no. 17 in President's Materials Policy Commission, *Resources for Freedom* (Washington: GPO, 1952), v. 5, *Selected Reports to the Commission*, p. 137. This paper was condensed from a report prepared by Horst Mendershausen.

[24] *Barron's*, July 9, 1956.

purchases as a means of relieving depressed conditions in lead and zinc mining. Congress, also, when it authorized the bartering of surplus agricultural materials for strategic materials, diverted stockpiling from its true objective, making it a means of furthering the farm program. Congress, moreover, must bear the responsibility for authorizing contracts for the purchase of additional supplies of tungsten, asbestos, fluorspar and columbium, although long-term stockpile goals for all of these materials except fluorspar had already been filled. These purchases, according to Felix Wormser, then Assistant Secretary of the Interior, were clearly a subsidy to domestic producers. According to a newspaper report, he told the House Subcommittee on Appropriations for the Interior Department that "generally speaking, we do not need the production which comes as the result of this act for the present building of defense and defense-related items."[25]

Is Stockpiling An Anachronism?

Disturbing criticism of the stockpiling program comes from students of military science and of international affairs who are concerned not with the costs of the program nor with its prostitution for political purposes, but with its usefulness for national defense. In the decade following the enactment of the Stockpiling Act of 1946, two events, the development of thermonuclear weapons and the emergence of Russia as a world power, made necessary the re-examination of previously held conceptions of defense policies. "Since World War I," Henry A. Kissinger has remarked, "our strategic doctrine has always been built around the proposition that our forces-in-being at the beginning of a war need only be large enough to avoid disaster and that we could then crush the enemy by mobilizing our industrial potential after the outbreak of hostilities."[26]

Our industrial potential has strategic significance only

[25] As quoted in *Journal of Commerce,* February 1, 1957.
[26] *Nuclear Weapons and Foreign Policy* (New York: Council on Foreign Relations, 1957), pp. 90-91.

if we are invulnerable to direct attack and have allies strong enough to hold the line while we are mobilizing. But the atomic and hydrogen bombs have demolished the first assumption, and the decline in the power of our European allies and the rise of the U.S.S.R. have weakened the second. Now that Russia has the power to destroy our industrial installations directly, our industrial potential becomes relatively unimportant, compared with our forces-in-being.

In the same vein, Klaus Knorr has written:

> Military experts agree that, in the event of unlimited war with thermonuclear weapons — at present possible only between the United States and the U.S.S.R. — the decisive blows will be dealt right at the start, within a matter of days or a few weeks. The main purpose of our strategic air force is to deter such a war altogether by being ready to inflict, at a moment's notice, instantaneous and unprecedented destruction on any aggressor. This power to deter, and to wage all-out war should it break out, rests entirely on military force in being before the outset of hostilities. If there should be any second phase in such a war — the phase of the broken-backed war — it must likewise be fought by means of forces available at the start, because the United States itself will immediately suffer immense destruction of its population and its capacity to produce. Present estimates of civilian casualties range in the tens of millions and it is assumed that more than one-third of our productive capacity will be knocked out and more than another third paralyzed for a considerable period of time. Under these circumstances, any mobilization base will be irrelevant once war is precipitated. For one thing, there will be no time to convert it to wartime production; for another, this "base" will be nearly ruined or at least crippled.[27]

An all-out war with thermonuclear weapons, however, is not the only or the most likely possibility; for such wars present stockpiles have excessive quantities of some materials and not enough of others. The United States must also be prepared for wars of limited scope and duration

[27] Klaus Knorr, "Import Restrictions and National Security: A Problem in American Policy," *Foreign Trade Policy,* a compendium of papers collected for the House Subcommittee on Foreign Trade Policy (Washington: GPO, 1957), p. 650.

fought not for unconditional surrender, but for limited objectives. A war of limited objectives may or may not involve the use of nuclear weapons. Such a conflict, as long as it remains "limited," would not require large-scale industrial mobilization. Firms normally engaged in production of military goods would expand their operations. The need for some strategic materials would increase, but without giving rise to dangerous shortages. For in such a war at least some of the channels of international trade would remain open. Hostilities might interrupt trade with the Middle East, with Southeast Asia and with the Far East. But the United States would still be able to draw supplies from Canada, Mexico and the Caribbean, and probably from South America as well, and from Africa, south of the Sahara. One can never be sure, of course, that a limited war will not develop into an all-out war fought with thermonuclear weapons, but that case we have already considered.

Stockpiling Re-examined

Re-examination of the goals of the stockpiling program, as well as their implementation, was the task which Gordon Gray, Director of the ODM, assigned in October 1957 to an advisory committee of distinguished private citizens, bankers, businessmen, retired military officers, educators and scientists, with Holman D. Pettibone, a Chicago banker, as chairman.

The Committee found, in January 1958, that the Strategic and Critical Stockpile held materials valued at $6.2 billion, but this sum did not adequately represent the extent of the government's involvement in stockpiling activities. It had $750 million worth of materials on hand in Defense Production Act inventories and had contingent obligations to purchase up to $1,750 million more under outstanding contracts. In addition, the Supplemental Stockpile held strategic materials, obtained in exchange for surplus agricultural commodities, valued at $400 million.

To get a complete picture of the accumulation under

government ownership of commodities needed in war, one should add the Federal Civil Defense Administration's stocks of survival and relief necessities, valued at $200 million, the Atomic Energy Commission's stocks of fissionable and source materials, equipment and supplies held by the military services, the National Industrial Reserve consisting of industrial plants either in operation or in stand-by condition, an inventory of machine tools valued at about $3.5 billion, and finally the $5.6 billion of agricultural commodities held by the Commodity Credit Corporation, with additional quantities pledged against loans of $1.6 billion.

The Committee's report[28] proposed a number of minor improvements, such as the upgrading of materials and the declassification of information regarding stockpile goals, quantities on hand and under contract. The major recommendations had to do with the selection of materials for stockpiling, the amounts to be retained, the disposal of excess supplies, and the relation of stockpiling to national economic policy.

Laying emphasis on the need to modify the stockpiling program so as to take account of the possibility of an attack with nuclear weapons, the Committee recommended that a store of products essential for survival and relief, especially food, medical and sanitation supplies, should be provided. The Committee's suggestion in this matter went far beyond the usual limits of the stockpiling program, invading the field of civil defense. Supplies of strategic and critical materials, the Committee stated, would be useful in a period of recovery and rehabilitation following a nuclear attack. Thus, by implication, it recognized that in nuclear warfare the original purpose of stockpiling metals and other materials, viz., their use in production of military goods, would have vanished.

To fit the present stockpiling program to the needs of *limited wars,* the Committee recommended substantial

[28] *Stockpiling for Defense in the Nuclear Age,* A Report to the Honorable Gordon Gray, Director of the Office of Defense Mobilization by the Special Stockpile Advisory Committee, January 28, 1958.

changes. Advances in military strategy and logistics, it found, had reduced the direct military requirements for many common industrial materials. Consumption of most materials in a national emergency, it should be assumed, would be "about equal to the normal rate of consumption by existing industrial capacity." This and other passages in the report sustain the criticism that the stockpiling program has been preparing the nation for *the last war*, by impounding great quantities of the materials which proved useful in that conflict. The report stressed the need to give more attention to the accumulation of stocks of the newer high-temperature and special-purpose materials. "Instead of relying on past use patterns, possible needs 5 to 10 years hence must be surveyed and stockpiles built up as need is indicated."[29]

The Committee approved the present plan of determining the amounts to be stockpiled by the estimated shortages in a 3-year emergency period. It also recommended that, in the case of metals and minerals, supplies from sources outside the "general North American area" should be discounted and that Greater Security Stockpile Goals should be set up to implement this suggestion.

The Committee found that in certain directions stockpiling had been carried too far. Government inventories of several materials (not identified) already exceeded even the maximum estimated requirements, i.e., the Greater Security Stockpile Goals. Moreover, the government was committed by contracts running several years into the future to purchase additional quantities of strategic materials at a cost of $1,750,000,000. To check the accumulation of unwanted materials, the Committee suggested that reasonable settlements might be negotiated, "possibly involving payments for cancellation of rights to make future delivery to the Government, when such action would not jeopardize expansion projects essential to national security."[30]

How to get rid of excess materials already in the stockpile presented a tougher problem, for which the report

[29] Same, p. 9.
[30] Same, p. 15.

presented no clear-cut solution. Congress made it easy for the Director of the ODM to acquire materials for the stockpile, but both legislative restrictions and executive policies have made it difficult to get them out. The Committee recognized the need to simplify and make more flexible the process of disposal. It therefore recommended that executive policy in this matter be revised, and that Congress be requested to modify existing legislation so as to permit the disposal of stockpile surpluses, without the necessity of obtaining its express permission.

Assuming that Congress would act as requested, the Committee recommended that perishable materials (such items as wool and rubber) held in the stockpile in excess of maximum requirements should be sold or otherwise disposed of. The practical import of this recommendation, however, was somewhat reduced by the proviso, "when this can be done without causing serious domestic or foreign economic disruption, or international political situations contrary to the interests of the United States."[31]

The Committee denounced the diversion of stockpiling from its original purposes in an attempt to regulate the nation's economy. "In some instances," the report stated, "stockpile procurement has been used to maintain essential productive capacity that had been threatened by economic problems. Procurement for the stockpile, however, is not necessarily either the best way or the only way of maintaining essential productive capacity." Alternative ways, it suggested, were "possible tariff adjustments, imposition of quotas, tax concessions, and the installation of Government-owned equipment in privately-owned plants."[32] The members of the Committee, however, seem to have doubted whether Congress would adopt the suggested self-denying ordinance, for they added this sentence: "If stockpile procurement is used primarily to accomplish domestic or foreign economic objectives, such activity should be clearly explained to the public."[33]

The Committee's blunt endorsement of stockpiling for

[31] Same.
[32] Same, p. 12.
[33] Same.

stockpiling's sake was sound doctrine which, however, is hard to reconcile with the Committee's equally outspoken support of the barter program. The Committee, the report stated, "concurs in the existing practice of acquiring metals and minerals, beyond the quantities considered essential for defense purposes, when they can be obtained in exchange for United States stocks of agricultural surpluses." [34] Yet it can hardly be denied that to employ stockpiling as a means of supporting the farm program is an attempt to use it to regulate an important sector of the nation's economy, a practice which the Committee condemned.

The International Materials Conference

In the early months of the Korean war the United States dealt with the problem of raw materials unilaterally. But eventually the need for joint action with other United Nations countries became apparent. The need was met by the establishment in February 1951 of the International Materials Conference.

The impact of greatly increased demand for materials, the supply of which in the short run had little or no elasticity, inevitably raised prices. The upward movement was exaggerated by the activities of speculators. In the first 12 months after the invasion, the prices of all raw materials in world trade showed an average rise of 50 percent. The price of Australian wool, which in the six months before the Korean attack had averaged 86 cents a pound, had risen to $1.89 by March 1951. Prices of tin, rubber, Egyptian cotton, jute and cordage fibers had either doubled, or almost doubled, in this period. A continuation of the price inflation threatened to weaken the economies of the nations which were opposing aggression in Korea. Primary-producing countries were rejoicing in a sudden access of prosperity which, however, threatened their long-run economic development and their political stability.

For these results, blame was concentrated on the very large American imports, both for private and public account, and particularly purchases for the strategic stock-

[34] Same, p. 11.

pile. A number of countries protested formally to the State Department. The United Kingdom, for example, complained of stockpile purchases of zinc and of export restrictions on sulphur and cotton. In fact, in the early months of the war it seemed that the principal member of the United Nations, indifferent to the needs of its associates, had adopted a policy of importing as much as possible and exporting as little as possible.[35]

In early 1951, the go-it-alone policy was abruptly changed so as to recognize the principle of collective defense.[36] Its implementation took the form of participation in the International Materials Conference. The Conference was not an operating agency. It was established:

> to provide a framework of international consultation in which the major producing and consuming countries of the free world could review the supply and demand position of important commodities, could seek to reach agreement on action to be taken by governments for increased production and more effective conservation and use of the commodities, and could develop agreed measures for equitable distribution of the available supplies.[37]

[35] "The reduction of molybdenum exports from the United States . . . seems to have been accompanied by a policy of importing as much tungsten as possible. Since the two metals are substitutes for each other within certain ranges, the policy could not have been more successful in creating difficulties for tool-steel producing partners of the collective defense alliance if it had been designed with that end in view." H. H. Liebhafsky, "The International Materials Conference in Retrospect," *Quarterly Journal of Economics,* v. 71, no. 2 (May 1957), p. 275. In this section I have drawn liberally from Dr. Liebhafsky's excellent article. See also Richard P. Stebbins, *The United States in World Affairs, 1951* (New York: Council on Foreign Relations, 1952), pp. 222-225; and his volume for 1952, pp. 89-91; also *Survey of United States International Finance,* 1953, by Gardner Patterson and others (Princeton: Princeton University Press, 1954), pp. 261-263.

[36] A directive of the Office of Defense Mobilization (May 29, 1951) committed the United States to a policy of international allocation of scarce materials (including supplies produced in the United States) among the countries resisting aggression in Korea. The guiding principle was defined as "an equitable distribution of the resulting burdens and sacrifices." The text of the directive is given in "The International Materials Conference," by Willis C. Armstrong, *Department of State Bulletin,* v. 25 (July 2, 1951), pp. 29-30.

[37] Willard L. Thorp, in a letter reprinted in *Department of State Bulletin,* v. 26 (February 18, 1952), p. 277.

The Conference consisted of a Central Group, the Secretariat, and a number (7 in all) of commodity committees. The latter, after examining conditions of supply and demand, recommended plans for distribution directly to the 28 participating governments. The latter accounted for over 90 percent of the Free World's production and consumption of the 14 commodities chosen for consideration, viz., copper, lead, zinc, manganese, nickel, cobalt, tungsten, molybdenum, sulphur, cotton and linters, pulp and paper, and wool. Oil was not in short supply. The United States had already established import monopolies on rubber (December 1950) and on tin (March 1951). In order to make its purchasing of these materials more effective, this country proposed that they should be subject to international allocation, but was unable to reach any agreement with other consuming and producing countries.

Two characteristics distinguished the IMC from its predecessor in World War II, the Combined Raw Materials Board: (1) The Conference was a world-wide, multilateral agency, whereas the Board comprised only the United States and the United Kingdom; (2) the IMC had no machinery for enforcing its recommendations but had to rely on voluntary compliance. The two members of the Board, on the other hand, through their control of shipping, dominated the movement of materials from producing to consuming countries.

The Conference soon abandoned programs of conservation and expansion of production, concentrating on distribution of available supplies. In this field its accomplishments were substantial. Except in the case of wool, where the opposition of Australia and other Commonwealth countries could not be overcome, the Committees were able to reach agreement, and their recommendations were loyally carried out by member governments. The United States accepted restriction on the amount of molybdenum it should retain, and on imports of tungsten. It agreed to recommendations regarding the export of sulphur and to limitations on consumption and imports of copper, zinc, nickel and cobalt. Assurance of continuing supplies reduced hoarding and panic-buying of scarce commodities. Planned distribution strengthened the economies of the allies and supported their collective war effort. Furthermore, international allocation did away with the ill will engendered by competitive bidding, and helped to mitigate the irritation caused by aggressive American purchasing in the first six months of the war.

In shifting from a policy of isolation to one of international collaboration, the Truman administration aroused strong opposition in Congress. Certain members complained that insufficient allocations of copper and other minerals had caused unemployment in fabricating industries and had unduly restricted the civilian economy. Curtailment of supplies, they said, had interfered with stockpiling and had obstructed the nation's war effort. Behind these objections, and others of a more specious character, there lurked deep-seated suspicion of foreign countries and a reluctance to collaborate with them in economic matters, even for purposes of collective defense.

Spokesmen for the administration attempted to set the record straight. Manly Fleischmann, Administrator of Defense Production, pointed out that the United States had not been "short-changed" in the division of supplies. Instead, in recognition of our great mobilization effort, allocations to the United States had regularly been much larger than the country's prewar share of the international supply.[38] But he did not succeed in convincing the opposition, and in the summer of 1952 Congress attempted, by amendments to the Defense Production Act, to take the United States out of the IMC. Defeated in these moves, it succeeded in attaching to the bill appropriating funds for the State Department a proviso that none of the funds should be used to meet expenses incurred in participating in the work of the Conference. The action was futile, for the Department could have used funds from other sources, and, besides, as prices of strategic materials fell and short-

[38] "An International Materials Policy for a Free World," *Department of State Bulletin*, v. 26 (February 25, 1952), pp. 297-302.

ages disappeared, the useful work of the Conference was approaching its end. During late 1952, various committees began to dissolve. The last, the Manganese-Nickel-Cobalt Committee, disbanded at the end of September 1953.

International Commodity Agreements

Countries that export raw materials, seeking to avoid injury to their economies from fluctuations in world market prices, on various occasions have invited the United States to join with them in agreements for price stabilization through international controls of production or trade, or both. With respect to such intergovernmental agreements the United States has pursued no clearly defined policy. In public opinion they are usually condemned as restraints of trade which if practiced by business firms would be illegal. Students of trade policy question their efficacy in bringing about greater price stability than would exist in their absence.

Objections to U. S. participation in international commodity agreements were summarized in the report of the Randall Commission as follows:

> The Commission does not believe that extensive resort to commodity agreements will solve the problem of price instability; and it believes that such agreements introduce rigidities and restraints that impair the elasticity of economic adjustment and the freedom of individual initiative, which are fundamental to economic progress. . . . The Commission finds the same objections to the proposals for unilateral buffer stock action by the United States to stabilize world prices of raw materials and foodstuffs.[39]

The United States government, nevertheless, in order to give legitimacy to its domestic wheat subsidy program and if possible to reduce its cost, has participated in a series of international wheat agreements. Collaboration with Cuba and other sugar-exporting countries in the International Sugar Agreement affords a means of regulating imports of that commodity so that they do not interfere with controls

[39] Commission on Foreign Economic Policy, *Report to the President and the Congress* (Washington: GPO, 1954), p. 35.

on domestic production. With respect to raw materials in general, the United States on balance is an importing nation and hence might lose rather than gain by taking part in schemes which, in the guise of price stabilization, might actually raise commodity prices.

The United States government sends observers to the annual meetings of the International Rubber Study Group, but has consistently declined to enter any agreement to stabilize rubber prices. The government has declined also to take part in the International Tin Agreement.

Postwar Tariff Policy

During World War II and in early postwar years industrial materials were in short supply and prices were high. Under these conditions, foreign competition did not appear harmful. But after the 1952 slump in prices, following the Korean boom, domestic producers appealed to the President, via the Tariff Commission and the ODM, for increased tariff protection. Except in the case of oil the President did not grant the relief requested but instead provided substitute remedies.

In 1954 he set aside a majority report from the Tariff Commission recommending an import fee of 10 cents a pound on raw wool, to be added to the existing customs duty.[40] The producers of fluorspar also were disappointed when the President, after a split decision by the Tariff Commission, declined to raise the import duty on their product.[41] Also in 1954, the President turned down a unanimous report from the Tariff Commission advising him to raise import duties on lead and zinc. Instead, he directed that the industry be given relief through increased purchases of the metals for stockpiling. This remedy having been applied and proven ineffective, the mining companies in the spring of 1957 asked Congress to raise the duties. The President supported the proposed legislation, but Congress declined to act. The industry then filed a second application with the Tariff Commission on which that

[40] See Chapter 8, p. 229.
[41] See Chapter 7, p. 209.

body again, in April 1958, acted favorably. At this writing (May 1958) it appears that the President will again offer the domestic producers a substitute, this time in the form of a subsidy.[42]

Independent oil producers based their plea for increased protection from import competition on grounds of national defense, appealing to an amendment to the 1955 Trade Agreements Extension Act. The amendment, which was designed for their benefit, authorized the President to "adjust" imports of any commodity when he found that such imports threatened to impair the national security. Upon the advice of the Director of Defense Mobilization, the President caused an inquiry to be made, as a result of which he *requested* American companies to restrict their imports of foreign oil. At first the "voluntary restrictions" applied only to imports into East Coast and Gulf Coast ports, but in December 1957 they were extended to oil brought into California and other West Coast states. Although backed by threats of compulsory quotas, the new restrictions on oil imports were only partially successful. Most of the importing companies eventually acceded to the government's requests, but a few disregarded them. Difficulty arose also in apportioning equitable quotas to newcomers in the oil-importing business. Independent oil companies, dissatisfied with the voluntary program, pressed for legal quotas. The international companies, however, which did most of the importing objected that such action would bring too large an extension of government intervention in the oil business. This evidently is also the attitude of government.[43]

Export Controls

Since 1948 the U. S. Department of Commerce, on grounds of national security, has restricted exports of certain industrial materials to the U.S.S.R. and its satellites in

[42] See Chapter 4, pp. 99-100.

[43] For a full account of the restrictions on oil imports, see Chapter 10, pp. 317-320.

Eastern Europe. Also on security grounds, exports to Communist China are prohibited, in accordance with the 1950 embargo on trade with that country. On economic grounds, the Department imposes controls on exports of raw materials and other commodities whenever it deems such action necessary "to protect the domestic economy from the excessive drain of scarce materials." It has restricted exports of iron and steel scrap at the request of American steel makers, who complained that shipments to markets abroad were responsible for shortages of an essential steel-making material, and for unreasonably high prices. Examination of the facts in the case[44] shows that no substantial injury resulted from the exports. The restrictions, however, aroused resentment in importing countries in Western Europe and in Japan, where steel makers depended heavily on supplies of American scrap. Faced with this conflict of interest, the Department decided in favor of the domestic steel industry. Under threat of legal action, the principal importing interests agreed to limit their takings of American scrap by "voluntary" quotas. The Department's action raised grave doubt whether the power to control exports, except where the national security is clearly endangered, should be entrusted to any administrative body.

It appears equally doubtful whether it is in the national interest to continue restrictions on exports of raw materials to the Soviet bloc and to Communist China. The U.S.S.R. has within its borders great resources of strategic materials, and what it lacks can, for the most part, be obtained from its satellites and from North Korea and Communist China. Furthermore, the American policy cannot be effective unless other Free World nations impose similar restrictions. Attempts to bring the policies of our allies into line have irritated them, without attaining a high degree of success. The fifteen countries which joined the United States in 1951 in an embargo on exports of strategic materials to Communist China later modified their policies. A particularly large loophole developed in the embargo in

[44] See Chapter 7, "Materials for the Iron and Steel Industry," pp. 183-185.

1956 when the British government permitted the export of rubber to China from Malaya and Singapore. Indonesia and other rubber-exporting countries then quickly lifted their prohibitions. (See Chapter 9, pp. 279 to 281.)

Dr. Alexander Eckstein has written:

> The maintenance of strategic and related trade controls entails some economic loss for all concerned: the United States, the free world as a whole, the Soviet Union and its satellites, and China. . . .
>
> In over-all resource terms, the net loss resulting from a reduction in trade through the enforcement of controls may be considered as quite small for both sides, though it is possibly greater for the Soviet bloc than for the free world as a whole. However, the Soviet bloc, with its relatively greater capital scarcities, may be considered as a greater loser because free-world controls make it somewhat more difficult than would otherwise be the case to acquire some types of capital equipment freely or promptly. Yet there is a real question as to how much effect all this may have on the military capabilities of the Soviet Union or the bloc as a whole.
>
> Granting that strategic trade controls may have a more adverse economic effect upon the Soviet bloc than upon the free world does not of course mean that all countries or areas within the two camps are affected equally. Their effect upon the United States may be negligible, while upon Japan, Hong Kong, Burma and Ceylon it may be quite appreciable. These very differences in their economic impact give rise to one of the chief complications which beset the whole field of trade controls. In the United States these measures are mostly considered as an inexpensive yet fairly effective foreign policy instrument. Among our allies, and even more in the uncommitted areas, they enjoy varying degrees of unpopularity. While trade controls may appear to be cheap in economic terms, they may be quite costly, politically, to the United States.[45]

Dr. Eckstein's skeptical attitude is particularly applicable to controls on trade in raw materials. Since the controls do not seriously check Soviet economic advancement, they have little or no value as bargaining counters.

* * * *

[45] *Moscow-Peking Axis* by Howard L. Boorman and others (New York: Council on Foreign Relations, 1957), pp. 99-100.

The following chapters, 4 through 10, constitute a series of case studies in national policy. They consider in detail the application to a number of important materials of the various measures of national policy already described in this and the preceding chapter.

Chapter 4

NATIONAL POLICY ON LEAD AND ZINC

IN BOTH peace and war, lead and zinc occupy a strategic position in the American economy. The consumption of both metals by American industries in the past generation has greatly expanded, but meanwhile the output of domestic mines has fallen, both relatively and in absolute terms. United States mines produced in 1956 one-half as many tons of lead as in 1925 and about 75 percent as much zinc. The widening gap between primary production and consumption has been filled by recovery of secondary (scrap) metal and by imports. Increased dependence on supplies of foreign lead and zinc is shown below:

Year	*Net imports as percent of reported consumption*[a] *Lead*	*Zinc*
1937–39 (average)	.2	5.9
1946–50 (average)	30.4	26.9
1951–55 (average)	38.5	43.9
1956	39.5	53.4

[a] Not including amount stockpiled; including old scrap.

In postwar years, national policy on lead and zinc has been the subject of long-continued controversy. The principal questions at issue have been:

(1) Does the national interest, economic or strategic, or both, require that domestic production of lead and zinc (a) be increased, (b) be maintained at some given level?

(2) If government assistance is required, in what form should it be provided, by tariff protection, by subsidies or in some other way?

The American Lead-Zinc Industry

Lead and zinc differ widely in chemical composition and in their uses, but are often closely associated in geological formations. Occasionally, as in Southeastern Missouri, lead ores are found free from zinc, and certain zinc ores mined in Eastern states contain no lead. But usually in the United States the two metals are obtained from the same ores, although the proportions vary from mine to mine and from district to district. The same business interests are usually engaged in mining, milling and concentrating both lead and zinc ores, and often in smelting and refining them.

Companies engaged in mining lead and zinc fall into two divisions: (1) The small operators whose activities are confined to exploring and developing ore bodies in the United States. They own no foreign mines, and no smelters, either at home or abroad. (2) Large companies which have mines in foreign countries, as well as at home, and which import, smelt and refine in this country imported ores and concentrates.

In 1952 the U. S. Tariff Commission found 912 lead-zinc mining operations in the United States. Of these, 242 accounted for over 95 percent of total mine output. The lead and zinc ores from these mines were concentrated in about 120 mills. Business ownership and management in the lead-zinc industry showed a high degree of concentration. The 10 largest producers of lead accounted for about 65 percent of the total output. In zinc, 10 companies had 62 percent of the total mine output. Seven firms that appeared in both groups accounted for over half of the combined output of zinc and lead ores. Smelting and refining constitute the second stage in preparing unmanufactured lead and zinc.[1] In 1952, 12 concerns operated 18 primary zinc smelters and six companies operated 13 primary lead smelters. These plants are in many cases situated near markets at some distance from the mines.

The largest firms engaged in producing lead and zinc ores and concentrates are integrated[2] concerns that own

[1] Some ores and concentrates are used in pigments and chemicals without smelting or refining.

[2] There is little "forward integration." Unlike the situation in the copper industry, the fabrication of lead and zinc products, except in a few instances, is conducted by firms independent of the mining and smelting companies.

and operate smelters. The Tariff Commission reported that in 1952 more than half the country's output of lead and zinc ores was produced by companies also engaged in smelting and refining. These companies process foreign ores as well as the product of their own mines. Hence, smelting capacity in the United States is much greater than is necessary to process the lead and zinc output of domestic mines.

The recovery of secondary metal from lead and zinc scrap constitutes a third division of the industry which has assumed greatly increased importance in postwar years. Several hundred firms smelt and refine lead and zinc scrap, but the bulk is smelted in 20 to 30 plants which process also a wide variety of other secondary metals.

Geography of U. S. Lead and Zinc Mining

Eighteen states reported lead and zinc production in 1956. The mine output of recoverable lead and zinc in the three principal producing areas is shown below:

States	*Lead* (short tons)	*Zinc* (short tons)
Western states (principally Idaho, Utah, Colorado, Montana, Washington, Arizona and New Mexico)	197,758	304,437
West Central states (Kansas, Missouri and Oklahoma)	143,768	60,560
States east of the Mississippi (principally Illinois, New Jersey, New York, Tennessee and Virginia)	11,300	177,343
Total	352,826	542,340

Southeastern Missouri, long the principal lead-producing district, contributed over one-third of the national total. In the Western states, zinc is mined principally in Montana, Idaho, Utah and Colorado. Among the West Central states, Oklahoma and Kansas are the principal zinc producers and east of the Mississippi, New York and Tennessee. The richness of ores (recoverable metal content per ton of crude ore mined) varies rather widely from one region to another. Lead ores in 1952 yielded 2.4 percent in the Western states, 1.1 percent in the West Central states, and 0.2 percent in the states east of the Mississippi. For zinc, the yields were 4.1 percent, 0.7 percent and 4.5 percent, respectively.

In the Western states, mining and milling required much more labor (man-hours per ton of crude ore mined) than in other areas. Labor requirements are lowest, the Tariff Commission reported, "in the Tri-State and Southeastern Missouri districts; the large open stopes and other physical conditions in these districts permit the use of mining methods and large-scale mechanization that cannot be as effectively employed in mining the richer but smaller and less accessible ore bodies in the Western States."[3] The Tri-State district comprises Kansas, Oklahoma and Southwest Missouri.

Products and Uses

About one-third of the annual consumption of lead goes into electric storage batteries. For this and other uses, automobile manufacturing takes about 40 percent of total lead consumption. Other important uses are in lead sheathing for all kinds of cable (telephone, public utility, etc.), in the manufacture of tetraethyl lead, an antiknock agent in gasoline, in paint pigments (red lead, litharge, white lead and miscellaneous compounds), and in building construction (pipes, calking, etc.). Other uses are in solder, ammunition and in type metals. Short-wave radiation does not penetrate lead. Hence, it is widely used for shielding X-ray equipment and recently in atomic energy installations.

The quantities consumed in the principal uses in 1956 are shown on the following page.

Zinc is used principally as a protective coating on steel, to prevent corrosion, and in various nonferrous alloys. The automobile industry uses about 30 percent of all the zinc annually consumed in the United States, in base alloys for

[3] U. S. Senate, *Lead and Zinc Industries,* Report of the U. S. Tariff Commission on Senate Resolution of July 27, 1953, 83rd Cong., 2d sess., Doc. no. 119 (Washington: GPO, 1954), p. 226.

	Short tons
Storage batteries	370,771
Cable covering	134,339
Solder	75,290
Ammunition	44,438
Bearing metals	28,321
Type metal	26,709
Other metal products	180,489
Tetraethyl lead	191,990
Paints and pigments	120,370
All other	37,000
Total, all uses	1,209,717

die-cast parts[4] and for assemblies for pumps, carburetors, etc. The average passenger car contains about 65 pounds of zinc. Other uses for zinc die-castings are in vacuum cleaners, washing machines and miscellaneous hardware. Out of total 1956 consumption of 1 million tons of slab zinc, 44 percent was used for galvanized products, 35 percent in zinc-base alloys, principally for die-castings, 12 percent in brass products and the remainder, 9 percent, in rolled zinc, zinc oxide and other products.

Trends in Demand and Supply

In postwar years domestic supplies of lead and zinc have failed to keep pace with the expansion in the requirements of American industries. Consumption of lead by American industries increased from 915,000 tons in 1925 to 1,238,000 tons in 1950, a gain of over one-third in 25 years, but subsequently the upward trend seems to have halted. Consumption of zinc in 1950 was 1,149,000 tons, a gain of more than 50 percent over 1925. The rate of increase in zinc consumption, also, has slowed. In 1956 it was only 15 percent greater than in 1950.

The peak of the output of domestic lead mines was attained in the years 1925-29 when it averaged 662,000 tons.

[4] Die-casting has been defined as "the process of producing accurately dimensioned, sharply defined, smooth-surfaced parts by forcing the molten zinc-alloy metal under pressure into metal dies or molds. Die-casting is probably the fastest of all casting processes, and is often employed where large quantities of duplicate castings are involved and rapidity of production is important." U. S. Senate, *Lead and Zinc Industries,* cited, p. 191.

In the depression of the 1930's, output declined to less than 300,000 tons. Economic recovery, and the high prices generated by enlarged use in World War II, produced a second production peak of 500,000 tons in 1942. After a postwar decline, a third peak was reached in 1950. Since that year, notwithstanding vigorous government assistance,

Table 4

LEAD:[a] U. S. PRODUCTION, NET IMPORTS, SUPPLY AND CONSUMPTION, 1937-39, 1946-1956

(in thousands of short tons, lead content)

Year	*Production*		*Net*	*Supply (production plus net*	*Reported*
	Primary	*Secondary*[b]	*imports*	*imports)*	*consumption*[c]
1937–39 (av.)	416	221	1	638	631
1946	335	345	135	815	956
1947	384	445	221	1,050	1,172
1948	390	433	331	1,154	1,134
1949	410	464	411	1,185	958
1950	431	428	560	1,419	1,238
1951	388	442	225	1,055	1,185
1952	390	412	641	1,443	1,131
1953	342	429	452	1,223	1,202
1954	325	425	477	1,227	1,095
1955	338	449	449	1,236	1,213
1956	353	446	478	1,277	1,209

[a] Including lead ores, flue dust and matte, lead bullion, pigs and bars, scrap and dross, type metal and antimonial lead.
[b] Old scrap.
[c] As reported to the Bureau of Mines; does not include lead added to government stockpiles.
Sources: U. S. Bureau of the Census; U. S. Bureau of Mines; U. S. Tariff Commission

the trend of lead production has been downward (see Table 4 and Chart C). In 1956, primary production of lead stood at 353,000 tons, practically the same figure as had been registered 20 years earlier. The record output of zinc was reached in 1926 at 775,000 tons, and this production was again almost attained during World War II. Zinc also suffered a postwar decline which brought the output of do-

CHART C

LEAD: U. S. PRODUCTION (PRIMARY AND SECONDARY), IMPORTS AND CONSUMPTION, 1937-39, 1946-1956
(in thousands of short tons, lead content)

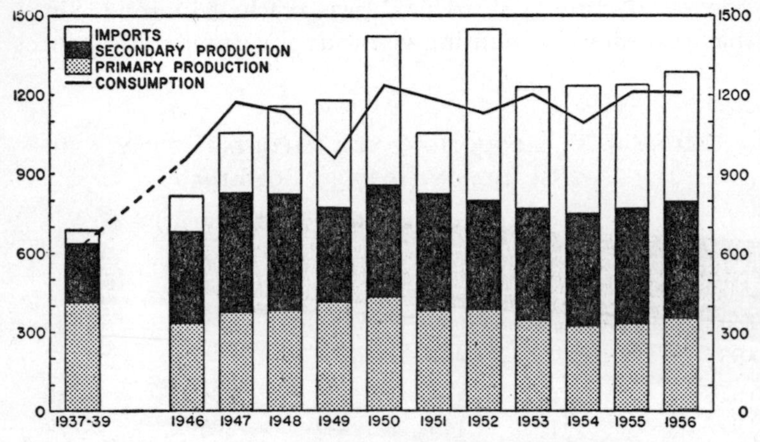

Source: U. S. Bureau of the Census, U. S. Bureau of Mines

mestic mines down to 542,000 tons in 1956, a figure slightly below that registered in prewar years.[5] (See Table 5.)

Recovery of Secondary Metals

The gap between the output of lead from American mines and consumption by American industries has been closed partly by recovery of secondary metal and partly by imports. In 1956, secondary metal (old scrap) supplied 35 percent of total U. S. supply; newly mined lead furnished 28 percent; and net imports, 37 percent.

Lead has a high degree of resistance to corrosion and a low melting point. Its principal use is in storage batteries which have a comparatively short life, about two years. Hence the proportion of lead annually recovered from old scrap to the yearly output of newly mined metal is higher than for any other nonferrous metal. The Paley Commission estimated that, out of every 100 pounds of lead con-

[5] At the end of 1957 lead and zinc were being produced at annual rates of 334,000 and 520,000 tons, respectively.

Table 5

ZINC:[a] U. S. PRODUCTION, NET IMPORTS, SUPPLY AND CONSUMPTION, 1937-39, 1946-1956

(in thousands of short tons)

Year	*Production*		*Net imports*	*Supply (production plus net imports)*	*Reported consumption*[c]
	Primary	*Secondary*[b]			
1937–39 (av.)	576	40	39	655	664
1946	575	77	260	912	1,001
1947	638	75	261	974	981
1948	630	74	208	912	996
1949	593	52	222	867	826
1950	623	74	386	1,083	1,149
1951	681	68	290	1,039	1,126
1952	666	75	637	1,378	1,212
1953	547	64	671	1,282	1,342
1954	473	73	618	1,164	1,181
1955	515	42	563	1,120	1,469
1956	542	43	706	1,291	1,323

[a] Including zinc-bearing ores, scrap, dross and skimmings, and blocks, pigs and slabs.

[b] Old scrap.

[c] As reported to the Bureau of Mines; does not include zinc added to government stockpiles.

Sources: U. S. Bureau of the Census; U. S. Bureau of Mines; U. S. Tariff Commission

sumed, 76 pounds were "potentially recoverable," and 24 pounds were "dispersed," as, for example, the lead added to gasoline and used in paint. Of the 76 pounds of recoverable lead, 60 pounds are actually reclaimed and recycled.[6] In postwar years (except 1949 and 1950), the output of secondary lead[7] has substantially exceeded the output of domestic mines. The increasing importance of this source of supply in relation to primary production is shown in Table 4.

[6] President's Materials Policy Commission, *Resources for Freedom* (Washington: GPO, 1952), v.2, *The Outlook for Key Commodities,* p. 42.

[7] In secondary metal, only "old scrap" is included, i.e., lead which has been discarded after going through processes of manufacture. New scrap has been excluded in order to avoid double counting.

The supply of scrap lead shows less variation in response to cyclical influences than the output of the newly mined product.

Unlike a mine, which closes if the price of lead makes operation unprofitable, a factory that uses lead will continue to market its scrap lead, even if the price is very low; plant scrap must be disposed of, and usually it is more profitable to deliver to a smelter than to a waste dump. Cheap labor also facilitates the collection of scrap during periods of depressed economic activity; however, when a depressed state of industrial activity delays replacement of worn or obsolete lead items, the quantity of scrap entering the market is lessened.[8]

It should be kept in mind that the supply of secondary metal depends on total consumption, which includes imported metal as well as the product of domestic mines. Thus, recovery of scrap has risen in postwar years while domestic production was falling.

Secondary zinc is not a large factor in the total domestic supply of that metal. Much of it—for example, the zinc used in galvanizing—is not recoverable; hence the annual supply of scrap does not increase proportionately with the growth of domestic consumption. (See Chart D.)

Postwar Depression in the Domestic Mining Industry

American producers of lead and zinc and other nonferrous metals experienced serious postwar disturbances. "Nonferrous metals have undergone over fifteen years of wildly fluctuating demand, uncertain markets, erratic stockpiling or liquidation of stocks by various governments, attempts at control by governments, and widespread work stoppages. Metal producers have learned to expect, and to live with, the unexpected."[9] In the United States and in foreign countries, productive capacity had been enlarged in World War II and again during the Korean war. In 1951 the United States government, anticipating a long

[8] U. S. Bureau of Mines, *Mineral Facts and Problems,* Bulletin 556 (Washington: GPO, 1956), p. 433.

[9] R. H. Ramsey, "Outlook for Nonferrous Metals," *Conference Board Business Record,* v. 12, no. 10 (October 1955), p. 382.

CHART D

ZINC: U. S. PRODUCTION (PRIMARY AND SECONDARY), IMPORTS AND CONSUMPTION, 1937-39, 1946-1956

(in thousands of short tons)

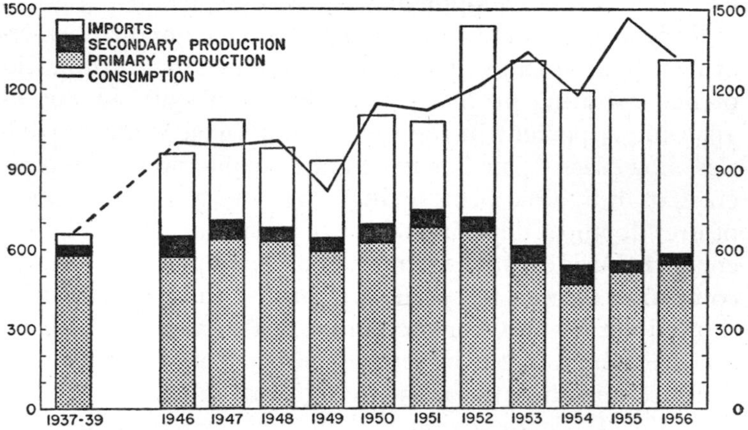

Source: U. S. Bureau of the Census, U. S. Bureau of Mines

war, had entered into long-term contracts with producers at the high prices then prevailing; in some cases these contracts provided for deliveries extending into 1959. After the decline of military demand, civilian consumption did not increase enough to provide a market for the expanded productive capacity.

Two reports of the Tariff Commission,[10] describing the condition of the lead and zinc industries in 1952-1953, found indications of depression in rapidly falling prices, declining production and rising unemployment. "Between 1947 and 1952 employment in the lead and zinc mines in this country fluctuated between 19,000 and 23,000 workers. After the end of the Korean emergency, and before the President announced the expanded stockpile program in August 1954 for these two important metals, employment

[10] U. S. Tariff Commission, *Lead and Zinc,* Report to the President on Escape-clause Investigation no. 27 (Washington: Author, 1954); and *Lead and Zinc Industries,* Report of the U. S. Tariff Commission on Senate Resolution of July 27, 1953, 83rd Cong., 2d sess., Doc. no. 119 (Washington: GPO, 1954).

in these mines had dropped to 16,400 workers."[11] In less than two years, 179 lead and zinc mines had either closed or curtailed their operations. In this number were 40 major operations. The mortality rate among small mines in an exploratory or development stage was particularly high.

Reports submitted to the Commission by 95 firms operating 185 mines and 67 mills showed a decline in the ratio of net operating profits to net sales from 23.6 percent in 1950 to 5.3 percent in the first half of 1953. Wide disparities, however, existed between the profit-and-loss experiences of individual firms owing to geological factors (grade of ore, depth of deposits, width of veins) as well as differences in business management. For example, in 1952, 57 companies showed net operating profits and 38 companies showed net losses. Over the period of two and a half years, however, the number of reports showing high profit ratios declined and the number with high loss ratios increased.[12]

In the Tri-State region and in the Western states, the industry suffered worst. In March 1955 a representative of the small mine operators of Kansas, Oklahoma and Southwestern Missouri told a Senate committee that many mines had been abandoned and that 50 percent of the lead and zinc miners in the Tri-State district were out of work.[13] New Mexico's entire lead-zinc mining industry in December 1953 was almost entirely shut down. Mr. Otto Herres, representing the lead and zinc mining industry at the Senate committee's hearings, testified: "During the past 2 or 3 years, one-fourth of all the lead-zinc miners in the United States have lost their jobs and industry has reached depression lows."[14]

In Utah in 1948, 74 operators reported production of lead and zinc, but in 1954 only seven. These were the

[11] U. S. House, Committee on Ways and Means, *Lead and Zinc*, Hearings, 85th Cong. 1st sess. (Washington: GPO, 1957), p. 168.

[12] See *Lead and Zinc Industries*, report of the U. S. Tariff Commission to the Senate (1954), cited, pp. 39-42.

[13] Testimony of Tom Kiser before the Senate Committee on Finance, in *Trade Agreements Extension*, Hearings, 84th Cong. 1st sess., on H.R. 1 (Washington: GPO, 1955), p. 622.

[14] Same, p. 607.

largest enterprises. In Park City, Utah, the center of an important mining district, a writer for the *New York Times* reported that population fell from 2,250 to about 1,800 in three years. "Main Street stores are shuttered, once neat homes stand vacant, their dooryard gardens overrun with weeds. . . ." The writer, however, observed little or no hardship. He found that the mine workers had been absorbed in other industries in Utah and in neighboring

CHART E

LEAD: U. S. WHOLESALE PRICES, ACTUAL AND IN TERMS OF 1947-49 DOLLARS, 1936-1957
(in cents per pound)

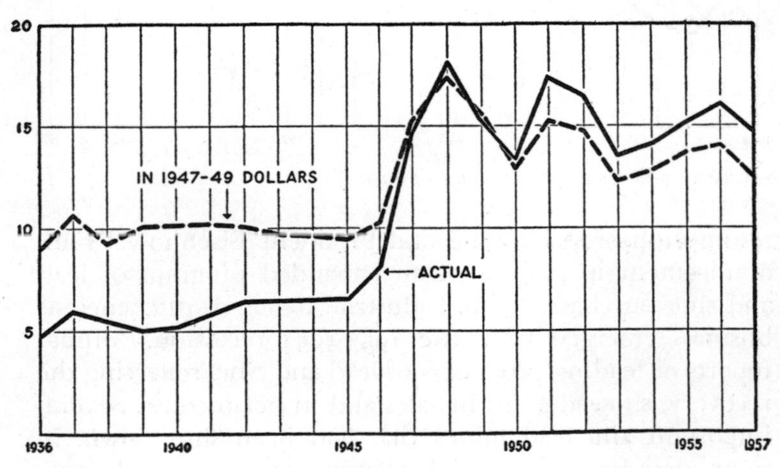

Source: *Engineering and Mining Journal*

states. Unencumbered families had pulled up stakes and had gone to work in copper mines, steel mills, railways, factories and farms. "Park City old timers who own homes along the town's steep streets now 'commute' twenty-seven miles by the Canyon Highway to Salt Lake City for jobs."[15]

The years 1954-1956 witnessed a substantial improvement. In 1954 prices of lead and zinc began a steady upward movement (see Charts E and F) as the result of the

[15] *New York Times,* November 1, 1953. This community, which at one time numbered 7,000, had begun to decline 10 or 15 years earlier.

CHART F

ZINC: U. S. WHOLESALE PRICES, ACTUAL AND IN TERMS OF 1947-49 DOLLARS, 1936-1957
(in cents per pound)

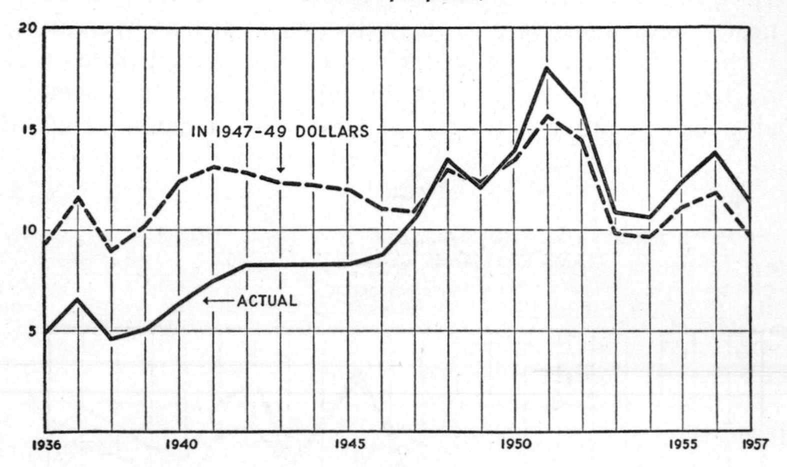

Source: *Engineering and Mining Journal*

resumption of stockpiling and President Eisenhower's announcement in August of an expanded program of lead and zinc purchases. Also, industrial demand quickened as business emerged from the 1953-1954 recession. Annual reports of leading producers of lead and zinc, reflecting the recovery, showed gains in sales and in net income. Several important zinc-lead mines that had been shut down, in some cases for as long as three years, resumed production in 1955.

The recovery, however, was short-lived. In early 1957 depression again hit the lead and zinc producers. Between May and July the price of zinc which had been at 13.5 cents a pound since January 1956 dropped to 10 cents, the lowest level in three years. Lead fell from 16 to 14 cents. In the Western states, many small mines either curtailed production or closed altogether. Even the larger companies began to restrict mining and smelting operations. The slump in prices was precipitated by a shift in stockpiling policy both in the United States and in the United Kingdom. The American government in late December 1956 temporarily suspended the barter program whereby it had been acquiring lead and zinc from foreign countries in exchange for surplus agricultural products. By this action it pulled a prop from under world market prices. At the same time the United Kingdom announced that it would sell stockpiled lead and zinc. The fall in prices was not checked by expanding consumption in the American or in foreign markets.

Trends in United States Demand for Lead

It seems certain that in the next quarter century the demand for lead will increase with the expansion of the American economy, although probably not proportionately. Between the years 1937-1939 and 1956, consumption increased only 90 percent, although in that period total industrial production increased 150 percent.

Compared with all commodities, lead in 1956 was 40 percent more expensive than in prewar years. The change in relative prices has stimulated widespread substitution of cheaper materials which in some uses have proved more effective than lead. Plastics and aluminum, and combinations of these materials, are being used in place of lead for sheathing cables,[16] titanium in paints, aluminum foil in some types of packaging. In storage batteries experiments have been made with the use of nickel and cadmium in place of lead. The nickel-cadmium battery has a longer life, but a higher initial cost. Since both nickel and cadmium are "scarce" materials, this substitution may be of dubious value from the point of view of national interest. The Paley Commission's report expressed the opinion that "substitution away from lead has already proceeded so far . . . that the over-all opportunity for further substitution is relatively limited."[17] On the other hand, new uses for lead in which this metal has unique advantages may develop. For example, some installations for the development of atomic

16 By 1954 half of the cable produced for the Bell Telephone System was covered with polyethylene.

17 *Resources for Freedom,* v. 2, cited, p. 40.

energy, particularly in ships and railway locomotives, will require lead as a shield against harmful radiation.

Sources of Lead Supply—Outlook for Domestic Production

Future supplies of lead will come from three sources: domestic mines, secondary recovery and imports. All three will be affected by price changes, but the response will vary in each case according to the conditions of supply. Moreover, government policies may stimulate domestic output and restrict imports.

Lead mining is an old industry in the United States, dating back to early Colonial days. Some deposits have been actively exploited for at least a hundred years. During this time the richer and more accessible ores have been depleted. The decline in the output of the Southeast Missouri district is a case in point. Under the stimulus of rising prices, new technical developments in mining and milling might bring submarginal ores into production. Improvements in manufacturing, in transportation and in the marketing of fabricated products would, indirectly, have the same effect. At higher prices, much lead could be recovered from slag heaps which accumulated at smelters before the flotation process was used to separate lead from zinc.

The Bureau of Mines estimated in 1956 that the United States had 2,500,000 tons of lead in "developed reserves," and an additional 5,000,000 tons of "inferred reserves." The Paley Commission fixed total reserves of lead (measured, indicated and inferred) at 7,100,000 tons of recoverable metal and measured, or proved, reserves at 1,000,000 tons, the equivalent of less than three years' production.[18] Lead mining companies consider these estimates too conservative, an opinion which seems to be shared by the U. S. Bureau of Mines. A leading economic geologist, however, considers all estimates of lead reserves unreliable.

[18] "Proved reserves" have been defined as parts of mined deposits which are well defined in extent and content and which can be exploited commercially at given levels of product prices and factor costs.

"The largest mining companies keep their figures confidential; reserves cannot be even roughly estimated by anyone who does not have access to company maps and assay data."[19]

The Commission, in view of the lack of significant recent additions to known lead deposits, took a pessimistic view of future lead production in the United States. Its conclusion was that "it should be possible for the industry to maintain production somewhere close to the 1950 rate [431,000] tons for perhaps the next half dozen years or so, given the favorable market conditions expected."[20] After that period, assuming no discovery of a major new district, it anticipated that annual domestic mine output of lead might decline to between 200,000 and 300,000 tons by 1975, and that a still further decline might be expected after that date. The decline of 18 percent in domestic output of lead which actually took place, from 431,000 tons in 1950 to 353,000 tons in 1956, seems to indicate that the Commission erred on the side of optimisim. The U. S. Bureau of Mines prophesied an average annual output of 300,000 tons of lead from domestic mines in the 10 years 1956-1965.

Imports of Lead

Imports of lead into the United States consist principally of (1) ores and concentrates, and (2) refined lead in pigs and bars. In addition, there are relatively small imports of type metal (alloy of lead, antimony and tin), and reclaimed lead, scrap and dross. The quantities (lead content) imported in 1956 are shown below:

Lead imports	*Short tons*	*Percent of total*
Ores and concentrates	196,182	40.3
Refined lead (pigs and bars)	261,557	53.7
Other	29,011	6.0
Total	486,750	100.0

[19] W. H. Voskuil, *Minerals in World Industry* (New York: McGraw-Hill, 1955), p. 218.
[20] *Resources for Freedom,* v. 2, cited, p. 41.

Five countries, Australia, Mexico, Peru, Canada and Yugoslavia, now supply over 80 percent of the lead (including scrap) entering the United States for consumption. The amounts (lead content) imported from each of these countries in 1946 and 1956 are shown below:

Country of origin	*1946 imports* In short tons	*1946 imports* Percent of total	*1956 imports* In short tons	*1956 imports* Percent of total
Australia	16,435	12.0	117,802	24.2
Mexico	43,893	32.1	95,689	19.7
Peru	19,896	14.5	92,080	18.9
Canada	36,336	26.6	51,410	10.6
Yugoslavia	—	—	38,655	7.9
All other	20,273	14.8	91,114	18.7
Total	136,833	100.0	486,750	100.0

Source: U. S. Bureau of the Census

In the 10-year period, imports from the three leading Western Hemisphere suppliers failed to keep pace with total imports. In 1946 Canada, Mexico and Peru had furnished 73 percent of all U. S. imports of unmanufactured lead. Ten years later they supplied only 50 percent. In 1956, imports from two major overseas suppliers, Yugoslavia and Australia, made up one-third of the total.

Lead Production in Foreign Countries

The total world production of lead in 1956 was estimated by the Bureau of Mines at 2,420,000 tons. Production outside the United States and Soviet Russia was 1,777,000 tons; the growth since prewar years was about 450,000 tons. The output of mines in the major producing countries is shown on the following page.

Estimated production for the Soviet Union was 290,000 tons in 1956. The table shows that, with the exception of the United States and Russia, all of the leading producers of lead are in varying degrees industrially underdeveloped. Canada consumes about 35 percent of its mine output of lead; Australia and New Zealand, about 20 percent; Yugoslavia, 8 percent; Mexico, 4 percent. Lead consumption in Peru is negligible. On the other hand, practically all the heavily industrialized countries of Western Europe pro-

Country	*Mine production of lead* (in 1,000 short tons, lead content) *1935–39* (average)	*1947–51* (average)	*1956*
In the Western Hemisphere:			
United States	390.5	400.7	352.8
Mexico	246.9	242.7	220.0
Canada	228.7	167.2	189.0
Peru	45.2	69.0	133.5
In Europe:			
Yugoslavia	76.1	78.2	96.3
Germany[a]	84.8	38.6	72.1
Spain	44.9	36.8	66.8
Italy	39.1	37.2	53.2
In Africa:			
Southwest Africa	11.0	34.8	109.4
French Morocco	15.0	45.4	95.5
In Southeast Asia:			
Australia	279.1	239.8	333.7
World total[b]	1,715.2[c]	1,710.0	2,420.0
Total, excluding U. S. and U.S.S.R.[b]	1,324.7	1,206.1	1,777.2

a West Germany in 1947-51 and 1956.
b Estimated.
c Excludes the U.S.S.R.
Sources: United Nations, U. S. Bureau of Mines

duce some lead, but not nearly enough for their requirements. Western Europe's lead deficit is approximately 600,000 tons annually. Hence, lead enters actively into import and export trade. Between 60 and 70 percent of the annual mine output of the world ordinarily crosses international borders at least once, either as ore or as metal.

Between 1947-1951 and 1956, the Bureau of Mines' estimates indicate an expansion of about 570,000 tons in world lead production, outside the United States and the U. S. S. R. In the Western Hemisphere, the growth occurred principally in Peru, from 69,000 to 133,500 tons. Canada showed a gain of slightly over 10 percent, while Mexican output was nearly 10 percent less. The Australian gain in this period is impressive, and also that of various areas in Africa where production increased by 155,000 tons. Western Europe's long-established lead industry showed rapid postwar recovery.

In postwar years the United States has bought between

25 and 30 percent of the mine output of foreign countries. In prewar years we took less than three percent. The leading producing countries in postwar years have become heavily dependent on the American market. In 1956, the United States took the following proportions of the mine output of five leading suppliers:

Country	*Percent of mine output*
Peru	69
Yugoslavia	40
Mexico	39
Australia	35
Canada	24

Prospects for Rising Real Costs of Lead

Writing in 1952, the Paley Commission's experts had this to say about the future of lead production: "In view of the outlook for a scarcity of newly mined lead throughout the free world for a good part of the next 25 years, total lead supplies are expected to be short. The United States may therefore expect to find it difficult to obtain its desired imports through 1975."[21]

The authors realized that market conditions were abnormal when they were writing. Defense needs for lead were being piled on unusually large civilian demand. Nevertheless, they foresaw that even under more normal conditions the pressure of increasing demand on inelastic supply would result in rising real costs. They cited the pessimistic outlook of geologists and mining engineers regarding new discoveries and suggested the possible need for adjusting demand to supply by scaling down lead consumption, as, for example, in gasoline.

American mining interests have claimed that the Paley report overestimated the future consumption of lead. They have also charged that its figures for domestic production were too low. Andrew Fletcher, president of the St. Joseph Lead Company, the largest domestic producer, in 1952 estimated 1975 consumption at 1,420,000 tons, 530,000 tons less than the Paley Commission's estimate. He foresaw do-

21 *Resources for Freedom,* v. 2, cited, p. 44.

mestic mine production of 375,000 tons, which is 75,000 tons above the Commission's maximum estimate, plus scrap recovery at a higher level than the Commission's prediction. Thus, his calculations reduced the 1975 gap between domestic consumption and the output of U. S. mines from 900,000 to 200,000 tons.

In the United States, future supplies of lead may come to market as a by-product of zinc mining. This will also probably be true of new mines recently opened in eastern Canada and in Peru. Elsewhere in the world no major new sources of lead are in prospect.

Imports of Zinc

Zinc is imported principally in the form of ores and concentrates, to be processed in American smelters and refineries. Of total 1956 imports of 731,100 tons, 66 percent was ores and concentrates and 33 percent zinc blocks and pigs. There has been no significant change in the ratio in postwar years, but with the growth in total imports the tonnage of foreign ores received for smelting and refining in this country has increased from 198,000 tons in 1946 to 486,000 tons in 1956.

Canada, Mexico and Peru are the chief foreign suppliers of zinc. Imports from these countries in 1956 amounted to 586,800 tons, or 80 percent of the total. Comparative figures for 1946 are shown below:

	1946 imports		*1956 imports*	
Country of origin	*In short tons*	*Percent of total*	*In short tons*	*Percent of total*
Canada	167,800	54.7	265,800	36.4
Mexico	69,800	22.8	216.900	29.7
Peru	33,200	10.8	104,000	14.2
All other	35,700	11.6	144,400	19.7
Total	306,500	100.0	731,100	100.0

Source: U. S. Bureau of the Census

The Outlook for Zinc

The prospects for zinc are brighter than for lead. That is to say, there is a greater probability that new supplies will be forthcoming at a rate proportionate to the increased demand. Consequently, no significant increase in the real cost of zinc is in prospect. This optimistic forecast is based on (1) the expectation of continuing U. S. production at about the average 1950-1956 level; (2) a moderate rate of increase in consumption by American industries; and (3) prospects for considerable additions to world supplies without increase in real costs.

Consumption of zinc, the Paley Commission estimated, would grow from 1,156,000 tons in 1950 to 1,600,000 tons in 1975, a gain of about 40 percent. This represents a slowing of the rate of increase; in the previous 25 years it had been about 50 percent. The principal increases will probably take place in galvanized sheet steel which is finding growing use in air-conditioning, heating and ventilating installations. New markets for rolled zinc are opening in shipbuilding and in offshore oil drilling. The automobile industry is using more zinc per car. On the other hand, the possibilities for substitution are wider than in the case of lead. Already aluminum is replacing zinc in die-casting, one of its major uses. Magnesium may replace rolled zinc in dry cells and engraving plates.

Zinc ores occur more frequently than lead ores. The typical deposits are larger and richer. In mixed lead-zinc deposits, the zinc content usually exceeds that of lead in the ratio of 2 to 1. Domestic reserves are larger than lead reserves,[22] and the discovery record also is better. Large recent increases in production have come from newly opened mines in Tennessee. New techniques in smelting, which have raised the percentage of recovery of metal from concentrates, will add to the supply.

Looking at the 1915-1950 record, the Paley Commission found that the domestic zinc-mining industry had "maintained a fairly constant ability . . . both for short-term peaks and for longer periods of sustained, high-level output."[23] It noted the depletion of zinc reserves in the Tri-

[22] According to a 1950 estimate of the Bureau of Mines, "indicated" recoverable reserves were 6,530,000 tons and "inferred" reserves were 9,800,000 tons. Both figures refer to metal content.
[23] *Resources for Freedom,* v. 2, cited, p. 46.

State district, where output declined from 258,000 tons in 1941 to 79,000 tons in 1949. (The 1956 output was 60,600 tons.) The area still has large unmined deposits, "but the ore is low grade and the part that can be mined profitably by present mining methods is rapidly nearing exhaustion."[24] In other districts, however, a large number of small mines are emerging which are able to profitably exploit mixed ores by the new flotation process. Important additions to reserves have been made in New York, Tennessee, Washington and Idaho.

Nevertheless, the Commission anticipated that the maximum domestic mine production of zinc would not exceed 700,000 tons per year. This ceiling now seems high. The 1954 output dropped to 473,000 tons, the lowest figure in twenty years. The increase to 542,000 tons in 1956 was not sustained; estimated production in 1957 had fallen to 520,000 tons. The American Zinc Institute, in its 1955 review of the industry, saw no indication of the return of domestic mine output to the higher levels of earlier years.

U. S. consumption of zinc in 1975, the Paley Commission estimated, would be about 1,600,000 tons. This estimate was based on the assumption that demand for zinc in 1975 would be nearly 40 percent greater than in 1950, an increase amounting to about two-fifths the expected rate of growth in total production of goods and services. It took into account both the increasing use of zinc in galvanizing and for other purposes and also the growing substitution of aluminum in place of zinc in die-casting, and the use of aluminum sheets in roofing in place of galvanized iron.

Zinc Production in Foreign Countries

The Bureau of Mines estimated total world production of zinc in 1956 at 3,330,000 tons, of which 351,000 tons was attributed to the U.S.S.R. The output of mines in the major producing countries in 1935-1939, 1947-1951 and 1956 is shown on the following page.

[24] W. H. Voskuil, cited, p. 223.

Country	Mine production of zinc (in 1,000 short tons)		
	1935–39 (average)	*1947–51* (average)	*1956*
In the Western Hemisphere:			
United States	564.1	633.1	542.3
Canada	252.2	294.4	419.4
Mexico	164.7	210.9	274.4
Peru	24.6	83.6	167.4
In Europe:			
Poland[a]	122.0[b]	108.0	138.0
Italy	92.2	86.7	134.9
Germany[c]	187.3	59.0	101.8
Spain	51.1	60.8	96.0
In Africa:			
Belgian Congo	4.4	67.6	126.2
French Morocco	2.5	8.2	43.0
In Asia:			
Australia	215.4	210.8	311.3
Japan	49.1	48.8	135.2
World total	1,931.5[d]	2,240.0	3,330.0
Total, excluding U. S. and U.S.S.R.	1,367.4	1,468.9	2,436.7

[a] Smelter production; conjectural.
[b] 1937-39 average.
[c] West Germany in 1947-51 and 1956.
[d] Excludes the U.S.S.R.
Sources: United Nations, U. S. Bureau of Mines

The outlook for future foreign supplies of zinc is far more favorable than for lead. Many known deposits abroad are not yet exploited and there is good reason to expect continued discoveries in the future. Since World War II, large reserves of low-cost zinc have been developed in Morocco, in the Belgian Congo and in South West Africa. An ore body recently discovered in Brazil may turn out to be one of the world's largest and richest deposits. The Paley Commission observed that "the world is currently in the midst of a boom in the development of zinc mines."[25] Zinc reserves, measured and indicated, in the Free World outside the United States, were estimated by the U. S. Geological Survey, as of 1950, at 35 million tons of recoverable zinc. Reserves of this order of magnitude, the Paley Commission believed, should make possible a doubling of world

[25] *Resources for Freedom,* v. 2, cited, p. 48.

zinc production in the 25 years 1950-1957, with little or no increase in real costs. The Commission qualified its prediction, however, by this condition: "provided political and economic circumstances also can be made favorable."[26]

National Policies on Lead and Zinc

National policies designed to assure adequate supplies of lead and zinc, in peace and war, are expressed in a wide variety of federal statutes and administrative regulations. They provide for (1) assistance to the domestic mining industry by technical services of the U. S. Bureau of Mines and the Geological Survey; (2) depletion allowances and other tax incentives; (3) grants of federal funds for exploration and discovery; (4) subsidies to American companies to promote the expansion in certain foreign countries of lead and zinc production; (5) stockpiling, including barter transactions; (6) restriction of imports through tariff legislation.

Tax incentives (item 2) have been discussed in Chapter 2 and items 3 and 4 in Chapter 3. This chapter will deal with the two most controversial aspects of national policy as applied to lead and zinc, viz., stockpiling and import restrictions.

Stockpile Programs[27]

Government acquisition of lead and zinc through purchases and barter deals had resulted, by the end of 1956, in the accumulation of about one million tons of each of these metals. These acquisitions were designed not only to provide emergency supplies but also to assist the domestic lead and zinc industry by withdrawing from domestic and world markets excess quantities of these metals. Active buying of foreign lead and zinc after the attack on Korea was reflected in the imports of 1952 and 1953. Under the new long-term stockpiling program, additional large purchases

[26] Same, p. 45.
[27] For a general discussion of the stockpiling of strategic materials, see Chapter 3, pp. 38-54.

of domestic lead and zinc[28] began in 1954. In August of that year, President Eisenhower, rejecting the Tariff Commission's recommendation, declined to raise import duties on lead and zinc. Instead, he suggested the purchase for the strategic stockpile of 200,000 tons of newly mined domestic lead and 300,000 tons of zinc as a means of strengthening and protecting the domestic mobilization base. These purchases were credited by business as well as official sources with an immediate effect on prices. The President's Cabinet Committee on Minerals Policy stated in a November 1954 report:

> The very announcement of the new stockpile policy gave a firmness to the lead and zinc markets. When a purchase program was inaugurated under this new policy, the market prices of both commodities rose substantially. The price for lead is now approximately 20% above the low point of February, 1954, and for zinc approximately 24% higher.[29]

The revival of business activity in the United States in 1954 and 1955 and rising European demand explain in part the upswing in metal prices, but traders were convinced that government acquisitions for stockpiling were important factors in sustaining the market, particularly for zinc, both foreign and domestic. The *Journal of Commerce* remarked, October 16, 1956, that "the chief visible source of strength in recent months has been stockpile purchasing" and importing under the barter program. "Without the two stockpile programs, it is generally conceded that the market would have declined this year, and it might well have done so even in the boom year 1955." The *Metal Bulletin* (London) said, October 23, 1956, that stability in the world zinc market "is dependent to a consider-

[28] Regarding these purchases, the Director of the ODM said: "We just don't take it [lead and zinc] from abroad at all, because we feel that the program should contribute to a strengthening of the domestic mobilization base." U.S. House, Committee on Banking and Currency, *Defense Production Act — 1956,* Hearings, 84th Cong., 2d sess., on H.R. 9852 (Washington: GPO, 1956), p. 11.

[29] *Report of the Cabinet Committee on Minerals Policy* (Washington: Author, November 30, 1954), p. 1 of letter of transmittal.

able extent on U. S. barter deals, 100,000 tons being thus absorbed during August."

The withdrawal from domestic and world markets of hundreds of thousands of tons of lead and zinc in 1954-1956 temporarily raised prices, but it did not stimulate long-range investments in exploration and development of new ore bodies.[30] Andrew Fletcher, President of the St. Joseph Lead Company, in an address before the Colorado Mining Association, February 1956, said: "The stockpile program has . . . met the test of effectiveness and feasibility as far as the market price was concerned, but unless our Government is willing to assure that stockpiling will be continued for five or even ten years and is willing to take the world surplus production of lead and zinc, then the stockpiling program falls far short as an automatic or fair device."[31]

The distrust shown by Mr. Fletcher and others of stockpiling as a means of supporting the lead and zinc industries was justified. In April 1957 the temporary suspension of the barter program precipitated a sharp fall in the prices of both metals, with resulting contraction of production. Entire responsibility for the slump, however, should not be laid on the stockpiling program. The announcement at the end of 1956 that the United Kingdom would sell lead and zinc from its stockpiles and the stagnant condition of demand were contributory causes. The Office of Defense Mobilization announced on March 31, 1958 that no further purchases of zinc would be authorized for the U. S. strategic stockpile. A similar announcement was made for lead on May 26, 1958.

Tariff Policy

The Tariff Act of 1930 imposed duties on unmanufactured lead and zinc as follows:

[30] See testimony of Miles P. Romney, Manager, Utah Mining Association, and Howard I. Young, President, American Mining Congress, *Trade Agreements Extension,* Hearings, Senate Finance Committee, on H.R. 1 (1955), cited, pp. 334, 1394.

[31] Reprinted in *Engineering and Mining Journal,* v. 157, no. 3 (March 1956), p. 76.

Unmanufactured lead:	
Lead-bearing ores, flue dust, and mattes of all kinds.	1½¢ per lb. (lead content)
Lead bullion or base bullion, lead in pigs and bars, lead dross, reclaimed lead, scrap lead, antimonial lead, antimonial scrap lead, type metal, all alloys or combinations of lead, n.s.p.f.	2⅛¢ per lb. (lead content)
Unmanufactured zinc:	
Zinc-bearing ores of all kinds, except pyrites containing not more than 3 percentum zinc.	1½¢ per lb. (zinc content)
Zinc in blocks, pigs, or slabs, and zinc dust.	1¾¢ per lb. (zinc content)
Old and worn-out zinc, fit only to be remanufactured, zinc dross and zinc skimmings.	1½¢ per lb. (zinc content)

The margin between the rates on ores and on the refined product is more than sufficient to compensate for losses incurred in converting the ore to refined metal. The Tariff Commission in 1954 reported that only a small fraction of the differential represented compensation for metal lost in smelting; the remainder constituted tariff protection on processing operations.

Tariff duties seem to have had little effect in restricting imports in the past 25 years, owing to (1) the reductions made in trade agreements; (2) the rise in prices of lead and zinc, which lowered the burden of the specific rates; and (3) the large proportion of imports which, at various times and for various reasons, entered duty-free. Trade agreements with Canada (1939) and Mexico (1943) and the Torquay agreement (1951), taken together, cut in half the 1930 import duties on lead, both ores and refined products. They reduced the zinc duties by 60 percent.[32] The rise in lead and zinc prices would have brought about a radical reduction in the burden of the specific duties, and in the protection afforded to domestic lead-zinc producers, even had trade agreements made no changes in the rates.

[32] In 1950 upon the termination of the trade agreement with Mexico the lead duties reverted to the 1930 level, effective January 1, 1951. Six months later, the Torquay agreement restored the reduced rate.

The combined effect of price increases and rate reductions between 1939 and 1956 is shown below:

	Equivalent ad valorem rate (in percent)	
	1939	*1956*
Lead-bearing ores	42.9	5.7
Lead pigs and bars	114.9	7.2
Zinc-bearing ores	78.9	10.9
Zinc blocks, pigs or slabs	57.2	5.3

Duty-free Imports

During World War II, large quantities of lead and zinc were imported free of duty for government use. After the war, when shortages arose, in 1948 and again in 1952,[33] Congress suspended the duties on lead. Lead, for government use, was imported free of duty in postwar years, and also for smelting and refining and export, and as a product of the Philippines. As a result of these exemptions, 45 percent of the unmanufactured lead imported in the years 1946-1953 paid no duties.

Almost all unmanufactured zinc imported during World War II entered free of duty for government use (for stockpiling and distribution to fabricators) ; imports for smelting, refining and export paid no duty during the war or in postwar years. In order to encourage imports, Congress suspended the duties on zinc ore and slab zinc in February 1952. They were reimposed in July 1952 when zinc prices fell below 18 cents. In the period 1946-1953, 33 percent of the zinc imports entered duty-free.

Tariff Commission's Investigations, 1953-54

In September 1953, lead and zinc mining interests applied to the Tariff Commission for increases in tariff duties, alleging that the greatly increased imports were injuring their industry. The Commission promptly ordered an escape-clause investigation. Several months earlier, in

[33] The 1952 act (*Public Law* no. 257, 82d Cong.) carried a proviso that duties should again be imposed when the average price of lead for a calendar month should fall below 18 cents. This occurred in May 1952, and lead again became dutiable in June.

response to Senate and House resolutions, the Commission had undertaken a more general investigation of the lead-zinc industry. In its report[34] of the general study, issued April 19, 1954, the Commission made no recommendations on rates of duty. Two Commissioners, however, expressed the opinion that higher rates of duty would be of little benefit to the lead-zinc industry. Commissioner Edminster held that restricting imports could do little to raise the level of domestic prices because of (1) the depressing effect which a higher American tariff would exert on world prices; (2) the possibility that American consuming industries would substitute other metals for lead and zinc; and (3) particularly in the case of lead, the elasticity in the supply of secondary metal. Increased duties, he pointed out, would injure the domestic smelting and refining industries which were occupied in smelting foreign ores, particularly zinc, as well as domestic ores. United States investors in foreign lead and zinc mining operations might also suffer.

The Commission's report showed that differences in wages were not a decisive element in the competition between American and foreign producers of lead and zinc.

Average hourly earnings of production and related workers at the Canadian mines and mills, taken as a group, were only slightly less than the average in the United States, whereas average hourly earnings of the Mexican workers were very much smaller than those of workers in either the United States or Canada. Data received from Australia show that average hourly earnings of production and related workers at the large lead and zinc mines in that country are similar to those in the United States and Canada.[35]

Reports which the Commission received from three Canadian and two Mexican companies indicated that their average labor costs *per ton of crude ore mined* were somewhat higher than the average for United States companies. "However, because of the much higher value of products per ton of ore mined in Canada and Mexico, the labor cost per dollar's worth of products was much less than in the

[34] *Lead and Zinc Industries*, cited.
[35] Same, p. 254.

United States."[36] The explanation the Commission found in the fact that "the ore mined by lead and zinc mines in Canada and Mexico (as well as in other principal foreign countries exporting lead and zinc to the United States) has a much higher recoverable content of lead and zinc than that mined in the United States. In addition, the ores mined in these countries have a substantially higher recoverable content of silver, and in Canada and Mexico of gold and copper as well."[37]

Commissioner Ryder noted that the United States lead-zinc industry was about a century old.

> The United States . . . has exploited its lead and zinc resources for a much longer period, and much more intensively, than have the countries which are the principal sources of United States imports. This difference between the older lead and zinc industries of the United States as compared with the newer lead and zinc industries of the principal supplying countries is a factor of major importance with regard to the competitive position of the United States.[38]

The Struggle for Increased Protection

In its report on the escape-clause application, May 21, 1954, the Tariff Commission was unanimous in finding that increased imports had injured the domestic lead-zinc industry. Evidence of injury was found in declining mine output, unemployment, falling prices and low average business profits. The Commission therefore recommended that the President increase by 140 percent the rates then in force on lead, and that he raise zinc duties by 200 percent. The new rates would have exceeded those in the Hawley-Smoot Tariff by about 20 percent. But because of the intervening great increases in market prices, the rates the Commission proposed, when converted to a percentage of the 1953 foreign values of the imports, would still have been moderate.

[36] Same, pp. 253-254.
[37] *Lead and Zinc,* Report on Escape-clause Investigation no. 27, cited, p. 26.
[38] *Lead and Zinc Industries,* cited, p. 96.

President Eisenhower rejected the Tariff Commission's recommendation. In explaining his action he implied that the lead-zinc industry, like other sectors of the national economy, was suffering not from imports but from the readjustment "from war-stimulated levels of prices and production. . . ." He recognized the need for maintaining a strong and vigorous domestic mining industry, for the production of strategic and critical materials, but he doubted whether increased tariff protection would bring the expected benefits. "The increase in duties," he said, "would probably have only a minor effect on the price of lead and zinc in this country. There is a real question as to whether the tariff action would have important consequences in reopening closed mines. Moreover, the increase in the tariff would most likely depress the prices of these metals outside the United States." As a further reason for not accepting the recommendations of the Tariff Commission, the President added: "Since the benefits to be derived from the increase of the tariff on lead and zinc are so uncertain, I am not prepared to seek them at the expense of the serious adverse consequences that would follow for our international relations. . . . Moreover, it must be recognized that our economy requires substantial quantities of imported lead and zinc to augment domestic production in peace-time, and that the United States relies on nearby friendly nations to assist us in meeting fully our mobilization requirements in wartime."[39]

Instead of raising tariff duties, the President announced that he would strengthen and protect the domestic mobilization base by increased purchases of newly mined domestic lead and zinc under the long-term stockpile program, and by the acquisition of metals of foreign origin for the supplemental stockpile. But domestic lead-zinc mining interests, recognizing that stockpiling was necessarily a temporary device, continued to press for restriction of imports.

Toward this goal there were three possible approaches:

[39] Letter to Chairman Millikin of the Senate Finance Committee and Chairman Reed of the House Ways and Means Committee; White House press release, August 20, 1954.

(1) a second application to the Tariff Commission; (2) an appeal to the Office of Defense Mobilization; and (3) an attempt to obtain Congressional action. These choices really boiled down to two: whether to appeal to the President, to whom all recommendations of the Tariff Commission and the ODM had to go for final decision, or to go to Congress. The Tariff Commission's procedures were time-consuming, and, even if its recommendations were again favorable, the President might reject them. Moreover, making a case before the ODM threatened to be difficult. Appearing before that body, the industry would have to prove not only that imports were causing injury, but also that lead and zinc mining qualified as an industry essential to national defense. So, although the industry had consistently maintained that it deserved government assistance because of "security implications," its spokesmen decided not to base their claim for increased protection exclusively on that ground.

The Appeal to Congress

Going to Congress might get quicker action, but that route also was hazardous. In 1934 the legislative branch had delegated limited tariff-making powers to the executive, and in 20 years thereafter had not intervened to raise or lower rates of duty on any commodities. Trusting, however, to support from Representatives and Senators from Western states, the industry chose the legislative approach. The President fell in with this plan and gave it strong endorsement. Accordingly, in June 1957 the Secretary of the Interior submitted to Congress a proposal for "import-excise taxes"[40] on lead and zinc. These were sliding-scale taxes, varying with market prices of the metals, to be imposed in lieu of existing import duties. The rates were designed to afford substantially increased tariff protection. At hearings before House and Senate committees, spokes-

[40] A somewhat similar proposal had been included in Secretary Seaton's *Long-Range Minerals Program* (June 4, 1957). The use of the term "import-excise tax" was a misleading attempt to differentiate the proposed new restrictions on imports from tariff duties. In the Internal Revenue Code excise taxes are considered as customs duties.

men for the State Department, the Departments of Labor, Treasury and Commerce, and in addition the Director of the Office of Defense Mobilization, supported the proposed legislation. The only discordant note was sounded by the Tariff Commission which warned that the new taxes would contravene obligations of the United States under GATT, and that this country would find it difficult to offer compensatory concessions to injured nations.

In 1954, the Department of State had opposed similar legislation when introduced by Representative Simpson of Pennsylvania, giving the following reasons:

1. It is neither necessary nor desirable to establish this kind of protection for the lead-zinc industry. The difficulties in the industry are short run in nature and are not due to inability to compete effectively with foreign producers. The foreign lead and zinc industry now faces the same problems of adjustment.

2. If serious injury is threatened for domestic producers, the escape clause procedures under the Reciprocal Trade Agreements Act provide an adequate remedy.

3. The proposed measure would increase the instability in the lead and zinc market, and encourage unwarranted speculation.

4. It would establish artificial barriers against imports of materials which the American economy needs and normally acquires from abroad.

5. It would discourage the production of lead and zinc in Mexico and Canada, on the availability of which the United States would have to depend in the event of emergency.

6. It would increase the costs of the American consuming industry.

7. It could injure American investors in foreign mining enterprises.

8. It would injure markets for American exports of a great variety of other goods.

9. It would repudiate international commitments undertaken by the Government of the United States.

10. It would be inconsistent with the action already taken to extend the Reciprocal Trade Agreements Act for 1 year and during that time to make a joint study by the Congress and the administration of our trade policy.[41]

41 Reprinted in *Lead and Zinc,* Hearings before the House Committee on Ways and Means (1957), cited, p. 68.

At the 1957 hearings, the Acting Assistant Secretary of State for Economic Affairs stated that his Department now advocated raising the duties on lead and zinc, but he found it difficult to explain to questioning committee members the reasons for the reversal of opinion.[42]

On grounds of national security the lead and zinc industry does not qualify for additional tariff protection. This seems to have been the opinion of Dr. Gordon Gray, Director of the Office of Defense Mobilization, the official charged by Congress with special responsibility in this matter. At the hearings, Dr. Gray supported increased tariff protection on lead and zinc as "helpful in maintaining a healthy domestic industry"; but, under questioning, he declined to commit himself on the matter of defense. He said, ". . . we look upon this bill as one which properly would safeguard and assist a healthy domestic peacetime mining industry and . . . I have not been in a position to make a finding that imports of lead and zinc at the present time do affect the national security."[43]

Seven Senators and 16 Representatives from Western states favored the proposed legislation, as did spokesmen for the lead and zinc industry. On the other hand, companies engaged in smelting imported, as well as domestic, ores argued that the large mining companies which produced the bulk of the domestic output of lead and zinc ores needed no additional protection against foreign competition. Sliding-scale duties, they said, would not stabilize prices, as the proponents of the legislation claimed, but on the contrary would induce greater instability.[44] They asserted that the higher duties would injure U. S. relations with supplying countries and referred to the representa-

[42] See testimony of Hon. Willis C. Armstrong, Acting Assistant Secretary of State for Economic Affairs, same, especially pp. 69-78.

[43] Same, p. 45. The opinion of the Defense Department as expressed by a minor official was that increased protection for the lead and zinc industry was a reasonable solution for advancing the total national interest. In response to leading questions from a committee member, he agreed that lead and zinc were necessary for national defense. Same, pp. 84-85.

[44] Experience of England and other countries supports this view. On the operation of sliding-scale import duties, see Gottfried Haberler, *The Theory of International Trade* (London: Hodge, 1936), pp. 343-344.

tions made on this subject by Canada, Mexico, Peru and Australia. Lead and zinc were among Mexico's leading exports. Out of a total 1956 product valued at $150 million, 90 percent was exported, mostly to the United States. The increased tariff rates, according to some estimates, would close half the mines. To the Peruvian lead and zinc industry, hard hit like the Mexican by price declines in world markets, the proposed duties caused serious concern.

At the close of the hearings the Chairman of the House Ways and Means Committee informed President Eisenhower that he and 14 Democratic members of the committee would not agree to the bill. He warned the President not to ignore the procedures for tariff increases provided in the Trade Agreements Act, reminding him that if Congress acted on lead and zinc it would have to deal with many other industries seeking tariff relief. Thereupon, the Senate Finance Committee dropped its plan for a straight tariff increase of 3 cents a pound on lead and zinc. A minority report by Senators Paul H. Douglas and Albert A. Gore denounced in forceful language the proposed increase in the lead and zinc duties which, they said, undermined the trade agreements program. They predicted it would "open the flood gates" to a host of other increases. "We will indeed have opened Pandora's box," they said, "and in the process, the reciprocal trade program will go down the drain."[45]

The lead and zinc case bids fair to become the *cause célèbre* in postwar tariff controversy. On April 24, 1958, the Tariff Commission repeated its finding of four years earlier, that imports were causing serious injury to American producers. The finding was unanimous, but the six Commissioners could not agree on their recommendations. The three Republican members advised the President to raise the import duties to the legal maximum.[46] In addition, they advised the President to restrict imports of lead to 221,700 tons a year and zinc to 325,600 tons.

[45] As quoted in *Journal of Commerce,* August 20, 1957.

[46] The recommended duties are compared below with the rates of the 1930 Act and those in effect, April 1958:

If adopted, this recommendation would have cut back lead imports to less than one-half the average of the four years 1953-1956, and zinc imports would have been restricted in about the same proportion. The Democratic members rejected the proposals for quotas and recommended that the duties should be raised only to the rates established in the Tariff Act of 1930.

Subsidies Proposed

The Commission's findings and recommendations put the President in a quandary. Many of the reasons he had advanced four years earlier against raising the import duties on lead and zinc were still valid. It was still doubtful whether raising the tariff would give the domestic industry the relief it sought, and the adverse effect on United States relations with supplying countries was more certain than ever. As a substitute for higher tariffs, the President in 1954 had directed the ODM to increase its purchases of domestic lead and zinc for the strategic stockpile. In April 1958 this alternative course was no longer open, for the ODM had announced that the stockpile goals would soon be attained. In its dilemma the administration brought forward a third possible means of providing additional assistance to the lead and zinc industry, namely, subsidies. Four days after the Tariff Commission's report was made public, the Secretary of the Interior presented to the Senate Interior and Insular Affairs Committee a plan for annual "stabilization payments" to producers of lead and zinc and certain other minerals. The payments, which would be continued for five years, would guarantee producers a price of 14.75 cents a pound on 350,000 tons of lead, and 12.75 a pound on 550,000 tons of zinc. (In April 1958 lead was selling in primary markets at 12 cents and zinc at 10 cents.)

	Act of 1930 rates	*April 1958 rates*	*Recommended rates*
		(cents per pound)	
Lead ore	1.50	.75	1.80
Lead, refined	2.12	1.06	2.55
Zinc ore	1.50	.60	1.80
Zinc, refined	1.75	.70	2.10

In its main features the minerals stabilization plan closely resembled the incentive payments accorded to wool growers in the National Wool Act of 1954 (see pages 234 to 240). In both cases the subsidy represented a substitute for *added* tariff protection, not a device for replacing existing import duties. It might be added that the lead and zinc miners, as well as the wool growers, would have preferred increased restrictions on imports.

The Reform of National Policy

In earlier pages this survey has shown that the United States, in the past 20 years, has become increasingly dependent on imports of lead and zinc. In this period, mine production of domestic zinc showed no increase and lead production declined by nearly 15 percent, but, meanwhile, the consumption of both metals by American industries doubled. We have seen that the causes of the industry's decline were (1) the progressive depletion of the best domestic ore reserves; (2) the competition of more profitable mining and other enterprises for labor and capital; (3) the substitution by industrial consumers of other materials, particularly aluminum and plastics; and (4) most important, the competition of low-cost lead and zinc from the richer ore deposits of Canada, Mexico, Peru and other foreign countries.

Lead and zinc are listed as strategic commodities, but the American industry has not based its appeals for restriction of imports on grounds of national security. In fact, it would seem impossible to justify additional government assistance to the domestic industry on such grounds.[47] In case of war, the country could draw immediately on its large stockpile. Imports from Canada and Mexico, countries within the United States defense orbit, could be promptly expanded with no danger of interruption by enemy action. In these countries ore reserves of higher grade than the domestic are abundant, and it seems that

[47] Dr. Gordon Gray, Director of Defense Mobilization, implied as much in his testimony before the House Ways and Means Committee. See p. 97.

American industry can confidently rely on continued access to their supplies. The mining of lead and zinc in the United States is carried on by several hundred firms, of which a small group, about a half dozen, accounts for half the annual output. It is quite possible that the most efficient of the large operators would be able to continue in business in the face of competition from abroad without government assistance, and in a war emergency their operations could be expanded so as to supplement imports and stockpile supplies. In other words, this small group of large, low-cost firms would constitute an "adequate mobilization base."

Chapter 5

NATIONAL POLICY ON COPPER

COPPER STANDS first among nonferrous metals in the value of annual output; in tonnage used every year, it is surpassed only by aluminum. Yet, before World War II copper was not listed among strategic or critical raw materials, for the United States was then one of the world's largest producers and exporters of the metal. After the war the situation was reversed. Acute shortages occurred in 1951-1953 and again in 1954-1955. Copper prices rose rapidly, outstripping the general rise in commodity prices and diverging sharply from the price trend in other nonferrous metals and steel.

Government intervened on several occasions, and in a variety of ways, to "stabilize" the market. It released copper held in government stocks and diverted to industry copper destined for the national stockpile. Export controls were employed to prevent the drain of supplies of refined copper and scrap to foreign markets. Prices were subject to legal control in 1951-1953. When legal controls were lifted, leading producers attempted to pursue a policy of price stability. In 1955, supplies of copper in the American market were far from adequate to meet requirements of fabricating industries, and in early 1956 the New York price of copper reached 47 cents a pound, the highest point in 80 years. The short-supply situation proved only temporary, and by the end of the following year, copper prices had fallen to 26 cents. Copper became a drug on the market, and producers began to cut back the output of their mines in the United States, in South America and in Africa. In early 1958, available supplies of copper appeared adequate for foreseeable demands both for military and civilian needs. This turn of affairs gave rise to demands for the restoration of the import tax which, since April 1947, had been in abeyance.

Postwar Trends in Trade, Production and Consumption

World War II marked a transition in United States trade in copper, as in oil, lead and zinc, and other raw materials, from an export to an import basis. In 1935-1939, *average net exports* had been 60,600 tons; in 1946-1950, *net imports*[1] averaged 382,000 tons, and in 1952-1956, 391,300 tons. (See Table 6.)

Table 6

U. S. IMPORTS AND EXPORTS OF COPPER,[a]
1925-29, 1935-39, 1946-1956
(in thousands of short tons, copper content)

Year	*Imports*[b]	*Exports*	*Net imports*
1925–29 (av.)	391.1	471.0	(79.9)[c]
1935–39 (av.)	263.2	323.8	(60.6)[c]
1946	396.4	53.6	342.8
1947	413.9	148.7	265.2
1948	507.4	147.3	360.1
1949	552.7	146.3	406.4
1950	690.4	154.6	535.8
1951	489.1	141.2	347.9
1952	618.9	183.7	435.2
1953	676.1	144.6	531.5
1954	594.8	294.1	300.7
1955	594.1	238.6	355.5
1956	595.7	262.1	333.6

[a] Ore, concentrates, matte, blister, refined copper, scrap.
[b] Imports are general imports, not imports for consumption.
[c] Net exports.
Source: U.S. Bureau of the Census

[1] Net import figures (imports minus exports) fail to show the substantial volume of foreign copper-bearing materials that are regularly imported for smelting and refining, and then exported. This business was encouraged in prewar years, when raw copper was dutiable, by tariff provisions permitting smelting and refining in bond. Large smelters were established, particularly on the Atlantic seaboard, to process copper of foreign origin. In 1956, 362,400 tons of copper were refined from foreign ores, matte, etc.

United States mine production of copper, which was 625,800 tons in 1935-1939, reached a peak of slightly over 1,000,000 tons in 1942 and 1943. After a sharp postwar decline, the annual output of domestic copper mines in the years 1951-1955 remained fairly stable. The range was between 900,000 and 1,000,000 tons, except for 1954 when output fell to 835,500 tons. (See Table 7.) The 1956 output, 1,100,300 tons, was the highest on record.

Table 7

U. S. PRODUCTION OF COPPER, 1925-29, 1935-39, 1946-1956

(in thousands of short tons, copper content)

Year	*Primary*	*Secondary*[a]	*Total*
1925–29 (av.)	885.8	347.5	1,233.3
1935–39 (av.)	625.8	341.5	967.3
1946	608.7	406.5	1,015.2
1947	847.6	503.4	1,351.0
1948	834.8	505.5	1,340.3
1949	752.8	383.5	1,136.3
1950	909.3	485.2	1,394.5
1951	928.3	458.1	1,386.4
1952	925.4	414.6	1,340.0
1953	926.4	429.4	1,355.8
1954	835.5	407.1	1,242.6
1955	998.6	514.6	1,513.2
1956	1,106.2	468.5	1,574.7

[a] Old scrap; see note, p. 106.
Source: U.S. Bureau of Mines

Concentration and large-scale operations characterize the domestic copper industry. Three dominant producers, Kennecott, Phelps Dodge and Anaconda, in 1955 reported a combined output of 752,000 tons, about 75 percent of the U. S. total. An additional 15 percent was furnished by six smaller companies, and the remaining 10 percent was divided among a large number of small producers.

The largest copper companies are vertically integrated. They own, or control, smelters, refineries and fabricating businesses. (The three largest firms are said to control 65 percent of the American facilities for producing brass and copper wire.) Two of the three leaders in the industry have large investments in foreign copper mines and smelters, particularly in Chile and in Peru. Two-thirds of Anaconda's total output is derived from foreign mines and one-fourth of Kennecott's. Phelps-Dodge, the third company, has only recently made investments in foreign mines.

The total supply of copper (primary and secondary metal) available for consumption in the United States in the past two decades rose from an annual average of 900,000 tons in 1935-1939 to 1,910,000 tons in 1956. (See Chart G.)

CHART G

COPPER: U. S. PRODUCTION (PRIMARY AND SECONDARY), IMPORTS, EXPORTS AND SUPPLY, 1925-29, 1935-39, 1946-1956

(in thousands of short tons, copper content)

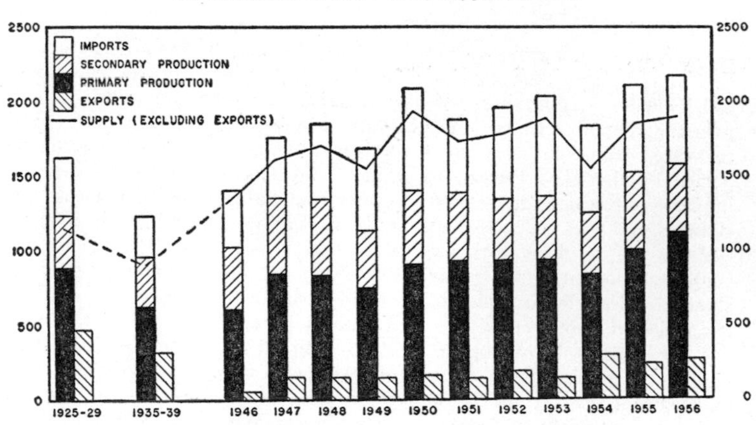

Source: Tables 6 and 7

Most of this increase, however, took place in the first half of the 20-year period. Since the end of World War II, the gain in supply, as measured by the comparison of three-year averages, has been less than 15 percent, from 1,560,000 tons in 1946-1948 to 1,773,600 in 1954-1956.[2] In the same period the index of industrial production showed a gain of nearly 40 percent.

Per capita consumption of copper in the United States, as estimated by trade sources, shows a slight decline in the postwar decade, from 25.4 pounds in 1946, to 22.2 in 1956. Domestic copper mines, secondary metal and net imports contributed to the total annual supply as follows:

Year	*Total supply* (1000 tons)	Ratio to total supply (percent) *Mine production*	*Old scrap*	*Net imports*
1951	1,734.3	53.5	26.4	20.1
1952	1,775.2	52.1	23.4	24.5
1953	1,887.3	49.1	22.7	28.2
1954	1,543.3	54.1	26.4	19.5
1955	1,868.7	53.4	27.5	19.0
1956	1,908.3	57.6	24.9	17.5

In 1925-1929, domestic mine production averaged 77 percent of total supply; in 1935-1939, 69 percent; and in 1946-1950, 48 percent.

2 Estimates of domestic consumption vary because of variations in methods of computing the supply of secondary copper. Trade statisticians usually take account only of the metal recovered from old scrap by primary refiners. In my calculations, I have included also the copper recovered from old scrap by secondary refiners and brass mills, as reported by the U.S. Bureau of Mines. To this sum I have added net imports (equivalent in refined copper) and have made adjustments for changes in stocks privately held at the beginning and end of each year.

From the resulting estimates of annual consumption, the amounts of copper accumulated each year by government in the national stockpile should be deducted in order to get a more accurate approximation of the quantities of copper used by American industries. Official statistics do not show amounts of copper held in national stockpiles, but estimates from trade sources seem to crystallize around a figure, as of early 1956, of 950,000 tons. At the beginning of 1949, according to unofficial estimates, the stockpile held only 110,000 tons of copper, most of which consisted of material transferred at the end of World War II from various government stocks. In the five years, 1951-1955, it is believed that 450,000 tons were added. If these estimates are in general correct, the amounts of stockpiled copper which should be subtracted from apparent annual supply, in order to arrive at an approximate figure for civilian or industrial consumption, should be larger at the end of the postwar period than at the beginning. Thus the calculation reinforces the conclusion that copper consumption in the United States has shown but slight gain since the end of World War II.

Copper finds its principal peacetime use in the electrical manufacturing industry in the production of generators, motors, switchboards and transmission lines for light and power. Copper alloys, such as bronze and brass, are widely used in the manufacture of automobiles, in shipbuilding and in construction. In World War II, copper was used principally for the manufacture of munitions, tanks, military airplanes and naval vessels. A large bomber required one ton of copper, and a battleship 1,000 tons. In 20 minutes of action, a 37-millimeter antiaircraft gun used up one ton of copper; a 50-plane squadron consumed approximately 7 tons of copper in a minute's firing.[3] In 1951-1953, defense requirements for copper took about 20 percent of all shipments of copper-base mill and foundry products. In future wars copper may prove a less important metal. Battleships have become obsolete, and missiles, to some extent, may replace airplanes. Also, in munitions other metals are being substituted for copper.

Imports. In prewar years the bulk of the imports were concentrates and blister copper brought into the country for smelting and refining. During postwar years, owing largely to policies adopted by exporting countries, about one-third of the enlarged imports have already been refined abroad. In 1956, out of total imports of 595,747 tons, 122,174 tons consisted of crude copper, 276,085 tons were unrefined black blister and converter copper, and 191,745 tons of refined metal.

Chile, the principal source of imported copper, furnished an annual average of 274,600 tons in 1952-1956. (See Table 8.) Other Western Hemisphere sources were Canada, 98,800 tons; Mexico, 53,800 tons; Peru, 26,800 tons; Cuba, 18,400 tons; and Bolivia, 4,000 tons. The United States normally imports about 65 percent of Chile's total copper production, virtually all of it from properties controlled by the Anaconda and Kennecott companies. About one-third of Canada's production comes to the

3 Testimony of John A. Danaher, Hearings, *Copper Import Tax Suspension,* before the Senate Finance Committee, 83rd Cong., 1st sess. (Washington: GPO 1953), p. 40.

United States and from 50 to 85 percent of the output of other Western Hemisphere countries. In case of national emergency, the United States could supply all its copper requirements from domestic sources plus imports from countries in this hemisphere. These countries in 1952-1956 furnished about 75 percent of all imports.

Table 8

U. S. IMPORTS[a] OF UNMANUFACTURED COPPER, BY COUNTRIES, 1949-1956

(in thousands of short tons, copper content)

Country of origin	*1949*	*1950*	*1951*	*1952*	*1953*[b]	*1954*[b]	*1955*[b]	*1956*
Chile	285	292	268	362	281	267	226	237
Canada	83	82	55	82	104	88	100	120
Mexico	65	63	48	51	66	51	48	53
Peru	22	29	10	11	27	22	31	43
Northern Rhodesia	27	87	44	28	88	62	74	28
Cuba	16	23	22	20	18	18	20	16
All other	55	114	42	65	93	87	95	99
Total	553	690	489	619	676	595	594	596

a General imports. Data include copper imported for immediate consumption, plus material entering country under bond.
b Imports of scrap copper (amounting to 7,800 tons in 1953; 4,700 tons in 1954; and 12,600 tons in 1955) not distributed by countries.
Source: U. S. Bureau of the Census

Exports. Exports of copper,[4] which averaged 324,000 tons in 1935-1939, were only 130,000 tons in 1946-1950. The annual average in 1952-1956 was 225,000 tons. Copper in all forms was subject to export control throughout the postwar years (see p. 122), and until late 1956 no licenses were issued for exports of copper refined from domestic ores. Hence the exports have consisted almost entirely of copper smelted and refined in the United States from concentrates and blister copper of foreign origin.

4 Including ores, concentrates, refined copper and scrap. In addition, substantial quantities of copper were exported indirectly in the form of wire and in various manufactured products, such as electrical goods and automobiles.

Copper Prices

Copper prices in the postwar decade pursued an erratic course, with periods of enforced stability alternating with rapid change. The trend was more strongly upward than the movement of the general price level, so that, in terms of other commodities, copper was considerably more expensive in 1956 than 10 years earlier. (See Table 9.)

Table 9

COPPER: U. S. WHOLESALE PRICES, ACTUAL AND IN TERMS OF 1947-49 DOLLARS, 1929-1956

(in cents per pound)

Year	*Actual price*	*Price in 1947–49 dollars*	*Year*	*Actual price*	*Price in 1947–49 dollars*
1929	18.1	29.2	1944	11.8	17.5
1930	13.0	23.2	1945	11.8	17.1
1931	8.1	17.1	1946	13.8	17.5
1932	5.6	13.3	1947	21.0	21.8
1933	7.0	16.4	1948	22.0	21.1
1934	8.4	17.2	1949	19.2	19.4
1935	8.7	16.7	1950	21.2	20.6
1936	9.5	18.1	1951	24.2	21.1
1937	13.2	23.5	1952	24.2	21.7
1938	10.0	19.6	1953	28.8	26.2
1939	11.0	22.0	1954	29.7	26.9
1940	11.3	22.1	1955	37.5	33.9
1941	11.8	20.8	1956	41.8	36.6
1942	11.8	18.4			
1943	11.8	17.6			

Source: Actual price — *Engineering and Mining Journal*
Price in 1947-49 dollars — Calculated from U. S. Bureau of Labor Statistics series.

During World War II, government controls fixed the price at 12 cents per pound (electrolytic, New York). But the supply coming on the market at that price was far from adequate to meet the greatly increased demand. Premium prices were consequently granted on copper produced in excess of assigned quotas from high-cost mines, and from high-cost areas in other mines. During the period, February 1942-June 1947, when the Premium Price Plan was in effect, copper prices, including premiums, averaged 14.3 cents per pound. With the end of price control in November 1946, prices advanced rapidly, leveling off in early 1947 at 22 cents.

The scramble for copper induced by the Korean war brought about a second period of price control. At the end of January 1951, maximum prices were fixed for individual producers at the highest prices they had received during the preceding month.[5] For the bulk of the sales this meant a ceiling of 24.2 cents per pound. During the period of compulsory price stabilization, which lasted until February 1953, the price of copper in free markets abroad rose rapidly, and a considerable spread developed between New York and London. To prevent the diversion of foreign copper from the American market, price premiums were again introduced. In 1951-1952, copper of foreign origin was sold in the United States at 3 cents above the ceiling. Premium prices were also paid on copper from certain American mines, under maintenance-of-production contracts.

With the removal of price control in early 1953, New York prices rose sharply to 30 cents, and the gap between domestic and foreign prices disappeared temporarily.[6] But in 1955 it reappeared. London prices had risen rapidly in the fourth quarter of 1954 as a result of mounting European demand. But American producers kept their prices at the 30-cent level until February 1955, and then raised them only gradually, so that they lagged behind the London market. (See Chart H.) This policy aroused complaints both at home and abroad. In the United States

[5] At this time the National Production Authority was given the power to restrict inventories, reduce consumption, and direct the flow of copper and copper scrap. Later in 1951, the Defense Production Administration placed copper raw materials under complete allocation control.

[6] No free market price for copper was quoted in London until August 1953. Until then the British government had controlled purchases and sales.

CHART H

U. S. AND U. K. WHOLESALE PRICES OF COPPER (ELECTROLYTIC), 1939-1945 (YEARLY AVERAGES) 1946-1956 (QUARTERLY AVERAGES)
(in cents per pound)

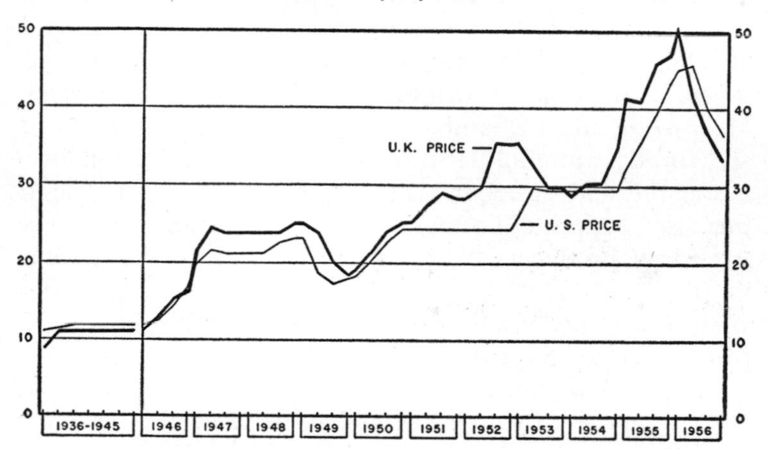

Source: *Engineering and Mining Journal;* Great Britain, Central Statistical Office

small copper mining enterprises, whose selling price was based on New York quotations, charged that they were being robbed of profits. The Chilean government complained of the low yields in dollar exchange from copper exported to New York by the major American companies from their Chilean mines. Accordingly, for a time Chile restricted copper exports to the United States to one-third of the country's output.

In August 1955, the major American copper companies put their price up, first to 40 cents and then to 43 cents a pound. In February 1956, the price hit 47 cents, the highest figure recorded since 1872. London prices, however, were still higher, so the American market did not attract increased quantities of foreign metal. Acting in response to complaints of the copper fabricating industries, the U. S. government postponed deliveries of copper to the national stockpile, authorized sale of metal from stocks accumulated under the Defense Production Act and tightened export controls on copper and copper-alloy scrap.

In July 1956 the United Kingdom, which had released 65,000 tons of copper from its stockpile in 1955, announced that 36,000 tons more would be released before the end of March 1957.[7] American fabricators staged a buyers' strike, living off inventories in anticipation of lower prices. Meanwhile the demand for copper from the American and foreign automobile industries had fallen off. Furthermore, the end of labor troubles in the mines indicated increased supplies. To meet the new conditions, the large American producers dropped their prices from 45 cents in June to 41 cents in July and to 36 cents in November 1956. Continued decline in 1957 brought the New York price down to 26 cents at the end of the year.

Copper is a standardized commodity which moves in large quantities in international trade. But the behavior of prices in postwar years, particularly in 1953-1956, seemed to indicate the absence of a world price for this metal. United States imports in postwar years amounted to 20 percent of total world production, and 30 percent of world production excluding the United States. Since 1947 foreign copper had entered the U. S. market duty free.[8] Transport charges from South America to consuming centers in Western Europe and in the United States were about equal. Under these conditions, one would expect that, except in periods when the United States or other governments enforced price control, copper would have sold in New York and London at approximately the same prices. Yet Table 10 indicates (1) that throughout the 10-year period New York prices were regularly lower, at times much lower, than the London quotations; and (2) that the movements in the two markets were not closely synchronized. The initiative for price change generally came from London, with the New York market showing a lag, at times, of several months.

[7] In August 1957 the British government announced that it would release a further 27,000 tons.

[8] Except for the period July 1, 1950-April 1, 1951, when a tax of two cents a pound was in effect.

Table 10

AVERAGE WHOLESALE PRICE OF COPPER (ELECTROLYTIC), IN THE UNITED STATES AND IN THE UNITED KINGDOM, BY QUARTERS, 1946-1956

(in cents per pound)

		First quarter	*Second quarter*	*Third quarter*	*Fourth quarter*
1946	U. S.	11.8	12.5	14.2	16.8
	U. K.	*11.2*	*12.8*	*15.1*	*16.4*
1947	U. S.	19.8	21.6	21.2	21.2
	U. K.	*21.6*	*24.6*	*23.9*	*23.8*
1948	U. S.	21.2	21.2	22.6	23.2
	U. K.	*23.8*	*23.8*	*23.8*	*25.2*
1949	U. S.	23.2	18.5	17.2	17.9
	U. K.	*25.2*	*23.9*	*20.1*	*18.5*
1950	U. S.	18.2	20.1	22.5	24.2
	U. K.	*19.1*	*21.1*	*24.0*	*25.3*
1951	U. S.	24.2	24.2	24.2	24.2
	U. K.	*25.3*	*27.5*	*29.1*	*28.4*
1952	U. S.	24.2	24.2	24.2	24.2
	U. K.	*28.4*	*29.9*	*35.6*	*35.5*
1953	U. S.	26.2	29.8	29.6	29.6
	U. K.	*35.7*	*32.6*	*29.9*	*29.7*
1954	U. S.	29.7	29.7	29.7	29.7
	U. K.	*29.0*	*30.3*	*30.6*	*35.1*
1955	U. S.	31.8	35.7	39.3	43.2
	U. K.	*41.4*	*41.2*	*45.9*	*46.9*
1956	U. S.	45.0	45.6	40.0	36.7
	U. K.	*50.7*	*41.9*	*37.2*	*34.8*

Source: U. S. Prices — *Engineering and Mining Journal*
U. K. prices — Great Britain, Central Statistical Office

These apparent anomalies in price behavior may have several explanations. The quoted New York producers' prices do not represent all transactions in the New York market. Independent smelters often sell copper at prices which more closely approximate the London quotations. Furthermore, the lack of agreement between the world market price of copper and the price at which the American Big Three companies sell their product in New York was related to the latter's desire to maintain stable prices, having in mind, perhaps, price patterns in the steel and aluminum industries.

The Outlook for Demand

The substitution of plastics, steel, aluminum and other materials for copper may have more than temporary effects on demand. Most significant is the shift from copper to aluminum in certain uses, notably in electrical equipment. Before World War II, aluminum at 20 cents cost twice as much, pound for pound, as copper. During the war aluminum fell while copper was controlled, so that in 1946 they sold at approximately the same price. In postwar years copper has become the more expensive metal. (See Table 11 and Chart I.) The price differential against copper in 1952, when the Paley report was published, was between four and five cents. At that time aluminum had already displaced copper almost completely in high-tension power transmission. It was entering the field of urban power dis-

Table 11

U. S. WHOLESALE PRICES OF COPPER (ELECTROLYTIC) AND ALUMINUM (PRIMARY, 99%), YEARLY AVERAGES, 1926-1956

(in cents per pound)

Year	*Copper*	*Aluminum*	*Year*	*Copper*	*Aluminum*
1926	13.8	27.5	1941	11.8	16.5
1927	12.9	25.8	1942	11.8	15.0
1928	14.6	24.3	1943	11.8	15.0
1929	18.1	24.3	1944	11.8	15.0
1930	13.0	23.8	1945	11.8	15.0
1931	8.1	23.3	1946	13.8	15.0
1932	5.6	23.3	1947	21.0	15.0
1933	7.0	23.3	1948	22.0	15.5
1934	8.4	22.2	1949	19.2	17.0
1935	8.7	19.5	1950	21.2	17.6
1936	9.5	19.0	1951	24.2	19.0
1937	13.2	19.8	1952	24.2	19.4
1938	10.0	20.0	1953	28.8	20.9
1939	11.0	20.0	1954	29.7	21.8
1940	11.3	18.8	1955	37.5	23.7
			1956	41.8	26.0

Source: *Engineering and Mining Journal,* American Metal Market

CHART I

U. S. WHOLESALE PRICES: COPPER (ELECTROLYTIC) AND ALUMINUM (PRIMARY, 99%), YEARLY AVERAGES, 1926-1956
(in cents per pound)

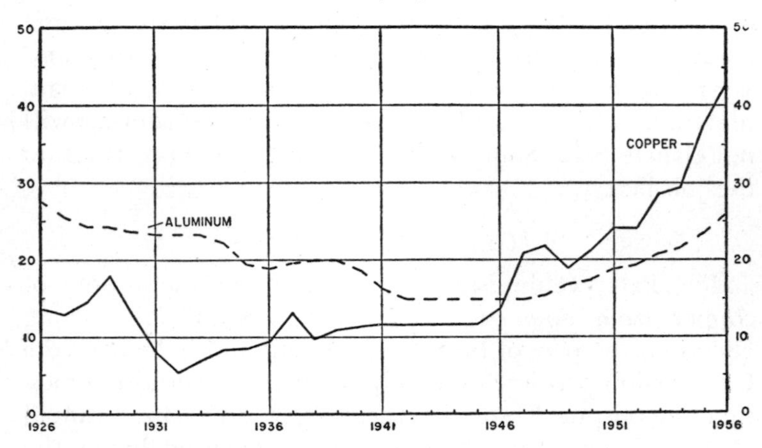

Source: Table 11

tribution, and its use was beginning in the windings of small motors and large generators. Substitution of aluminum is limited, however, by its lower electrical conductivity (60 percent of copper) which means that aluminum components must be larger. Hence, the use of the cheaper metal necessitates the redesigning of equipment.

The Bell Telephone Laboratories, in 1954, reported spectacular reduction in the use of copper: "In long-distance transmission, 50 years ago it required 350 pounds of copper per mile of voice circuit; this was reduced to 54 pounds in 1917, to 7.3 pounds in 1938, to 3 pounds in 1948, and 1 pound in the new L-3 carrier system of today. In the radio-relay system that now spans the continent for long-distance voice and TV transmission, no copper is used between the towers."[9]

In some automobile parts, aluminum and stainless steel

[9] Statement by R. M. Burns, in Hearings before the Senate Subcommittee on Minerals, Materials and Fuels Economics, *Stockpile and Accessibility of Strategic and Critical Materials* . . . , 83rd Cong., 2d sess., pursuant to S. Res. 143 (Washington: GPO, 1954), pt. 11, p. 402.

have been substituted for copper and brass. In building construction a declining rate of copper consumption per unit of new building appeared after 1947. On the other hand, the growth of the electronics industry and the development of nuclear power installations will require large amounts of copper. The fall in copper prices in 1956 and 1957 may set in motion a return to copper, but many manufacturers who switched to more price-stable materials will not change back. Some have discovered that substitutes do the job better.

Outlook for Supply

The Paley Commission's projections of the supply of copper *from domestic mines* were pessimistic. "Strong efforts on the part of both Government and industry," the Commission predicted, "will be required to sustain domestic mine output. Even with these efforts an average annual output of 800 thousand tons a year, somewhat below the mine production of 1950 and 1951, is the highest that can be safely counted on over the next 25 years." [10] Actually, in the years 1951-1955 American copper mining enterprises, aided by government loans and purchase contracts and stimulated after 1953 by rapidly rising prices, produced an annual average of over 920,000 tons. Their 1956 output was 1,106,000 tons.

Present domestic reserves of copper are estimated at 25,000,000 tons of copper metal, recoverable under present economic and technological conditions, but the progressive depletion of the richer deposits has already brought about a rise in real costs. In 1953 the average grade of copper ores mined was .85 percent, that is, 17 pounds of metal from one ton of ore. In 1900 the average had been five percent—100 pounds per ton. Profitable mining of lean ores has been made possible by large-scale mechanized operations. As early as 1948, three-quarters of the U. S. output came from vast open pits where it was scooped up

[10] President's Materials Policy Commission, *Resources for Freedom* (Washington: GPO, 1952), v. 2, *The Outlook for Key Commodities*, p. 33.

by huge electric shovels. It seems doubtful whether further improvements in mining and handling ore, or in milling and concentrating, will make possible the exploitation of ores now considered submarginal.

Since 1890, very few new copper deposits have been discovered in the United States. The prospects of finding large deposits the Paley Commission did not consider bright. It reported:

> . . . virtually all the remaining store of known occurrences of copper mineralization in this country were explored during the Second World War and since, and those that proved to be commercial have been or are being prepared for production. These new deposits will permit a short-run increase in over-all productive capacity, but are expected soon to be offset by a depletion elsewhere that will tend to keep total, long-run productive capacity at roughly the present level. Further, the copper industry appears already to have exploited fairly exhaustively the possibilities provided by advances in technology to date. On the geologic score, the prevailing view is that, with present techniques and knowledge, the chance of further discovery outside the known districts is small. Revolutionary advances in the techniques of copper discovery would, of course, result in substantial alteration of the domestic reserve and production situation.[11]

Secondary, or scrap, copper forms an important addition to the supply of newly mined domestic metal. Between 60 and 75 percent of the copper which enters into consumption as manufactured products is eventually recovered as scrap. In the years 1951-1955, recovery of old scrap[12] averaged 425,000 tons annually. In its projections of future U. S. supplies of copper, the Paley Commission assumed that old scrap would furnish 28 percent, i.e., 700,000 tons of metal in 1975. Its 1975 balance sheet for copper was:

[11] Same, p. 35.

[12] New scrap, waste material from manufacturing processes, defective castings, clippings, turnings, etc., is not regarded from a long-range viewpoint as constituting an addition to the annual copper supply. To include it would involve double counting because of the shortness of the production-recovery cycle. The cycle for old scrap, metal articles discarded because they are worn out, obsolete or damaged, ranges from 10 to 40 years.

Projected consumption:	2,500,000 tons
Projected supply from domestic sources:	
From domestic mines:	800,000 tons
From old scrap:	700,000 tons

According to this calculation, the gap to be filled by (net) imports in 1975 would be 1,000,000 tons, an increase of about 665,000 tons over the 1956 figure.

Foreign Production

The total production of the world's copper mines (see Table 12) in 1956 was about 3.75 million tons. Of this

Table 12

WORLD MINE PRODUCTION OF COPPER, SELECTED YEARS

(in thousands of short tons, copper content)

Country	*1937–39* (average)	*1943*	*1946*	*1951*	*1955*	*1956*
United States	709	1,091	609	928	999	1,106
Canada	287	288	184	270	326	356
Mexico	51	55	65	61	60	60
Chile	406	561	398	420	478	540
Peru	40	37	27	36	48	49
Northern Rhodesia	236	281	211	352	395	445
Belgian Congo	146	173	159	212	259	276
All other, except U.S.S.R.	379	358	214	345	450	502
U.S.S.R.[a]	109	143	165	280	385	416
Total world[a]	2,363	2,987	2,032	2,904	3,400	3,750

[a] Estimated.

Sources: U. S. Bureau of the Census, American Bureau of Metal Statistics

amount, the United States production was about 30 percent. The five principal producing countries in the Western Hemisphere (the United States, Canada, Mexico, Peru and Chile) supplied 2,111,000 tons, 56 percent of the total, and two African countries, Northern Rhodesia and the Belgian Congo, 720,000 tons, or 19 percent. Soviet Russia was credited with 416,000 tons, 11 percent of the total.

"Indicated" reserves of copper in foreign countries,

outside the U.S.S.R., have been estimated [13] at 190 million tons of recoverable copper. Proven reserves are about 87 million long tons of copper metal. According to the Bureau of Mines, 90 percent of the world's resources of unmined copper are in five regions: south-central Africa, Chile, western United States, eastern Ontario and southern Quebec in Canada, and Kazakhstan, U.S.S.R. The African deposits include very large amounts of copper ore with 3-6 percent metal content, which contrasts with the U. S. average of less than 1 percent. Chilean deposits have large tonnages averaging 3 percent copper. The differences in yield do not indicate, however, differences in mining costs, for in both South America and Africa underground mines predominate, whereas in open-pit American operations large tonnages of low-grade ore are handled at low costs.

The problem of increasing production abroad is not the discovery of new reserves but the fuller exploitation by new capital investment of those known to exist. In Northern Rhodesia, a great, new power development on the Zambesi River, financed by a loan of $86 million from the International Bank for Reconstruction and Development and by loans of $56 million from copper companies and the Rhodesian government, will "pave the way" for a 40 percent expansion in copper production by 1960. Anaconda announced in October 1956 that it was spending $100 million for improvements in its Chilean copper mines. In the Toquepala Valley in southern Peru, three U. S. companies have joined forces to develop copper deposits estimated to contain one billion tons of ore assaying a little over 20 pounds of copper to the ton. Half of the total investment of about $200 million will be provided by a loan from the U. S. Export-Import Bank. Initial production, about 120,000 tons per year, is scheduled for 1960.

The Copper and Brass Research Association has estimated that 48 copper expansion projects already under

[13] By the International Geological Congress. See *Central African Examiner,* December 7, 1957, p. vi, Supplement.

way in various parts of the world at the beginning of 1956 will add, by 1958, almost 500,000 tons to the world's yearly output. Geographic distribution of these projects is shown below:

Area	*Number of projects*	*Scheduled additions to 1955 production* (tons)
United States	7	148,000
Canada	15	103,450
South and Central America	7	42,550
Africa	10	137,100
Other[a]	9	27,570
Total free world	48	458,670

[a] Includes Australia, the Philippines, Austria, Norway and Israel.
Source: *New York Times,* January 3, 1956.

Tariff Protection

Tariff protection on copper in 1869-1894 coincided with a period of rapid growth of the industry, but the restriction of imports in reality was not a causal factor of importance. "The extraordinary progress of the industry was obviously due to the discovery and exploitation of great natural resources,—resources so rich and so tempting that the same effects on production, prices, and international trade would have come about, whatever the rates of duty."[14] After 1894, when copper was put on the Free List, the industry continued to expand until, at the beginning of the 20th century, the United States had become the largest copper-producing country in the world and copper had become a leading article of export. Under these conditions there seemed to be no occasion for restricting imports. Nevertheless, the collapse of foreign and domestic markets in the Great Depression led to the imposition in 1932 of an import tax[15] of 4 cents a pound on refined copper and the metal content of copper-bearing ores.

Over a period of 25 years the tax has had little effect on either import trade in copper or on the fortunes of domes-

[14] F. W. Taussig, *Some Aspects of the Tariff Question* (Cambridge: Harvard University Press, 1924), p. 165.

[15] Like the excise tax on imported oil, the copper tax was in all but name an import duty.

tic producers. Before World War II, when the United States was a net exporter of copper, most of the imports entered free of tax for refining and export. The bulk of the taxed copper was manufactured into products which were later exported with benefit of drawback. During World War II, imports were largely for government use and again bore no tax. Immediately after the armistice, shortages of copper developed and in April 1947 the import tax on copper materials was suspended. The tax on copper scrap had been suspended five years earlier, and neither of these taxes has since been reimposed. The original suspension was for three years, but later acts have continued the policy of free trade in unmanufactured copper until June 30, 1958. The suspension of the duty, by virtue of a 1951 amendment (*Public Law* no. 38, 82d Congress), was made to depend on the maintenance of copper prices at no less than 24 cents a pound. If the price should fall below that figure, the President was required to revoke the suspension. Under these conditions, the reductions in the copper tax in trade agreements had little practical significance.[16] Price changes also reduced the potential effectiveness of the copper tax. In 1932, when copper was selling on the London market at 5 cents a pound, the 4-cent tax on copper was equivalent to an 80 percent duty on the foreign value of the imports. But in 1956, when the average London price was 35 cents, the reduced tax, had it been in effect, would have amounted to only 5.7 percent.

While copper was in short supply and prices high, domestic producers did not ask to have import taxes restored on foreign copper. In fact, in 1953, 11 companies, including small as well as large enterprises, went on record as not opposing the continued suspension of the tax. But following the 1956-1957 slump in demand and in prices, protectionist sentiment revived. At the end of 1957, the price of copper in New York had fallen to 25 cents. By dropping their quotations to 24 cents, the major U. S. companies

[16] In 1949 the General Agreement on Tariffs and Trade cut the duty to 2 cents. The 1957 GATT provided for a series of three successive annual reductions, bringing the tax on June 30, 1958, to 1.7 cents.

could have brought the import tax into operation. They refrained from doing so, however, and instead supported bills introduced in January 1958 by a group of Senators and Representatives from seven copper-producing states, which would impose a 4-cent tax to be applied as long as copper sells for less than 30 cents a pound.[17] In coming to this decision, the leading copper-producing firms had to resolve certain internal conflicts of interest. As miners and smelters of domestic ores they would naturally favor the restriction of imports. But two of them also import large quantities of copper from their South American mines, and the third has recently invested in a foreign copper mining enterprise. Hence they have an interest in maintaining free trade in copper. Their investments in fabricating plants in the United States would, it seems, also incline them to favor free trade in the raw material. Nevertheless, on balance they seem to have concluded that a protective policy would be to their advantage.

Copper was one of the metals included in the Domestic Minerals Stabilization Plan proposed, April 29, 1958, by Secretary of the Interior Seaton. According to his five-year plan, the government would guarantee domestic copper producers a price of 27 1/2 cents a pound on a maximum annual production of 1,000,000 tons.

Export Controls

Postwar controls on the export of copper are based on the Export Control Act of 1949,[18] but, before the statute took effect, exports of refined copper and copper matte, copper scrap and various forms of fabricated copper had been embargoed to the U.S.S.R. and its satellites, for reasons of national security. The 1951 general embargo on trade with Communist China prevents exports of copper to that country. The 1949 Act also authorized the Department of Commerce to apply short-supply controls which it

[17] In April 1958 Secretary of the Interior Seaton, speaking for the Eisenhower administration, recommended that Congress restore the import tax on copper.

[18] See Chapter 3, pp. 60-62.

has alternately relaxed and tightened, according to conditions prevailing in the domestic copper market.

During the Korean war, the allocation of export quotas among various recipient countries raised questions of politics as well as economics. The problem, explained in a 1951 report of the Department of Commerce, was "to strike a fair balance between conserving needed supplies for domestic use and helping to meet essential needs of friendly countries."[19] The Department felt compelled to permit exports of copper products to copper-producing countries so as to make sure of continued imports of the raw material. "Refined copper and copper manufactures," the report explained, "must also be exported from the United States to meet requirements abroad of special projects devoted to petroleum production, nonferrous metal mining operations and related power and transportation facilities. Failure to meet such needs might jeopardize these important enterprises and so result in reduced United States imports of a wide range of vitally needed materials. Finally, other friendly countries allied with us in the mutual defense effort must be allocated copper to help maintain their defense programs."[20]

After the shortages of 1951 and 1952 ended, exports of refined copper and copper scrap were freed, in September 1953, from short-supply restrictions. Export licenses were freely issued, except for shipments to Iron Curtain countries and to Communist China. But the period of free exports lasted little more than a year. In October 1954 controls were reimposed, and in February 1955 all exports of copper refined from ores *of domestic origin* were prohibited. These tightened controls, the Department explained, were necessitated by the shortage of copper. Demand had risen both in the United States and in foreign countries, and at the same time labor troubles had curtailed production. "In this situation," according to the Department, "continuation of exports at prevailing rates

[19] *Export Control,* 14th Quarterly Report of the Secretary of Commerce (Washington: GPO, February 28, 1951), p. 2.
[20] Same.

threatened to have adverse effects on important segments of the domestic economy."[21]

In effect, the restrictions on the exports of copper scrap constituted an intervention by government in the market on behalf of the brass mills and other consumers of the secondary metal. It was an attempt to compensate them for the injury they suffered from the price policies of domestic copper producers. The latter, as we have seen, for a number of years kept the New York price of refined copper below the London quotations. Under these conditions, it became profitable to ship scrap abroad. The consequent rise in the domestic price of scrap put a squeeze on the brass mills whose selling prices were tied to the domestic price of refined copper.

Short-supply restrictions on copper exports remained in force until late 1956. At that time the Department of Commerce, recognizing that the metal was no longer in short supply, raised quotas for copper scrap and restored the open-end quota on refined copper produced from materials of domestic origin. Prohibition on copper exports for security reasons still remained in force.

Expansion of Domestic Production

The Defense Production Act of 1950 authorized government aid for the expansion of copper production from both domestic and foreign mines. Government purchase contracts assured a market for nearly 1.5 million tons over a 10-year period, at prices subject to escalation provisions to cover certain increases in costs. For qualified properties exploration loans were granted amounting to 50 percent of estimated costs. Copper companies were awarded certificates of necessity, permitting accelerated amortization ("fast write-offs") for income tax purposes. In addition, like the oil companies and lead and zinc mining enterprises, they benefited by depletion allowances based on a percentage of gross sales.[22] As the result of these various

[21] *Export Control,* 31st Quarterly Report of the Secretary of Commerce (Washington: GPO, July 1, 1955), p. 15.
[22] See Chapter 2, pp. 21-27.

types of assistance, projects were initiated soon after the start of hostilities in Korea which aimed at the addition of 300,000 tons to U. S. productive capacity.

The mobilization goal for the copper industry, established by the Office of Defense Mobilization in February 1952, was an annual supply of 2,270,000 tons, including production of domestic mines, scrap and imports. In late September 1956 the ODM announced that the goal had been attained. Thereupon, the program for the expansion of domestic mine production was formally ended. No further fast write-off permits were to be issued.

Stockpiling, the Chilean Episode

Copper was not considered a strategic or critical material in the years before World War II, and at the time of the attack on Pearl Harbor the U. S. government had no stockpile of copper. Unlike lead and zinc, the U. S. copper industry suffered no postwar depression; except for a short period in 1949-1950, the metal continued in short supply and prices rose steadily. Under these circumstances, the accumulation of copper in the national stockpile proceeded slowly. Because of market shortages, the Office of Defense Mobilization found it necessary in 1955 to defer deliveries of copper purchased for the stockpile and to divert the metal to industry. Fabricating industries, complaining of high prices and shortages, asked for the release to the market of stockpiled copper, but the ODM refused, citing the need for Congressional approval. At the end of 1957, the minimum objective for copper had not been attained, although at that time, according to unofficial estimates, the stockpile held about 1,000,000 tons.

The circumstances of the purchase of 100,000 tons of Chilean copper in 1954 illustrate the interrelation of raw materials policy and foreign policy in general. Prominent among U. S. objectives in dealing with Chile in early post-Korea years were: (1) to assure the continuance of large annual imports of Chilean copper, for the national stockpile and for the needs of American industries; (2) to secure better treatment at the hands of the Chilean government for American corporations, particularly Kennecott and Anaconda, which had large investments in Chilean copper mines (specifically, this meant the removal of discrimination in taxation and in the administration of exchange control); (3) to prevent the U.S.S.R. from acquiring copper from Chile, and from extending its influence in the government and in the labor movement of that country; (4) to assist Chile to rescue its economy from chronic inflation.

On its side, Chile aimed at getting maximum revenues from the U. S. copper companies. It wanted, also, to make copper exports yield the largest possible amounts of foreign exchange. Hence, Chile objected to controls imposed by the U. S. government on copper prices, and found equally obnoxious the price stabilization policies adopted by U. S. copper producers.

Each side held strong cards. Chile, through its control of exports, was in a position to cut down the supply going to the United States. On the other hand, the United States, the principal market for the major product of the Chilean economy, could depress Chilean prices by reimposing its 1932 copper import tax, or by restricting imports by quotas.

The U.S.S.R. played the role of an interested, but perhaps not entirely innocent, bystander. Unverified reports credit the Russians with standing ready to purchase substantial amounts of Chilean surplus copper, either directly or through intermediaries. Moreover, Communist influence, it was reported, played a part in the strikes of the mine workers that curtailed copper production in Chilean mines. Had only economic matters been involved in the negotiations between the two countries—the quantity of copper to be bought and the purchase price—a quicker settlement might have been reached. But discussions of Chile's tax legislation, and of her relations with the U.S.S.R., touched upon sensitive areas of national sovereignty where international agreement is always difficult.

On May 7, 1951, the State Department announced[23] that agreement had been reached on the following points:

(1) American mining companies would expand copper production in Chile so that supplies of copper going to the United States would be increased.
(2) Chile agreed to reserve no more than 20 percent of the output of American companies for its own use and for export to countries other than the United States.
(3) "Chile," the agreement read, "will take steps to limit such exports to essential requirements of friendly countries and will take the necessary measures to insure that such copper will not be re-exported, and will make no sales to countries of the Soviet bloc."
(4) In recognition of Chile's need "for additional dollars in order to maintain its economic stability and support its own effort for participation in hemispheric defense," the U. S. government agreed that Chilean copper might be sold in the United States at 3 cents per pound above the ceiling on domestic copper.

No agreement could be reached, however, on the reform of taxation of American companies or on removing discrimination in exchange rates.

Chile denounced the agreement in May 1952, after barely a year of operation. But after disposing of small lots of copper at the high prices prevailing on the world market, the Chilean export monopoly found its experiment had failed. It had accumulated a large supply of copper, 80,000 to 100,000 tons, and its foreign exchange receipts had diminished rather than increased. Chile's "stockpiling," however, had aggravated the acute shortage of copper in the American market. Consequently, the United States was willing to make a major concession by abolishing price controls on copper of foreign origin. Chile, in August 1953, in order to get rid of its embarrassing copper surplus, made a formal offer of 65,000 tons at

[23] State Department Press Release 367, May 7, 1951. The quotation in the text is taken from the release. Other sources for the following paragraphs are press reports in the *New York Times,* August 8 and 27, November 7, 10, 11, 21, 1953, and March 26 and October 12, 1954; *New York Herald Tribune,* November 1, 1953; *Christian Science Monitor,* December 4, 1953; and *Times* (London), October 22, 1953.

30 cents, the world market price. The United States rejected this offer and again demanded the immediate reform of the Chilean mining laws so as to remove discriminatory treatment of American companies. It insisted also as a precondition of the copper purchase that Chile should carry out its 1951 agreement to prohibit sales of copper to countries in the Soviet orbit.

Chile eventually made these concessions, but not as a formal *quid pro quo*. After a delaying action, the Chilean senate in December 1953 voted to bar sales from its copper stocks to Iron Curtain countries, but it was not until May 1955 that the Chilean government, in its so-called New Deal legislation, removed the obnoxious features of its laws taxing foreign mining enterprises and discrimination in conversion of dollars to pesos. Meanwhile, more than a year earlier, the United States had fulfilled its part of the bargain by taking 100,000 tons of Chile's hoard of copper at 30 cents a pound.

* * * *

This brief survey has revealed no present need for government assistance to the copper industry, either by import tariffs, stockpile purchases or subsidies. Both production and prices in 1956 reached all-time highs. Although the general business recession in 1957 was responsible for a downturn in prices and in production, in the postwar period as a whole domestic copper mining has shown moderate but steady expansion. The industry is in the hands of a few large, integrated companies, well managed and financially strong. Domestic production, it is true, has not kept pace with consumption, so that American fabricating industries have become increasingly dependent on supplies of copper mined abroad. But this does not indicate the need, in the national interest, of subsidizing the domestic industry. With a million tons of copper in its strategic stockpiles, the country is protected against immediate war emergencies. Copper production in the Western Hemisphere, in Chile, Peru, Mexico and Canada, is undergoing rapid expansion, promising increasing supplies of the metal, without burdensome increases in real costs. If enemy action should reduce imports, the loss could be offset by expansion of domestic production, by the substitution of aluminum and other materials, by restrictions on consumption for civilian use, and by enlarged recovery of secondary copper.

The proposed restoration of import taxes on copper, after ten years of free entry, cannot be justified on grounds of national defense. It would give Latin American republics added cause for resentment, thus weakening the bonds of collective security. Moreover, the tariff, like stockpile purchases of domestic copper and other types of subsidy, weakens the American economy by diverting its resources to less efficient uses, and by hastening the depletion of nonreplaceable resources weakens the country's defense potential.

Chapter 6

THE PROBLEM OF NICKEL

"NICKEL HAS an unusual combination of qualities – strength, hardness, toughness, ductility, resistance to corrosion, and maintenance of strength at high temperatures. When alloyed with other metals, those qualities are largely imparted to the resulting material. When alloyed with nonferrous metals, nickel also provides pleasing whiteness, magnetism, electrical qualities, and special desired coefficients of expansion. It so strengthens, toughens, and improves the alloys of which it is a part that effective substitutes are difficult to find."[1] These properties are the clue to the demand for nickel for peacetime industries. They explain also why nickel in wartime holds a high priority among strategic and critical materials.

Nickel is one of the newer metals, having been first produced in New Caledonia about 1865 and in Canada in 1886. Impetus for production on a large scale came first in the 1890's when naval authorities of France, England and Germany learned of the superiority of nickel steel over carbon steel in armor plate for battleships. Nondefense uses were soon discovered, but from the late 19th century until after World War I the demand for nickel came primarily from military and naval establishments.

With the end of hostilities in 1918, and the subsequent naval disarmament program, the nickel market collapsed. Thereupon the International Nickel Company, which had acquired world leadership in the industry, began a vigorous and intelligent campaign to develop new peacetime uses for its product. By alloying steel and nonferrous

[1] U. S. Bureau of Mines (with the cooperation of the Geological Survey), *Nickel,* Materials Survey compiled for the National Security Resources Board (Washington: GPO, 1952), p. 1-3.

metals with nickel, the company developed new products and opened up wide markets in engineering, in building construction and in households, in hospitals and other institutions. The results were spectacular. Sales revived and, by 1939, 85 percent of the world's annual output was absorbed by civilian production.

A Canadian economist wrote in 1937: "Nickel is a minor and by no means irreplaceable material in modern warfare."[2] But his opinion soon proved false, for in World War II the military uses of nickel again became predominant. In fact, during that struggle practically no nickel was available for peacetime purposes. But after V-J Day there was no disarmament comparable to that which followed the First World War. The conquered nations, it is true, were compelled to disband their armed forces and to cease the production of armaments and munitions. The victors also, for a few years, reduced the number of men under arms and cut down defense budgets. But the conflicts of interest and purpose which arose between the United States and its allies, on the one hand, and the U.S.S.R. on the other soon checked this trend. After the Russian seizure of Czechoslovakia, Congress set in motion a rearmament program providing for the renewal of conscription and enlarged expenditures for the armed services. The attack on South Korea in June 1950 caused a scramble for all strategic materials, including nickel.

New weapons had caused changes in the art of warfare. The introduction of the atomic bomb seemed to call for greater reliance on airplanes and less on ground troops. The new look at defense policy emphasized deterrent power, "massive retaliation," rather than building up local defenses. Put together, these changes called for larger numbers of aircraft with higher speed, each containing more pounds of nickel. In 1954, the Department of Defense reported that nickel "comes closest to being a true 'war metal.' It deserves first priority among materials receiving conservation attention. Since the start of the

[2] Alex Skelton in *International Control in the Non-Ferrous Metals,* by William Y. Elliott and others (New York: Macmillan, 1937), p. 176.

Korean War, nickel has remained the world's most critical material; this condition is likely to continue for some time."[3]

This was the situation in 1954, and, in fact, in 1955 and 1956 military demands (including stockpiling) took almost half the available supply of nickel, thus creating an acute shortage of the metal for civilian uses. But at the end of 1957 supplies had increased, the military had reduced its take to 25 percent of the total, and nickel was again in the position it had occupied 20 years earlier, a metal whose uses were predominantly in the field of peacetime production.

Problems of Postwar Policy

The key problem of postwar policy was how to get more nickel. A secondary aim was to build up new sources of supply, in Cuba and Canada, so as to reduce dependence on a single firm which dominated world trade in nickel, the International Nickel Company. A third objective was to apportion to best advantage the available supply. This involved determining how much should be stockpiled, how the remainder should be divided between defense and nondefense industries and how nondefense nickel should be apportioned among thousands of firms producing articles for civilian use.

The characteristic feature of the postwar nickel problem was the need to rely for practically all the supply on the output of mines and facilities situated in a foreign country and owned by a foreign corporation, the International Nickel Company of Canada, Ltd. (In 1955 it was estimated that if all the nickel in the United States were mined and processed it would last at the current rate of consumption for only nine months.[4]) Reliance upon the foreign source

[3] U. S. Department of Defense, Office of Assistant Secretary of Defense (Supply and Logistics), *Annual Materials Conservation Report* (Washington: Author, 1954), p. 4.

[4] James H. Pinkley, of the General Services Administration, in *Defense Production Act,* Progress Report No. 33, Hearing before the Joint Committee on Defense Production, 84th Cong., 1st sess. (Washington: GPO, 1955), p. 6.

apparently posed no problem of national security,[5] for Canada had agreed that its resources were to be shared for purposes of joint defense. The Canadian nickel, however, was not automatically available. The Canadian corporation which controlled practically all the developed reserves was not subject to American jurisdiction, or vulnerable to the many types of pressures which the government of the United States can exert on a domestic business enterprise.

The Demand for Nickel

No material has been found which can economically be substituted for nickel as a catalyst in the hydrogenation of fats and oils and in the refining of petroleum. In 1956 about 32 million pounds of nickel (13 percent of total consumption of new metal) were used in electroplating steel and other metals. On many kinds of electrical appliances, plumbing fixtures and other hardware, and the "bright work" on automobiles, chromium is deposited on a thin undercoating of nickel.

About three-quarters of the annual consumption of nickel goes into alloys, either with iron and steel or with nonferrous metals (copper, tin, zinc, magnesium and aluminum). Monel metal, an alloy of copper and nickel, has been widely used where resistance to corrosion is essential, in chemical plants and oil refineries, in laundry and kitchen equipment. Alloys of nickel with bronze are used for ship propellers. The special magnetic and electrical properties of iron-nickel alloys explain their widespread use in telephone equipment. It is now virtually impossible to find telephone apparatus in which nickel is not playing a significant role. The largest and fastest-growing use of nickel is in stainless steel and other ferrous alloys. Nickel gives added strength and durability to the steels used in bridges and in building construction, in the

[5] The concentration of production in a single small area, the Sudbury basin, involves the hazard of destruction by long-range ballistic missiles. But this hazard would be equally present if the ore bodies were in the United States.

gears and bearings of internal combustion engines, in automotive transmissions and in railway rolling stock, and in drilling cutters in oil wells.

Nickel and nickel alloys are extensively used in atomic energy projects. The principal military use, accounting for 30-40 percent of the military total, is in heat-resistant alloys, containing as high as 80 percent nickel. Steels with a lower nickel content are used in the construction of ships, vehicles, weapons, ammunition and other military "hardware."

The post-Korea rearmament program made exceptional demands on the nickel supply because of the development of nuclear weapons, increased reliance on air power, and the development of planes powered by gas turbines and jet engines. For the new types of engines, metals were required which could withstand red heat (approaching 2,000 degrees Fahrenheit) and great stress. These qualities were furnished by alloys containing chromium, nickel and other additive metals. The average amount of nickel required for a piston-type engine for military aircraft has been estimated at 330 pounds. For jet engines the corresponding figure would be 1,300 to 1,600 pounds.

Postwar changes in the uses of nickel by American industries, both for defense and civilian production, are shown in Table 13. The table indicates that in the period, 1946 to 1956, total consumption gained about one-third (from an average of 170 million pounds in 1946-1948 to 220 million in 1954-1956). Meanwhile, however, the index of industrial production rose nearly 40 percent and the combined index of production of nonferrous metals about 60 percent. There was, in fact a continuing shortage of nickel for civilian consumption. Domestic production being negligible, practically the entire supply was obtained from imports which did not increase fast enough to keep pace with the rapidly expanding demand for defense production, for stockpiling and for ordinary peacetime uses. The available supply was not big enough to go around. Military requirements, which had priority, absorbed a rapidly growing share of the total.

Table 13

U. S. CONSUMPTION OF NEW NICKEL, BY USES, 1946-1956
(in millions of pounds)

Year	*Ferrous*[a]	*Non-ferrous*[b]	*Alloys*[c]	*Electro-plating*	*Other*	*Total*
1946	73.2	51.8	13.6	18.6	4.0	161.0
1947	73.4	54.7	10.3	19.2	3.6	161.5
1948	84.6	56.1	12.3	29.8	4.5	187.1
1949	57.6	39.6	8.1	28.3	5.6	139.3
1950	87.1	58.8	11.4	34.8	7.1	200.0
1951	83.9	53.9	14.8	11.7	9.1	173.4
1952	97.9	64.0	16.0	13.2	11.6	202.8
1953	90.9	61.6	16.4	28.5	13.9	211.4
1954	76.3	56.1	13.2	29.6	14.3	189.5
1955[d]	100.3	51.3	17.3	31.7	17.8	218.3
1956[d]	100.5	62.9	21.4	31.8	35.4	252.0

a Including stainless and other steel and cast iron.
b Including copper-nickel alloys, nickel-silver, aluminum and manganese alloys, Monel metal, Inconel.
c Special high-temperature and electrical-resistant alloys.
d Preliminary.
Source: U. S. Bureau of Mines

In 1948 defense agencies[6] took from the market 7 million pounds of primary nickel, between 3 and 4 percent of the total available supply; in 1956 the defense share, including stockpiling, was approximately 124 million pounds, or 43 percent. Meanwhile, although the total available supply had increased from 192 million pounds to 290 million, the quantity of primary nickel consumed in nondefense industries fell from 185 million pounds to 166 million.[7] (It is worth noting that the amounts of nickel made available for nondefense uses in 1956 included 77 million pounds of government nickel which had been diverted from the stockpile.) Estimates for 1957, if we assume no additions to the stockpile, indicate a reduction

[6] See Office of Defense Mobilization, *Defense Mobilization in a Full Economy* (Washington: Author, 1957), p. 21.
[7] These amounts, it should be noted, refer only to *imported, primary* nickel. They do not include small quantities of domestic production of primary nickel or scrap.

in the amounts reserved for military purposes to 75 million pounds, 25 percent of the total available supply. (See Table 14.)

Table 14

NICKEL: U. S. SUPPLY AND CONSUMPTION FOR MILITARY AND CIVILIAN PURPOSES, 1948-1957

(in millions of pounds, nickel content, except percentages where noted)

Year	Total available supply	For military purposes[a]		For civilian use[b]	
		Amount	% of supply	Amount	% of supply
1948	192	7	3.6	185	96.4
1949	153	18	11.8	135	88.2
1950	200	14	7.0	186	93.0
1951	187	74	39.6	113	60.4
1952	213	108	50.7	105	49.3
1953	234	111	47.4	123	52.6
1954	262	130	49.6	132	50.4
1955	277	135	48.7	142	51.3
1956	290	124	42.8	166	57.2
1957 (est.)	305	75	24.6	230	75.4

[a] For defense production plus stockpiling; after diversions to industry.
[b] Including diversions of government-owned nickel. These were:
1954 — 5.5 million pounds
1955 — 29.9 " "
1956 — 76.8 " "
1957 — 117.0 " "

Source: 1948-1956 — Office of Defense Mobilization, *Defense Mobilization in a Full Economy* (Washington: Author, 1957), p. 21
1957 — ODM Press Release no. 612, October 3, 1957

The Sources of Supply

The total Free World production, outside the United States, of primary nickel in 1956 was about 449 million pounds. Of this amount the United States imported 284 million pounds, or 63 percent. In addition to the imports, small amounts of primary nickel are regularly produced in the United States as a byproduct of copper refining and from a few small deposits of nickel ore. All of this production, amounting to about 13 million pounds, was covered in 1956 by government contracts. From a nickel-cobalt-copper separation plant at Fredericktown, Missouri, the National Lead Company agreed in 1951 to produce and sell to the government 4,631 tons of nickel at the rate of 925 tons per year. At Riddle, Oregon, a deposit of silicate ore is estimated to contain 20 million tons of ore with a content of 1.2 percent nickel. From this ore the M. A. Hanna Nickel Smelting Company undertook in 1953 to furnish the government over a 9-year period with 125 million pounds of nickel contained in ferronickel.

Nickel in Scrap

Nickel recovered from scrap furnishes an increasingly important addition to the available domestic supply of the metal. "Revert" scrap, that which is generated within the plants of steel producers and other "melters," is almost fully recovered, furnishing a substantial part of their total nickel supply. Recovery from the operations of fabricators of nickel products is much less complete, owing to the cost of segregating nickel-bearing from other scrap. Obsolete material (junk) yields only insignificant amounts of nickel. But the shortage of primary nickel and the rising price of scrap greatly stimulated its recovery. Thus in the fiscal year 1956 producers of iron and steel alloys, nickel and copper-base alloys and ingots reported purchases of scrap with a nickel content of 59 million pounds. This was over one-third of their receipts of new nickel and 23 percent of total U. S. consumption of the primary metal.

Imports

Table 15 shows the nickel content of postwar imports and comparative figures for earlier years. The stimulus of increased military demand is apparent during World War I and, in more pronounced form, in World War II. The table shows also the slump in demand for nickel in the depression years of the 1930's. For six years following World War II, imports showed no upward trend. But as a result of the war in Korea, American rearmament and stockpiling they rose in 1952-1956 by over 30 percent, from 218 to 284 million pounds.

Table 15

NICKEL IMPORTED INTO THE UNITED STATES, 1910-1956
(in thousands of pounds)

Yearly averages	*Nickel content* (estimated)
1910–14	38,213
1915–19	62,932
1920–24	29,144
1925–29	52,239
1930–34	37,080
1935–39	85,634
1940–44	218,000
Years	
1945	214,866
1946	185,000
1947	161,435
1948	192,800
1949	182,146
1950	182,694
1951	186,380
1952	217,700
1953	237,474
1954	265,036
1955	285,116
1956	283,724

Note: In the data above no deduction has been made for small amounts of nickel imported from Canada and processed in the United States which were later exported to the United Kingdom.
Source: U. S. Bureau of the Census

Canada in 1956 supplied 79 percent of the imports, and Cuba nearly 11 percent. Norway supplied 24 million pounds of nickel refined from Canadian ores. Of total imports in 1956, 75 percent was in the form of refined metal.

Foreign Production

Geologically, nickel is not a scarce metal. It is more widely distributed in the earth's crust than even the "base" metals, such as lead, zinc and copper. But concentrations of deposits of nickel which can be economically exploited are rare, being found principally in five countries, Canada,

New Caledonia, the Union of South Africa, the U.S.S.R. and Cuba.[8] Hence, judged by price nickel *is* scarce.

In August 1957 the bulk of the supply sold in U. S. markets for 74 cents. At that time nickel sold for about three times the price of copper and more than five times the price of lead.[9] Figures for world production in postwar years are shown in Table 16.

Table 16

FREE WORLD PRODUCTION OF PRIMARY NICKEL, 1946-1957

(in millions of pounds, nickel content)

Year	*Canada*	*United States*	*Cuba*	*New Caledonia*	*Other*	*Total*
1946	192.1	0.7	24.8	6.4	2.6	226.6
1947	237.3	1.3	4.4	6.3	2.3	251.6
1948	263.5	1.6	—	7.6	1.2	273.9
1949	257.4	1.4	—	5.5	1.4	265.7
1950	247.3	1.7	—	9.3	2.1	260.4
1951	275.8	1.5	—	9.2	3.5	290.0
1952	281.1	1.3	17.8	19.0	2.8	322.0
1953	287.4	1.2	27.7	26.0	5.7	348.0
1954	322.5	1.7	29.1	26.0	4.7	384.0
1955	349.9	7.6	30.3	36.0	6.2	430.0
1956	357.5	13.4	32.1	51.0	8.0	462.0
1957[a]	360.0	17.0	45.0	40.0	6.0	468.0

[a] Estimated.
Source: U. S. Bureau of Mines, U. S. Department of Commerce

[8] Philippine iron ores contain large amounts of nickel which, however, cannot at present be economically exploited, or perhaps in the foreseeable future. The Office of Defense Mobilization estimated (July 1956) total Philippine nickel ore reserves at 550 million tons, containing 4.4 million tons of nickel.

Venezuela has ores of high nickel content which have not been exploited because of high labor costs.

[9] The price disparity between nickel and certain other nonferrous metals had diminished since prewar years:

	Ratio of nickel price to prices of			
	Copper	*Lead*	*Zinc*	*Aluminum*
1937–39 (av.)	2.8	6.0	5.9	1.6
1954–56 (av.)	1.7	4.2	5.2	2.7

In the late 19th century, when European countries and the United States first began to use nickel steels for armor plate, they obtained the metal from the French island of New Caledonia, where ores containing 10-15 percent nickel had been discovered in 1865. Even after the exhaustion of the richest deposits, current operations are reported to yield 3-5 percent. Despite the relative richness of the ores and low mining costs, the development of the mines has been handicapped by lack of coal, shortage of labor and especially by the high cost of transporting the product to far-distant markets in Western Europe and the United States. No reliable estimate of reserves is available but the remaining tonnage of high-grade ore is thought to be small when compared with that in Canada and Cuba.

Production in Russia dates from the early 1930's. The Soviet Union, after Finland's cession in 1944 of its mines at Petsamo, became one of the world's major producers of nickel. According to a 1956 estimate Russian mines were producing about 90 million pounds a year, an amount which fully supplies domestic consumption and may permit some exports to satellite countries.

Cuba

Cuba has the world's largest known reserves of nickel, variously estimated to contain between 17 and 24 million tons of metal. The nickel content of ore at Mayari has been found to be 1.2 percent; at Moa Bay, 1.35 percent; and at Nicaro, 1.42 percent. Open-pit operations reduce mining costs, but the exploitation of the ores has been retarded by the lack of an economical process of recovering by-product minerals, iron, cobalt and chromium. This handicap has been partially overcome by a sulphuric acid leaching process, developed by the Freeport Sulphur Company, which makes possible the recovery of cobalt.[10]

Canada

For the past half century Canada has been the principal source of the world's nickel production. Most of the Cana-

[10] Further discussion of the development of the Cuban nickel ores will be found on pp. 148-151.

dian metal has come from the mines of the International Nickel Company in the Sudbury district in the province of Ontario. For more than 50 years the sulfide nickel-copper ores in this area have been the principal source of supply for the United States. In 1956 INCO produced 286 million pounds of nickel, 80 percent of the total Canadian output and 62 percent of total Free World production. In the Sudbury basin alone this company owned 130,000 acres of mineral lands, in which it operated five underground mines and two open pits. In addition it had concentrators, smelters and refineries and hydroelectric plants in Canada, refineries in England and Wales, and rolling mills and foundries in England and Scotland. Investments in the United States were represented by a rolling mill at Huntington, West Virginia and a foundry at Bayonne, New Jersey.

With a capitalization of $443 million in 1956, and about 20,000 workers, it was the third largest Canadian corporation and one of Canada's largest employers of labor. Its growth and success are intimately associated with the prosperity of the entire country. Nevertheless INCO is truly "international." It was organized in New Jersey in 1902 as a consolidation of a number of companies engaged in producing nickel in the United States, Canada and New Caledonia. In 1926 the corporate structure was altered and a Canadian subsidiary, International Nickel Company, Ltd., became the parent company.[11] Its main business office is in Copper Cliff, Ontario; offices are provided for its principal executives in New York City, also. The president and 11 of the 24 members of the board of directors, as well as its chairman, are citizens of the United States. Americans own 45 percent of the stock, Canadians, 35 percent, the remainder being held by English and other investors. Its ownership of the world's largest body of developed nickel ores, adjacent to the world's largest market, has given it a dominant position in Canadian and United

[11] For information on the early history of the company see Eugene Staley, *Raw Materials in Peace and War* (New York: Council on Foreign Relations, 1937), pp. 276-279.

States markets. In addition to nickel, the Sudbury ore contains other valuable metals, copper, cobalt, platinum and other metals in the platinum group, as well as gold and silver. Recently iron ore has been recovered.

In May 1946, the U. S. Department of Justice filed a complaint against INCO, alleging (1) that it had established a monopoly in interstate commerce in nickel and (2) that it had entered into agreements with leading foreign producers "to impose limits on world production, to fix world-wide prices, and to allocate and restrict sales in world markets." The case did not come to trial. Instead, a consent decree required INCO "to sell, for a period of 20 years, basic nickel raw materials at prevailing market prices to any producer of rolling mill products containing nickel that wished to purchase such materials." Concerning the decree, a Senate subcommittee expressed the opinion that it "did almost nothing to affect the basic monopoly INCO enjoys over the sale of nickel and nickel products in the United States."[12]

Plans announced in late 1956 call for the expansion within a few years in INCO's annual capacity to 385 million pounds of nickel, an increase of 100 million over the 1956 production. This will be accomplished primarily by an investment of $175 million in developing two new nickel mines in the Mystery-Moak Lakes area in Northern Manitoba, 400 miles north of Winnipeg. A concentrator, smelter and refinery will be built, and a new town to house 8,000, including 2,000 employees. Power will be supplied by a hydroelectric plant to be constructed by the Manitoba government. The company will assist in financing a 30-mile railroad spur to the lines of the Canadian National Railways. Initial production is scheduled to begin in 1960, with full production attained in the following year.

The greatly increased production in the Sudbury area during the past 20 years has been made possible princi-

[12] U. S. Senate, Preparedness Subcommittee of the Committee on Armed Services, *Nickel*, Fourth Report, 82d Cong., 1st sess. (Washington: GPO, 1951), p. 5.

pally by the use of lower-grade ores. Hence the ore mined has shown lower average yields, but total reserves and their nickel-copper content have increased. In the five years, 1950-1954, the company mined twice as many tons of ore for each ton of nickel-copper deliveries as in 1935-1939.

A second change has been an increasing emphasis on underground mining.[13] With the exhaustion of deposits easily accessible by surface operations, the company has been forced to open deep shafts. In 1956 the latter produced 14,350,000 of the 15,510,000 tons of ore mined. The resulting upward trend in costs has to some extent been offset by a series of major technological improvements, in mining and milling methods and in refining. Despite the rise in the prices of both nickel and copper, sales of both metals increased. Over the 10-year period, nickel sales rose from 201 to 286 million pounds and copper from 150 to 271 million. The result of these changes was a steady increase in net earnings from $29.7 million in 1946 to $96.3 million in 1956. Converted to dollars of 1946 purchasing power, the increase in earnings in the 10-year period was $47 million.

World War II and the subsequent rearmament programs of the United States and other Western powers weakened the position of the International Nickel Company. Contracts with the U. S. government enabled a second company, Falconbridge Nickel Mines, Ltd., to expand its operations. The third Canadian producer, Sherritt Gordon Mines, Ltd., built a refinery with the aid of a government contract. In 1956 Falconbridge sold 43 million pounds of nickel and Sherritt Gordon 19 million. The mounting demand for nickel stimulated exploration and led to the discovery of new Canadian deposits in northwestern Ontario, in the Hudson Bay area, and in the Yukon and in Manitoba.

Price Policies

The predominant position which INCO has occupied in the world's nickel markets made it possible for the

[13] During World War II there was open-pit mining at Sudbury, but both before and after the war the mining has been primarily underground.

company to maintain stable prices over long periods. In the years 1929-1941, when prices of other metals showed wide fluctuations, INCO sold most of its nickel at the generally going contract price of 32 cents a pound. On January 1, 1939, the price was reduced to 31 1/2 cents, reflecting the drop of 1/2 cent in the U. S. import duty.[14] This price remained in effect for eight years, until November 1946, when it was raised to 35 cents. A reduction to 33 3/4 cents occurred in January 1947, again in response to a further reduction in the duty of 1 1/4 cents per pound. The upward trend of nickel prices is shown in Table 17 and Chart J.

Price trends over the past 20 years show that the competitive position of nickel has worsened in relation to other steel-alloying elements:

	Prices			*Increases*	
	Average 1936–38	*End of 1946*	*June 1957*	*1936–38 to 1957*	*1946 to 1957*
	(cents per pound)			(percent)	
Nickel	32.00	35.00	74.00	131.3	111.4
Molybdenum	80.00	80.00	128.00	60.0	60.0
Ferro-vanadium	270.00	270.00	320.00	18.5	18.5
Ferro-chromium:					
Low carbon	20.00	23.00	39.50	97.5	71.7
High carbon	10.33	14.50	27.75	168.6	91.4
	(index, 1947–49 = 100)			(percent)	
Wholesale prices	53.2	91.6	117.4	120.7	28.2

Note: Nickel was decontrolled on November 10, 1946; the other alloying elements, on June 12, 1946.
Sources: Nickel prices—International Nickel Company
Other prices—*Iron Age*
Wholesale price index—U. S. Department of Labor.

INCO's market price is not an accurate measure of the postwar cost of nickel to the U. S. government or to non-defense industries. In order to bring out larger supplies the government made advances to domestic and foreign producers and purchased their nickel at premium prices.

[14] INCO has regularly made it a practice to pay the U. S. duty, adding it to the price quoted to U. S. consumers.

Private firms, to supplement their allotments of market-price nickel, had to buy additional amounts at much higher prices in gray and black markets.[15] A multiple-price situation developed.

"During the period 1950-1956 other producers [i.e., other than INCO], notably French and Japanese, regularly sold nickel in U. S. markets at whatever the traffic would bear. Prices ranged from $1.10 per pound up to $2.75 with reports of some sales at even higher prices. In today's market [late 1956] primary nickel is sold at a variety of prices. About 85 percent of the primary nickel coming into the U. S. is sold at the 64 1/2 cent 'market' price. The 15 percent balance is sold at premium prices ranging up to $2.50 per pound." [16] Nickel contained in nickel-bearing scrap was selling in 1956 for as much as $2.25 per pound, more than three times the cost of the "free-market" price of the new metal. By the end of 1957, the supply of market-price nickel being adequate, industrial concerns no longer bought at premium prices, and the price of nickel-bearing scrap dropped below the market price of the new metal.

Table 17

INCO CONTRACT PRICE TO U. S. BUYERS FOR ELECTROLYTIC NICKEL, 1946-1956

(in cents per pound)

Year	*Price*[a]	*Year*	*Price*[a]
1946	31.5–35	1952	56.5
1947	35	1953	60
1948	33.75–40	1954	60–64.5
1949	40	1955	64.5
1950	40–48–50.5	1956	64.5–74
1951	50.5–56.5		

[a] F.O.B., Port Colborne, Ontario; includes U. S. duty.
Source: International Nickel Company of Canada, Ltd.

[15] Gray-market transactions were not illegal. They consisted of sales and purchases of high-priced metal imported from France and Japan, as well as metal recovered from scrap. The black market was supplied by nickel illegally diverted by defense contractors.

[16] *Nickel Handbook and Commercial Outlook for 1957,* by Herman B. Director Associates (Washington: Author, 1956), Sec. 4, n.p.

CHART J

U. S. WHOLESALE PRICE OF PRIMARY NICKEL, 1926-1956
(in cents per pound)

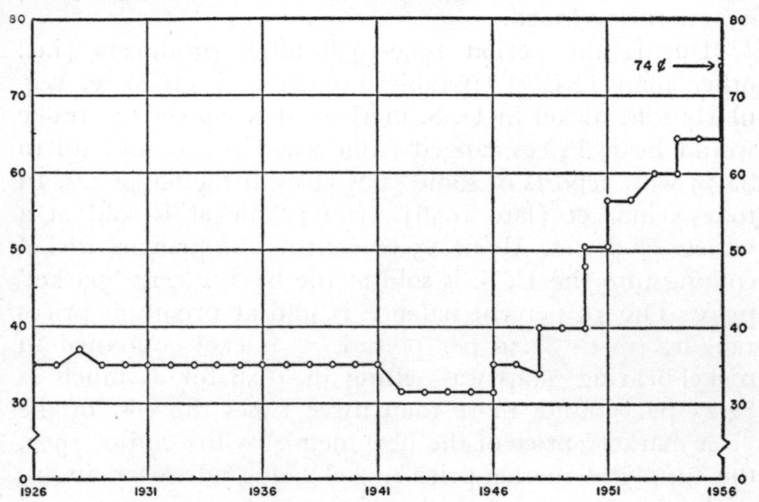

Source: International Nickel Company of Canada, Ltd.

National Policy on Nickel

The postwar problem of national policy with respect to nickel centered on the provision of supplies adequate for the rapid expansion of the civilian economy. The Korean war and the rearmament program meant increasing use of nickel in defense industries, and at the same time the mounting tension in international relations called attention to the need for adding nickel to the strategic stockpile. These needs had priority; when they had been taken care of, remaining supplies of nickel did not satisfy the requirements for stainless steel and other alloys, for nickel plating and all the other peacetime uses of the metal.

In dealing with the nickel shortage government policies had several purposes: (1) to increase the supplies from domestic and foreign sources; (2) to see to it that available supplies were wisely apportioned between defense production and the national stockpile, on the one hand, and production for peaceful uses, on the other; (3) to allocate equitably among private firms the nickel destined for peacetime uses. During the Korean war a fourth consideration received attention, viz., the maintenance of a just balance between American needs and those of friendly foreign countries.

As a means of stimulating nickel production the government engaged in nickel mining in Cuba and entered into a large number of contracts with producers, principally in Canada, for exploration and research and for the expansion of production. In seven years, 1950-1957, the United States invested $789 million in its nickel expansion program. The gross value of purchase contracts was $655 million and of research contracts $6.6 million. In addition the government invested over $100 million in nickel production at Nicaro, Cuba. The probable ultimate cost to the government of the nickel program, 1950-1957, has been estimated at about $124 million.[17]

Only limited use has been made of rapid tax amortization and incentives for exploration of new sources of domestic supply because of the lack of workable ore deposits and the scarcity of American producers. For the same reason the tariff has not figured in the nickel expansion program.

Nickel and the Tariff

In the American tariff refined nickel is dutiable, but nickel ores, nickel oxide and matte are on the Free List.[18] The rates on nickel, and on manufactures of nickel, imposed by the Tariff Act of 1930 were substantially reduced in subsequent trade agreements, as shown below:

	1930	*1957*
Pigs, ingots, etc.	3¢ lb.	1¼¢ lb.
Bars, rods, sheets, etc.	25%	12½%
If cold-rolled, cold-drawn, etc.	35%	17½%
Tubes and tubing	25%	6¼%
If cold-rolled, cold-drawn, etc.	35%	8¾%
Manufactures of nickel	45%	22½%

[17] *Report of the Attorney General,* pursuant to Sec. 708(e) of the Defense Production Act of 1950, as amended (Washington: Author, August 9, 1957), p. 44.

[18] Nickel ore is rarely shipped in international trade; it is usually reduced before shipment to nickel matte (an intermediate product of 54-78 percent nickel) or nickel oxide (containing about 75 percent nickel).

Aside from a few small mines, domestic production of nickel was practically nonexistent; hence there was obviously no question of building up a domestic nickel-mining industry by the restriction of imports. Officials responsible for nickel policy did not have to consider how far they should rely on domestic and how far on foreign sources of supply. They were free to put their maximum efforts on getting as much nickel, as economically as possible, from abroad. In this respect nickel has presented U. S. policy makers with a simpler problem than did certain other materials, such as lead, zinc, copper, coal and oil.

The Tariff Act of 1930, following a precedent established in earlier legislation, uniformly imposed higher duties on refined metals than on ores and concentrates, in order to promote smelting and refining in this country. This seems to have been the purpose in making refined nickel dutiable, even though the ore was on the Free List. (Similarly ores of antimony, cadmium and chromite enter free of duty, and the refined metals are dutiable.) Within recent years, the U. S. import duties on nickel have been too low[19] to furnish any incentive for the construction south of the border of facilities for processing Canadian ores. The ample supplies of cheap electric power in southern Ontario give Canada a decisive cost advantage. Moreover, the Ontario and the Canadian governments, aware of the threat implied in the U. S. tariff, would make every effort, by subsidies, export taxes or other means, to retain the refineries at Port Colborne.

The Development of Cuban Nickel Mines

In its endeavors to obtain large supplies of nickel from foreign sources the U. S. government in 1942 undertook the production of nickel in Cuba. Long before World War II, mining engineers had known of the existence of large deposits of nickel in eastern Cuba. But they considered that exploitation was not commercially feasible, because of the difficulty in separating the nickel from the

[19] In 1956 the import duty of one and three-fourths cents a pound was equivalent to 2.5 percent of the foreign value of the refined imports.

other metals, iron, cobalt and chromium, with which it was associated.

In 1940-1941, however, an American corporation, the Freeport Sulphur Company, became interested in Cuban nickel and conducted pilot-plant refining operations in Texas. In 1942 Freeport through its wholly owned subsidiary, the Nicaro Nickel Company, completed acquisition of large claims in Cuba with the assistance of the Reconstruction Finance Corporation and contracted with the U. S. government for the construction in Cuba of the facilities necessary for mining the ore and extracting nickel oxide. The plant, which cost $33 million, had a rated capacity of 30 million pounds. For 40 months, 1943-1947, it was operated for the U. S. government by the Nicaro company under a management-fee contract. Freeport furnished the ore from its Cuban mines without payment.

In the final year of operation the plant was producing at an annual rate of about 25 million pounds, an amount equivalent to 15 percent of U. S. consumption. The total output for the three and one-third years of operation was something over 60 million pounds. "Though production fell short of the theoretical rated capacity, it was a material supplement to the critical nickel supply, and was reportedly a good record of production and at a reasonable wartime cost." [20]

On March 31, 1947, the operation was discontinued, and the plant was put in stand-by condition. At this time the emergency in nickel seemed to be past, consumption of nickel in most uses was falling, and the Canadian metal was available at a price less than Nicaro's costs.

Reactivation of the Nicaro Plant, 1952

Within three years, however, the outbreak of war in Korea revealed the inadequacy of supplies of many raw materials, particularly nickel. The price of the Canadian

[20] U. S. House, Committee on Government Operations, *Inquiry into the Expansion and Operation by General Services Administration of the Government Nickel Plant at Nicaro, Cuba,* 84th Cong., 2d sess., House Report no. 2390 (Washington: GPO, 1956), p. 4.

product, which at the beginning of 1948 was 33 3/4 cents a pound, rose to 40 cents in July; in May 1950 it was increased to 48 cents and to 50 1/2 cents in December of that year. An obvious way of meeting the shortage was to resume production at the government-owned plant at Nicaro. The Department of the Interior had recommended this action in May 1948, but Congress did not provide funds for rehabilitation until August 1950, two months after the attack on Korea. A further two years elapsed before the plant came again into full operation. The plant was operated, under a five-year management contract, by the Nickel Processing Corporation, owned by a Dutch company, by the National Lead Company and by Cuban interests. The Dutch having withdrawn, National Lead acquired control.

In December 1953, the ODM authorized a 75-percent expansion at Nicaro designed to raise its capacity to 49 million pounds. The completion of the project in March 1957 at a cost of $37 million, $6 million under the original estimate, brought the government's total investment to somewhat less than $90 million.

Nicaro's production, in terms of nickel content,[21] in the years 1953-1956 was:

Year	Pounds
1953	27,700,000
1954	29,100,000
1955	30,275,000
1956	32,123,000

After one year's operation of the reactivated plant, a report of the General Services Administration observed:

> So far, it can produce nickel at a cost, including plant depreciation, below the current market. Whether it could make a profit in nickel markets of the future is something that the next year or two may decide, especially in view of some newer potential process developments and improvements.[22]

[21] Nicaro at first produced only nickel oxide. Later the oxide in the form of sinter was shipped to the Crum-Lynne (Pennsylvania) refinery of the National Lead Company for conversion into metallic nickel pig.

[22] As quoted in *Inquiry into the Expansion and Operation by General Services Administration of the Government Nickel Plant at Nicaro, Cuba,* House Report no. 2390 (1956), cited, p. 6.

In 1955 the costs of producing nickel oxide at Nicaro were between 48 and 49 cents a pound, including administrative expense and an allowance for plant depreciation. These costs did not include provision for taxes or interest on the government's investment. The market price for nickel metal at that time was 64 1/2 cents and for the oxide a few cents less.

The Hoover Commission, after studying the Nicaro operation, reported (1955): "At present, the project provides stockpile nickel on a basis of operating costs. The difference between these costs and the higher Canadian monopoly price provides a substantial saving." The Commission gave qualified approval to the continuance of the government's operation of the Nicaro plant. The present form of operation it thought appropriate while the government stockpile was being built up and as long as the United States was so largely dependent on a single source of supply, i.e., on INCO. After the stockpile requirements have been met, the entire Nicaro operation should be reviewed "in the light of all relevant matters, including production costs and the prevailing circumstances of supply and demand for nickel."[23] The U. S. Attorney General reported, on August 9, 1957, that "the basic expansion and operation of Nicaro to date has been extremely successful."[24] The operations, he said, had been run at a profit.

Purchase Contracts

The Defense Production Act of 1950 made it possible for the U. S. government to enter into long-term agreements with producers abroad and at home for the delivery of nickel to the national stockpile. An important, long-term aim of the contracts was to expand productive capacity abroad, thus assuring this country more ample supplies for defense and civilian uses.

[23] Commission on Organization of the Executive Branch of the Government, *Business Enterprises Outside of the Department of Defense,* Staff Study (Washington: Author, 1955), p. 84.

[24] *Report of the Attorney General* (August 9, 1957), cited, p. 32.

There was little possibility, as we have remarked before (see p. 132), of developing nickel production from domestic ores. Nevertheless, in 1953 the Defense Materials Procurement Agency advanced about $25 million to the Hanna Nickel Smelting Company to develop a deposit of nickel ore at Riddle, Oregon, and agreed to purchase from the Hanna Company ferronickel with a metal content of 125,000,000 pounds, at 85-90 cents per pound, subject to escalation. In late 1951 the government contracted with the National Lead Company to furnish 9,261,000 pounds, over a period of six and one-half years, of nickel from a copper mine at Fredericktown, Missouri. The price was 54 cents.

The first substantial contract[25] with a foreign producer was that signed, after several years of sporadic bargaining, with Falconbridge Nickel Mines, Ltd. of Canada. In December 1947 Falconbridge had offered the Bureau of Federal Supply 150 million pounds of nickel to be delivered over a 10-year period. But although the Bureau promptly recommended the purchase, the U. S. Munitions Board turned it down on two grounds: (1) because small deliveries were provided for in the early years of the contract, and (2) because acceptance would preclude purchases on a shorter-term basis from the major Canadian supplier, the International Nickel Company.[26] However, in 1948, a five-year contract was signed covering the delivery of 40 million pounds.

The Munitions Board in March 1950 rejected a second Falconbridge proposal because the term of the contract was too long, in view of uncertainties in stockpile objectives. When several months later, two days before the

[25] The Economic Cooperation Administration in 1950 had contracted with La Société le Nickel for nickel from New Caledonia to the value of $965,000. The metal was to be furnished over a number of years in repayment of a credit for purchasing conveying and mining equipment.

[26] In a letter written several years later, the acting chairman of the Munitions Board gave a third reason. He said that the Board was unable to guarantee the financing over the 10-year period. (Letter reproduced in *Nickel,* Fourth Report of the Senate Preparedness Subcommittee, 1951, cited, p. 25.)

Korean attack, Falconbridge made a third offer, the Board allowed it to lapse without formal action. The explanation offered later was that all available funds had already been "programmed" for the acquisition of other materials.

In January 1951 the United States agreed to buy 50 million pounds of Falconbridge nickel, to be delivered over a period of ten years with payment at the current market price. As an inducement to expand production, the Defense Materials Procurement Agency made the company an advance of $6 million. A second contract, signed in 1953, provided for the delivery of 100 million pounds of nickel before June 30, 1962. To compensate Falconbridge for undertaking the development of its nickel reserves, this contract provided a premium of 40 cents in excess of the market price at the time of delivery. Both the 1951 and 1953 contracts carried options for additional deliveries by the company. If all options should be exercised, the total deliveries of nickel which might be made through 1967 would be 275 million pounds.

A stockpile purchase contract made it possible for a third Canadian company, Sherritt Gordon Mines, Ltd., to undertake exploration and production of nickel from ore deposits at Lynn Lake, Manitoba, and to build in Alberta a refinery with a capacity of 20 million pounds. The contract, dated April 19, 1951, called for the delivery before the end of 1958 of 80 million pounds of nickel, if all options should be exercised, at the market price at the time of delivery.

The largest available source of nickel was the Sudbury operation of the International Nickel Company. From 1946 to the middle of 1952 eight small contracts were made with this company, calling for the delivery of about 50 million pounds of nickel, at the market price or less. But no significant purchase was made from this source until September 1952 when the United States agreed to take an additional 54 million pounds. A larger contract, signed in May 1953, covered the purchase of 120 million pounds of nickel at 89 cents. The premium of 25 cents over the market price was an incentive to install separate processing equipment for lower-grade ores. An escalation clause in the contract later brought the price up to 97 cents a pound. The first deliveries were to be made in December 1953 and January 1954. The U. S. government also agreed to buy the copper produced in connection with its nickel purchase at 27 cents, which was below the market price.

In 1953 the Defense Materials Procurement Agency made ten separate contracts providing for expansion of nickel production. Altogether they added up to about 486 million pounds to be provided over a ten-year period. But the expansion of production required large capital investments in mining machinery and equipment, in conveyers and other transportation facilities, before additional ore could be taken out. In some cases new mills and refineries had to be built. Hence the rise in available supplies came only slowly. In 1951, when the new program got under way,[27] the United States had received from all sources 187 million pounds, and in 1956, 290 million. The gain, 103 million, came almost entirely from projects sponsored by the U. S. government or stimulated by government assistance. Nevertheless, a careful analysis by a leading authority[28] characterized the 1956 supply as "wholly inadequate" and stressed the need for further expansion of production.

The Joint Congressional Committee on Defense Production in May 1956 urged the ODM to use all its powers to encourage greater production of nickel. In response, the Office announced a new "expansion goal" calling for an annual supply of 440 million pounds to be available by 1961.[29] To achieve this goal, the ODM authorized the use of rapid tax amortization and the negotiation of government purchase contracts at 1956 market prices. In certain

[27] A great expansion of INCO's production had begun in 1950. The company's deliveries, from stocks as well as from new output, increased by 47 million pounds over 1949.

[28] John R. Townsend, director of Materials and Standards Engineering for the Sandia Corporation.

[29] Earlier goals had been fixed at 264 million pounds (January 1952) and 380 million (November 1952).

instances, payment of premium prices[30] was authorized to cover unusual development costs in bringing new production into being as quickly as possible. Meanwhile, until additional supplies were forthcoming, the ODM authorized diversion to industry of all nickel scheduled for delivery to the government.

The first purchase contract under the new expansion program was signed March 8, 1957 with the Cuban American Nickel Company, a subsidiary of the Freeport Sulphur Company. It permitted the delivery, before June 30, 1965, of a maximum of 271 million pounds of nickel and 24 million pounds of cobalt. For the nickel which it "calls" the U. S. government will pay 74 cents or the market price, whichever is higher, and for the cobalt, $2.00. For the nickel which Freeport "puts" to the government, it will pay 74 cents. The government's purchase obligation will expire 30 days after the company's cumulative sales to all its customers amount to 271 million pounds or, alternatively, as soon as accumulated annual cash returns, after deductions for taxes and depreciation, amount to $98 million. The nickel will be produced from ore mined and concentrated at Moa Bay and refined at a plant to be constructed in Louisiana. The company estimates the total investment required for plant and other facilities at more than $100 million. Tax amortization certificates will be issued covering 80 percent of the facilities. Initial production is scheduled for the summer of 1959.

The Stockpiling Program

Stockpiling of nickel, which began in 1946, at first proceeded slowly. During the Korean war practically all the available nickel was taken for defense production so that it was not until 1953 that stockpiling really got under way. Actual figures of amounts of nickel put into the stockpile are not made public, but a rough estimate may be made by

[30] The ODM reported that of the 650 million pounds of nickel under contract as of June 30, 1955, 379 million were purchased at premium prices. As of June 30, 1956, the government's contracts covered more than 1 billion pounds.

subtracting U. S. consumption, as reported by the Bureau of Mines, from total available supply, as reported by the ODM. The results of this calculation, which takes no account of changes in Defense Production Act inventories, are presented below:

Year	*Millions of pounds*	*Year*	*Millions of pounds*
1950	0	1954	73
1951	14	1955	59
1952	10	1956	38
1953	23	1957	0

The estimates of the *Wall Street Journal* (March 13, 1956) for 1954 and 1955 were 80 million and 84 million pounds, respectively.

In order to relieve the scarcity of nickel for civilian use, the ODM in 1954 began to divert to nondefense industries some of the nickel purchased for stockpiling. These diversions rose from 5.5 million pounds in 1954 to 76.8 million in 1956. All the nickel scheduled for delivery in 1957 to the stockpile and DPA inventories was diverted, thus adding to the amount available to industry some 115 to 120 million pounds. In October 1957 the ODM announced that it would divert to industry all of the nickel scheduled for delivery to the stockpile in 1958.

Allocation and Conservation

During World War II nickel was one of the first metals to require allocation. Nonessential uses were banned, and even some essential uses had to be curtailed. All restrictions had been lifted by August 1945, and from that date until the attack on Korea the use of nickel was subject to no controls. Late in 1950, the National Production Authority reintroduced restrictive measures, and at the beginning of the new year allocation and priorities control orders went into effect and remained in force until November 1953. At that time they were replaced by a voluntary allocation conducted by the United States subsidiary of the principal Canadian producer under the supervision of the U. S. Department of Commerce. Under this system the various components of the supply were distributed as follows:

(1) *Market-price nickel.* In 1956 about 230 million pounds, 80 percent of the U. S. supply of primary nickel available to American industry, was sold at INCO's market price. The bulk of this portion of the supply came from three Canadian companies. International Nickel provided 81 percent of market-price nickel; Falconbridge, 2½ percent; and Sherritt Gordon, 4 percent. The remaining 12½ percent was shipped from the American government's plant at Nicaro.

When the U. S. government freed nickel from legal control, it asked International Nickel to take over the task of allocating its output to nondefense users, after filling all "defense-rated" orders. Following the principle of distribution established by the National Production Authority, INCO did not attempt to distinguish between more essential and less essential end-uses but instead made its allocations on historical bases, i.e., on each customer's average monthly consumption during two periods, August-October 1953 and 1948-1950. The company did not, however, apply the rule with mathematical precision. It examined its customers' requirements periodically, seeking to make adjustments to current needs. In order to prevent them from unfairly increasing their allotments, it requested them to supply information on the amounts of nickel which they secured from other sources,[31] but without disclosing the form in which the nickel was obtained or the company furnishing it.

The nickel oxide produced at the government's plant at Nicaro was sold by the operating company, principally to the steel industry in the United States, at market prices. These sales were supervised by the Business and Defense Services Administration (U. S. Department of Commerce) to make sure that they did not "warp the equity of the dis-

[31] U. S. Department of Commerce, *Interim Report on Nickel . . .* (Washington: Author, 1956), pp. 12-13. A fuller description of INCO's distribution methods will be found in *Report of the Attorney General* (August 9, 1957), cited, pp. 57-63.

tribution patterns" which producers, i.e., the Canadian companies, were trying to maintain.[32]

(2) *Premium-price nickel.* To distribute equitably the premium-price nickel diverted from government contracts to industry was virtually an impossible task. Producers' premium nickel sold at four or more different price levels, depending on their contracts with the government.[33] Varying amounts were available at each price. One form of the product, ferronickel, was usable only by the steel industry. In addition to market-price and premium-price nickel, users were able legally to obtain nickel in the gray market (market-price nickel) and, illegally, black-market nickel.

To cope with the scarcity of nickel, consuming industries undertook programs of conservation and substitution. In the Department of Defense's Materials Conservation Program nickel was given top priority. Under this program about 9 million pounds of nickel were saved in 1952 and 2½ million pounds in 1953. The savings were accomplished principally by "downgrading," i.e., reducing the nickel content of ferrous and nonferrous alloys used in armament, ammunition and other forms of military hardware. Similar methods of conservation were practiced by producers of goods for civilian use. Manganese was substituted for nickel in stainless steel, and in some cases nickel was entirely replaced by chromium. Where heat resistance was essential, "clad" steels were used in which a layer of stainless steel was permanently bonded to a sheet of carbon steel. By the addition of small amounts of boron and other intensifiers, steel was given hardness without the use of nickel.

Monel metal, a nonferrous alloy containing about two-thirds nickel, was replaced in food service equipment, in laundries and in textile factories with stainless steel with only 8-10 percent of nickel. The Bell Telephone System

[32] U. S. Congress, Joint Committee on Defense Production, *Study of Supply and Distribution of Nickel,* Progress Report no. 36, 85th Cong., 1st sess. (Washington: GPO, 1957), p. 26.

[33] In 1956 premium prices were paid to Falconbridge, 77 cents to 87 cents on one contract and $1.04 to $1.14 on another; to International Nickel, about 95 cents; and to the Hanna Company, about $1.15 (for ferronickel).

reported in 1952 that metallurgical and engineering studies had reduced its consumption of nickel over a 10-year period by 65 percent. In two years, 1950-1952, its requirements were reduced by almost a million pounds. The savings were accomplished by substitution and conservation, and by improvements in designs and in manufacturing techniques. By 1956, however, efforts at conservation seemed to have "reached an area of diminishing returns." Further efforts, according to expert opinion, "would not appreciably affect the supply situation." [34]

Restrictions on Exports

Export controls were applied to nickel soon after the Korean war broke out. For the third quarter of 1950 the Department of Commerce fixed an over-all export quota for exports of primary nickel, nickel alloys, nickel manufactures and nickel scrap at 1,022,000 pounds (gross weight). The quota was cut in half in the first quarter of 1951.[35] A year later the quarterly quota was fixed at 100,000 pounds, nickel content.

In imposing export controls the United States was aiming to safeguard its own supply of nickel, and its products, for the benefit of defense and nondefense industries. But it had to take account also of the needs of friendly countries, particularly those which normally were dependent on imports of nickel products and scrap. In fact, the United States in 1951-1953 was bound, by its membership in the International Materials Conference, to honor the minimum requirements of "dependent" nations.

The control of nickel scrap posed difficult administrative problems, because of the great variety of grades and qualities. At one time, the export regulations provided separately for 13 groupings of nickel and nickel-bearing scrap. Certain types of scrap, it was found, could not be economically processed in this country. Consequently regulations

[34] *Study of Supply and Distribution of Nickel*, Progress Report no. 36 of the Joint Committee on Defense Production (1957), cited, p. 9.

[35] Exclusive of nickel converted in the United States from Canadian matte and ingots and exported to the United Kingdom under special licensing.

were devised to permit them to be exported with provision for partial return of the recovered metal. In the first quarter of 1957, for example, the export quota on nickel-copper alloy scrap was 500,000 pounds. Licenses for that amount were granted with the proviso that not less than 90 percent of the nickel content would be returned in the form of metal. Exports of other kinds of nickel-bearing scrap were embargoed. Other nickel products remained under open-end licensing. For security reasons no licenses were issued for exports to the U.S.S.R. and satellite countries or to Communist China.

Evaluation of National Policy

Between 1950 and 1957 the total annual supply of nickel available to the United States increased from 200 million to 300 million pounds. The gain was very largely the result of the stimulation of production in Cuba and Canada by means of government purchases and loans. A secondary result of these transactions was to build up new sources of supply. In 1950 the International Nickel Company furnished 95 percent of the U. S. supply; in 1956 its share was 66 percent. Nevertheless, in spite of these accomplishments, no aspect of national policy on raw materials has aroused more criticism than the failure in postwar years to provide supplies of nickel adequate for civilian use as well as for the national stockpile and for defense production.

In the emergency produced by the attack on South Korea, stockpile and defense requirements jumped in less than a year from 14 to 74 million pounds. To supply this new demand, plus civilian needs, the available supply of nickel was "woefully inadequate." The rearmament program which Korea set in motion made new demands on nickel. Changes in military planning, involving increased construction of jet-powered airplanes and guided missiles, prolonged the nickel shortage. Since military needs had priority, manufacturers of goods for civilian consumption had either to curtail their operations or to introduce substitutes for nickel in their products. They were hampered by end-use restrictions and by allocations, at first under government regulation and later, after end-use restrictions had been removed, by rationing carried out by the principal supplying company under government supervision. Their cost calculations were confused by the need of buying portions of their raw material supply at widely differing prices. Discouraged by the outlook, they relaxed research activities designed to find new uses for nickel.

The causes of the postwar shortage of nickel are to be found, first, in the failure of the government to act promptly at the close of World War II to stimulate increased production in the principal supplying countries, Cuba and Canada. After the attack on Korea, it failed to devise and enforce methods for the most effective use of the available supplies.

The postwar shortage of nickel was not unpredictable. It should have been clear that V-J Day had not brought a settled peace. Moreover, technological developments in World War II, particularly the jet engine, the gas turbine and atomic energy developments, were bound to open up new fields for the use of heat-resistant and corrosion-resistant metals, in industries supplying the needs of the civilian population as well as of the armed services. Hence it seems that a prudently far-sighted policy would have taken steps at once to see that nickel was accumulated in the national strategic stockpile and would have undertaken by advance planning to provide an ample and continuing supply from abroad.

Stockpiling

In the years before the Korean crisis, the U. S. Munitions Board repeatedly rejected offers from Canadian companies to supply the metal on long-term contracts. On this account a Senate subcommittee laid on the Board much of the responsibility for the nickel shortage which developed during the Korean war. Recognizing that public opinion, the Budget Bureau and Congress were in some degree culpable, the subcommittee said: "The sum of proper criticism of the Munitions Board is that it has been complacent where it should have been vigilant; it has been quiet where it should have spoken loudly; it has been timid where it should have been bold—or on occasion brash." [36] Later, in 1953 when nickel was in short supply, the government insisted on continuing deliveries to the stockpile.

Mismanagement of Nicaro Project

It is now apparent that the discontinuance of nickel production at Nicaro, Cuba in 1947 was a serious mistake. The end of the war need not have ended the government's operations in this field. (The United States continued in the business of producing synthetic rubber until 1955.) After two years of operation the Nicaro plant was supplying 25 million pounds of nickel a year, 15 percent of total U. S. consumption, at costs which, in comparison with market prices, were not unreasonable. The development of the Cuban project had furnished a valuable second source of supply for intermediate products. There were no refineries at Nicaro, and hence it was not a likely target for enemy attack. Even if the continuance of government ownership was inadvisable, continued production at Nicaro might have been arranged by selling the plant to private investors. In fact, however, numerous offers from business firms were rejected as unsatisfactory by the War Assets Administration, to which the property was transferred in July 1947.

The attack on Korea aroused new interest in Nicaro, but three years elapsed before the plant was again brought into production. In 1950 a Senate subcommittee called attention to the government's failure to rehabilitate its Cuban nickel extraction plant and condemned its "very leisurely approach to this problem." Another Congressional committee, reviewing the situation in 1956, found evidence that private and political influence had been responsible for unnecessary and costly delay in letting the principal construction contract. The delay, it estimated, had cost the United States at least 10 million pounds of nickel at a critical time. The amounts paid to engineering

[36] *Nickel,* Fourth Report of the Senate Preparedness Subcommittee (1951), cited, p. 22.

firms for their services in connection with the expansion of the plant, the committee found, were excessive.[37]

Negotiations with Canadian Producers

The largest nickel mines in the world were in the Sudbury basin in Canada, easily accessible to U. S. industries by rail and lake transportation. The availability of Canadian nickel in time of crisis seemed to be assured by Canada's strategic position and guaranteed by bilateral agreements.[38] Hence it would seem that immediately after World War II a far-sighted national policy would have provided for prompt agreements with Canadian companies, looking toward the expansion of their production and exports to this country. But the U. S. Munitions Board and later the General Services Administration were slow in tapping the Canadian supplies. The Board handled its negotiations with the Falconbridge company in slipshod fashion. The International Nickel Company, which in 1950 produced 95 percent of the Free World's total, was the most promising source of additional supplies for American industries and for the national stockpile. Yet no substantial contract was signed with INCO until September 1952, and it was May 1953 before the purchase of 120 million pounds was negotiated.

[37] See Report no. 2390 of the House Committee on Government Operations (1956), cited, pp. 24-25. Minority members of the committee issued a blanket rejection of the report which, however, did not challenge specific findings or conclusions. Charges that favoritism and political influence played a part in the award of Nicaro contracts were made in an article by Herbert Solow in the August 1955 issue of *Fortune,* "GSA: Washington's Most Durable Mess." The charges were denied by GSA officials in hearings before the Joint Committee on Defense Production in August 1955.

[38] An agreement negotiated by the State Department with the Canadian government in October 1950 provided that the two governments should cooperate "in all respects practicable, and to the extent of their respective executive powers, to the end that the economic efforts of the two countries be coordinated for the common defense and that the production and resources of both countries be used for the best combined results." (State Department Press Release no. 1103, October 26, 1950.) From October 1951 to September 1953 the International Materials Conference allocated nickel to Free World countries. The Conference's action, which was purely advisory, seems not to have restricted exports from Canada to the United States.

In 1947 and 1948, when the world market was dull, the major Canadian producer was eager to make a contract to furnish nickel for the American stockpile. But in later years, when the market revived, the prospect was less attractive. By 1950 INCO was operating its Sudbury mines at capacity. Its ability to export "quick" nickel to the United States was limited by its obligations to customers in other countries, particularly in Europe. Moreover, the expansion of capacity necessary for the completion of large, long-term contracts involved considerable risk. The INCO management, recalling the company's difficulties when the nickel market collapsed after World War I, wished to avoid a repetition of that disaster. In addition, it foresaw that rapid, large-scale expansion would encounter technical difficulties. Because of the rapid wartime depletion of ores obtainable by open-pit operations, the company had begun, a few years after the end of World War II, to extract a larger proportion of its ore from underground operations. The company's officers, moreover, hesitated to imperil later operations by invading its reserves at too rapid a rate.

Allocation of Available Supplies

The Senate Preparedness Subcommittee in 1950 recommended that "nonessential uses of nickel be promptly restricted *on the basis of order of essentiality* [italics supplied]; that certain uses of nickel be banned entirely, particularly in coinage and certain types of electroplating. . . ." Steel makers, it recommended, should be required to reduce the nickel content of alloy steels. The Department of Defense should "intensify its program of conserving the use of nickel for military orders. . . ." The National Production Authority was urged to set in motion a drive to increase collection of nickel-bearing scrap metals.[39] In 1951

[39] *Nickel,* Fourth Report of the Senate Preparedness Subcommittee (1951), cited, p. 22. The attitude of the subcommittee is illustrated by its reference to the use of nickel in automobile construction. "The largest single end-use of nickel is the automobile. Nickel is used in the metal trim and in vital working parts such as gears, steering parts and crankshafts. In the light of the current shortage of nickel and the difficulty of substantially increasing the supply, as well as in the light of the shortages of other

and 1952 the nickel shortage grew worse. Yet the recommendations of the subcommittee received only scant attention. The Treasury continued to use nickel in its coinage,[40] and only moderate progress was made in nickel conservation and in scrap collection.

The Defense Production Act of 1950 gave the National Production Authority, an agency of the Department of Commerce, broad and flexible powers to establish priorities and to allocate scarce materials. In a 1953 amendment Congress restricted these powers somewhat, but left the Authority free to impose end-use restrictions, to provide set-asides for independent small business and to employ other controls, *so long as they fell short of general control of distribution of the material in the civilian market.* It permitted general controls of a material, however, upon a finding by the President:

> (1) that such material is a scarce and critical material essential to the national defense, and (2) that the requirements of the national defense for such material cannot otherwise be met without creating a significant dislocation of the normal distribution of such material in the civilian market to such a degree as to create appreciable hardship.[41]

In accordance with this authorization the NPA, in December 1950, set quotas for individual firms at 65 percent of their use of nickel in the first six months of 1950. When, after a few months, this limitation proved inadequate it prohibited, or substantially reduced, the use of nickel and nickel-bearing alloys in some 400 products and applications. Later in 1951, working in connection with producers of nickel and nickel-bearing alloys, it further reduced civilian consumption by "restricting the nickel

---

materials used in large volume in the automobile, we may soon be faced with a choice of riding in shiny new automobiles or defending our very lives." (p. 20)

[40] The 5-cent piece contains 25 percent nickel. During World War II when nickel was eliminated in coinage, the saving in one year amounted to 860 tons of nickel.

[41] U. S. Senate, Committee on Banking and Currency, *Defense Production Act Amendments of 1956*, 84th Cong., 2d sess., Report no. 2237 (Washington: GPO, 1956), p. 9.

content for specific end uses to the minimum amount judged necessary for the satisfactory performance of the service for which each use was intended." [42] This general procedure, however, was modified in allocating nickel for electroplating. Instead of dealing individually with several thousands of small firms, NPA allocated nickel to their suppliers, requiring them to distribute the metal to their customers "in an equitable manner."

When, in November 1953, nickel was decontrolled, the government asked the International Nickel Company to allocate supplies of nickel to American nondefense industries in accordance with the method established by the NPA. The company allowed the Department of Commerce to supervise its methods of distribution, and to examine its books for this purpose. At this time, neither the company nor the government fully anticipated the difficulties which lay ahead. It was assumed that with the signing of the armistice in Korea the demand for nickel for defense production and for stockpiling would decrease so that supplies for civilian production would soon be adequate. But this optimistic forecast proved wrong. Actually, beginning in 1953 the amounts of nickel taken by government for military purposes expanded rapidly. Estimated amounts going into stockpiles and defense production inventories rose from 10 million pounds in 1952 to 73 million in 1954. Large additional supplies were taken by the government in 1955 and 1956. (See table, p. 156.) The result was that the amounts of nickel available for civilian use increased much less rapidly than did the needs of consuming industries.

Criticism of Allocation

The resulting shortage of nickel gave rise to many complaints, particularly from small firms in the electroplating industry, the job-platers. From all sections of the country they presented to their Congressmen and to government officials hardship cases and charges of unfair treatment.

[42] *Study of Supply and Distribution of Nickel*, Progress Report no. 36 of the Joint Committee on Defense Production (1957), cited, pp. 22-23.

They claimed that because they were not getting their fair share of market-price nickel they were being forced to pay exorbitant prices in gray and black markets. A representative of the Department of Defense complained that mills engaged in defense production were claiming more nickel than they were actually using.[43] Officials of the Department of Commerce, which had assumed responsibility for supervising the distribution of nickel by the International Nickel Company, replied that the size of the gray market had been exaggerated and denied that allocations were unfair. The Department opposed the suggested re-establishment of government rationing of nickel. The chairman of the Senate Committee on the Armed Services, on the other hand, suggested that the need for legal controls be reviewed. The Senate Subcommittee on Small Business went even further, calling on the President to restore legal controls on nickel distribution.

To some extent the criticism of nickel allocation was exaggerated; the nickel situation became a football of domestic politics. Hence one can find in testimony before Congressional committees, and even in the committees' reports, inaccurate statements and biased opinions. A more reliable source is the report of a special investigation made in 1956 by the Department of Commerce. In this report[44] the Secretary of Commerce restated the Department's view that the distribution of primary nickel by producers had in general been carried on in a fair and equitable manner. He found that the International Nickel Company had treated its small customers in an "eminently fair manner." He recognized, however, that suppliers of electroplating materials had followed unfair practices in allocating nickel to small firms. The system of allocating nickel on the basis

[43] The extent of this "defense disparity" was greatly exaggerated in 1957 by the Senate Preparedness Investigating Subcommittee which reported that consumption had exceeded estimated requirements by 60 percent; an official of the Department of Commerce estimated that less than one-half of one percent of the quantity of nickel moving in commerce had been illegally diverted.

[44] The report was dated December 31, 1956; it appeared as a committee print of the Joint Committee on Defense Production, *Study of Supply and Distribution of Nickel,* Progress Report no. 36 (1957), cited.

of past consumption was found to be unsatisfactory, because it tended to freeze the pattern of production, failing to make provision for shifts in consumption and technological advance. In a flexible system these factors would normally change the status, both absolute and relative, of various nickel-using industries and of member firms.

Nevertheless the Department did not advocate the reestablishment of legal control of end-uses of nickel, and thus evaded discussion of the basic question: Should government have transferred to a private corporation the responsibility for allocating nickel to civilian users? From the point of view of public policy this action seems to have been wrong. National defense requirements had created serious shortages in civilian supply which threatened to, and actually did, cause dislocations and hardships. Government was already deeply involved, through its control of the Nicaro output and of the nickel produced under premium-price and stockpile contracts, in the distribution of nickel to consuming industries. Under these conditions it was a mistake, I believe, to have attempted to wash its hands of responsibility for allocations.

From a bureaucratic point of view, the informal "partnership of control" had its advantages, for government officials had no legal responsibility for allocations and hence were immune to criticism. Moreover, the arrangement saved the government "tremendous clerical manpower." Technically, the International Nickel Company was well equipped for the task of allocating nickel. For years it had supplied the bulk of the American market. Its sales force was intimately acquainted with the needs, business methods and buying habits of its 700 to 1,000 active customers. But something more than business efficiency was involved. The allocation of a critically important raw material to users for civilian production involved policy decisions which for some of them, especially small firms, might be vital.

The ODM argued, negatively, that the continuance of legal restrictions on the use of nickel would not relieve the shortage or alleviate the hardships of the users. It favored abandonment of controls on the grounds that competition in a free market was "a major factor in the maintenance of a strong and dynamic economy." But in the case of nickel this argument was curiously irrelevant, because of the dominant position of the major producer.

An official of the Department of Commerce, in hearings before the Senate's Select Committee on Small Business, said:

> It has been advocated by some that the Government should reimpose controls on the use and distribution of nickel for all purposes. We would vigorously resist this since Government controls would not increase the total supply of nickel, and the Government would be placed in the position of injecting itself directly into the private affairs of a great many business firms. Furthermore, with Government controls, it would probably be necessary, as I have pointed out earlier, to restrict or prohibit the use of nickel for decorative or nonfunctional purposes. If this should be the case, the Government would be making the decision as to which private business establishments were more important than others, which is a function of Government generally abhorrent to our basic concept of a free enterprise economy.[45]

Under questioning he admitted that the International Nickel Company in its allocations had to make the decisions which he felt it would be "abhorrent" for government to make. Nevertheless he approved of the transfer of the allocation function to INCO.

The Outlook

The Paley Commission in 1952 foresaw a long-continued shortage of nickel. Free World demand for 1975 it had estimated at 528 million pounds, and had observed that the projected requirements would be "difficult to meet." But recent events have proved the Commission's estimates of future supplies to have been much too conservative. Within a few years, according to official and private estimates, feast may take the place of famine in the nickel mar-

[45] Statement of Frederick H. Mueller, Assistant Secretary for Domestic Affairs, Department of Commerce, in *Supply and Distribution of Nickel.* Hearings before the Senate Select Committee on Small Business, 84th Cong., 2d sess. (Washington: GPO, 1956), p. 113.

ket. The change, due to come in 1959 or 1960, may be sudden. Large, new supplies then will be available from several sources. The Manitoba mines of the International Nickel Company are scheduled to be producing 75 million pounds in 1960. An additional 25-30 million pounds will then be available from INCO's Sudbury mines. At approximately the same time, the Freeport Sulphur Company expects to be marketing nickel from its new Cuban operation. Moreover, the U. S. government's recently expanded plant at Nicaro, Cuba, may have an output in 1960 of 50 million pounds. Putting these facts together, and allowing for small increments from other sources, the U. S. Department of Commerce in August 1956 predicted a total Free World production in 1960 of 606 million pounds of nickel, distributed as follows:

Year	*Canada*	*U. S.*	*Cuba*	*New Caledonia*	*Other*	*Total*
		(in millions of pounds, nickel content)				
1957[a]	360	17	50	40	6	473
1960[b]	400	20	130	50	6	606

[a] Estimated. Includes anticipated increased production of 20,000,000 pounds of nickel by the Nicaro, Cuba, plant.
[b] Estimated. Includes proposed expansion announced by Office of Defense Mobilization.
Source: *Interim Report on Nickel* (August 15, 1956), cited.

The prediction of Dr. John F. Thompson, chairman of the International Nickel Company, was somewhat higher. In 1956 he estimated that within five years total Free World capacity for nickel production would be 650 to 675 million pounds. He predicted that, if defense demands remained at 1957 levels and if stockpiling was not resumed, the 1956 rate of civilian consumption would have to be increased by 75 percent. In preparation for the new situation, INCO is undertaking to recover markets lost to other metals during the years of shortage and is seeking out new uses for its products.

At the end of 1957 it seemed fairly certain that in the next 20 or 25 years the supply of nickel would be adequate for the growing peacetime needs of American industry. The measures taken rather tardily by government agencies during the Korean emergency had eventually altered the supply situation to the advantage of American industries. In 1957, instead of being dependent almost exclusively on a single foreign supplier, they were able to obtain nickel from two additional Canadian firms, and they could look forward to receiving within a few years substantial supplies from new, large-scale developments in Cuba.

The future of INCO's competitors, however, was somewhat uncertain. They were benefiting by U. S. government contracts, some of which provided for purchases at premium prices. How long would they be able to maintain their positions in the market, once these contracts had expired? The fate of the U. S. government's operation at Nicaro was still undecided. In view of the impending surplus of the metal, would the government continue in the nickel business? If not, would private enterprise be willing to take over?

The government's immediate problem at the end of 1957 was to dispose of a surplus of perhaps 25 million pounds of nickel in Defense Production Act inventories. To transfer the metal to the strategic stockpile would serve no useful purpose, for the stockpile already had enough of the metal. Gradual liquidation of the stocks under careful management so as to avoid unnecessary disturbance of the market seemed the only feasible alternative.

Action was needed, also, to prevent further accumulation of nickel in publicly owned stocks. The government was committed to purchase over a period of years several hundred million additional pounds of the metal, under contracts which permitted suppliers to "put" the nickel to the government at a "floor" price. The situation obviously called for negotiations looking toward cancellation of the contracts under agreed terms.

The uncertain factor in framing future policies for nickel, as well as for other materials, is the danger of war. In the case of nickel the problem is simplified by the absence in this country of significant reserves of nickel-bearing ores. There is, therefore, no question, as in the case of other nonferrous metals, of assisting a domestic industry so as to provide an adequate mobilization base. For its wartime supplies of nickel, the country must rely (1) on the stockpile, the first line of defense, (2) on making the best use of available supplies by prompt and vigorously applied measures of allocation, price control and scrap collection, and (3) above all, on access to the output of mines in Canada and in Cuba. It is clearly a matter of national interest that production should be maintained at a high level in both countries, and that they should not in any way impede our access to their output. This amounts to saying that the provision of adequate wartime supplies of nickel hinges upon the ability of the United States to retain Cuba and Canada as partners in a system of collective defense.

Chapter 7

RAW MATERIALS FOR THE IRON AND STEEL INDUSTRY

THE IRON and steel industry provides illustrations of practically all the problems of national policy which arise in the field of raw materials. In some of the materials for this industry, coal for example, the country is self-sufficient; in a second category we find nickel, of which practically the entire supply is imported. Between these extremes are materials like manganese, tungsten and fluorspar which are supplied partly from abroad and partly from mines in the United States. Scrap iron, a material of first-class importance, falls into none of these categories. In postwar years the United States has become the world's largest exporter of iron and steel scrap. The problem of policy concerns the limitation of exports, not of imports.

The capacity of the iron and steel industry to devour materials is prodigious. In 1956 its furnaces were fed with 134 million tons[1] of iron ore, 68 million tons of coke, 80 million tons of iron and steel scrap and 34 million tons of limestone. In terms of metal content manganese consumption was about 800,000 tons; fluorspar, 262,000 tons; nickel, 59,000 tons; and tungsten, 2,000 tons. For many of these materials, the iron and steel industry furnished by far the largest market. It took the entire available supply (imports as well as domestic shipments) of iron ore and iron and steel scrap, 90 percent of the coke, 90 percent of the manganese, practically all of the tungsten and nearly half of the nickel.

[1] For many of the commodities treated in this chapter the Bureau of Mines reports its statistics in long tons. The American Iron and Steel Institute uses both long and short tons, as does the Department of Commerce. In this chapter statistics have been given in short tons (2,000 pounds) except where otherwise stated.

No questions of national policy arise with respect to limestone or coking coal. For the foreseeable future, adequate supplies of these materials will be available from domestic sources. Transportation costs will preclude imports. Nickel is the subject of a separate chapter in this study. The present chapter will be devoted to iron ore, iron and steel scrap, manganese, tungsten and fluorspar.

Iron Ore

Domestic supplies

With respect to supplies of iron ore a significant change has taken place in the last half century. In northern Minnesota the rich iron ores of the Mesabi range have been rapidly depleted, so that the end of the supply of the richest and most easily accessible ores is in view and an increasing proportion of the annual output is now drawn from underground operations. In 1947-1951, 75 percent of the iron ore produced was of direct-shipping grade, i.e., immediately usable without concentration; in 1956, only 61 percent. Thirty years of research and experimentation, resulting in new mining and processing techniques, made it possible to begin large-scale exploitation of the immense reserves of taconite[2] in the Lake Superior region. With new drilling and crushing machinery and new concentration processes, iron of high grade is now extracted from 20-25 percent ore. The federal government provided assistance by allowing accelerated amortization of new investment for tax purposes, and the state of Minnesota imposed on taconite production a severance tax which was only a small part of the amount charged on high-grade iron ore. In 1956, shipments of taconite concentrates (over 60 percent iron) were about 5 million tons.

[2] Taconite is a compact, siliceous rock in which iron oxide is so finely disseminated that it cannot be concentrated by simple methods of benefication such as crushing, screening, washing, etc. It has been estimated that the Lake Superior region contains 30 billion tons of taconite ore averaging about 30 percent iron.

Supplies from abroad

The increasing dependence of the United States on imports of iron ore is shown below:

Year	*Ore consumed*	*Imports*	*Percent from imports*
	(in millions of short tons)		
1944	116.2	.5	.4
1950	119.8	9.3	7.8
1956	134.0	34.1	25.4

Canada supplied 1.2 million tons in 1946; in 1956, 15.4 million tons. Four South American countries, Venezuela, Peru, Chile and Brazil, furnished 15.5 million tons. Over one million tons came from Liberia, a new source which was insignificant in 1947-1951.

From the standpoint of national security, as well as the future growth of the American iron and steel industry, the rapid development of the extensive Canadian iron ore reserves is of first-class importance. Before World War II, practically no iron ore was mined in Canada, but in 1956 that country, with an output of 22 million tons, was the fourth largest producer in the world, surpassed only by the United States, Russia and France. In Newfoundland, in the Quebec-Labrador Iron Belt and in Ontario, north of Lake Superior, there are vast deposits of high-grade ore (estimated at 3 billion tons) which can be used directly in furnaces, and extensive deposits of low-grade, iron-bearing material usable after concentration. Production is capable of rapid expansion. The Canadian Department of Mines has estimated that within ten years the country's iron ore output may be in the range of 52 to 67 million tons.

The opening of the St. Lawrence Seaway, now scheduled for 1959, will make it possible for the United States to receive by inland waterways—free from the danger of enemy action—important additions to its domestic supply of iron ore. The Seaway, moreover, will reduce substantially the transportation costs on the important new supplies from Labrador and northern Quebec to the U. S. steel industry in the Great Lakes area. In winter months the

Seaway will be closed to navigation, but iron ore can be stored without deterioration.

The need for imports

There seems no doubt that the supplies of iron ore available to the United States will be adequate for the future needs of American industry. The Paley Commission in 1952 estimated U. S. consumption of iron ore in 1975 at 200 million tons, a figure which has found general acceptance in the iron and steel industry. Domestic ore production, according to the U. S. Bureau of Mines, after reaching 144 million tons in 1955-1960, will decline to 129 million in 1970-1975. To close the widening gap between domestic supply and the requirements of the steel mills, an increasing volume of supplies from abroad will be needed. Imports in 1975 are estimated at 76 million tons, close to 40 percent of consumption.

Under conditions of peaceful trade there seems no doubt that foreign countries can supply the American deficit without an advance in real costs. In time of war hostile action might deprive us of some part of the ore now obtained from South America and Cuba. But shipments from Canada through the St. Lawrence Seaway would not be vulnerable to enemy attack, and the output from mines in Labrador now being developed and in northern Quebec could be readily expanded. Also, under wartime pressures domestic production, both of direct-shipping ores and those concentrated from low-grade taconite, could be enlarged.

Improved techniques in mining and processing ore can still further increase the availability of domestic ore. These are matters which can be left to private enterprise, with the assistance of the research staffs of the Bureau of Mines and other government agencies. The development of iron ore production abroad has been undertaken by American companies without the aid of U. S. government purchase contracts or loans. In Canada the government, we may assume, will interpose no serious obstacles to the export of iron ore or to American investments in iron mines. As respects other countries, the protection of such investments from oppressive taxes and discriminatory exchange regulations and labor legislation may prove a major concern of American policy.

Iron and Steel Scrap

Congress in 1949 gave the Department of Commerce broad powers to control exports. The Department's use of these powers with respect to exports of iron and steel scrap has raised substantial questions of national policy.

Eighty-one million tons of scrap iron in 1956 made up one-half of the metallic material used in iron and steel production. "Home scrap," waste material recycled within the industry, furnished about 44 million tons. The balance, nearly half the total supply, was "purchased scrap." Of the latter, prompt industrial scrap furnished 15 million tons in the form of trimmings, clippings, etc. The remainder, about 22 million tons, was "obsolete scrap" consisting of material salvaged from wrecked buildings, steel rails and freight cars, automobile bodies and obsolescent and worn-out machinery. The problem of national policy centers on this type of scrap, which constitutes the bulk of the exports.

The United States, because of its rapid, large-scale industrial development, generates every year more ferrous scrap than any other country. Its reservoir of scrap, the supply actually and potentially available, is probably greater than in any other country. But the United States is also the world's leading producer of iron and steel, and on that account is the largest consumer of scrap. Open-hearth furnaces, the biggest consumers, use scrap and pig iron (hot metal) in roughly equal proportions. In iron foundries, the charge of scrap in 1956 averaged 65 percent of the total charge. Electric steel furnaces use a still larger proportion of scrap.

How scrap collection is organized

Scrap collection and sale is an extensive, well-organized industry. Some 4,000 small business firms buy scrap from farmers, peddlers, automobile wreckers and other local sources. In their junk yards they assemble and prepare the material which they sell in carload lots through brokers, who deal directly with steel mills and foundries. Only a few of the largest brokers have any export business. The smaller dealers complain that, with the increasing size of brokerage firms and the decline in their number, competition in the scrap market has been restricted. A single firm, according to testimony presented to a Congressional committee in 1957, controlled half of the entire business in purchased scrap. To some extent this trend toward concentration is the result of the mechanization of the processes of handling and processing scrap which requires increasingly large investments of capital. But the growth of big business in this field has been accelerated also by the use of exclusive contracts with steel mills, tie-in arrangements and other business practices of at least doubtful legality. The Federal Trade Commission in 1954 filed a complaint that two firms in the scrap industry had conspired with 16 iron and steel producers to suppress competition and create a monopoly in the interstate purchase and sale of iron and steel scrap. The Commission has held hearings over a period of several years but without coming to a decision.

Combination is characteristic also of foreign trade in scrap. The bulk of the exports to continental Europe is handled by a combination of three firms. Five firms export to England and six to Japan. In each of the principal importing areas all American scrap is bought by a single official or semi-official agency.

Foreign trade in scrap fluctuates with the ups and downs of the steel industry in this country and abroad. Before World War II the United States regularly exported more scrap than it imported, but in most of the years from 1943 to 1951 imports exceeded exports. A small export balance again developed in 1952 and in 1953, and after that a great outflow of scrap began which eventually resulted in 1957 in the limitation of U. S. exports, by the so-called voluntary agreement of the principal importing countries.

For several years after World War II the Department of Commerce had imposed restrictions on exports of scrap to all countries except Mexico and Canada.[3] The embargo on exports to the Soviet bloc and to Communist China rested on considerations of national security. The refusal to issue licenses for exports to other countries was justified on the grounds that the sales of scrap abroad would injure the domestic economy.

But in late 1953 the reason for the controls seemed to have disappeared, for scrap was no longer in short supply. Owing to a down-turn in business activity steel mills in the United States had slackened their purchases of scrap, prices had fallen and supplies had accumulated in the hands of dealers and consumers. Consequently on October 1 the Department removed its restrictions and announced that exports of iron and steel scrap would be licensed to virtually all countries in the Free World. The outgoing shipments which followed were unprecedented. (See Table 18.)

Table 18

U. S. EXPORTS OF IRON AND STEEL SCRAP, BY COUNTRY OF DESTINATION, 1947-51, 1952-1956

(in thousands of short tons)

Year	*Canada*	*Mexico*	*All other*	*Total*
1947–51 (av.)	124.1	90.1	12.3	226.5
1952	195.4	135.1	30.9	351.4
1953	76.8	156.4	76.6	309.8
1954	48.5	224.4	1,406.3	1,679.2
1955	429.8	258.5	4,441.7	5,130.0
1956	708.5	304.7	5,284.7	6,297.9

Source: U. S. Bureau of the Census

When in 1954 economic recovery in Japan and in Western Europe greatly enlarged the demand for iron and steel, increased use of scrap gave foreign producers the quickest way to expand their output. Since domestic supplies of scrap were inadequate, they began to buy in the newly opened United States market. The result was that our exports rose from 300,000 tons in 1953 to 6,300,000 tons in

[3] No licenses were required for exports to Canada; licenses were freely issued for exports to Mexico.

1956. Meanwhile, however, the American steel industry, having recovered from the short-lived recession of 1953-1954, itself needed more scrap. Reflecting the increased domestic plus foreign demand, scrap prices rose from $23-$28 per long ton in early 1954 to over $60 at the close of 1956. Average yearly prices, 1945-1957, are shown in Table 19.

Table 19

U. S. WHOLESALE PRICES OF IRON AND STEEL SCRAP, 1945-1957

(heavy melting, Pittsburgh)

(in dollars per long ton)

Year	*Price*	*Year*	*Price*
1945	20.00	1952	44.00
1946	20.82	1953	41.08
1947	36.30	1954	29.83
1948	41.33	1955	40.54
1949	32.07	1956	53.50
1950	39.26	1957	47.67
1951	45.18		

Source: U. S. Bureau of Labor Statistics

In this situation American steel makers urged that the Department of Commerce reimpose export restrictions. Between late 1953 and early 1957 they made at least 20 separate appeals and representations on this subject. Firms engaged in exporting scrap protested that restrictions were unnecessary. The Department agreed and declined, until 1957, to modify its policy, except in minor details. Meanwhile, however, two Congressional committees conducted hearings in which the Department's administration of export controls was subjected to searching examination and at times to severe criticism.

At the 1957 hearings on the extension of the Export Control Act, representatives of the steel industry insisted that exports had caused a shortage of scrap, thereby injuring the smaller integrated companies, particularly, and weakening the country's "mobilization base." In reply, the Department pointed to large inventories of scrap as proof that no shortage existed. The cause of high prices it found in abnormally large domestic demand rather than in exports. Moreover, it disclaimed authority to restrict exports unless they threatened injury to the entire national economy. The fact that certain steel producers were "in a squeeze" did not, it held, warrant action in their behalf. Assistant Secretary McClellan turned aside the suggestion that the Department, by a liberal construction of the Export Control Act, might help the petitioners "on the grounds of security."

In the hearings, foreign policy aspects of export control received some attention. Counsel for the scrap dealers asserted that the Department of Commerce, by denying sorely needed critical material to foreign friends and allies, had hampered the country's foreign policy. A representative of the steel industry recognized that our foreign policy required us to promote capacity steel production in friendly countries in Western Europe and elsewhere, but he criticized government for leaning too far toward an international point of view.[4]

The House Committee on Banking and Currency, in its report, after observing that exports could not be permitted to continue at the rate of 5 million tons a year, added:

> The committee realizes that the needs of our allies abroad must be considered. It would be too disruptive of our international relations to cut off scrap exports completely at this time.[5]

But, by a curious turn of reasoning, an officer of the Department of Commerce, and also an executive of a steel company, argued that by restricting exports the United States would promote the best interests of Western Euro-

[4] Testimony of Robert W. Wolcott, Lukens Steel Company, in Hearings before the House Committee on Banking and Currency, *Regulation of Exports,* 84th Cong., 2d sess., on H.R. 9052 (Washington: GPO, 1956), p. 117.

[5] U. S. House, Committee on Banking and Currency, *Extension of Export Control Act of 1949,* Report no. 1998, 84th Cong., 2d sess. (Washington: GPO, 1956), p. 4.

pean countries who otherwise might "build up an unreasonable dependence upon us for scrap." [6]

In 1954 the Department of State began conversations with the purchasing agencies in principal importing countries, the European Coal and Steel Community, the United Kingdom and Japan, urging moderation in their purchases of scrap in American markets. When these appeals for voluntary action brought no results, the Department of Commerce moved toward compulsion. For a number of weeks, beginning in February 1957, it refused to issue licenses for export of iron and steel scrap, except for hardship cases. The Department explained that its resumption of licensing on March 26 did not indicate a "lessened concern for prospective needs of domestic users" but was designed to permit steel operations abroad to continue while discussions of U. S. export policy on scrap were under way.

Pressure was again brought to bear on the importing countries by the Department's announcement in early May that, pending the outcome of negotiations, exports of heavy melting scrap[7] to the United Kingdom, Japan and the European Coal and Steel Community would be restricted to the tonnage shipped to them in 1956. A four-cornered international tug of war then ensued. The Japanese and the Europeans were pulling to get as much scrap as possible for their respective industries. U. S. scrap dealers were struggling to preserve valuable export markets. On the other side, the American steel and iron industry was endeavoring to keep in the country as large a supply as possible of an essential raw material. The Department of State

[6] Testimony of B. Campbell Blake, Connors Steel Division, H. K. Porter Company, in Hearings before the House Select Committee on Small Business, *Small-Business Problems Relating to Iron and Steel Scrap,* 85th Cong., 1st sess. (Washington: GPO, 1957), p. 310. See also the testimony of Assistant Secretary McClellan, p. 374.

[7] Heavy melting scrap refers to scrap "salvaged from relatively heavy shapes, such as structural material from buildings, railroad cars, and freight cars. This type of scrap is usually uniform in grade and metallurgical composition; hence it is a grade of scrap preferred by the steel industry because of its ability to be refined into steel of a given grade and composition in a minimum time." *Report on Iron and Steel Scrap by the Department of Commerce,* Committee Print of the House Banking and Currency Committee, 85th Cong. (Washington: GPO, 1957), p. 3.

became involved because of the possible effect of export restrictions on the economies of friendly foreign countries. At the center of these conflicting forces was the Department of Commerce where decisions had to be made.

The outcome was that the foreign interests were brought to terms. On June 18, 1957 the Department announced a "voluntary" agreement whereby importing interests in Japan, the United Kingdom and Western Europe agreed to limit their 1957 purchases of heavy grades of iron and steel scrap to 113 percent of their respective 1956 imports.

Considerations of national security afforded no justification for restricting exports of scrap. The Office of Defense Mobilization does not include scrap in its list of strategic and critical materials. No scrap has been accumulated in the national stockpile.

On economic grounds, the case for restriction is not convincing. The Export Control Act of 1949 authorized the Department of Commerce to control exports in order to protect the national economy from an excessive drain of scarce materials and to reduce the inflationary impact of abnormal foreign demand. The use of such vague terms in the statute as "excessive" and "abnormal" gave the administering agency wide discretion. Nevertheless, it would be difficult to prove that the scrap exports in 1955, 1956 and early 1957 actually had reached a point where they endangered the national economy. The growth of the exports in relation to the volume of scrap annually consumed by steel mills and foundries is shown below:

		Consumption		*Exports as percent of consumption of*	
Year	*Exports of scrap*	*All scrap*	*Purchased scrap*	*All scrap*	*Purchased scrap*
	(in thousands of short tons)			(percent)	
1953	310	77,131	35,410	.4	.9
1954	1,679	61,354	25,769	2.7	6.5
1955	5,130	81,375	35,796	6.3	14.3
1956	6,298	80,315	37,000	7.8	17.0
1957[a]	3,931	40,279	17,142[b]	9.8	22.9[c]

[a] January-June.
[b] Net receipts.
[c] Percent of net receipts of purchased scrap.
Source: U. S. Bureau of Mines, U. S. Department of Commerce

Evidence was produced at Congressional hearings, and by the Department of Commerce, showing that in the years of heavy exports scrap was not in short supply, i.e., that it could be obtained by purchasers able and willing to pay market prices. Actually, in the years 1954-1957, when exports were largest, the proportion of scrap to pig iron used in furnaces steadily increased.

The steep rise in scrap prices after 1954 was typical of all industries in which supply cannot be readily expanded to meet a sudden increase in demand. Considered over a longer period, the rise in scrap prices, when compared with other price movements, should have given no cause for alarm. In the ten-year period beginning in 1947 when wartime controls were removed, we find that scrap prices increased 50 percent. In the same period the price of iron ore advanced 125 percent and pig iron 80 percent. In 1956 the average composite price of finished steel products was 75 percent above the 1947 level, and the wholesale price index of metals and metal products was 63 percent higher.

It is difficult to find any basis, in fact or in logic, for the contention that restriction of exports of scrap was necessary in order to prevent the depletion of this country's reserves of obsolete scrap. Scrap, unlike virgin ore, is a renewable resource; the supply is like a reservoir which is continually drawn upon and continually replenished.[8] No one knows how much obsolete scrap exists at any time in the reservoir, or how much can be recovered. Estimates of the amount which is technically recoverable vary widely. How much would be *worth recovering* at any given level of scrap prices is still more uncertain. Moreover, the future inflow of scrap into the national reservoir is determined by technological changes affecting the rate of obsolescence of capital goods, which cannot be accurately predicted. The same

[8] During this process, it is true, the quality of the scrap in the reservoir, as well as the quantity, undergoes change. The present trend in output of steel mills toward a larger proportion of light products will mean that, after a time lag, they would supply a larger proportion of receipts of obsolete scrap. The concentration of export demand on the heavier types of scrap, moreover, tends to change the contents of the reservoir in the same direction.

is true of the developments in the metallurgy of iron and steel, some of which may lessen and others increase the demand for scrap.[9]

But even if reliable and comprehensive data indicated that the nation's supply of obsolete scrap was in danger of depletion, export controls would not supply a sufficient remedy, perhaps no remedy at all. Restrictions on the amount of scrap which can be sold abroad do not conserve the country's supply unless they are accompanied by restrictions on domestic consumption. Otherwise they merely change the proportions of the total annual crop of scrap consumed at home and abroad.

Manganese

The American iron and steel industry uses about 95 percent of all the manganese consumed in the United States. For every ton of steel produced, 10 to 15 pounds of manganese are used, principally to counteract the effect of sulphur. For this purpose it is not practicable to replace manganese with any other material. Titanium or zirconium might be substituted, but in war or any other emergency, when manganese is scarce, these metals are even scarcer. Much larger quantities of the substitutes would be needed, and the change-over would raise technical difficulties. Manganese is also an "additive" metal. A ton of finished steel may contain 20 to 280 pounds of manganese, to provide added strength and resistance to abrasion. In this use it is technically possible to substitute other metals, tungsten for example. But here again economic conditions impose severe limitations.

In many nonferrous alloys, with copper, nickel, aluminum and magnesium, manganese adds strength and resistance to corrosion. In addition to metallurgical uses, man-

9 A survey prepared by the Battelle Institute for the Department of Commerce has greatly enlarged our information on the demand-supply situation, present and prospective, in scrap. The Institute, however, has warned that its data were far from satisfactory and that conclusions drawn from them should be only tentative. The Institute's survey was reprinted in *Report on Iron and Steel Scrap by the Department of Commerce* (1957), cited, pp. 25-91.

ganese has other important applications. It is indispensable in the manufacture of the common dry-cell battery, and has many uses in the chemical industry.

The presence in Soviet Russia of 60 percent of the estimated world supply of high-grade manganese, as well as 35 to 40 percent of the intermediate grade, is a significant fact. Russia, the source of more than a third of the manganese used by American industries in prewar years, and now the world's largest producer, has exported no manganese directly to the States since 1949.[10] India has taken her place as the principal supplier, furnishing nearly 30 percent of the total. Imports from the principal supplying countries in 1946 and 1956 are shown in Table 20.

From the point of view of national defense, the great distances which separate the American steel mills from their major suppliers of manganese are significant. The Western Hemisphere has only a small fraction of the Free World's manganese production and reserves. For example, the total annual output of the four most important producers in that area, Cuba, Mexico, Brazil and Chile, even if all of it were available to American industries, would furnish less than one-half of U. S. needs.

The domestic supply

Domestic reserves of manganese include "manganese ore" containing 35 percent or more manganese, "ferruginous manganese ore" with a metal content ranging from 10 to 35 percent, and "manganiferous iron ore" which contains less than 10 percent manganese. Manganese ore containing 35 percent or more metal is scarce in the United States; most deposits are too small to be worth mining. Low-grade ores, however, are found in almost every state in the Union. Arizona, Minnesota and Maine have large deposits, and in South Dakota there are said to be over 2 billion tons of ore testing less than one percent metal. In

[10] In cutting off shipments to the United States, the U.S.S.R. may have sought to retaliate against the American embargo on exports of strategic materials. In late 1953 it was reported that Russian manganese and chrome had been offered in the American market, but at prices which did not attract buyers.

Table 20

U. S. IMPORTS OF MANGANESE ORE, 1946 AND 1956
(in short tons, manganese content)

	1946	*1956*
Western Hemisphere:		
Cuba	77,469	100,437
Brazil	38,985	99,296
Mexico	18,570	83,087
Other	65,229	13,508
Total	200,253	296,328
Africa:		
Gold Coast (Ghana)	145,981	149,338
Union of South Africa	113,037	121,682
Belgian Congo	—	77,958
Other	1	89,387
Total	259,018	438,365
Asia:		
India	160,958	293,977
Other	—	5,003
Total	160,958	298,980
Soviet Union:	121,754	—
All other:	—	3,940
Total[a]	741,983	1,037,613

[a] In addition, the manganese content of imports of ferromanganese was 26,000 tons in 1946 and 130,300 tons in 1956.
Source: U. S. Bureau of the Census

1956, mines principally in Montana, Nevada, Virginia and Tennessee produced 344,700 tons of manganese ore of 35 percent or more manganese.

Production of high-grade ore in the United States in the past 50 years has shown wide fluctuations. In wartime the industry, aided by government, has expanded rapidly, but equally rapid contraction has taken place after the emergency support was removed. Thus in World War I ore production rose from an average of 2,900 tons in 1910-1914 to 342,600 tons in 1918, and fell back to 15,000 tons in 1922. In World War II production rose to 247,600 tons in 1944 and fell in 1951 to less than half that amount. Remobilization programs after the attack on Korea lifted production in 1956 to the record figure of 344,700 tons. In that year domestic mines supplied 14 percent of total ore consumption. (See Table 21.)

Table 21

U. S. SUPPLY AND CONSUMPTION OF MANGANESE ORE (35+ PERCENT MANGANESE), 1951-1956

Year	Domestic mine shipments	General imports		Net supply[b]	Consumption[c]	Mine shipments as % of consumption
		Ore	Ferromanganese[a]			
	(in thousands of short tons)					(percent)
1951	105.1	1,767.6	241.0	2,104.3	2,121.0	5.0
1952	115.4	2,668.8	126.5	2,898.0	1,918.0	6.0
1953	157.5	3,501.0	252.0	3,900.7	2,254.0	7.0
1954	206.1	2,165.7	116.1	2,477.5	1,658.0	12.4
1955	287.3	2,078.2	242.7	2,607.6	2,378.0	12.1
1956	344.7	2,235.4	488.4	3,056.0	2,420.0	14.2

[a] In terms of ore; includes manganese metal and miscellaneous alloys.
[b] In terms of ore; excludes ore and ferromanganese exports ranging from 9.3 to 12.7 thousand tons; includes manganese metal and miscellaneous alloys.
[c] Consumption of ore, plus ferroalloy imports in terms of ore adjusted for changes in ferroalloy stocks.
Source: U. S. Bureau of the Census, U. S. Bureau of Mines

Tariff policy

World War I revealed the inadequacy of domestic supplies of manganese. In an attempt to build up the American industry, the Tariff Act of 1922 made imported ore dutiable at $20 per ton of manganese content, a rate which was over 100 percent of foreign value. During the fourteen years in which this rate was in effect, it seems to have had no appreciable effect either in checking imports or in stimulating domestic production. In 1936 a trade agreement with Brazil cut the duty in half,[11] but whatever results this

[11] A leading producer later complained that the reduction in the duties had made his million-dollar property, the most modern mill in the United States with developed reserves, valueless over night. "I simply walked away and left it. Junk, overnight." Testimony of J. Carson Adkerson of the American Manganese Producers Association, before the House Ways and Means Committee, *Trade Agreements Extension Act of 1953*, Hearings, 83rd Cong., 1st sess. (Washington: GPO, 1953), p. 1598.

action might have had were more than offset by the purchasing of domestic manganese ore for government stockpiling under the Act of June 7, 1939.

In 1948, a second tariff cut, from $10 to $5 per ton, gave indication that the restriction of imports was no longer a significant feature of national policy on manganese.

Assistance to domestic producers

The growth of shipments of high-grade ores from domestic mines in the five-year period 1951-1956, from 105,100 to 344,700 tons, can be attributed directly to various measures of government assistance. The Defense Minerals Exploration Administration made loans to aid promising projects, but the principal stimulus was provided by government purchases. The General Services Administration, beginning in June 1951, offered to purchase up to 18 million long-ton units[12] of low-grade manganese ore. In addition, the agency offered to buy from small producers 19 million units (later increased to 28 million) of contained manganese. Terminal dates for deliveries were June 1958 and January 1, 1961. The prices which the government offered, $2.30 per unit of 48-percent ore and $2.00 for 40-percent, were $1.30 in excess of the current market quotations. (See Table 22.) With this incentive, deliveries through June 30, 1956 amounted to 22.4 million units.

Table 22

RANGE OF U. S. MARKET PRICES FOR MANGANESE ORE

(metallurgical grade ore, 48% Mn content)

Year	*Per long-ton unit of contained manganese*
1948	$ .67–$ .73
1949	.73– .84
1952	1.22– 1.27
1953	1.10– 1.22
1954	.75– 1.10
1955	.82– 1.15
1956 (est.)	1.17– 1.65

12 A long-ton unit is 1/100 of a long ton, or 22.4 pounds.

Stimulation of production abroad

To encourage the development of Mexican manganese resources, the Defense Materials Procurement Agency in 1953 signed contracts with a number of small producers in that country for 500,000 long tons of low-grade ore to be delivered within three years to a processing depot in Texas.

Production of manganese in Brazil, which averaged about 150,000 tons in early postwar years, was greatly enlarged as the result of purchase contracts and Export-Import Bank loans to Brazilian companies in which American steel companies have large interests. In 1952 the Bank authorized a line of credit of $67,500,000 to a company in which the Bethlehem Steel Company had a 49-percent participation. A related contract provided for the purchase by the GSA of 400,000 long tons of Brazilian manganese and set a floor price for production up to 5,500,000 long tons.

After five years of exploration and development, including the building of a 120-mile railroad, the Bethlehem Steel Company began mining Brazilian ore at Amapa in early 1957. The mine is scheduled to produce 600,000 tons of unusually high-grade (45 percent) ore annually, two-thirds of which will go into the U. S. stockpile. In 1951 the Export-Import Bank offered to lend $30 million to assist in the development, by the United States Steel Corporation, of manganese mines in Matto Grosso. The conditions of the loan, however, did not meet with the approval of the Brazilian government, and the project was dropped. In 1957 the American company made an arrangement with the Brazilian holder of the mining concession, with the cooperation of the Bank of Brazil. Neither the Export-Import Bank nor other U. S. government agencies are participating in this project. Production is scheduled to begin in early 1958, at a rate of 50,000 tons yearly.

Stockpiling

When World War II ended, the U. S. strategic stockpile contained a white elephant, in the form of 129,000 long tons of manganese of such low grade that the steel industry could not have used it "without a drastic disruption of production processes."[13] When stockpile purchases were renewed after the Korean attack, the government continued to buy domestic ore so low in manganese content as not to be usable in steel manufacture.[14] Later it was found that only one-third of the government's holdings of manganese was of the 40-percent grade required by stockpile specifications.

At the end of 1954 the "minimum" stockpile goal for manganese had been filled, and the ODM announced that the stocks on hand, together with scheduled deliveries, were adequate to meet full mobilization requirements, even if some of the major sources of supply, such as India and Africa, should be completely cut off. It therefore began, whenever possible, to cancel or reduce supply contracts. Later new minimum and long-term objectives were set up. In 1956, government stocks of manganese of metallurgical grade greatly exceeded the minimum stockpile objective and were 90 percent of the long-term objective. In addition to the strategic stockpile, the supplemental stockpile contained manganese acquired by barter of surplus agricultural commodities.

Problems of manganese policy

As far as peacetime supplies are concerned, manganese, it seems, poses no questions of national policy. The Paley Commission in 1952 estimated that American industries in 1975 would require 2.5 to 2.7 million tons of ore of 46-percent manganese. This estimate of consumption now appears conservative, for consumption of manganese ore for the five years 1951-1955 had already risen to 2,066,000 tons and in 1956 to 2.4 million.

About 15 percent of our manganese supply now comes

[13] Hearings before the House Subcommittee on Mines and Mining, *Strategic and Critical Minerals and Metals*, 80th Cong., 2d sess. (Washington: GPO, 1948), p. 31.

[14] The minimum specifications, at first 18 percent, were lowered in 1954 to 15 percent.

from mines in this country. Some of the domestic production is supported by premium-price contracts, all of which will expire before 1961. Informed sources agree with the opinion expressed in 1952 by the Paley Commission that under normal commercial conditions domestic production cannot be expected to increase. The Commission's experts reported that the 1951 cost of mining and treating domestic ores, so as to extract a product comparable to the imports, would be at least twice and in some cases more than four times the landed cost of the foreign ore.[15]

Foreign ores are not only cheap; they are abundant. The world outlook for expansion of manganese output is favorable. During World War II new sources of supply were developed in French Morocco, the Union of South Africa and Cuba, and in the older producing areas, India and the Gold Coast, output was increased. According to the Paley Commission:

> The expansion of manganese production [abroad] is much less difficult and costly than for many other metals. Manganese ores usually occur on or near the surface and are cheaply excavated by hand or power shovels. Furthermore, these ores do not require crushing and elaborate concentration; a washing operation is usually sufficient to remove most of the waste material.[16]

The average grade of imported ores has declined, but the Commission nevertheless concluded that the increased production needed to satisfy rising world demand would not encounter rising real costs.

The United States draws 85 percent of its supply from abroad, but is not greatly dependent on a single source. Seven countries in 1956 supplied 90 percent of all imports of manganese, ranging in importance from Mexico with 7.7 percent of the total, to the Gold Coast with 13.9 percent and India with 28.6 percent.

15 The only domestic ores which could be competitive are those at Butte, Montana, which have a high yield of valuable by-products, lead, zinc and silver. There is little prospect that new reserves of high-grade ore will be uncovered.

16 President's Materials Policy Commission, *Resources for Freedom* (Washington: GPO, 1952), v. 2, *The Outlook for Key Commodities*, pp. 23-24.

The policy problem hinges on the danger that war might cut off foreign supplies. Manganese is a bulky commodity; the yearly imports run to 2 or 3 million tons of ore. Moreover, most of the foreign supply would have to be transported over thousands of miles of salt water. There is little manganese to be had in Canada or Mexico, and the entire Western Hemisphere at present supplies less than 30 percent of total U. S. imports. The strategic stockpile of manganese is designed to provide for the immediate needs of American industry if, in an emergency, overseas supplies should be cut off. The problem of policy is to find the most effective and economical means of maintaining in peacetime a manganese industry large enough to serve as a mobilization base and capable of rapid wartime expansion.

For this purpose, high protective tariffs have proven ineffective. The use of import quotas is inconsistent with the principles of our commercial policy and, like high tariffs, would offend friendly and the uncommitted countries whose good will it is important to maintain unimpaired. Purchase contracts at premium prices, the present form of subsidy, should be discontinued as soon as stockpile objectives have been attained. The maintenance of a domestic industry of minimum dimensions necessary for a mobilization base should be supported by direct payments to producers.

Subsidies, however, should constitute only a part of the government's manganese program. It should actively promote research in better methods of utilizing manganese in steel making, in the recovery of manganese from the slag dumps which surround steel mills, and in economical processes of upgrading domestic ores. In terms of ore consumed, the smelting of ferromanganese as at present conducted is inefficient. Over 15 percent of the manganese in the furnace charge is lost in slag and in flue dust. If economical techniques could be discovered this waste material might prove a valuable supplement to domestic ore supplies. The Paley report, assuming 700,000 tons of manganese as the annual requirement of the steel industry, estimated that the complete recovery from flue dust would furnish each year about 60,000 tons of metallic manganese. "Another 60,000 tons of manganese would still be lost annually in the ferromanganese slags, and future research could no doubt lower materially this source of waste."[17]

Tungsten

National policy on tungsten in postwar years afforded an extreme example of the successful use of purchase contracts to stimulate a domestic mining industry. In fact the policy might be called too successful. The owners of tungsten mines, stimulated by premium prices, produced more than ever before. The U. S. government by its purchase contracts stimulated production abroad, with the result that imports of foreign ores also increased. But the gain in U. S. consumption was not at all equivalent to the increase in available supply. The surplus went into the national stockpile, so that by 1957 the ODM could report that its supply of tungsten was sufficient for six years' consumption, even if all foreign sources should be cut off. Nevertheless, Congress in June 1956, responding to pressure from Western Senators, continued the purchase of tungsten, for the subsidy program had led to the opening of new high-cost mines and, in old mines, the extension of operations into marginal areas. Thus, like the protective tariff, it had created a vested interest in its perpetuation.

Defense and civilian uses

Tungsten, like nickel, is a relatively new metal. Its use in high-speed tool and die steels dates from the end of the last century. About 25 years later came the introduction of sintered tungsten carbide as a high-speed cutting tool. Tungsten is also used in filaments for light bulbs and television tubes, and in electrical contact points in the timing devices of internal combustion engines. Because it has the highest melting point of any metal, over 6,000 degrees Fahrenheit, tungsten promises to have increasingly wide application where stability at high temperatures is re-

[17] *Resources for Freedom,* cited, v. 4, *The Promise of Technology,* p. 46.

quired, in guided missiles, in jet engines and in atomic reactors.

U. S. consumption of tungsten in 1956 was distributed as follows:

	Percent of total
In steel and other alloys	45
In carbides	35
As pure metal	13
Miscellaneous	7

The strategic importance of tungsten in armament production, which first became apparent in World War I, was greatly emphasized in World War II when the Germans employed armor-piercing shells of tungsten carbide. The Second World War also developed jet engines and gas turbines which used superalloys containing tungsten and other metals.

Sources of supply

The postwar years have shown rapid gains in domestic shipments of tungsten from mines. Imports in 1956 were also much larger than at the end of the war.[18] But although

[18] In Table 23, imports are "imports for consumption." Later in the text, I refer to "general imports." The latter are imports received in the United States in a given year, part of which go into consumption during the year and the remainder into bonded warehouses. Imports for consumption include withdrawals from warehouses during a given year as well as current imports going into consumption in that year. Differences between these classifications of imports of tungsten ores and concentrates are shown below:

U. S. Imports of Tungsten
(1,000 pounds, contained tungsten)

Year	*General imports*	*Imports for consumption*
1949	7,357	6,274
1950	8,342	16,147
1951	7,533	6,377
1952	16,985	17,406
1953	28,994	27,683
1954	22,989	24,132
1955	20,789	20,646
1956	21,857	20,860

The excess of imports for consumption over general imports in 1950 resulted from withdrawals from warehouses of supplies which had ac-

the total available supply rose from 11.8 million pounds of contained tungsten in 1946 to 34.9 million in 1956, consumption by American industries gained only 2.6 million. The annual surplus of supply over consumption is roughly equivalent to the amount added to government-owned stocks and inventories. (See Table 23.)

Table 23

U. S. SUPPLY AND CONSUMPTION OF TUNGSTEN, 1946-1956

(in thousands of pounds, contained tungsten)

Year	*Shipments from mines* (1)	*Imports for consumption*[a] (2)	*Available supply* (3)	*Consumption* (4)	*Estimated additions to government owned stocks*[b] (5)
1946	4,942	6,869	11,811	6,458	5,353
1947	2,945	6,018	8,963	7,812	1,151
1948	3,838	7,548	11,386	8,853	2,533
1949	2,632	6,274	8,906	4,958	3,948
1950	4,588	16,147	20,735	6,597	14,138
1951	5,973	6,377	12,350	11,410	940
1952	7,244	17,406	24,650	8,634	16,016
1953	9,128	27,683	36,811	7,734	29,077
1954	13,030	24,132	37,162	4,037	33,125
1955	15,619	20,646	36,265	8,967	27,298
1956	14,027	20,860	34,887	9,061	25,826

[a] See p. 195, footnote 18, for description of imports.
[b] Stockpile plus DPA inventories.
Note: No account has been taken of small changes in producers' and consumers' stocks.
Sources: Col. 1—U. S. Bureau of Mines
Col. 2—U. S. Bureau of the Census
Col. 3—calculated by adding cols. 1 and 2
Col. 4—U. S. Bureau of Mines
Col. 5—calculated by subtracting col. 4 from col. 3

Domestic tungsten reserves, measured and indicated, have been estimated at 4,230,000 short-ton units of tungsten trioxide; practically all of the ore has a tungsten

cumulated over a period of several years. I have used general imports as the best means of showing the shift in sources of tungsten imports during the Korean war, but in comparing the volume of imports with the level of domestic consumption I have used imports for consumption.

content of less than 1 percent. In 1955 eight companies produced 70 percent of the entire domestic supply; at the end of 1957 only three companies were operating mines, viz:

Company	*Location of mines*
Tungsten Mining Corporation	Henderson, North Carolina
Nevada-Massachusetts Company	Mill City, Nevada
Union Carbide Corporation	Bishop, California

A small addition to the domestic supply came from the mines of the Climax Molybdenum Company at Climax, Colorado, where tungsten was produced as a by-product.

China, which has about 80 percent of the world's reserves, supplied 4.9 million pounds, 67 percent of all the tungsten imported into the United States in 1949. The following year, as a result of the war in Korea,[19] imports from China dropped to 394,000 pounds, less than 5 percent of the total. But increased purchases from Bolivia and other South American countries, the Republic of Korea, Australia, Spain and Portugal filled the gap, so that consumption of tungsten by American industries showed no decline.

The outbreak of the Korean war gave the signal for a scramble on the part of industrial countries for the Free World's supply of tungsten. The intensity of the competition is evidenced by the rise in price within a few months, from $17.50 to $86 per short-ton unit (20 pounds). In 1949 the United States had received 2.5 million pounds of tungsten (general imports)[20] which, when added to domestic shipments, gave this country 27 percent of the Free World's supply. The next year, with general imports of 7.9 million pounds, the proportion was 63 percent. The United States then agreed to recommendations by the Tungsten-Molybdenum Committee of the International Materials Confer-

[19] The United States in December 1950 imposed an embargo on all exports to Communist China. But before it became effective, receipts of tungsten from that country had practically disappeared. The unilateral action of the United States was converted into a multilateral obligation by the United Nations resolution of May 1951.

[20] In order to present comparable figures from 1949 through 1952, imports from China have been excluded.

ence[21] which reduced its 1951 take to 45 percent. In 1952 world production expanded so rapidly that the IMC allocation of tungsten for that year permitted U. S. imports of 17 million pounds, which, when added to increased domestic shipments, gave this country 56 percent of Free World supply.

In case of war the United States could not rely upon adjacent countries to supply much of its tungsten requirements. In 1956, Canada and Mexico furnished only 26 percent of consumption. However, Bolivia in that year was the largest single source of imports, and the combined imports of all the Western Hemisphere countries exceeded total U. S. consumption by 3 million pounds. The distribution by foreign sources of supply in 1956 is shown below:

Country of origin	*Imports for consumption, 1956* (1,000 pounds, tungsten content)	
Western Hemisphere		11,972
Bolivia	4,146	
Argentina	2,164	
Brazil	2,107	
Canada	1,704	
Other	1,851	
Republic of Korea		3,081
Australia		1,850
Portugal		1,341
All other		2,616
Total		20,860

Source: U. S. Bureau of the Census

Assistance to foreign producers

The high level of tungsten imports after 1951 was the result, in part at least, of U. S. policy. Contracts were made by the General Services Administration to buy tungsten from producers in the Republic of Korea, Canada, Argentina, Mexico and Bolivia. The Export-Import Bank made loans to producers in Argentina, Peru and Bolivia to assist them in providing tungsten for the U. S. national stockpile. Leading producers in Thailand received an RFC loan for the same purpose. In early 1955 there were outstanding

[21] See pp. 54-58.

35 U. S. contracts calling for the production abroad of 6 million units (120 million pounds) of tungsten trioxide. For a large portion of the supply the government is said to have paid $65 per short-ton unit, $2 more than the domestic purchase price.

Tariff protection for the domestic industry

For the protection of the domestic industry, which developed during World War I, the Tariff of 1922 made imports of tungsten dutiable at 45 cents a pound (metallic tungsten content). The Act of 1930 raised the duty to 50 cents, 120 percent of foreign value, where it remained until 1948 when a multilateral trade agreement reduced it to 38 cents. The lowered duty remained in effect until December 1950, when China withdrew from the General Agreement on Tariffs and Trade. That action restored the 50-cent rate on imports of tungsten from all countries.[22] In 1956 it was equivalent to only 18 percent of the foreign value of the imports.

During World War II the tariff on tungsten had no practical significance since all the imports were for government account. After 1951 government purchases figured largely in imports; in 1956 they accounted for about one-half of the total. For domestic producers of tungsten, the tariff has been reduced to relative insignificance by the government's purchase program which has given them a subsidy amounting to several times the duty.

Direct assistance to domestic producers

The Defense Minerals Exploration Administration provided loans for exploration and discovery of tungsten deposits, covering 75 percent (later 50 percent) of expenditures for these purposes. Loans on 118 contracts in 1951-1956 amounted to $3,230,000.

In early 1951 the ODM authorized, under the Defense Production Act of 1950, the purchase from domestic pro-

22 Bills introduced in the 82d Cong., 1st sess., providing for the temporary suspension of tungsten duties during the Korean emergency, failed of passage.

ducers of 3 million units (60 million pounds) of tungsten trioxide. This quantity, over 15 times the average annual output of American mines (1947-1950), was to be delivered within five years, i.e., before June 30, 1956. The offered price, although $10 less than the current market quotation, was more than double the average price of the preceding year. With this incentive, domestic producers stepped up their operations and completed their deliveries by the expiration of the offer.

In mid-1956, the national stockpile of tungsten was full; both short-term and long-term goals had been attained. The Director of Defense Mobilization stated:

> Even without any access to foreign or domestic sources of supply in the event of war, we would have enough tungsten in the stockpile to meet total requirements for approximately a five-year period.[23]

Under these circumstances he declined to take responsibility for further purchases. Congress, nevertheless, at the insistence of Senators from Western states, in 1956 authorized a new tungsten program. In *Public Law* no. 733 it directed the Department of the Interior to purchase before December 13, 1958 an additional 1,250,000 units (25 million pounds). The new price, $55 per unit, gave sellers a premium of $20 over current market quotations.

The continuance of a domestic purchase program was subjected to severe criticism. An official report pointed out that 49 producers actually had participated in the program and, of these, 9 received 87 percent of the funds. One of them, after receiving $10 million, condemned the stockpiling of tungsten as "an out-and-out boondoggle."

The outlook

In early 1957 Senators from certain Western states predicted that if government subsidies, in the form of purchase contracts, were withdrawn, the domestic tungsten industry would not last three months. This prediction came very near the truth. Congress failed to renew the appropriations

23 Quoted in *Chemical and Engineering News,* June 11, 1956.

for the purchase program, and at the end of the year production from domestic mines had practically ceased. The price of foreign tungsten delivered in New York (including duty) had fallen to $22 per short-ton unit, the lowest level since early 1950. At this price the situation of the American mine owners was precarious, excepting one company which produced tungsten as a by-product of molybdenum. Until government policy crystallized, the three other remaining companies were continuing operations rather than incur losses consequent upon closing and reopening the mines.

The great demand for tungsten and the high prices induced by the Korean war stimuated increased output of tungsten in many foreign countries. In 1950 the Free World total, outside the United States, was 15 million pounds. Two years later it had risen to 36 million. With the collapse of the Korean boom in 1953 and, in later years, the expiration of U. S. purchase contracts, some foreign mines were closed. But Free World production outside the United States remained at a high level. The 1956 estimate was 35 million pounds.

The prospects for further expansion are clouded by political uncertainties. Some of the world's largest deposits are in Asian countries vulnerable to Communist pressures, in South Korea, Burma and Thailand. In China there is plenty of tungsten of excellent quality; for several years after 1951, because of the United Nations embargo, it was diverted from the Free World market to Russia.[24] But the United Kingdom, West Germany and other countries have now relaxed their controls on trade with China. Should this trend continue, we may expect that tungsten of Chinese origin will reappear in world markets. Such an event would put at rest fears of an impending world shortage. Nevertheless the control of a substantial part of the world's output by a Communist dictatorship would give rise to apprehension of another sort, namely, that the Chinese might use their control for political reasons, adding to or

[24] Liberal use of Chinese tungsten may explain the rapid advance of Russian production of jet airplanes and ballistic missiles.

diminishing the supply, in order to upset the economies of the United States and other importing nations, or to drown competing sources of supply in a flood of cheap tungsten. Uncertainty on the latter score is said to constitute an obstacle to investment in tungsten mining in some countries.

A prescription for national policy

Tungsten policy, like policy on manganese, hinges on considerations of national defense. Two questions must be answered: (1) how large a domestic tungsten industry do we need, and (2) how can it best be maintained? The defense authorities, the only authoritative source of information on the first question, will not give a quantitative answer. They say only that the industry must be large enough to provide "an adequate mobilization base." They have indicated, also, that without government assistance domestic production of tungsten would not satisfy this requirement. This brings us to the consideration of the second question: How can an industry essential to national defense best be maintained?

No amount of tariff protection could build up a self-supporting tungsten industry in this country, i.e., one that could eventually stand on its own feet without protection. Even if mechanization of mining and milling operations should reduce labor costs to a competitive level, the absence in this country of ore deposits of a size and richness comparable to those in Bolivia, Brazil and other tungsten-exporting countries would still constitute a permanent and decisive handicap. This a priori conclusion is fortified by experience, by the lack of progress in the industry over the long period in which it was protected by high duties. Moreover a tariff, for a number of reasons, is not the best way to maintain a defense industry.[25] Import duties place the burden of cost on the consumers of the protected product, not where it properly belongs, on the whole body of tax-

[25] For fuller exposition of this argument see my *What the Tariff Means to American Industries* (New York: Council on Foreign Relations, 1956), pp. 127-129.

payers. Also, no specific performance is required from the beneficiaries, the protected firms.

Payment of subsidies in some form seems the best method of maintaining a tungsten industry of the minimum dimensions declared by the ODM, or other competent authority, to be necessary for a mobilization base. It has been proposed that the government, instead of aiming at continued production of domestic tungsten, should allow the mines which cannot compete with imports—practically all of them—to shut down. It would then pay an annual subsidy to the owners of the best-equipped and best-situated mines to cover the cost of pumping, repairs and upkeep of above-ground facilities. Thus by the expenditure of a few million dollars annually the mines could be maintained in stand-by condition. Within six months, should an emergency arise, they could be brought into full production. The difficulty with this scheme lies in keeping together the engineering and management staffs during the stand-by period.

A more practicable plan, in fact, the only one which would maintain the desired production at minimum cost to the community, would be to make direct payments from the U. S. Treasury to tungsten miners as incentive to produce stipulated tonnages. In his Domestic Minerals Stabilization Plan, Secretary Seaton proposed that Congress guarantee for a period of five years a price of $36 per short-ton unit of tungsten or an annual production of 375,000 units. In this Plan, however, the subsidy supplements rather than replaces tariff protection.

Fluorspar

In fluorspar, the demand-supply situation in postwar years epitomized the general situation in raw materials, viz., the failure of domestic production to satisfy the expanding demands of American industry, and the country's growing reliance on foreign sources of supply. The course of fluorspar policy followed lines already familiar to readers of this and earlier chapters. Faced in 1950 with a shortage of fluorspar, executive agencies made purchase contracts with domestic and foreign producers. Stimulated by premium prices they opened new mines and enlarged old operations, so that at the end of 1957 the government had acquired practically all the fluorspar it needed in its stockpiles.[26] Market prices meanwhile had fallen and domestic producers pleaded for the continuation of the subsidy.

Measured by the tonnages consumed each year, or in dollars, fluorspar is not an impressive item in the American economy. The entire 1956 consumption was 621,350 tons, valued at something less than $40 million. For the steel and aluminum industries, however, fluorspar is an essential raw material [27] for which no practicable substitute has yet been found.

Just before World War II domestic mines were shipping each year about 150,000 tons, which was 90 percent of total consumption. By 1956 their output had more than doubled (see Table 24), but meanwhile American industries had

Table 24

U. S. SUPPLY AND CONSUMPTION OF FLUORSPAR, 1937-39, 1946-50, 1951-1956

(in short tons)

Year	*Domestic shipments*	*Imports for consumption*	*Available supply*[a]	*Reported consumption*	*Surplus of supply*[b]
1937–39 (av.)	148,135	24,329	171,057	162,067	8,990
1946–50 (av.)	295,477	96,091	390,545	371,388	19,157
1951	347,024	181,275	527,126	497,012	30,114
1952	331,273	352,503	683,101	520,197	162,904
1953	318,036	359,569	676,838	586,798	90,040
1954	245,628	293,320	538,305	480,374	57,931
1955	279,540	363,419	642,085	570,261	71,824
1956	329,719	485,552	805,205	621,354	183,851

[a] After subtracting exports ranging from 1,400 tons in 1937-39 to less than 200 tons in 1956.

[b] Represents principally addition to national stockpiles and DPA inventories; includes also additions to consumers' inventories.

Source: U. S. Bureau of the Census, U. S. Bureau of Mines

[26] As of June 1957 the stockpile inventories had not been reported as filled. However, these inventories, plus stocks in other government accounts and materials on order, taken together probably amounted to the total of the stockpile goals.

[27] About 5½ pounds of fluorspar are used for every ton of steel and 120 pounds per ton of aluminum.

expanded their demand for fluorspar nearly 300 percent. Thus the proportion of consumption supplied by domestic mines fell to 50 percent.

Changes in domestic production

The over-all figures in Table 24 conceal some rather important developments. Before World War II, the iron and steel industry accounted for nearly 75 percent of total consumption of fluorspar. The great expansion of the aluminum industry in the war years and thereafter gave rise to a much enlarged demand for hydrofluoric acid. In 1956 almost half the total supply of fluorspar was used for this purpose, and over half of the shipments from domestic mines. In the chemical industry also, a variety of new uses developed for hydrofluoric acid, particularly in the manufacture of fluorine compounds.

Closely related to the postwar development of new uses for fluorspar was the westward movement of the industry. Traditionally, fluorspar production had been concentrated in an area along the Ohio River, in southern Illinois and western Kentucky, but after World War II output from this area declined both in absolute tonnage and in relative importance. The reasons are found partly in rising costs in Kentucky and Illinois mines, owing to exhaustion of surface deposits and the necessity of resort to underground mining. Frequent flooding of the mines in this area also handicapped production. But the growing importance of fluorspar production of Western states, principally Montana, Colorado, Nevada, New Mexico and Utah, is related also to the changing character of the demand. Most of the Western deposits, except in Utah and Montana, are better adapted for the production of the acid than the metallurgical grade.[28]

[28] Calcium fluoride content determines in general the three commercial grades of fluorspar—acid, ceramic and metallurgical. Where fluorspar deposits contain a relatively high proportion of other minerals (chiefly silica), as in most of the Western states, the fluorspar "can be freed from these impurities only by relatively fine grinding and the use of the flotation process. Such deposits are suitable for the production of acid and ceramic fluorspar where the cost of mining and milling and access to markets justifies exploitation." (U. S. Tariff Commission, *Fluorspar* [Washington:

Assistance to foreign producers

Imports of fluorspar in 1956 were 485,500 tons, five times the average receipts of the immediate postwar years. Mexico in 1956 supplied 65 percent of the foreign fluorspar. Other important sources were Spain, Italy and West Germany. The rise in imports after 1950 was in large part the result of U. S. government purchase contracts and other measures of assistance to foreign producers. The latter included a grant of the equivalent of $1 million in counterpart funds to the largest Italian producer of fluorspar to construct a flotation mill. The funds were repayable in acid-grade fluorspar to be delivered to the U. S. stockpile. The following year the Export-Import bank lent Spain $400,000 for a similar purpose. A Canadian firm operating mines in Newfoundland got a loan from the Defense Materials Procurement Agency for the construction of a large modern mill at Wilmington, Delaware. Fluorspar concentrates processed at this mill from Canadian ore went into the U. S. stockpile under a contract ending in 1957. A barter agreement with a large Mexican producer made possible a substantial addition to his plant capacity. The amounts of foreign fluorspar added to government stocks as the result of these transactions are shown below:

Fluorspar Imported for Government Account
(in short tons)

Year	Tons
1950	2,700
1951	22,700
1952	55,600
1953	109,400
1954	50,800
1955	12,400

Source: U. S. Department of Commerce

Author, 1955], p. 52.) Although the steel industry and ceramic manufacturers use some fluorspar of the highest purity, the bulk of the supply containing over 97 percent calcium fluoride is used in the manufacture of hydrofluoric acid. Ceramic grades, which account for the smallest proportion of consumption, usually have 94-97 percent calcium fluoride. Both ceramic and acid grades are normally sold in finely ground form. Metallurgical grades must be in gravel or lump form to provide the necessary fluxing properties in the basic open-hearth process. They may contain as little as 70 percent calcium fluoride.

When in late 1950 a severe shortage of acid-grade fluorspar developed, the Department of Interior entered into exploration and development contracts with a number of American firms. The Defense Materials Procurement Agency, to meet the needs of an aluminum expansion program, also made contracts with domestic firms for the delivery of substantial quantities of acid-grade fluorspar at guaranteed prices.

President Eisenhower declines to raise import duties

Toward the end of 1953 the collapse of the Korean boom in raw materials brought a sharp decline in the market price for fluorspar. Owners of mines within this country who were supplying the government on uncompleted contracts feared that when purchases for the stockpile ceased they would be exposed to the competition of low-cost foreign fluorspar, some of it from mines subsidized by their own government. To forestall this situation fluorspar producers sought higher tariff protection. They first applied to the Tariff Commission in 1953, requesting that the 1930 import duty on acid-grade fluorspar, which had been reduced in trade agreements, be restored.[29] This application, however, they subsequently withdrew. The Tariff Commission, in response to resolutions of the Senate Finance Committee, made two investigations of the domestic fluorspar industry. Its first report (June 1955) was of a general

[29] The rates imposed by the Tariff Act of 1930 were $8.40 per long ton of fluorspar containing not more than 97 percent of calcium fluoride, the metallurgical grade. An agreement with Mexico (1943) reduced this duty to $6.30, but upon termination of the agreement in December 1950 the $8.40 rate was restored.

On the acid grade, of which very little was produced at home, the 1930 rate was only $5.60. In 1951, under the General Agreement on Tariffs and Trade, this rate was cut to $2.10. Meanwhile improved methods of treating Western fluorspar ores had made possible greatly enlarged production of acid-grade concentrates, so that in 1956 the output exceeded that of the metallurgical grade and the price per ton was about 50 percent higher. Thus an anomalous tariff situation had arisen. The major product with the higher unit value was dutiable at one-fourth the rate imposed on the less important, cheaper grade. The conversion of the specific rates to their ad valorem equivalents reveals an even greater discrepancy. Imports of acid-grade fluorspar paid duties in 1955 equivalent to 6.1 percent of foreign value, whereas the cheaper metallurgical grade paid 56.0 percent.

character. In the second (January 1956), which dealt only with the acid grade, three Republican Commissioners found that increased imports threatened serious injury to domestic producers and recommended that the import duty be raised from $2.10 per long ton to $5.60, the 1930 rate. The three Democrats on the Commission, however, found no evidence in the trend of prices, profits, wages or employment that increased imports had caused serious injury to the American industry. Regarding profits these Commissioners said:

> The information that has been feasible to obtain in the investigation indicates that *none* of the fluorspar mining and milling operations, that contributed substantially to the domestic production of acid grade fluorspar in recent years and that would be likely in immediate future years to contribute substantially to such production, are clearly unprofitable under presently prevailing conditions. The available information further indicates that under present conditions the operations of *most* of the acid grade fluorspar producing plants that are currently operating are clearly profitable and that *some* are extremely so.[30] [Italics in original.]

They concluded that the industry's fears that the end of the stockpiling program would bring disaster were unfounded. Government purchases, they predicted, would be a considerable factor in total demand until the end of 1958. Before that time, they expected that increased demand for hydrofluoric acid in the production of aluminum and in the increased production of fluorine compounds by the chemical industry would open up important new commercial markets.

The domestic industry, these Commissioners admitted, was not doing as well in 1955 as in the boom years 1950-1953. But a finding of injury, they believed, should not be based on short-run considerations but on a comparison of conditions over a longer term of years. Such a comparison afforded no indication that domestic producers were suf-

[30] U. S. Tariff Commission, *Acid Grade Fluorspar,* Report to the President on Escape-clause Investigation No. 42 (Washington: Author, 1956), p. 49.

fering from foreign competition. Accordingly, they recommended that no change be made in import duties. President Eisenhower accepted this recommendation.

Before the President's decision was made public the fluorspar producers, leaving no stone unturned, filed with the Office of Defense Mobilization an application for relief as an essential industry.[31] Action on this application is still pending.

Purchase contracts

In July 1956 Congress authorized[32] the purchase of 250,000 tons of acid-grade fluorspar produced by domestic mines at $53 per short ton. At this time the market price as quoted in trade journals was $47.50. The purchase, according to Secretary of Interior Seaton, was intended to remove from the market the surplus of fluorspar which had resulted from the completion of government stockpile contracts, to "provide time for consumption to catch up with supply, and for the industry to orient its operations to normal commercial markets."[33] Government buying for stockpile was still providing a floor under the domestic price of fluorspar of metallurgical grade. The Secretary expected that at the completion of the program this section of the industry would be "reoriented at reasonable price and production levels."

Problems of national policy

As the end of the present purchasing program draws near, the question will again arise whether the government should continue to subsidize fluorspar production. Domestic producers will urge that, without further measures of government assistance, imports will furnish an

[31] Under Section 7 of the Trade Agreements Extension Act of 1955, the "national security clause."

[32] In *Public Law* no. 733, 84th Cong., 2d sess., Congress appropriated $3,742,000 for this program which was to end in December 1958.

[33] Statement of Hon. Fred A. Seaton, Secretary of the Interior, before Senate Interior and Insular Affairs Committee, June 4, 1957. The completion of contracts does not necessarily imply that stockpile goals have been attained.

increasing proportion of the fluorspar consumed by American industries. This may well occur, and as a result some of the American producers may have to restrict their operations or shut down altogether. In competing countries, except Canada, wages paid in fluorspar mines and mills are much lower than in Kentucky, Illinois or Western states. Fluorspar deposits, also, are richer, especially in Mexico. Shippers of both Mexican and Canadian ores benefit by cheap water transportation.

From the point of view of the national economy, increasing reliance on imports of fluorspar could bring only gain. Production in the United States is an industry of small dimensions. The total number of persons employed in 1952, a year when mines and mills were fully active, was only 2,000. A substantial part of the annual output comes from "captive" mines, owned and operated by large manufacturers of steel, aluminum and chemicals. Whatever hardships were experienced locally from declining production would be offset by gains to the national economy. American industries would get cheaper supplies of an important raw material. Supplying countries, Mexico, Canada, Italy and Spain, would have more dollars to spend for American goods, including manufactures of iron and steel and aluminum.

On grounds of national defense there seems to be no good reason for subsidizing the domestic fluorspar industry. A stockpile of generous proportions provides adequate emergency supplies. They can be supplemented from easily accessible mines in Mexico and Newfoundland. In Mexico production has shown great possibilities of expansion in recently opened mines near the American border.

The Paley report, issued in the midst of the Korean war, expressed doubt whether the future supplies of fluorspar available to the United States and other countries in the Free World would be adequate for the expanding needs of their industries. The report projected a three-fold growth in U. S. consumption of fluorspar in the 25 years 1950-1975, basing its estimates on expected rates of increase in the aluminum and chemical industries. On the other hand, U. S. production, the Commission's experts believed, had passed its peak rate of growth, and only limited further expansion could be expected. The report hazarded the guess that in 1975 U. S. production might exceed the 1950 output by as much as 10 percent, rising from approximately 280,000 to about 300,000 tons. Actually, with the incentives provided by the government's purchases, production reached 341,000 tons in 1951 and in 1951-1956 averaged 301,000 tons. The Paley report stated: "At 1950 rates of consumption, presently known United States commercial reserves could 'support' United States demands for fluorspar for only about 15 years." [34] But a few years later, in 1956, the U. S. Geological Survey found, as a result of new discoveries in Western states, that reserves would support production at the average 1951-1955 rate for 30 years.

With respect to the possible expansion of Free World supplies, the Paley Commission's projections also seem to have been equally wide of the mark. Production in the Free World, *outside the United States,* the report estimated, might increase by 1975 to about double the 1950 level, which was in the neighborhood of 350,000 tons. Accordingly the 1975 output would be approximately 700,000 tons. Actually, production had exceeded this figure before the Paley report was off the press and in 1955 had reached 920,000 tons.

Free World Production of Fluorspar
(excluding United States)
(1,000 short tons)

1950	350
1951	600
1952	800
1953	830
1954	880
1955	920

Technological advance will force modifications of estimates of both future consumption and supply. New uses for fluorspar are developing, in the production of fluorine for nontoxic refrigerants, for propellants and in the pro-

[34] *Resources for Freedom,* v. 2, cited, p. 89.

duction of atomic energy. On the supply side, we may expect that the production of fluorine compounds from phosphate rock will supplement the output of natural fluorspar, if it should prove inadequate. On balance, we find no clear indication of long-run shortages in supply, and consequently no necessity for anticipatory measures of national policy.

Chapter 8

NATIONAL POLICIES AFFECTING WOOL

FOR THREE QUARTERS of a century wool growing in the United States has been a declining industry. World War II reversed the trend only temporarily, and between 1942 and 1956 sheep numbers fell from 49 million to 27 million and wool production from 455 million to 279 million pounds (in the grease).[1] In the same period, while total farm income increased by about 75 percent, income from sheep raising fell by 10 percent.

The decline in the sheep industry cannot be attributed to the lack of government assistance. For a period of 140 years wool growing has benefited from almost continuous tariff protection against foreign competition. In 1929, government loans and purchases were introduced as a further measure of assistance to the industry. But price-support policies designed to deal with "surplus" commodities proved ineffective when applied to wool, a product which has regularly been imported in large volume. In some years price supports seem chiefly to have benefited foreign wool growers by providing an unusually good market for their product in this country.

Domestic wool growers in 1953 demanded that the President impose quotas on wool imports, but the Tariff Commission recommended that he restrict the imports by adding "import fees" to the existing tariff duties. The

[1] Including both "shorn" and "pulled" wool. The latter is obtained from the carcasses of slaughtered animals. Unless otherwise noted, the production figures cited in the following pages refer to both pulled and shorn wool. Wool "in the grease" contains large amounts of sand, burrs and other foreign matter, in addition to natural fatty substances. The average clean yield of domestic production is estimated at 44 percent for shorn wool and 75 percent for pulled wool. Imported wools average considerably higher in clean content than the domestic.

President rejected this recommendation as an ineffective and unwise interference with international trade. Instead, he substituted for price supports direct payments from the U. S. Treasury to the wool growers. Thus a free market for wool, linked to world markets, was re-established in the United States. Direct payments constitute an innovation which, if applied to other farm products as well as wool, may be effective in reconciling the long conflict between an isolationist policy on farm products and minerals and a foreign economic policy which aims at the expansion of international trade.

Sheep Raising in the United States

For the study of the sheep industry, the United States is usually divided into two areas, the range states[2] and the "native states" which include the rest of the country. In 1957, there were 18,775,000 sheep shorn, 66 percent of the national total, on farms and ranches in the Western states and Texas. In this area the typical operation is the grazing of large flocks — 2,500 animals or more — on open range under constant supervision of a herder. Flocks graze on public lands at least part of the year, except in Texas where sheep of the range type feed in fenced pastures without herding. Rapid growth of the industry in Texas in the past quarter century has given it nearly one-fourth of all stock sheep and more than one-fifth of all breeding ewes. In the West some sheep, between 5 and 10 percent of the total number, are raised on small ranches, with less than 100 sheep each, under conditions similar to those in the native states. In the native states there were shorn in 1957 about 9,700,000 sheep and lambs, 34 percent of the U. S. total. Sheep raising in these states is conducted as a part of diversified farm enterprises in which sheep and wool usually contribute only a minor part of the total income. Small flocks, of 10 to 25 head each, are kept to check the growth of weeds, to utilize feed that otherwise might go

[2] The range states include 12 Western states (Washington, Montana, Oregon, Idaho, Wyoming, South Dakota, California, Nevada, Utah, Colorado, Arizona, New Mexico) and Texas.

to waste, and as a matter of habit. Farmers make little attempt to calculate their gain or loss from their flocks; consequently, the sheep industry in this region shows only a tardy response to changes in the price of wool, mutton and lamb.

Throughout the United States sheep raising is a joint-cost operation. Wool, which before 1920 furnished 50 to 60 percent of the total income, has now become the minor product, contributing less than 40 percent. Even in the West, where wool production is given more emphasis than in the native states, 65 to 70 percent of ranchers' total cash receipts is derived from sale of sheep and lambs.

The Postwar Decline in Sheep Raising and Wool Production

The recent downward trend in the sheep industry (see Table 25) should not be considered as an isolated phenomenon. More properly it should be regarded as a continuation, at a greatly accelerated pace, of a long-term downward trend, dating from the early 1880's.

In both the West and the native states there were far fewer stock sheep on farms and ranches in 1957 than in 1883. Seventy-five years ago each area had about 25,000,000 sheep, but in the native states the decline was faster so that when World War II came, they had only 30 percent of the national total. That proportion they have maintained in postwar years.

A 1953 report of the Department of Agriculture found six interrelated factors most significant in explaining the unprecedented decline in the production of sheep and wool between 1942 and 1950. They were:

(1) Scarcity of competent labor in an industry which is exceptionally dependent upon an adequate supply of specialized labor.
(2) Relatively low returns, high costs, and high risks with sheep compared with cattle.
(3) Inability to increase the efficiency of production at a rate comparable to other agricultural enterprises.
(4) Uncertainties as to the future arising from adverse price-cost relationships, the constant threat of imports and possible tariff

Table 25

U. S. PRODUCTION OF RAW WOOL AND NUMBER OF SHEEP ON FARMS, 1925-29, 1934-38, 1939-1957

Year	*Production of raw wool* (million pounds, grease basis)	*Number of stock sheep* (millions)
1925–29 (av.)	342	38.5
1934–38 (av.)	425	46.0
1939	428	45.5
1940	434	46.3
1941	453	47.4
1942	455	49.3
1943	444	48.2
1944	412	44.3
1945	378	39.6
1946	342	35.5
1947	308	31.8
1948	278	29.5
1949	248	26.9
1950	249	26.2
1951	254	27.3
1952	267	27.9
1953	274	27.6
1954	279	27.1
1955	276	27.1
1956	279	27.0
1957	269	26.5

Source: U. S. Department of Agriculture

reductions, and the possibility of reductions in grazing allotments.
(5) Losses from dogs and predatory animals at a time when competent help for protection against these hazards has been both scarce and expensive.
(6) Drought in some areas, especially the Southwest.[3]

Obviously, some of the factors listed above have less significance than others. Attacks of predatory animals, par-

[3] U. S. Department of Agriculture, Inter-Agency Wool Study Group, *Achieving a Sound Domestic Wool Industry,* A Report to the President of the United States from the Secretary of Agriculture (Washington: Author, 1953), p. 7.

ticularly coyotes in the range states, and of dogs in the native states have long been a sporadic source of loss to sheep growers. There seems to be no evidence that such attacks have recently increased in severity. Drought, also, periodically afflicts the sheep industry in the range states, especially in the Southwest.

The remaining causes of the decline in the sheep industry have more significance for the present study. Briefly, they are: (1) the industry's growing inability to compete for land, labor and capital with other farm enterprises in the United States; (2) inability to sustain competition with imported wool of superior quality produced at low costs in foreign countries; and (3) the failure of wool consumption to expand, owing in part to the substitution of synthetic fibers.

Competition with Other Farm Enterprises

In the West, sheep compete with cattle for the available range pasture and other feeds. The numbers of each kind tend to move in opposite directions, according to variations in prices and profits. When the ratio of the value per head of cattle to sheep rises, cattle numbers rise and sheep decline. In 1947, for the first time on record, cattle in the Western states and Texas were more numerous than sheep; in 1957, cattle were 24.6 million and stock sheep 16.2 million. In the native states, recent technological improvements have made sheep raising relatively less profitable than other occupations. Widespread use of power machinery has lowered the costs of field crops by increasing output per man-hour. Livestock enterprises, particularly dairying and hog raising, have benefited through the reduction in the costs of corn and other harvested feeds. But these improvements have done little or nothing to reduce the costs of raising sheep. In their rations such feeds, even in the native states, are a minor factor. For this and other reasons the average output per man-hour in sheep and wool production has remained practically constant in the past 20 years, whereas in all agricultural production the period has witnessed more than a 50 percent increase in labor efficiency.

Competition from Abroad

In 1935-1939, imported apparel wool furnished 21 percent of total U. S. supply; in 1957 the proportion was 38 percent. Between these dates some remarkable changes had occurred. (See Table 26 and Chart K.) The greatly enlarged wartime demands had been supplied principally by imports, which showed much more elasticity of supply than the domestic product.

In the years 1941-1945, foreign wool made up 63 percent

Table 26

U. S. PRODUCTION, IMPORTS AND SUPPLY OF APPAREL WOOL, 1925-29, 1935-39, 1940-1957

Year	*Production* (in million pounds, estimated clean basis)	*Imports*	*Total supply*	*Ratio of imports to supply* (percent)
1925–29 (av.)	166	81	247	32.8
1935–39 (av.)	207	56	263	21.3
1940	210	117	327	35.8
1941	220	328	548	59.9
1942	221	307	528	58.1
1943	216	382	598	63.9
1944	204	335	539	62.2
1945	188	409	597	68.5
1946	170	473	643	73.6
1947	153	259	412	62.9
1948	137	246	383	64.2
1949	120	155	275	56.4
1950	119	250	369	67.8
1951	119	272	391	69.6
1952	128	248	376	66.0
1953	133	166	299	55.5
1954	136	104	240	43.3
1955	134	113	247	45.7
1956	135	104	239	43.5
1957	129	78	207	37.7

Source: U. S. Department of Agriculture, U. S. Bureau of the Census

CHART K

U. S. PRODUCTION, IMPORTS AND MILL CONSUMPTION OF APPAREL WOOL, 1935-39, 1940-45, 1946-1956
(in millions of pounds, clean basis)

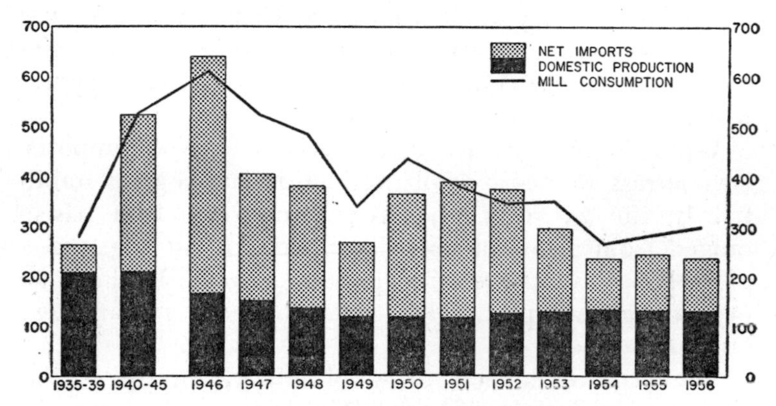

Source: U. S. Department of Agriculture, U. S. Bureau of the Census

of total supply, and in 1946, 74 percent. In postwar years imports show a steep and almost continuous decline. The 1957 receipts of foreign apparel wool were only 78 million pounds, approximately the imports of 1925-1929 and only 22 percent of the average of 1941-1945. For this decline both the downward trend in U. S. wool consumption and U. S. government policies share the responsibility. Government policy, in particular the National Wool Act of 1954, has been directly responsible for the decline in the share of total U. S. supply furnished by imports since that date. (See pp. 234-240.)

In general, wool imports are of three kinds. Apparel wool, consisting chiefly of wools finer than 44's,[4] with minor exceptions is similar to domestic wools and is directly competitive with them. A second category is made up principally of coarse, "improved" wools used in the

[4] The coarsest wools are 40's and under; the finest are 60's and over. Numerical designations of fineness indicate "the number of banks of single-ply yarn, each 560 yards long, which originally were or could be spun from a pound of 'top' (combed wool) of proper length and character." U. S. Tariff Commission, *Summaries of Tariff Information,* v. 11, pt. 1, *Wool and Manufactures* (Washington: GPO, 1948), p. 21.

manufacture of cheaper woven apparel fabrics, knit goods, blankets and upholstery fabrics. The third category includes coarse, "unimproved" wools, used almost entirely for floor coverings, which are produced in the United States only in very small quantities. Coarse wools for use in the production of carpets and certain other commodities enter free of duty. This study will deal only with apparel wool.

Wide fluctuations are characteristic of wool imports. By contrast, domestic wool production shows great stability. In the 25 years, 1932-1957, imports (clean basis) ranged from a low of 10 million pounds, in 1932, to a postwar peak of 473 million pounds in 1946. In the same period, domestic production varied between 119 and 221 million pounds.

The major influences on wool imports in the period since the beginning of World War II are to be found in a number of interrelated causes: (1) variations in the business cycle, (2) the decline in per capita wool consumption, and (3) government purchase and price-support policies. Import tariffs have lost much of their former significance.

Sources of Imported Wool

Five countries in the Southern Hemisphere, Australia, New Zealand, Union of South Africa, Argentina and Uruguay, in 1957 furnished 91 percent of American imports of apparel wool. In prewar years they supplied 80 percent. The quantities (clean basis) imported from each of these countries in 1934-38 and 1957 are shown below.

Country of origin	*1934–38* (average)	*1957*
	(million pounds)	
Australia	14	35
New Zealand	5	15
Union of South Africa	1	9
Argentina	11	8
Uruguay	7	4
All other	10	7
Total	48	78

Imports for intervening years are shown in Table 27.

Table 27

U. S. IMPORTS OF APPAREL WOOL, BY COUNTRIES, 1934-38, 1946-1957

(in millions of pounds, clean basis)

Year	*Australia*	*New Zealand*	*South Africa*	*Argentina*	*Uruguay*	*All other*	*Total*
1934–38 (av.)	14	5	1	11	7	10	48
1946	196	38	57	109	58	15	473
1947	124	22	20	50	37	6	259
1948	85	13	17	60	60	11	246
1949	57	10	14	24	41	9	155
1950	86	21	12	44	74	13	250
1951	121	25	24	28	58	16	272
1952	94	55	24	30	32	13	248
1953	46	23	11	49	29	8	166
1954	43	16	14	15	12	4	104
1955	53	15	17	12	12	4	113
1956	42	19	13	10	16	4	104
1957	35	15	9	8	4	7	78

Source: U. S. Bureau of the Census

Australia and the Union of South Africa supply most of the finer wools, merino and fine cross-bred. New Zealand and two South American countries furnish medium-grade wools. Australia, with 136 million sheep, is the world's leading wool producer. Its 1957 clip, 1.5 billion pounds (grease basis), was 30 percent of the world's wool production (56 percent of the total world output of fine quality merino wool). New Zealand's production in 1957 was 497 million pounds and South Africa's, 311 million. Argentina and Uruguay produced 409 and 209 million pounds respectively. (See Table 28.)

In Australia labor costs are lower than in the United States. Wages are lower, and less labor is required to tend flocks since the greater part of production is on fenced holdings whereas in the United States about half of the sheep are kept on open range. The alternative opportunities for the use of land, also, are less attractive in Australia, and the laws controlling land utilization are more favor-

Table 28

WOOL PRODUCTION IN THE FIVE PRINCIPAL EXPORTING COUNTRIES, 1925-29, 1934-38, 1946-1957

(in millions of pounds, grease basis)

Year	*Australia*	*New Zealand*	*Argentina*	*South Africa*	*Uruguay*	*Total 5 countries*
1925–29 (av.)	911	254	321	278	133	1,897
1934–38 (av.)	995	299	370	239	118	2,021
1946	977	367	515	210	176	2,245
1947	973	362	475	205	150	2,165
1948	1,031	367	419	219	144	2,180
1949	1,110	390	415	218	163	2,296
1950	1,118	390	430	228	185	2,351
1951	1,080	407	420	240	187	2,334
1952	1,281	418	407	257	190	2,553
1953	1,346	426	400	279	202	2,653
1954	1,283	455	364	281	198	2,581
1955	1,410	462	363	294	172	2,701
1956	1,565	491	392	301	174	2,923
1957[a]	1,463	497	409	311	209	2,889

a Preliminary.
Source: U. S. Department of Agriculture

able for raising sheep than in the United States. These advantages are only partially offset by the better market for lamb in the United States.

All the major foreign producers of fine and medium wools export the bulk of their product. (See Table 29.) Australia's sales abroad in the five years 1952-1956 averaged 1.1 billion pounds annually, which was 83 percent of production of those years. Wool exports in 1957, valued at the equivalent of $1,100 million, made up 50 percent of all Australian exports. Income from wool is vital in the Australian economy; it constitutes an appreciable part of the national income, and provides the predominant part of Australia's receipts of international currencies.

The United Kingdom for many years has furnished the principal market for Australian wool. The amounts taken by the leading purchasing countries in the 1955-1956 season were:

	Actual weight (million pounds)
United Kingdom	300
France	205
Japan	192
Italy	99
Belgium	97
West Germany	83
United States	65

Source: Australian Commonwealth Bureau of Census and Statistics

Russia occasionally has bought substantial quantities of Australian wool. These purchases have fluctuated widely; in both 1953 and 1954 they were 30 million pounds, but in 1955 only 400,000 pounds.

Table 29

EXPORTS OF RAW WOOL[a] FROM FIVE PRINCIPAL EXPORTING COUNTRIES, 1934-35 to 1938-39, 1948-49 to 1956-57

(in million pounds, actual weight)

Season	*Australia*	*New Zealand*	*South Africa*	*Argentina*	*Uruguay*	*Total 5 countries*
1934–35 to 1938–39 (av.)	827	274	231	302	101	1,735
1948–49	1,121	431	220	177	108	2,057
1949–50	1,204	413	179	360	165	2,321
1950–51	1,022	263	197	172	132	1,786
1951–52	906	464	214	92	50	1,726
1952–53	1,066	389	217	462	215	2,349
1953–54	1,071	390	229	189	122	2,001
1954–55	1,045	411	250	227	89	2,022
1955–56	1,152	406	261	255	161	2,235
1956–57	1,303	441	252	229	96	2,321

[a] Excluding wool on the skin.

Source: Commonwealth Economic Committee, International Wool Study Group

Consumption

The postwar record of mill consumption of wool in the United States shows continuous and rapid decline, from 610 million pounds in 1946 to less than half that amount ten years later. This short-run view, however, is misleading. Because of wartime restrictions on civilian use of wool, the backlog of accumulated demand explains the rise in consumption in 1946-1948 to an abnormal level. If, taking a longer view, we compare prewar consumption (average of 1935-1939) with the five-year average, 1953-1957, we find a gain of 9 million pounds, or 3.2 percent. The rate of gain, however, was less than the rate of increase in population, and consequently per capita consumption fell from a prewar average of 2.15 pounds to 1.76 pounds. Consumption figures for selected years are shown below.

Year	*Apparel wool* Estimated mill consumption (in million pounds)	*Estimated per capita consumption* (in pounds)
1935–39 (av.)	281	2.15
1946	610	4.31
1950	437	2.88
1957	243	1.42

For the decline in the consumption of apparel wool there were two principal causes: (1) changed living conditions affecting large sections of the American population; and (2) the rising real costs of wool and the increasing substitution of synthetic fibers. The more general use of central heating in homes, office buildings and stores was responsible for the use of clothing of lighter weight, i.e., fewer pounds of wool per yard. Closed automobiles equipped with heaters had the same effect. In the past 20 years new synthetic fibers, first rayon and more recently the noncellulosic materials, have found increasing acceptance in fabrics for both men's and women's clothing, alone or in combination with wool. At first the new fabrics were advertised as superior to 100-percent wool in style and durability. More recently, the reduction in the prices of the man-made fibers has introduced competition on a price basis.[5] (See Table 30.)

[5] For a fuller discussion of the increasing competition of synthetic fibers, see the author's *What the Tariff Means to American Industries* (New York: Council on Foreign Relations, 1956), pp. 149-150.

Table 30

U. S. CONSUMPTION OF WOOL AND OTHER FIBERS, 1925-29, 1935-39, 1946-1957

	Estimated mill consumption (million pounds)			*Estimated per capita consumption* (pounds)		
Year	*Wool*[a]	*Rayon and acetate*[b]	*Other man-made fibers*[b]	*Wool*[a]	*Rayon and acetate*[b]	*Other man-made fibers*[b]
1925–29 (av.)	350	[c]	—	2.94	[d]	—
1935–39 (av.)	377	45	—	2.93	.34	—
1946	738	209	10	5.21	1.48	.07
1947	698	259	3	4.85	1.79	.02
1948	693	303	5	4.73	2.07	.03
1949	500	211	10	3.35	1.41	.07
1950	635	396	22	4.18	2.61	.15
1951	484	411	32	3.13	2.66	.21
1952	466	370	47	2.97	2.36	.30
1953	494	357	54	3.09	2.24	.34
1954	385	434	64	2.37	2.67	.39
1955	414	561	105	2.50	3.39	.64
1956	441	474	127	2.62	2.82	.76
1957[e]	372	491	181	2.18	2.88	1.06

[a] Apparel and carpet wool, clean basis.

[b] Staple and tow; data represent domestic shipments plus imports.

[c] Less than 500,000 pounds.

[d] Less than .005 pound.

[e] Preliminary.

Note: Statistics of estimated mill consumption of rayon and acetate and other man-made fibers include amounts used for upholstery fabrics, carpets, etc., as well as for apparel. Hence for comparability it is necessary in this table to include in wool consumption carpet wool as well as apparel wool.

Source: U. S. Department of Agriculture

National Policies Affecting Wool

A complete catalogue of the various ways in which the federal government fosters the sheep industry would include the extensive research activities of the livestock experts of the Department of Agriculture, the statistical compilations of the Bureau of Agricultural Economics and the information and advice furnished to wool growers by the Agricultural Marketing Service. In addition, the federal government confers a valuable privilege on wool growers in Western states by permitting them to graze their flocks on public lands. To discuss these and many other features of national and state policy affecting the sheep industry would be impractical in this paper. It will deal with only three aspects of national policy: (1) the tariff on raw wool; (2) price-support programs; and (3) direct payments to wool growers and forward pricing, as provided in the National Wool Act of 1954.

Import Duties

Growers of wool have long been the beneficiaries of tariff protection. First imposed in the Act of 1816, import duties on raw wool have been continued almost without interruption. Since imports have furnished for many years a substantial part of American mill consumption, the wool duties, unlike those imposed on many farm products, have been "effective." They have raised domestic prices as well as the prices of foreign wools in United States markets. The duties on raw wool were built into the tariff on woolen and worsted fabrics and by this means were shifted, often in exaggerated form, to consumers.

The present import duties on apparel wool are based on the Tariff Act of 1930 which imposed a rate of 34 cents a pound, clean content.[6] In the early 1930's this rate was equivalent to about 100 percent of the foreign value of the imported wool. Duties on wools of the coarser, non-competitive types were reduced after 1934, in bilateral negotiations under the Reciprocal Trade Agreements Program, but until 1948 the domestic sheep industry successfully opposed all attempts to cut tariff duties on competitive apparel wools. The breakthrough came at the 1947 Geneva conference on trade and tariffs. At that meeting, the outcome of the multilateral negotiations hinged on the willingness of the U. S. negotiators to meet the demands of Australia and other wool-exporting countries. When it became known in Washington that the American delegation had agreed to a 25-percent reduction in the

[6] This was the basic rate on wools finer than 44's (in the grease or washed). Other rates were adjusted to this rate.

wool tariff, Congress, responding to the wishes of the wool growers, took steps to nullify the concession. President Truman, however, vetoed the legislation, and a reduced rate of 25½ cents per pound became effective as of January 1, 1948.

The benefits of tariff protection were further decreased as a consequence of the rise in wool prices. Between the early thirties and 1947 the foreign value of imported apparel wool doubled so that the ad valorem equivalent of the duty fell to about 50 percent. In 1956 the rate of 25½ cents a pound was the equivalent of a 22-percent duty on the most important category of imports.

The collapse of wool prices after the Korea boom, with imports continuing at a high level, gave rise to demands for increased tariff protection. In response, President Eisenhower, in July 1953, asked the Tariff Commission to determine whether wool was being imported "under such conditions and in such quantities as to render or tend to render ineffective, or materially interfere with, the price-support program."[7] On the same day the President asked the Secretary of Agriculture to analyze the factors retarding United States wool production and make "suggestions which will promote the development of a sound and prosperous domestic wool industry and at the same time permit an expanding world trade." The recommendations which he received from the two federal agencies differed widely. In February 1954 the Tariff Commission, by a majority of 4 to 2, found that wool imports were in fact "hindering and rendering ineffective" the price-support program. In accordance with this finding the Commission recommended that the President should add to the existing tariff on apparel wool an "import fee" of 10 cents a pound, but not exceeding 50 percent ad valorem.

The Commission's majority report stated in effect that the price-support program had failed. It had retarded the decline in domestic output but had failed to raise it to the goal of 360 million pounds of shorn wool (grease basis)

[7] In accordance with the provisions of Sec. 22 of the Agricultural Adjustment Act of 1933.

fixed by Congress in the Agricultural Act of 1949. The program had not fully succeeded even in maintaining the average farm price of wool at official support prices. In its attempts to do so the Commodity Credit Corporation had acquired large stocks of wool which it had not been able to sell in the market without incurring heavy losses. Domestic textile mills were using large quantities of foreign wools that were similar to domestic wools. The best way to stimulate domestic wool production, the Commission held, was to make imported wool more expensive. (Import quotas were dismissed as "impractical.") The Commission admitted that it could not determine precisely how large an increase in the tariff would be necessary to bring domestic production of shorn wool up to 360 million pounds a year (the 1952 figure was 230 million), but it promised to "keep the wool situation under constant surveillance . . . with a view to recommending whatever periodic change in fees seems appropriate under changing circumstances."[8]

While the Tariff Commission was making its investigation, the Department of Agriculture sent the President a report containing quite different advice. The Department agreed with the Commission that the price-support program was a failure, but it did not find higher import duties a satisfactory substitute:

> Programs which increase import restrictions [the report stated] tend to affect international trade. And, in the long run, programs such as increased tariffs or processing taxes which increase the cost of wool to mills will tend to detract from the competitive position of wool in relation to other fibers. Because of the pyramiding of costs all the way to the consumer, additional costs paid by consumers for woolen products under such programs tend to exceed the combined returns to producers and additional tariff or processing tax revenues accruing to the Government. Conversely, programs which lower costs of wool to mills tend to improve the competitive position of wool and benefit consumers.[9]

[8] U. S. Tariff Commission, *Wool, Wool Tops, and Carbonized Wool,* Report to the President (Washington: Author, 1954), p. 6.
[9] *Achieving a Sound Domestic Wool Industry* (1953), cited, p. ix.

The report discussed a variety of methods by which the domestic sheep industry might increase its efficiency in production and marketing, thereby improving its competitive position *vis-à-vis* other farm enterprises. These methods of self-help would not be adequate in themselves, however, to maintain a sound and prosperous sheep industry. They would need to be supplemented by government assistance. Among various possible types of government aid, the report indicated its preference for direct payments to wool growers.

President Eisenhower, on January 11, 1954, without waiting for the Tariff Commission's report, adopted the Department of Agriculture's suggestion and in a message to Congress recommended direct payments. Bills initiating the new program were promptly introduced, receiving strong support from the Department of Agriculture.

In declining to act on the Tariff Commission's recommendation, President Eisenhower said: "The enactment of this program [of incentive payments] by the Congress would eliminate the necessity for an increase in import fees or other limitations on wool imports, a course of action which I do not believe would best serve either the wool growing industry or the national interest."[10] He added: "I am confident that this new program will appreciably contribute to the achievement of a sound and prosperous domestic wool industry, an essential component of a healthy overall economy and a strong defense."

Price-Support Programs

During the 1930's steps were taken to supplement the tariff by other measures of assistance to wool growers. The National Wool Marketing Corporation and the Federal Farm Board lent growers a few million dollars in an unsuccessful attempt to check the fall in wool prices. Beyond these activities, and a modest loan program in 1938 and 1939, government did not again intervene in the wool market until after the outbreak of World War II. During the conflict, purchasing and price policies

[10] U. S. Tariff Commission, Press Release of March 4, 1954.

were undertaken not only in the interests of national security but also for the encouragement of the declining sheep industry. When in 1940 the War Department began large-scale purchases of woolen textiles, it applied Buy American policies. Supplying mills were required to use domestic wools, as long as these were available at prices not unreasonably higher than those of imported wools. An administrative order in November 1940 specifically permitted the use of foreign wools in military fabrics, but procurement officers continued to pay premium prices for cloths woven from the domestic product. As a result, prices of domestic wools rose above the duty-paid price of foreign wools, reversing the usual relationship.[11]

Influenced by rapidly increasing demand and rising prices, ranchers and farmers in both the West and the native states increased their flocks from 45,500,000 in 1939 to 49,300,000 in 1942, and their wool production from 428 to 455 million pounds. Responding to fears of a postwar collapse of the wool market, the Secretary of Agriculture in 1943, when military requirements began to fall off, directed the Commodity Credit Corporation to purchase at ceiling prices (about 42 cents a pound) the entire 1943 domestic wool clip and required growers to sell all their wool, with minor exceptions, to that agency. During the four years in which this policy was in effect, wool consumption by American textile factories remained at a high level, but an increasing proportion of the wool they used was of foreign, not domestic, origin. Although world prices of wool had fallen, the CCC was not authorized

[11] "The prices of domestic wools, which had averaged 10.7 cents per scoured pound lower than the duty-paid prices of imported wools of similar descriptions in 1936-39, averaged 4.7 cents higher in 1942 and 8.7 cents higher in the fall of 1943. Making allowance for the effects of differences in preparation and marketing of domestic and imported wools, it appears that the prices of domestic wools in 1943-44 were about 20 cents per scoured pound higher than the duties alone would have sustained. In 1945, the prices of domestic wools became even higher relative to the duty-paid prices of imported wools, chiefly owing to a fall in the delivered prices of imported wools because of the reduced rates of war risk insurance." U. S. Tariff Commission, *Summaries of Tariff Information*, v. 11, pt. 1, cited, p. 30.

until 1947 to sell its domestic holdings at prices competitive with foreign wools. After the wartime wool program came to an end, in April 1947, price supports on wool were resumed, but during the following seven years CCC loans and purchases had little effect, since farm prices of wool were regularly higher than the support level (see Table 31).

Table 31

U. S. WOOL PRICES RECEIVED BY PRODUCERS AND SUPPORT LEVELS, 1938-1957

(in cents per pound)

Year	*Received by producers*	*Support price*	*Year*	*Received by producers*	*Support price*
1938	19.1	18.0	1948	49.2	42.3
1939	22.3	18.0	1949	49.4	42.3
1940	28.4	—	1950	62.1	45.2
1941	35.5	—	1951	97.0	50.7
1942	40.1	—	1952	54.1	54.2
1943	41.6	41.7	1953	54.9	53.1
1944	42.3	42.4	1954	53.2	52.1
1945	41.9	41.9	1955	42.8	62.0
1946	42.3	42.3	1956	44.3	62.0
1947	42.0	42.3	1957	50.0[a]	62.0

[a] Preliminary.
Source: U. S. Department of Agriculture

The war in Korea was responsible for sky-rocketing prices of wool. (See Chart L.) Farmers who in early 1950 had been selling their wool on the average for 50 cents a pound got twice that amount a year later. The government made no attempt at this time to check the rise in wool prices. The Office of Price Stabilization, in its general price regulation of January 26, 1951, specifically exempted raw wool when sold by the producer. Similarly, the 1951 price stabilization amendment to the Defense Production Act of 1950 had no practical effect on wool prices. It provided that no ceiling was to be fixed on any agricultural product at less than 90 percent of the May 1951 price. At that time the average farm price of wool was $1.05 a pound, only 7 cents less than the highest price recorded in more than

CHART L

U. S. FARM PRICES OF WOOL, LAMBS AND BEEF CATTLE, 1939-1956

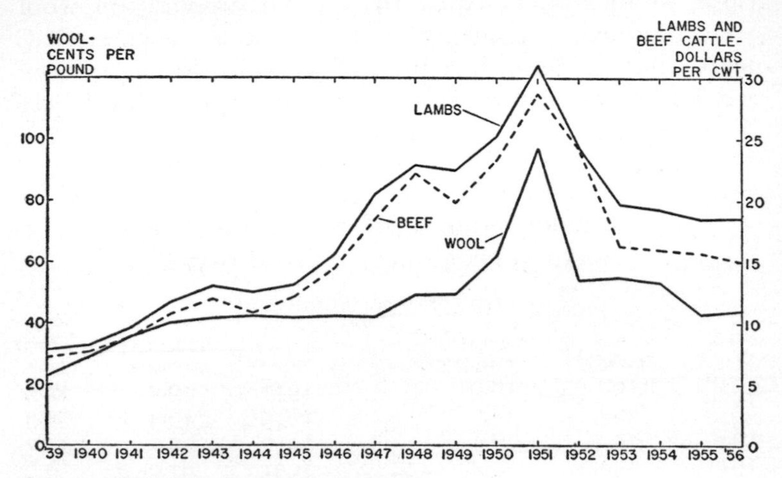

Source: U. S. Department of Agriculture

50 years. But the wool market had already begun to weaken, and within 12 months the farm price had fallen to 53 cents, which was about the pre-Korean level. In an attempt to check the price decline the CCC offered loans to growers at 54.2 cents and in 1952 and 1953 acquired over 100,000,000 pounds of wool.

By the end of 1953 government officials, and the wool growers themselves, were convinced that the price-support program had failed. In December 1953 the Department of Agriculture's wool study group reported: "Despite price supports, domestic growers' prices remain low relative to their costs and risks, and sheep and wool production remain unattractive compared with alternative enterprises."[12] The study group pointed out that, over the long run, price-support programs tend to stabilize producers' prices at or near the support level.

The wool acquired by the CCC must eventually be disposed of chiefly in the United States. If it is placed immediately on the open market, prices may be held down or depressed to a point

[12] *Achieving a Sound Domestic Wool Industry* (1953), cited, p. vi.

where current marketings by wool growers will continue to move to CCC, thereby creating new holdings. Likewise, if acquired wool is held until prices reach a certain level, the stocks impose a ceiling over the open market. This hampers growers in selling their current clip until this backlog is finally absorbed. Until the rise in prices is of sufficient duration and magnitude to absorb the backlog, the loan and purchase programs tend to hold returns to domestic wool growers at the support level.[13]

Several months later the Tariff Commission found that the price-support program had retarded the decline in the domestic output but had not been completely successful "even in maintaining the average price of wool at the support prices established by the Secretary. . . . The cost of conducting the program . . . has been greatly disproportionate to the overall results achieved . . . ."[14] In a later passage the Commission called attention to a still more serious defect from the point of view of the domestic industry. The price-support program, the Commission stated, "tends mainly to stimulate imports of wool rather than to expand domestic production. This consequence ensues because very large shares of the domestic output of wool go into and remain in Commodity Credit Corporation's inventory instead of going into consumption; consumption is therefore supplied increasingly by imports."[15] This view was expressed also in hearings before the House Committee on Agriculture. An official of the Department of Agriculture said, "We in effect have been holding the umbrella over imports of wool, and we have been taking over our own stocks while foreign wool has been coming in and taking the place that our wool normally would in the market."[16]

Representatives of the wool growers were thoroughly disillusioned. "The present wool-support program," said Ray W. Willoughby, President of the National Wool Growers Association, "is a recognized failure in the preservation of a sheep industry in the United States. The loan

[13] Same, p. 57.
[14] U. S. Tariff Commission, Report to the President (1954), cited, p. 4.
[15] Same, p. 12.

program has provided no incentive for improved or increased production. It is cumbersome, costly to the Government, and has created an unnecessary stockpile[17] which is now overhanging the industry. It has resulted in the Government control of grading, prices and marketing practices through decisions as to when and at what prices to sell the Government-owned wool. . . . American wool has been taken off the market and has been replaced by foreign wool. This has created a floor under the prices for wool produced in other countries and it has failed to properly help the American grower."[18]

President Eisenhower, as we have seen, had already rejected the Tariff Commission's recommendation for increased tariff protection for the wool industry and thus had made unavailable this familiar remedy for industries in distress. Obviously, a new policy was needed. This was forthcoming in the National Wool Act of 1954.[19]

The National Wool Act of 1954

The principal feature of the new wool policy initiated in 1954 was the abandonment of all attempts to support the farm price of wool by means of government loans or purchases, and the substitution of direct payments to growers. Congress did not make these payments mandatory; it directed the Secretary of Agriculture to "support the prices of wool and mohair, respectively, to the producers thereof by means of loans, purchases, payments, or other operations." The Secretary chose to employ direct payments.

The Act had a four-year term, from April 1955 through March 1959. During that time, the Secretary was required

[16] Testimony of Frank W. ImMasche, in U. S. House, Committee on Agriculture, *Wool Program,* Hearings on H.R. 7775, 83d Cong., 2d sess. (Washington: GPO, 1954), p. 39.

[17] The speaker was referring to the stocks held by the CCC and not the wool in the strategic stockpile.

[18] Testimony of Ray W. Willoughby, in U. S. Senate, Committee on Agriculture and Forestry, *Wool Program,* Hearings on S. 2911, 83rd Cong., 2d sess. (Washington: GPO, 1954), p. 45.

[19] Title VII of *Public Law* no. 690, 83d Cong., 2d sess. (Aug. 28, 1954). "Agricultural Act of 1954."

to fix the support price for shorn wool,[20] at levels which he considers necessary to bring domestic wool production up to certain specified minimum amounts. The new law declared it to be the policy of Congress:

. . . as a measure of national security and in promotion of the general economic welfare, to encourage the annual domestic production of approximately three hundred million pounds of shorn wool, grease basis, at prices fair to both producers and consumers in a manner which will have the least adverse effects upon foreign trade.[21]

Payments to growers were to be sufficient, when added to receipts of wool from their sales at market prices, to bring their total returns up to what they would have received had they sold their entire clip at the support price. To accomplish this purpose the Secretary of Agriculture was to announce in the spring of each year an average support-level price for wool in the grease. An official of the Department explained:

If the reported average price received by all producers for the year turns out to be below the previously announced average incentive price, the Secretary would establish the equivalent percentage increase required to bring the average farm price up to the incentive level. For example, if the incentive level was 60 cents and the reported United States average farm price for the year turns out to be 50 cents, the percentage payment to each wool grower to bring the national average received by growers up to 60 cents would be 20 percent.[22]

The "incentive" payment to each producer would then be equal to 20 percent of his net wool sales for the marketing year.

[20] Support prices for pulled wool and mohair are to be established at such levels in relation to shorn wool as will maintain "normal marketing practices" for pulled wool, and maintain approximately the same percentage of parity for mohair as for shorn wool.

[21] *Public Law* no. 690 (1954), cited, p. 14. If the support price is fixed between 90 and 110 percent of parity, the goal is 300 million pounds. But if the price is between 60 and 90 percent of parity the goal is raised to 360 million.

[22] Testimony of Hon. Ross Rizley, in *Wool Program,* House Hearings (1954), cited, p. 8.

Congress ingeniously linked the new incentive payments to the wool tariff. The 1954 Act limited total payments to growers to 70 percent of the amounts of tariff duties collected on imports of raw wool, plus the specific components of the duties on manufactures of wool.[23] Customs receipts are not earmarked for the incentive payments; they serve only to measure the amount of funds available for this purpose.

Three features of the new policy deserve special comment: (1) direct payments and forward pricing; (2) the link with the customs tariff; and (3) the quantitative goals. All of these had appeared in previous legislation; the novelty of the 1954 Act consists in bringing them together and applying them to wool.[24]

The National Wool Act of 1954 has been called "the Brannan Plan in sheep's clothing." Charles F. Brannan, Secretary of Agriculture, in April 1949 had recommended direct income payments to producers of certain nonstorable products. His plan would have allowed the prices of these commodities to fall to their natural market levels. If they fell below levels which the law defined as "fair," direct payments from the government would make up the difference. Forward pricing, an important feature of the new wool policy, also appeared in Secretary Brannan's proposals. Price-supporting schemes had been based on the farmers' needs, as indicated by receipts from past production, but in the National Wool Act of 1954 the incentive price to be paid on the wool clip of the coming season was to be announced in advance.

[23] This provision reads: "*Provided,* That the total of all such payments made under this Act shall not at any time exceed an amount equal to 70 per centum of the accumulated totals, as of the same date, of the gross receipts from specific duties (whether or not such specific duties are parts of compound rates) collected on and after January 1, 1953, on all articles subject to duty under schedule 11 of the Tariff Act of 1930, as amended." *Public Law* no. 690, cited, p. 15.

[24] Precedents for direct payments to farmers designed to stimulate production can be found in the benefits paid to farmers under the AAA and in the soil conservation program of the 1930's. The sugar program adopted in 1934 provided for subsidies to U. S. growers to be paid from the proceeds of a special excise tax. The purpose of the sugar payments, however, was to restrict, not to encourage, production.

A forward pricing approach is quite different from that of supporting prices at a fixed percentage of parity. The fixed percentage of parity looks to past price relationships, regardless of whether the resulting output is too much or too little. Forward prices and incentive prices presumably seek to guide production in desired directions.[25]

Relating the subsidy to receipts from duties levied on wool imports was a shrewd political maneuver.[26] It was frankly advocated as a means of concealing from the taxpayer the cost of the subsidy and, at the same time, of compensating the wool grower for the failure of the tariff to afford him adequate protection. The Executive Secretary of the National Wool Growers Association said:

Tariff rates now in effect would do double duty. Money collected on competitive foreign wool would be used to pay the grower the price he should receive but cannot receive because we have an insufficient tariff. This seems to us to be a much more reasonable approach to the problem than would a subsidy program designed to take dollars directly out of the taxpayers' pockets.[27]

The connection with customs receipts, moreover, tended to give the incentive payments a permanence they might not otherwise have possessed. For four years at least there would be no need to seek annual action by Congress. Conversely the connection of the subsidy with the tariff promised to forestall further downward revision in import duties on raw wool.

25 Murray R. Benedict and Oscar C. Stine, *The Agricultural Commodity Programs* (New York: Twentieth Century Fund, 1956), pp. 359-360.
26 The linkage of incentive payments to customs receipts appears to place a ceiling on the expenditures from the U. S. Treasury for the wool subsidy. Actually, however, the Act does not earmark customs receipts for payments to wool growers. In the four years, 1950-1953, 70 percent of the specific duties collected on all imports of wool and manufactures thereof (Schedule 11 of the Tariff Act of 1930) averaged $50 million annually. The Department of Agriculture calculated that payments to wool growers under the 1954 Act might be $15-30 million annually. In these calculations it was assumed that the payments would average 5-10 cents per pound. Actually, the payments on the 1955 clip amounted to $49.7 million, or 19.2 cents per pound.
27 Testimony of J. M. Jones in *Wool Program,* House Hearings (1954), cited, p. 52.

Merits of the 1954 Act

The new wool policy inaugurated in 1954 promises to be simpler and less costly in its administration than the preceding price-support program. It will eliminate the costs of acquiring and storing wool and also possible losses on the sale of the government stocks. Moreover, payments on a percentage basis should encourage wool growers to obtain the best possible price for their wool in the open market by improving the quality of their wool through better breeding and care of sheep, by better preparation of wool for market, and by giving more attention to marketing methods.

Of greater significance, from the point of view of national policy, is the re-establishment of a free domestic market in wool, linked with the world market. The price-support program had "priced wool out of the market," stimulating the substitution of synthetic fibers. Moreover, by raising the internal price of wool above the world market level, the price-support program subsidized imports. Thus it raised the consumers' costs of wool manufactures without effectively stimulating the domestic sheep industry, or even preventing its decline.

Faced with the generally acknowledged failure of price supports, the President had the choice of two major alternatives; he could restrict wool imports by raising tariff duties (the import "fees" recommended by the Tariff Commission were only a polite euphemism) or he could subsidize the wool growers directly with incentive payments. In choosing the latter type of assistance, he observed that it did not constitute a direct interference with imports of wool and hence did not endanger the continuance of friendly relations with Australia and other wool-exporting countries. The President's observation, however, was not altogether accurate. For if the incentive payments enabled American growers to put on the market an increased supply of wool at a given price, some imports would be displaced. If the result was to lower the market price, an expansion of consumption might take place which would be sufficient to absorb both the foreign and the domestic products. Otherwise, the subsidy, like the tariff, would strengthen the competitive position of the domestic producers. It should be kept in mind also that the direct-payments plan, although a substitute for *increased* tariff protection, did not replace the existing import duties on wool. Imported apparel wools still pay 25½ cents a pound duty, and the market price of domestic wools tends to exceed the world price by that amount.

With the incentive level fixed at 62 cents per pound, the tariff on wool could be reduced within limits, without injuring the wool producers. Actually, however, it seems probable that the new plan of assisting the wool industry will operate to deter tariff reduction. Lowering import duties would tend to depress the price of wool in the American market, making necessary increased incentive payments, in order to keep growers' returns at the predetermined parity level. Moreover, lowering the tariff presumably, but not necessarily, would cause the customs revenue from the specific wool duties to fall off at a time when the drain on these funds was increasing. Conceivably customs receipts might decline to a point where the 70-percent provision would be inadequate to cover the payments.

The average incentive level fixed by the Secretary of Agriculture for the clip to be marketed in 1955 was 62 cents per pound, which was 8.8 cents higher than the average 1954 farm price. Wool growers actually sold their 1955 clip at an average price of 42.8 cents, so in that year the subsidy amounted to 19.2 cents $(42.8 + 19.2 = 62)$. For the clips of 1956, 1957 and 1958 the incentive price was continued at 62 cents.

Incentive payments, like import duties and price supports, can be used to increase wool growers' incomes and to improve their economic position in relation to other farmers. But it is unlikely that the new program will prove any more successful than its predecessors in raising wool production, or even in checking its secular decline.[28]

[28] During the first three years of incentive payments the total production of wool (grease basis) averaged 275 million pounds, an increase of seven-

Between 1952 and 1957 domestic wool supplied an increasing proportion of U. S. consumption, but this did not necessarily indicate a strengthening of the competitive ability of the domestic sheep industry. After April 1955, when incentive payments were substituted for price supports, the entire domestic wool clip, now priced competitively, moved into market channels, whereas in the two previous seasons a large portion had gone into CCC stocks. Moreover, the CCC during the years 1955-1957 was liquidating its stocks of domestic wool. Thus the statistics of consumption of domestic wool showed increases although production continued to decline.

In one or two of its minor features,[29] the National Wool Act aims to improve methods of producing and marketing wool, but in general, like the tariff and price supports, its purpose is to prop up an inefficient and declining industry. In other words, the subsidy is designed to keep labor and capital in wool growing rather than to assist the shift to more efficient types of employment.

Wool and Defense

The preamble of the National Wool Act of 1954 declared it to be the policy of Congress *as a measure of national security* and in promotion of the general welfare to encourage the annual domestic production of 300 million or, under certain conditions, 360 million pounds of shorn wool, grease basis.[30] According to Senator Aiken, chairman of the Senate Committee on Agriculture and Forestry, 360 million pounds was "the amount we figured was necessary for the protection of the country in the

---

tenths of one percent over the average of the three previous years. Shorn wool production rose nine-tenths of one percent, from 234 million to 236 million pounds.

[29] By paying the individual grower a percentage of his net wool sales, the payments provided by the Act give him an incentive to improve the quality of his clip. The Act also provides for deductions from incentive payments to finance an educational campaign to increase consumption of lamb and wool.

[30] The Agricultural Acts of 1948 and 1949 had also fixed a production goal of 360 million pounds.

event of war."[31] The Senator did not reveal how the Committee arrived at this figure. The record does not show that advice was obtained or sought from the Office of Defense Mobilization or from the Department of Defense. Apparently, the production goals were based on estimates by experts in the Department of Agriculture of the numbers of sheep that the country's ranches and farms could "carry." Implicit in these estimates were certain assumptions about wool prices, but these were not stated. One analysis indicated that the country's grazing and feed resources "were sufficient for about 37 million head of stock sheep and still have the total of all grazing animals in balance with these resources." Annual production of shorn wool from 37 million sheep was estimated at 290 million pounds. Another analysis by the Department's experts indicated that "a balanced livestock population" would include 31 million sheep with an annual production of 260 million pounds of shorn wool.[32]

Actually, the defense argument for government assistance to the wool-growing industry, whether by tariff protection, by price supports or by incentive payments, has little or no merit. It is true that for 20 years, or longer, wool has been included in official lists of strategic and critical materials. It is also true that supplies of foreign wools are brought from great distances overseas, principally from Australia, New Zealand and from Argentina. Only small amounts could be obtained by land transport from Canada and Mexico. Nevertheless, if the entire external overseas supply should be cut off — an extreme assumption — the defense effort need not be greatly weakened. For great progress has taken place in the invention and commercial development of synthetic fibers—rayon, nylon, Dacron, Orlon, Acrilan and others. Although none of them now produced commercially possesses all the de-

[31] U. S. Senate, Committee on Agriculture and Forestry, *Foreign Trade in Agricultural Products,* Hearings, 83d Cong., 1st sess. (Washington: GPO, 1953), p. 475.

[32] *Achieving a Sound Domestic Wool Industry* (1953), cited, p. 43. For similar estimates, see U. S. Department of Agriculture, *Domestic Wool Requirements and Sources of Supply* (Washington: Author, 1950), p. 61.

sirable characteristics of wool—insulation, resiliency, ability to absorb moisture, and others—they have nevertheless proved satisfactory, either alone or in combination with wool, in a variety of civilian uses, in woven fabrics for men's and women's clothing, in knit goods, blankets, etc. Firms which have already produced a true artificial wool under laboratory conditions claim that within a few years they will be in a position to place it on the market in quantity. Military authorities have already modified procurement regulations so as to permit the admixture of synthetic fibers with wool in uniform cloths and in blankets.

Under these conditions it is difficult to justify continued government assistance to wool growers. With a stockpile of moderate dimensions to take care of immediate needs for natural wool plus rigid restriction on civilian consumption plus maximum use of synthetic fibers, the need for home-grown wool could be reduced substantially below the production goals fixed in the National Wool Act of 1954. In fact, as far as national security is concerned, there would seem to be no reason for continued government assistance to wool growers.

On economic grounds assistance is equally indefensible. In Australia, New Zealand, Argentina and elsewhere abundant supplies of high-grade wool are available at prices lower than American costs. The competitive advantages of the principal foreign producers in climate, supplies of cheap land and labor seem likely to persist for many years. Wool growing in the United States is not an infant industry; its disadvantages are not of the sort that can be overcome by tariff protection. Although benefiting by high rates of duty on imports, and by price supports, wool growing has declined continuously, except for war years, over a period of 75 years. There seems little probability that the recently introduced measures of increased government assistance in the form of incentive payments will reverse the downward trend. The removal of the subsidies would accelerate the decline, but not to the point of eliminating the sheep industry from the American economy.

The decline in wool prices resulting from the abolition of import duties would expand wool consumption, enabling the natural product to compete on more even terms with synthetic fibers. We should recall also that wool and lamb are joint products and that with decline in sheep numbers lamb prices would move upwards. As a result the total receipts from wool growing would probably not fall as rapidly as the price of wool.

The increased pressure of foreign competition might stimulate the more efficient and better-equipped sheep men to pay more attention to breeding so as to obtain heavier fleeces and to take greater advantage of grading and marketing services of cooperative organizations. In the native states, where wool and lamb are by-products of mixed farming enterprises, the removal of government supports would have less effect than on the specialized sheep ranches of the Western states.

Chapter 9

NATIONAL POLICY ON RUBBER

WHEN Pearl Harbor was attacked the American fabricators of automobile tires and other rubber products were dependent on imports from Southeast Asia for practically their entire supply of raw material. Synthetic rubber produced in privately owned plants furnished 8,000 tons, less than one percent of the industry's needs. Insurance against interruption of imports was provided by a small strategic stockpile and by inventories of rubber fabricators, amounting in all to about 500,000 tons, less than one year's peacetime consumption.

The fall of Singapore in early 1942 cut off 90 percent of U. S. supplies of natural rubber. Attempts to develop new supplies in Brazil and other Latin American countries and experiments with domestic planting of guayule and other rubber substitutes failed. Restrictions on civilian consumption, although more effective, were far from adequate. After 1940 a few government contracts were let for the construction of synthetic rubber factories, but as late as September 1942 the Baruch Committee reported that scarcity of rubber had produced a situation "so dangerous that unless corrective measures are taken immediately this country will face both a military and civilian collapse. . . ." [1]

Yet, within a little over two years, a synthetic rubber industry had been established capable of producing more than 1,000,000 tons annually. "In the short span of 3 years the Government, under the stress of a war emergency, lifted synthetic rubber technology from the test tube of

[1] Quoted in *First Report of the Inter-Agency Policy Committee on Rubber* (Washington: GPO, 1946), p. 16.

the laboratory and transformed it into a full-blown industry."[2] This has been called "one of the most spectacular industrial achievements of modern times."

Less spectacular, but equally remarkable, was the government's achievement in continuing the manufacture of synthetic rubber in the early postwar years, and in eventually transferring its plants to private ownership. The end of the war had found the United States in possession of 51 plants, representing a total investment of $700 million. Ten years later they all, with minor exceptions, had been transferred to private ownership, without loss to taxpayers and without disturbance to domestic or world markets. All controls over the uses of rubber had been abolished, and a free domestic market had been established in both the synthetic and the natural products.

The establishment of a giant rubber industry in the United States, capable of supplying nearly one-third of total world consumption of all kinds of rubber, has raised problems of foreign policy that concern particularly U. S. relations with the rubber-producing countries of Southeast Asia which, for the most part, are uncommitted in the East-West conflict. Since they market 30 percent of their output in the United States, they view with apprehension the rapid expansion of American capacity for synthetic production. They are concerned also with the beginnings of exports of American synthetic rubber to countries in Western Europe, exports which appear to pose a potential threat to some of their best markets.

The United States, moreover, is in a position to wield great power in the markets for natural rubber. Its accumulations in the strategic stockpile are now estimated at about 1.2 million tons, or two-thirds of the Free World's annual output. Technical advances in the production, synthetically, of a true natural rubber within a few decades may render this stockpile in large part obsolete. In that case its liquidation, unless skillfully managed, could cause serious disturbances in rubber markets.

[2] *First Report of the Attorney General on Competition in the Synthetic Rubber Industry* (Washington: GPO, 1956), p. 1.

The worries, however, are not all on the side of the countries producing crude rubber. The United States, despite the extraordinary rise of its synthetic industry, is far from self-sufficient in rubber. Its fabricating industries still use the natural product to the extent of 31 percent of total consumption (37 percent of total new consumption). They, and the economy in general, would suffer if the imports of crude rubber, now amounting to about 575,000 tons annually, should be cut off or substantially diminished. Hence the continuance of rubber production in Southeast Asia and elsewhere and continued access to supplies of the natural product are still objectives of U. S. policy.

The Synthetic Rubber Program

National rubber policy at the outbreak of World War II took three directions: (1) the conservation of supplies of natural rubber by stockpiling and control of civilian consumption; (2) attempts to grow natural rubber in the Western Hemisphere; (3) production of synthetic in government-owned plants operated by private companies.

Congress in June 1940 authorized the Reconstruction Finance Corporation to accumulate natural rubber in a national stockpile. A goal of one million tons was discussed unofficially; actually, however the wartime accumulation in government ownership never exceeded 400,000 tons. The Rubber Reserve Company, an affiliate of the RFC, became the sole importer of natural rubber, which it distributed to manufacturers. Beginning in early 1942, civilian consumption was rigidly controlled.

Also in June 1940, Congress gave the Department of Agriculture $500,000 to develop rubber plantations in tropical Latin America. But because of lack of technical experience, shortage of labor and the ravages of plant diseases the government-sponsored projects produced no significant amounts of rubber, either during the war or in postwar years. The Ford Company's attempts to grow rubber in Brazil, and Goodyear's in Costa Rica, were also unsuccessful. The government invested between $30 and

$40 million in planting some 30,000 acres in California with guayule, a rubber-bearing shrub. The operation was abandoned after it had yielded only 200 tons of rubber.[3]

The need for large-scale production of synthetic rubber was not recognized until after the fall of Singapore in early 1942. Plans were made soon thereafter for the investment of $650 million in construction of plants capable of an annual production of 877,000 tons. The Baruch Committee, in September 1942, gave specific content to these plans, specifying the kinds and amounts of rubber to be produced, the location of plants and the use of materials. It also recommended the target capacity of over one million tons annually. Most of the Committee's recommendations were adopted and within two years 40 plants built with government funds turned out about one million tons of rubber.

Synthetic rubber in prewar years had been produced on a substantial commercial scale only in Germany and in the Soviet Union. Total world production was about 70,000 tons of which 75 percent was manufactured in the U.S.S.R. The United States in 1942, however, did not have to start from scratch. The Firestone Tire and Rubber Company, which had begun experiments on synthetic rubber in the early 1930's, was operating a small plant when Pearl Harbor was attacked. Du Pont had begun to sell neoprene as early as 1931. The Standard Oil Development Company had discovered butyl rubber in 1937. Esso Standard in 1941 had under construction a $4.5 million plant which it turned over to the government and operated during the war under lease. Meanwhile the B. F. Goodrich Company in June 1940 had already manufactured and put on the market pneumatic tires made of more than 50-percent synthetic rubber produced in its own commercial plant. Thus the basic technical knowledge for the production of several types of rubber synthetically was already available in the United States. Small plants were in opera-

[3] Attempts to grow rubber in the Western Hemisphere are described in "Some Rubber-Planting Fiascos in Tropical America," by J. Fred Rippy in *Inter-American Economic Affairs,* v. 10, no. 1 (Summer 1956), pp. 3-24.

tion, but to develop them into large-scale commercial operations presented engineering problems of the first magnitude. It involved the investment of large sums of capital in an enterprise where the outcome was uncertain. The task which government performed was to mobilize the country's best talent in the field, to assume the risk and supply the capital.

In building up its new synthetic industry the government drew heavily upon the research and engineering staffs of the American synthetic chemical and petroleum industries. While they were laboring with problems of making the new rubbers, scientists in the rubber manufacturing industry were struggling to modify the techniques of manufacturing rubber products, tires, for example, so as to make serviceable products from the new synthetic material.

How Synthetic Rubber Is Made

Until recently, synthesizing rubber did not mean duplicating the natural product, as in the case of synthetic camphor or quinine. Rather it signified the production of a new substance with rubber-like properties. The chemical process, known as polymerization, consists in linking molecules of two or more substances so as to form more complex molecules (polymers) which possess the same chemical composition, but whose physical properties are different from the original materials.

General-purpose synthetic rubber (known also as GR-S or Buna S), the bulk of the American production, is made from two principal materials or feedstocks, styrene, a coal-tar intermediate produced by the synthetic chemical industry, and butadiene. The latter, which may be obtained either from petroleum or from alcohol, was supplied during the war in part by the oil refineries and in part by distillers of molasses and other agricultural products. Because of the higher cost of alcohol, butadiene is now made exclusively from petroleum.

The basic steps in the production of GR-S as described by the U. S. Tariff Commission are:[4]

1. *Emulsification* — About three parts of butadiene and one part of styrene are fed into a soapy-water solution and emulsified by vigorous stirring.
2. *Polymerization* — The combining of the butadiene and styrene molecules begins, a catalyst is added, and the temperature is raised to accelerate the reaction.
3. *Coagulation* — The latex is removed from the polymerization tank and placed in another tank after which sulphuric acid and a salt solution are introduced. The latex coagulates and rises to the surface of the tank.
4. *Collection* — The crumbs, or "flocs," of rubber are skimmed off, washed thoroughly, drained, dried, and pressed into blocks for shipment to manufacturers of rubber goods.

In addition to general-purpose rubber, two special types —butyl and neoprene—were made in the government's plants. Butyl, a copolymer of two chemical substancces, isoprene and isobutylene, is an inexpensive rubber impermeable to air, which at first was used almost exclusively for the inner tubes of automobile tires. Since the introduction of tubeless tires many new uses have been found, in cable insulation, adhesives, hose, conveyer belts and footwear. Butyl rubber has also been used experimentally in tire casings. Neoprene, derived from acetylene, sulphuric acid and salt, is well adapted for electrical insulation because of its resistance to heat, oil and oxidation. Buna N, the most expensive type, which was produced only in privately owned plants, is a copolymer of butadiene and acrylontrile; it is used where resistance to oil and gasoline is essential.

The Transition to Private Ownership

When Japan surrendered, the United States government had an investment of $700 million in facilities with an annual capacity of 1,100,000 tons of synthetic rubber,

[4] U. S. Tariff Commission, *Rubber,* War Changes in Industry Series, Report no. 6 (Washington: GPO, 1944), pp. 59-60.

including plants for producing the feedstocks, butadiene and styrene. The government had no intention of remaining permanently in the rubber business, but the transition to private ownership could not take place overnight. Continued government control was needed until a plan of disposal could be worked out which would safeguard the interests of rubber fabricators and the general public, and at the same time attract the investment of private capital.

It was difficult to forecast what measures of government support, if any, synthetic rubber production would require when under private ownership. Would the new owners produce enough to satisfy military and civilian demand? Should all the plants be sold, or should some be retained by government in stand-by condition? How could the government prevent the formation of a private monopoly which would threaten the interests of hundreds of small fabricators of rubber products, and of the millions of ultimate consumers of rubber end-products? Finally, there was the all-important question of the terms of sale. How much would private firms be willing to pay for the plants? How far could government hope to recover its investment?

In 1950 when plans for the transfer of the industry to private ownership seemed about to crystallize in legislation, the Korean war produced a new rubber shortage. So it was not until August 1953 that Congress finally enacted and the President signed the Rubber Producing Facilities Disposal Act.[5] By January 1955 the Disposal Commission created by the Act had worked out its program and had completed its negotiations for the sale of the plants remaining in government ownership.[6] Congressional approval, March 23, 1955, completed the process of transfer.

The period of government ownership was marked by important achievements both in business management and in technology. The selling price of general-purpose rubber, originally fixed at 50 cents a pound, was cut to 18.5

[5] *Public Law* no. 205, 83rd Cong., 1st sess. (Aug. 7, 1953).

[6] Between 1945 and 1953 the government had already disposed of 24 of the original 51 plants. Twenty-four plants were transferred to private owners in April 1955; two additional plants were sold in the following 12 months, and one then remained under lease.

cents in 1944, and maintained at that figure until 1950. Except in 1949 the average annual price was below the selling price of plantation rubber smoked sheets, the most nearly comparable grade of natural rubber. In January 1951 when the latter rose to 73.5 cents the government sold GR-S for 24.5 cents. The price was reduced to 23 cents in March 1952 where it remained until the end of the period of government ownership.

In the four years, 1943 to 1946, government operations showed net losses averaging about $50 million yearly. After that date small profits appeared. The final four years of government ownership produced net gains averaging $32 million. Including depreciation, the total operating losses for the 12 years of government ownership were $122 million.

Fears that the infant industry would not be able to survive without special measures of protection proved unfounded. Controls over allocation of rubber supplies and regulations requiring the use of certain minimum amounts or certain proportions of synthetic rubber in manufactured products were abolished in 1953. In April 1955 when the plants were sold to private business firms the new industry was able to stand on its own feet without subsidies or other measures of protection against the competition of natural rubber. In 1954, the last full year of government operations, synthetic rubbers supplied 52 percent of American consumption of new rubber.

Continued emphasis on research in rubber chemistry while the industry was under government ownership bore fruit in technological progress. Perhaps the most important accomplishment was the development in 1948 of "cold rubber," a new general-purpose product. Previously, polymerization had required temperatures of 120° Fahrenheit or above. The new product, which could be made at 41°, was easier to work in rubber mills. In some uses it proved superior to natural rubber, particularly in tire treads where it offered more resistance to abrasion.

Important economies in production were achieved in 1951 by two further technical innovations, the production of "oil masterbatch" and "black masterbatch" rubber. It was found possible at an intermediate stage to add mineral oil to cold synthetic rubber, in proportions ranging from 25 to 37 1/2 parts of oil to 100 parts of GR-S, without loss in the quality of the product. Thus one pound of oil costing 2 or 3 cents replaced a pound of rubber worth 23 cents. Additional savings were effected by the addition of 33 percent of carbon black at the polymerization stage. The oil-extended rubbers, however, involved higher costs in fabrication and hence sold at a lower price than GR-S.

When it sold its synthetic plants to private owners the government did not wash its hands of the new rubber industry. The Disposal Act of 1953 had authorized the transfer of the government's plants in a manner consistent with the development of a free competitive industry. Specifically, it required "That the disposal program should be designed best to afford to small-business enterprises and users, other than the purchaser of a facility, the opportunity to obtain a fair share of the end products . . . at fair prices." Furthermore, no producer was to possess unreasonable control over the manufacture of synthetic rubber or its component materials.[7]

In January 1955, when the Disposal Commission presented its program to Congress, considerable dissatisfaction was expressed with the implementation of these provisions. A minority report of the Senate Committee on Banking and Currency pointed out that about 88 percent of the capacity for producing GR-S and butyl rubber would be owned by four large rubber companies and three large oil companies. "The remainder . . . is in the hands of other relatively large rubber fabricators or users. It is from these sources that small-businessmen must obtain their supply of synthetic rubber."[8] The minority doubted whether guarantees provided in the sales contracts, that producers of GR-S should supply certain percentages of

[7] *Public Law* no. 205, 83rd Cong., 1st sess. (Aug. 7, 1953), Sec. 17.

[8] U. S. Senate, Banking and Currency Committee, *Disapproval of Proposed Sale of Government-Owned Rubber-Producing Facilities,* 84th Cong., 1st sess., Report no. 117 (Washington: GPO, 1955), p. 19.

their output to small business enterprises, would be of much practical value.

The report was equally skeptical regarding competition among the new owners. "These industries [rubber and oil]," it stated, "have been notorious in their disregard for antitrust laws, or Federal trade laws, or both. The hearings before committees of the Senate and the House are replete with documentation of court cases involving these industries with pleas of guilt or no contest to charges of price fixing, discounts, bonuses, classifications of customers, allocations of sales territories, etc. In short, the public record does not demonstrate a history of competitive actions but rather of concerted actions."[9]

The majority of the Committee recommended the adoption of the Disposal Commission's program, but took account of the minority's views by requesting the Attorney General to report to Congress each year for ten years on competition in the synthetic rubber industry under private ownership and on the treatment accorded to small business.

The Attorney General, in his first report, dated May 1, 1956, found that the experience of the first eight months of private ownership was "inadequate to provide a basis for a conclusion as to whether free and unfettered competition has been firmly established in this industry." A seller's market had enabled all the producers to sell their entire output with ease; most of the producers had had to allocate supplies to their customers. "Moreover," the Attorney General remarked, "it has been the experience of this Department in the reconstruction of competition in monopoly cases, an experience which parallels the transition of this industry from Government monopoly to competitive private enterprise, that a considerable period of time must elapse before it can be determined whether all of the effects of the monopoly have been fully dissipated."[10]

A year later the second report[11] found that a 50-percent

[9] Same, p. 21.

[10] *First Report of the Attorney General . . .* (1956), cited, p. 28.

[11] *Second Report of the Attorney General on Competition in the Synthetic Rubber Industry* (Washington: GPO, 1957).

increase, under private ownership, in the industry's capacity had accelerated the transition from a seller's to a buyer's market. New competitors seemed to experience no difficulty in gaining access to the industry, and no tendency was apparent toward greater concentration in ownership of productive facilities. Small business enterprises were able to obtain adequate supplies of general-purpose synthetic rubber at fair prices. On the other hand, the Attorney General considered the persistent stability and uniformity of prices to be an indication of "incomplete development of competition." He noted, however, some indications of rivalry based on service and quality, and he concluded that on the whole developments in 1956 indicated progress toward the establishment of a free, competitive synthetic rubber industry.

Congress originally had put the government into the rubber business in order to obtain supplies of a vitally necessary raw material. To make sure that under private ownership adequate supplies of rubber would be available, the Disposal Act required that every sales contract should contain a national security clause. In it the purchaser agreed to keep his plant in condition, for a ten-year period, to supply to the government a stipulated minimum output in time of emergency, or be ready on six months' notice to put the plant in condition to supply the required amount.

The Disposal Act also required the President to keep an eye on the functioning of the rubber industry in its first year under private ownership. In his report dated April 30, 1956,[12] President Eisenhower found that all the objectives of the disposal legislation, including the protection of national security, had been achieved satisfactorily. He pointed out that the plants in general were operating intensively. The industry was expanding its facilities and was making progress in the techniques of manufacture and in the development of new rubbers.

[12] *Message from the President of the United States,* in U. S. House, *Report Concerning the Nation's Rubber Requirements and Resources,* 84th Cong., 2d sess., Doc. no. 391 (Washington: GPO, 1956).

The Equation of Demand and Supply

National policy aims to make sure that in peacetime American manufacturers have enough rubber to satisfy the needs of consumers of end-products and that when war threatens, or actually occurs, the military effort is not weakened for lack of an essential raw material. In what follows we shall first analyze the trends in demand for rubber as indicated by the consumption of rubber products, and then consider the conditions of supply of both synthetic and natural rubber. Finally, we shall examine U. S. policies affecting the supply of rubber.

American industries in 1957 used 1,736,000 tons of rubber, of which 540,000 was natural, 929,000 synthetic, and 267,000 tons reclaimed from scrap. (See Table 32.)

Table 32

U. S. CONSUMPTION OF RUBBER, 1937-39, 1942-1957

Year	*Domestic consumption*				*Ratio of consumption of synthetic to consumption of:*	
	New synthetic rubber	*New natural rubber*	*Total new rubber*	*Total rubber, new and reclaimed*	*Total new rubber*	*Total rubber*
	(in thousands of long tons)				(in percent)	
1937-39 (av.)	—	524	524	675	—	—
1942	18	377	395	650	4.6	2.8
1943	171	318	489	780	35.0	21.9
1944	567	144	711	962	79.7	58.9
1945	694	105	799	1,040	86.9	66.7
1946	762	278	1,040	1,315	73.3	57.9
1947	560	563	1,123	1,411	49.9	39.7
1948	442	627	1,069	1,330	41.3	33.2
1949	414	575	989	1,212	41.9	34.2
1950	538	720	1,258	1,562	42.8	34.4
1951	760	454	1,214	1,560	62.6	48.7
1952	807	454	1,261	1,541	64.0	52.4
1953	785	553	1,338	1,623	58.7	48.4
1954	637	596	1,233	1,482	51.7	43.0
1955	895	635	1,530	1,842	58.5	48.6
1956	874	562	1,436	1,707	60.9	51.2
1957	929	540	1,469	1,736	63.2	53.5

Source: U. S. Bureau of the Census

The largest single use of *new* rubber, 926,000 tons, 63 percent of the total, was in tires and tire products for passenger cars, trucks, buses, airplanes and farm equipment. Other important uses were in the manufacture of conveyer and transmission belting, hose for air and liquids, specialized equipment for the printing and textile industries, in mining and construction, and in upholstery and footwear.

A rough estimate of uses of new rubber in 1955 according to major categories is as follows:

	(1,000 long tons)
Tires and tubes	941
Mechanical goods	155
Latex foam products	91
Shoe products	62
Athletic goods, toys, stationers' goods, sponge rubber	62
Insulated wire and cable	44
Footwear	26
Miscellaneous	150

In the years 1920-1957, the consumption of new rubber in the United States increased at the rate, compounded annually, of 5.5 percent. Largely because of the increased use of automobiles, the rate of growth was greater than that of gross national product. But in postwar years, 1946-1957, rubber consumption has risen at the rate of only 3.2 percent, which was practically the rate of growth of the gross national product in that period.

The Paley Commission in 1952 estimated 1960 consumption of new rubber at 1,800,000 tons. Four years later, government economists, applying a 3.5 percent rate to the average consumption of 1951-55, produced the following annual estimates:[13]

Year	*Long tons, new rubber*
1956	1,458,000
1957	1,507,000
1958	1,562,000
1959	1,616,000
1960	1,673,000

[13] Report of Ad Hoc Rubber Committee and Office of Defense Mobilization, Appendix A in *Message from the President of the United States,* House Doc. no. 391 (1956), cited, p. 8.

Actual consumption of new rubber, 1,436,000 tons in 1956, and 1,469,000 tons in 1957, has been somewhat less than was predicted.

Looking ahead a quarter century, the Paley Commission estimated 1975 "requirements" at 2,500,000 tons of new rubber. The President's advisers, surveying the situation four years later, accepted the Paley figure as "reasonable." Henry Aubrey believes it to be conservative, in view of revised estimates of population growth not available when the Paley report was prepared.[14]

Underlying all long-term estimates is the assumption, implicit or expressed, that technological progress will continue, but without introducing any radical reduction in costs or in the development of competing products. With regard to rubber prices, it is also assumed either that they will show no secular increase, or else that the demand for rubber will show a low degree of price elasticity. Since the demand for crude rubber is derived from the demand for a great variety of end-products, the latter assumption appears to be valid.

Recent developments in the use of rubber and substitutes, however, throw some doubt on the validity of extrapolations of past trends. First, a significant reduction has been taking place in the proportion of rubber consumed in tires. In 1945 tires accounted for 73 percent of total U. S. new rubber consumption; in 12 years the proportion had fallen to 63 percent. The explanation is found in improved technology which has provided more mileage per pound of rubber. The effects on rubber consumption have been offset thus far by increased demand for rubber in industrial products and in the development of new uses. Conspicuous has been the use of latex foam products in household and automobile upholstery and in bedding. Experiments have been made in the use of rubber in road building, but any extensive development in this direction would depend on a substantial decline in rubber prices.

[14] Henry G. Aubrey, *United States Imports and World Trade* (Oxford: Clarendon Press, 1957), p. 114.

The Demand for Rubber

American fabricators of tires and other rubber products in 1957 used 63 percent synthetic and 37 percent natural rubber.[15] During postwar years, these proportions have shown rather wide variations, depending largely on the fluctuations in the price of the natural product. The trend, however, has been toward increasing use, relative to total consumption, of the synthetic product.

For certain uses natural rubber gives better results than the synthetic product. In tires for heavy trucks, buses and airplanes it affords greater resistance to internal heat. Natural latex is preferred for articles made of foam rubber. On the other hand, general-purpose synthetic rubber is preferred for treads of passenger tires, for insulation of cables and for other industrial uses. Certain types of synthetic rubbers are more resistant to oil and grease; some are nonflammable while natural rubber burns easily. Synthetic rubbers may be colored in any shade desired and can be made impermeable to air. When vulcanized, silicone synthetic rubber will hold its properties over a wider range of temperatures than the natural rubber.

In discussions of the limits of substitution of synthetic for natural rubber, three groups of products are usually distinguished:

> Group I includes products for which natural rubber is preferred. They take one-fifth to one-third of total new rubber consumption.
>
> Group II includes the uses in which the synthetic product gives better results. They absorb somewhat more than one-third of total new rubber supply.
>
> Group III, the largest of all in point of rubber use, is a "twilight zone" in which the use of either natural or synthetic is determined by price or supply considerations.

Technological progress is limiting the value of these broad generalizations. The synthetic product is versatile;

[15] These are percentages of total new rubber consumed, not including reclaimed rubber, an inferior product having limited uses.

it is capable of modification. Each year new discoveries in the field of rubber chemistry are announced and new types of elastomers are developed, "tailor made" to the needs of particular industries.

B. F. Goodrich Company scientists in 1954 succeeded in producing in the company's laboratories the true molecule of tree-grown rubber. Later, the new "synthetic natural" rubber, called Ameripol SN, was made in a pilot plant and used experimentally in truck tires. The Firestone Tire and Rubber Company and Phillips Petroleum Company also have succeeded in producing synthetically products having characteristics nearly identical with those of natural rubber. An official report states:

> This material is a polyisoprene. The polyisoprene rubber corresponds quite closely with natural rubber in chemical composition and in molecular structure. It should, therefore, have approximately the same qualities and range of applications as natural rubber, although some nonrubber constituents of crude natural rubber not present in the synthesized product might have to be added to give full comparability.
>
> This major scientific achievement in the field of rubber holds great promise for the future. In the normal course, processes will be studied in pilot plants and improvements in processes worked out, before any large scale production is undertaken. It appears unlikely that large scale commercial production will be undertaken for the next few years.[16]

Tire manufacturers are experimenting also with polyurethane. This plastic rubber-like material, because of its high tensile strength, low heat loss and excellent age resistance, may offer stiff competition with natural rubber in tires for trucks and buses. It may produce passenger tires good for 100,000 miles.[17] Polyurethane can also be used in place of foam rubber in mattresses and upholstery.

Price Comparisons

In the competition between synthetic and natural rubber, prices have become an increasingly important factor.

[16] Report of the Ad Hoc Rubber Committee and Office of Defense Mobilization, Appendix A in House Doc. no. 391 (1956), cited, p. 10.

[17] H. L. Fisher, "Rubber," *Scientific American,* v. 195, no. 5 (November 1956), p. 88.

Since 1943 (except for 1949), the average annual price of the most nearly comparable grade of natural rubber has been higher than the price of general-purpose synthetic rubber. Comparative yearly averages are shown in Table 33.

Some observers familiar with conditions in Malaya and Indonesia believe that on efficiently conducted plantations

Table 33

U. S. WHOLESALE PRICE AND PRICE INDEX OF RUBBER AND WHOLESALE PRICE INDEX OF ALL COMMODITIES, 1942-1957

Year	*Wholesale price*		*Wholesale price index*		
	Natural rubber[a]	*Synthetic rubber*[b]	*Natural rubber*[a]	*Synthetic rubber*[b]	*All commodities*
	(cents per pound)		(1947-49 = 100)		
1942	22.5	50.0	111.9	270.3	64.2
1943	22.5	26.4	111.9	142.7	67.0
1944	22.5	18.5	111.9	100.0	67.6
1945	22.5	18.5	111.9	100.0	68.8
1946	22.5	18.5	111.9	100.0	78.7
1947	20.8	18.5	103.5	100.0	96.4
1948	21.9	18.5	109.0	100.0	104.4
1949	17.6	18.5	87.6	100.0	99.2
1950	41.3	19.0	205.5	102.7	103.1
1951	60.9	25.0	303.0	135.1	114.8
1952	38.6	23.5	192.0	127.0	111.6
1953	24.1	23.0	119.9	124.3	110.1
1954	23.4	23.0	116.4	124.3	110.3
1955	39.0	23.0	194.0	124.3	110.7
1956	34.3	23.0	170.6	124.3	114.3
1957	31.1	23.0	154.7	124.3	117.6

[a] Smoked sheets, New York.
[b] S-type rubber.
Source: U. S. Bureau of Labor Statistics, International Rubber Study Group, Rubber Manufacturers Association

natural rubber can be produced at 12 to 15 cents a pound. These costs, however, will have no effect on price as long as world markets will absorb the available supply at much higher prices. Further advances in rubber chemistry seem bound to eliminate differences in quality and to narrow the gap in prices. In the long run, the price of synthetic

CHART M

U. S. WHOLESALE PRICES OF NATURAL AND SYNTHETIC RUBBER, MONTHLY AVERAGES, 1946-1957

(in cents per pound)

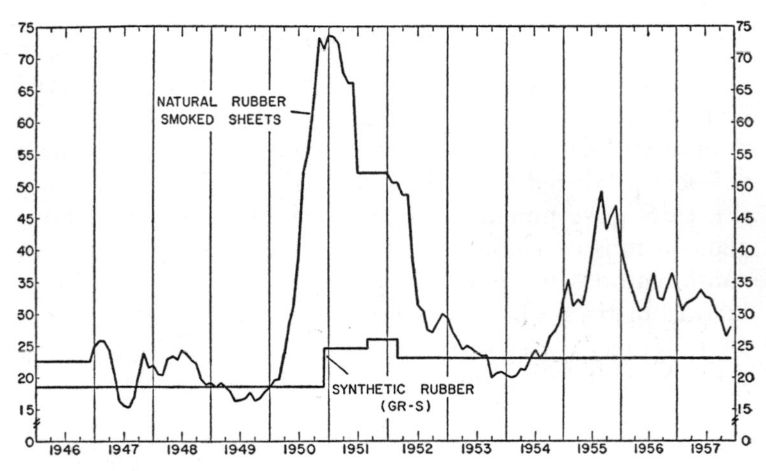

Source: Table 33

rubber will probably fix a ceiling on natural rubber prices.

Prices of natural rubber vary from day to day and even over a period of years show wide fluctuations. (See Chart M). They are particularly sensitive to political disturbances that obstruct or threaten supply. Thus after the attack on Korea the price rose from 27.8 cents (average price second quarter 1950) to 73 cents (average first quarter 1951). Changes in the internal political situation in Indonesia are soon reflected in rubber futures on the London exchange; over a somewhat longer period, booms and recessions in consuming countries, particularly the United States, raise or depress prices of all imported raw materials, including crude rubber.

In contrast, the prices of synthetic rubber have shown remarkable stability. In the years 1950-1957, only three changes took place. From 1944 to the end of 1950 the U. S. goverment sold GR-S produced in its plants at 18.5 cents a pound. In January 1951, when the average monthly price of natural rubber was 73.5 cents, GR-S was only at

24.5. In September 1951 it was raised to 26 cents, and in March 1952 reduced to 23 cents. Under private ownership, this price, except for minor and temporary changes, has been maintained.

Reclaimed Rubber

Rubber consumed in United States factories is derived from three sources: (1) natural rubber imported from Southeast Asia, Africa and other countries; (2) synthetic rubbers produced in the plants purchased in 1955 from the U. S. government; and (3) reclaimed rubber. About 280,000 tons of rubber reclaimed from scrap are used in combination with new rubber each year in the manufacture of tires, mats, hose and other industrial products. In 1952-1957 the amounts used showed a slowly declining ratio to the total consumption of rubber.

Year	*Tons of reclaimed rubber used*	*Percent of total U. S. consumption*
1937-39 (av.)	151,000	22.4
1952	280,000	18.2
1953	285,000	17.6
1954	249,000	16.8
1955	313,000	17.0
1956	271,000	15.9
1957	267,000	15.4

Should a serious rubber shortage develop, higher prices would induce increased collection and processing of scrap rubber. Statisticians, however, both in the rubber industry and in government, take it for granted that in the short run no great variations will occur in the amounts of reclaimed rubber put on the market and that over a longer period it will add a constant proportion to the available quantities of new rubber. Hence, they usually confine their estimates of future demand and supply to new rubber, natural and synthetic. Unless otherwise noted, this rule will be adopted in the following pages.

The Supply of Natural Rubber

Synthetic rubbers have not displaced natural rubber in the American market. Before World War II, when U. S.

CHART N

U.S. PRODUCTION, IMPORTS, EXPORTS AND SUPPLY OF RUBBER, 1937-39, 1946-1957

(in thousands of long tons)

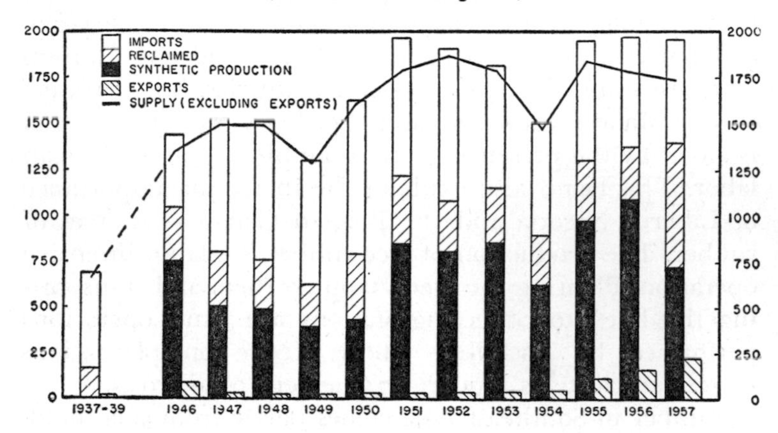

Source: U. S. Bureau of the Census

manufacturers were dependent entirely on natural rubber, imports were approximately 513,000 tons annually. After the war, expanding rubber consumption absorbed the growing production of the new synthetic rubber industry and still left room for 600,000-800,000 tons of imports. Scare buying and acceleration of stockpile purchases during the Korean war were responsible for unusually large imports, reaching 800,000 tons in 1950 and again in 1952. Since 1952 imports have declined. The average of the years 1953-1957 was 605,000 tons. (See Chart N.)

Malaya before World War II was the principal source of U. S. imports of rubber, furnishing 300,000 tons annually, or 60 percent of the total. Indonesia was second with 138,000 tons, 27 percent. Now the situation is reversed; Indonesia since 1952 has provided the larger quantities.[18]

[18] The amount of Indonesian rubber which goes to the United States is substantially larger than is indicated by official statistics. Indonesian rubber exported to Malaya is re-exported, after remilling, as a Malayan product. In addition, some of the rubber, smuggled out of Indonesia in order to avoid the export tax, eventually reaches the United States via Singapore. Trade sources estimate the amount of smuggled rubber at 2,500 tons monthly, in addition to an equal amount of "nonreported" exports.

Postwar import figures also reflect the increase in supplies coming from Thailand and Liberia. (See Table 34.)

The location of rubber growing is determined by both climate and economics. The necessary natural conditions, heavy, well-distributed rainfall (about 100 inches a year) and temperatures varying between 70° and 90° Fahrenheit, are found in many tropical countries. The production in Malaya, Indonesia and elsewhere in Southeast Asia is aided by the presence there of ample supplies of cheap labor. This factor also explains the increasing importance of Liberia, Nigeria and the Belgian Congo as sources of rubber. The production of tree rubber is a labor-intensive operation. Planting the trees, tapping them and transporting the latex to collecting stations are hand operations performed by unskilled labor. Hence on plantations wages constitute as much as 75 percent of all costs.

Rubber in Southeast Asia comes partly from smallholdings, under 100 acres each, and partly from rubber estates of much larger acreage. In the first quarter of the century, estates supplied the bulk of the rubber produced. Despite the benefits derived from the Stevenson scheme and other agreements for the control of rubber production, they suffered increasing competition from smallholders. The destruction of rubber groves during World War II affected principally the operations of estates and further lessened their relative importance. In Malaya, at present, they supply less than three-fifths of total output; in Indonesia, a little more than one-third. In Thailand rubber is produced entirely on smallholdings.

Rubber Production in Indonesia

Rubber growing suffered severely in Indonesia during World War II, exports practically disappeared, and in early postwar years recovery was hindered by the revolt against Dutch authority. Nevertheless, exports[19] rose from

(See the *Rubber Statistical Bulletin,* published monthly by the Secretariat of the International Rubber Study Group.)

[19] In the absence of accurate production statistics, export figures give the best indication of Indonesian production of natural rubber. The figures cited have been taken from *Rubber Statistical Bulletin.*

Table 34

U. S. IMPORTS OF NATURAL RUBBER,[a] 1937-39, 1946-1957

(in thousands of long tons)

Year	*Indonesia*	*Malaya*	*Thailand*	*Liberia*	*Indochina*	*Ceylon*	*All other*	*Total*
1937–39 (av.)	138	303	b	3	21	30	19	513
1946	36	205	10	22	67	18	30	388
1947	36	574	12	21	10	40	24	717
1948	114	456	81	25	5	55	4	740
1949	179	312	98	26	2	42	4	663
1950	215	365	106	29	21	63	10	809
1951	189	359	107	32	12	26	14	739
1952	309	306	104	39	16	23	12	809
1953	282	192	92	36	29	9	10	650
1954	240	155	106	37	50	6	9	600
1955	232	174	125	37	46	13	11	638
1956	206	170	112	39	30	7	19	583
1957	185	149	115	37	35	10	22	553

[a] Includes latex, guayule, gutta balata, jelutong, gutta percha and other guttas.
[b] Less than 500 tons.
Source: U. S. Bureau of the Census

something like 230,000 tons in 1946 to nearly double that amount in 1948 and 1949. (See Table 35.) In later years, the Korean boom in rubber prices and the promise of more settled political conditions under the newly established Republic of Indonesia brought continued growth. In recent years Indonesia supplied between 35 and 40 percent of all natural rubber entering into world trade.

In 1957, 37 percent of Indonesian rubber (252,000 tons) was produced on estates, situated principally on the island of Sumatra where British, Dutch, Norwegian, Chinese, Belgian and American companies own large plantations. Production from smallholdings in 1957 was 432,000 tons. In prewar years more rubber was produced on estates than on smallholdings, but the greater injuries suffered by the estates in the Japanese occupation and afterwards reversed the proportion. This change has been partly responsible for the stagnation in total Indonesian rubber production, because of the higher average yield per acre on the estates.

No substantial increase is expected in rubber exports from Indonesia during the next five to ten years, for several reasons: (1) replanting has been neglected and the new groves recently planted will require several years to come into maturity;[20] (2) the political situation does not encourage foreign companies to increase their investments in rubber plantations; (3) the economic outlook in the immediate future is somewhat uncertain owing to rising costs and the expansion of American capacity for the production of synthetic rubber.

The Indonesian government aims to promote economic development. Its leaders recognize the need for expanding production and exports of rubber because of their contribution to government revenues and supply of foreign exchange receipts. As part of a five-year plan of economic

[20] About seven years must elapse after the planting of a rubber grove before the trees are sufficiently mature for tapping. Maximum production of latex is attained at 12 years. At 30 or 35 years, declining yields and losses from disease end the economic life of rubber trees. If output is to be maintained, the groves should be replanted at the rate of about three percent annually.

Table 35

NET EXPORTS OF NATURAL RUBBER FROM PRINCIPAL PRODUCING COUNTRIES, 1935, 1940, 1945-1957

(in thousands of long tons)

Year	*Malaya*	*Indonesia*	*Ceylon*	*Vietnam*	*Cambodia*	*Thailand*	*Sarawak*	*British North Borneo*	*Africa*[a]	*All other*[a]	*World total*[a]
1935	417.0	282.9	54.3	28.7		28.3	19.3	8.9	6.[illegible]	28.2	873.7
1940	540.4	536.7	88.9	64.4		43.9	35.2	17.6	17.[illegible]	45.2	1,389.6
1945	51.6	4.3[a]	95.2	1.0		—	—	—	54.[illegible]	41.2	247.5
1946	366.9	230.0[a]	101.1	135.4		24.2	23.5	4.0	46.8	30.6	962.5
1947	640.1	287.0	82.5	50.5		52.6	35.6	15.0	38.[illegible]	30.7	1,232.5
1948	679.0	432.0	91.7	41.2		95.9	39.9	20.1	41.[illegible]	16.2	1,457.5
1949	679.1	422.1	90.5	40.9		94.2	38.9	19.5	44.8	10.0	1,440.0
1950	657.8	691.7	118.5	51.6		112.2	55.8	23.9	55.[illegible]	18.2	1,785.0
1951	608.2	793.8	103.6	52.3		108.8	42.5	21.7	72.[illegible]	19.1	1,822.5
1952	571.6	749.1	89.4	60.4		97.9	31.5	19.1	73.[illegible]	22.5	1,715.0
1953	569.7	674.0	96.7	70.6		95.6	24.0	16.8	77.[illegible]	15.6	1,640.0
1954	570.9	728.7	90.2	54.2	23.8	116.7	23.0	17.1	84.5	18.4	1,727.5
1955	631.9	721.1	97.4	61.4	25.8	130.2	39.4	20.1	98.0	17.2	1,842.5
1956	617.5	668.7	86.8	62.9	27.8	133.6	41.3	19.9	112.0	14.5	1,785.0
1957	638.9	666.5	94.0	72.5	30.6	133.0	41.0	19.9	110.6	18.0	1,825.0

a Estimated.

Source: U. S. Tariff Commission, International Rubber Study Group

development, new planting and replanting of rubber groves has begun on 260,000 hectares (650,000 acres) of smallholders' land. But increased production from this source cannot be expected before 1963. The social and economic policies of the new republic, although not as yet clearly defined, seem to favor the producers on smallholdings. In these holdings, which supply about 60 percent of Indonesian rubber, there are large acreages of over-age trees which must be replanted if rubber output is to be increased, or even maintained at its present level.

A vigorous program of replanting is also needed on the rubber estates, owned in large part by Dutch and British interests, which suffered severe injury during the Japanese occupation and the subsequent revolt against Dutch rule. Trees were overtapped or neglected, or even destroyed. Some estates were taken over by squatters who have successfully resisted efforts to evict them. British and Dutch rubber companies are well supplied with capital funds for replanting, but are deterred by unstable political conditions. They are not sure that the new republic can assert its authority and maintain law and order, particularly in the outer islands. They are worried by the hostile attitudes of ultranationalistic groups who, regarding absentee ownership of rubber plantations as a vestige of colonialism, advocate policies unfavorable to foreign investors, such as restrictions on the remittance of profits and on repatriation of capital. Foreign firms are subjected to pressure to hire Indonesians for administrative and technical positions. They find it difficult to get entry permits for foreign-born employees, although competent native personnel may not be available.

Wages of unskilled labor, although still low by Western standards, are rising as the result of trade union activity. Meanwhile, the companies contend, there has been no corresponding gain in productivity. Also in the background there is the threat that expansion of American production of synthetic rubber may oust natural rubber from its traditional markets in the United States and in Europe.

The Rubber Industry in Malaya

About four percent of the rubber acreage in Malaya was lost in the period of Japanese occupation, but much larger losses resulted from the destruction of buildings and machinery, particularly on the estates owned by Europeans. In spite of low world prices of rubber, which impeded rehabilitation programs in the early postwar years, the industry made a rapid recovery. By 1947 production and exports were nearly 20 percent above 1940, a high year, and by 1948 they had gained 25-30 percent.

World demand for rubber during the Korean war and the stockpiling programs of the industrial countries brought a boom in prices but no increase in Malayan production and exports. Malaya was the only major rubber-producing country which did not share proportionately in the seller's market of 1950-1951. After 1952, world consumption of natural rubber rose steadily, but it was not until 1955 that Malayan output again approached its early postwar level.

Year	*Malayan rubber production*	*Malayan rubber exports*	*Total world exports of rubber*	*Malayan exports as % of world exports*
	(in thousands of long tons)			
1940	544	540	1,390	38.8
1948	698	679	1,458	46.6
1950	694	658	1,785	39.9
1952	584	572	1,715	33.4
1955	639	632	1,843	34.3
1956	626	618	1,785	34.6
1957	639	639	1,825	35.0

A little less than half of Malayan rubber acreage belongs to individuals and family cultivators, known as smallholders. Officially, a smallholding is defined as an area of less than 100 acres, but most of the smallholdings are less than ten acres, and many less than three. In 1957 they accounted for 42 percent of Malayan rubber production.

Most smallholdings in Malaya produce rubber of inferior quality; programs for improving the smallholder's output and thereby increasing its value have made little progress. More than half of the trees on the smallholdings are over 33 years old, and two-thirds are over 25 years; nearly all of them are of a low-yield variety. In contrast, close to one-third of the estate acreage has been replanted with trees producing two to three times as much rubber as the ordinary trees. The average annual output per acre on the smallholdings is 350 pounds, but on the replanted acres of the large estates it rises to almost 800 pounds. For the whole country the average yield is estimated at 500 pounds.

Government policy since the early 1920's has discouraged the opening of new land for rubber planting. Between 1934 and 1947 new planting was prohibited; in the next eight years the government made very little land available for new planting because of its concern over "the fluctuating and uncertain fortunes of rubber and a consequent interest in more diversified land use, especially for lands which might be suitable for food crops."[21] In 1955, however, in response to insistent demands for new rubber acreage a small fund was set aside to assist smallholders to undertake new planting.

While restrictions on planting on new land were being successfully maintained in Malaya, similar policies were not so effectively enforced in Indonesia and Thailand, with the result that Malaya lost its position as the world's largest producer. In 1922, two-thirds of all rubber came from Malaya; the proportion is now about one-third. In the past 30 years rubber acreage in Malaya increased by about two-fifths, while in Indonesia the land under rubber is three times what it was in the mid-1920's.

The Malayan government has gone to great lengths since the war to encourage replanting, with higher-yielding trees, on *existing* rubber acreage. Because the smallholder is usually unable to bear the costs the government set up a fund, derived partly from its tax on rubber exports, from which it pays the smallholder 600 Malayan dollars (about

21 International Bank for Reconstruction and Development, *The Economic Development of Malaya* (Baltimore: John Hopkins University Press, 1955), p. 57.

$200) per acre over a period of years if he will replant with high-yield trees; this grant is applicable to one-third of his holding, or 10 acres, whichever is greater. Estates are offered a smaller grant per acre, up to one-fifth of their total acreage.[22] The smallholders have lagged far behind the yearly replanting goals set in 1952, because of the loss of income which they must undergo before the new trees come to maturity and because of technical difficulties in replanting small plots. They show an "understandable reluctance to uproot and replant a cultivated area when there are large unplanted areas near by. . . ."[23]

In 1954 two investigations of the Malayan rubber industry by a Mission of Enquiry[24] and by the International Bank,[25] emphasized the need for new planting as well as replanting. The Rubber Enquiry group pointed out that the allocation of new land for rubber cultivation would be the most effective way of providing fresh capital for the industry. It would permit the grower to plant high-quality trees while still obtaining income from his old holdings. The Bank's report suggested that the prospects for world consumption justified new planting as well as replanting. Much of the unoccupied land in Malaya, it said, was suitable only for rubber cultivation; hence there would be no conflict with policies of over-all agricultural development.

About 65 percent of the cultivated area of Malaya is planted in rubber; for both the agricultural estates and the smallholdings it is the principal crop. Its share of gross national product in the high year, 1951, was 27 percent; two years later, when prices had fallen, the proportion was only 12 percent. In 1956, export duties on rubber were

[22] In 1957, three-fifths of the government's investment in agriculture and industry was devoted to assisting rubber replanting, both on large estates and on smallholdings.

[23] P. T. Bauer, "Malayan Rubber Policy," *Political Science Quarterly*, v. 72, no. 1 (March 1957), p. 88.

[24] Mission of Enquiry into the Rubber Industry of Malaya, organized by the Malayan government and the Rubber Producers' Council which represents all rubber-producing interests in Malaya.

[25] Mission organized by the International Bank for Reconstruction and Development at the request of the governments of the Federation of Malaya, Singapore and the United Kingdom.

M$144 million (nearly U. S. $50 million). This amount, plus revenue from income taxes paid by the rubber industry, provided one-third of total government revenue. Net exports of rubber accounted for 58 percent of all 1956 export earnings and nearly half of all dollar exchange. Malaya, which buys about one-fifth as much as it sells to the United States, is one of the most important dollar earners in the British Commonwealth.

In recent years, efficient Malayan plantations have made substantial profits, but they recognize that the salvation of the industry depends upon planting the higher-yielding trees. If this program is carried through, "Malayan rubber will have nothing to fear from outside."[26] The International Bank urged that replanting be given the highest priority in programs of economic development. Its report stated:

> Cost data from a representative cross-section of rubber estates indicate that the production of high-yielding rubber on well-managed estates could continue to compete profitably with synthetic rubber even if prices of the latter were to fall well below present levels. Smallholdings on high-yielding rubber cultivated mainly with family labor or on a crop-sharing basis would be even less vulnerable to lower synthetic rubber prices.[27]

Other Foreign Production

In Africa low labor costs, nearness to European markets and stable political conditions have favored substantial investment in rubber production. Two leading American rubber manufacturing companies have obtained concessions for rubber plantations in Liberia, but only Firestone has actually begun production. This company, which began operations in Liberia in 1925 as insurance against restrictive agreements such as the Stevenson scheme, in 1955 had 100,000 acres in rubber in two plantations. It employed 25,000 workers who produced 38,000 tons of rubber, 90 percent of the total Liberian output. The average yield

[26] J. B. Perry Robinson, *Transformation in Malaya* (London: Secker & Warburg, 1956), p. 207.
[27] *The Economic Development of Malaya,* cited, p. 48.

per acre on the Firestone plantations, 1,048 pounds, was said to be the highest in the world.[28] In 1956 rubber exports from Liberia, valued at $30 million, were 68 percent of the country's total.

In the Western Hemisphere, in Mexico, Peru and Brazil, the small quantities of rubber produced are not sufficient for local consumption. Brazil, once the world's greatest source of rubber, now imports natural rubber from Southeast Asia and synthetic rubbers from the United States. The Firestone Company has announced the establishment of a 3,000-acre plantation in Brazil to supply material for its manufacturing plants in that country.

The Outlook

Regarding the future supply of synthetic rubber from American plants, all forecasts are optimistic. "Domestic consumers of rubber appear to have ample assurance that their future needs for synthetic rubber will be fully supplied by competitive private producers."[29] This reassuring official statement was based on the remarkable increase in production in the first year of private ownership (see Table 36) and on reported plans for expansion of facilities.

In his report on the first year's operations under private ownership, the Attorney General noted that an expansion program to be completed in 1957 would raise GR-S capacity by 50 percent over the April 1955 level. Actually, the new capital invested in the industry between April 1955 and the end of 1956 raised capacity for production of GR-S rubber from 737 thousand tons to 1,100 thousand tons. The Attorney General in his second annual report estimated that by the end of 1957 capacity would be about 1,400 thousand tons, or nearly double the April 1955 level. Trade sources estimate that American synthetic rubber factories will, by the end of 1958, have a total production capacity of about 1,700 thousand tons. Comparison of this

28 See Wayne C. Taylor, *The Firestone Operations in Liberia* (Washington: National Planning Association, 1956).

29 Report of the Ad Hoc Rubber Committee and Office of Defense Mobilization, Appendix A in House Doc. no. 391 (1956), cited, p. 14.

Table 36

WORLD PRODUCTION OF SYNTHETIC RUBBER,[a] 1942-1957
(in thousands of long tons)

Year	*United States*	*All other*	*Total*
1942	22	98	120
1943	232	119	351
1944	764	137	901
1945	820	46[b]	866
1946	740	67	807
1947	509	50	559
1948	488	44	532
1949	394	47	440
1950	476	58	535
1951	845	63	908
1952	799	79	878
1953	848	87	936
1954	623	93	716
1955	970	115	1,085
1956	1,080	131	1,211
1957	1,118	144	1,262

[a] Excluding the U.S.S.R.
[b] Excluding German production which in 1944 amounted to 102 thousand long tons.
Source: International Rubber Study Group, U. S. Bureau of the Census

figure with predicted consumption of new rubber (see page 256) shows that, if present plans are realized, the domestic rubber industry will be in a position in 1958 and 1959 to supply an amount equivalent to the consumption by the American rubber industry of both natural and synthetic rubber and still have a surplus of over 100,000 tons for export.

The growth, actual and potential, of the American synthetic industry seems to place a ceiling on imports of natural rubber, at least in the next five or ten years. But it does not necessarily constitute a threat to the continued expansion and prosperity of the growers of natural rubber. Until new plantings and replantings in Southeast Asia come to maturity, rubber production in that key area can hardly exceed the level of 1955-1957. For the enlarged production due to appear in 1960-1965 and thereafter, expanding markets outside the United States will be available. In the producing countries themselves, the manufacture of tires and other rubber products will take an increasing share of the output of crude rubber. Far more important will be the growing rubber consumption of Western Europe, Australia, Japan and South America which, it seems, will be satisfied principally by imports of natural rubber, a product which they can purchase with sterling.

Countries outside the United States raised their consumption of natural rubber from about 800,000 tons in 1948 to 1,330,000 tons in 1957. The outlook is for continued rapid growth, for their per capita consumption of new rubber is still low measured by American standards. Estimated consumption in 1957 was:

	Pounds per capita
United States	19.2
Australia	12.9
Canada	11.9
United Kingdom	10.4
France	9.4
West Germany	7.7
Japan	3.6
India	0.2

If we assume continued growth in national incomes in the major industrial countries, and freedom from major political disturbances, use of rubber in automotive transportation and for industrial purposes will continue to rise. Furthermore, many countries which in prewar years imported tires and other rubber manufactures are now establishing their own factories for which they will import rubber, principally the natural variety.

Outside of the United States and the Soviet Union, the use of synthetic rubber, in spite of recent gains, has not attained large volume. Consumption in the United Kingdom in 1957 was 57,000 tons; in Germany, 46,000; in France about 50,000: and elsewhere on the European Continent about the same amount. The obstacles are several. Foreign manufacturers of tires and other rubber products, except those affiliated with American companies, until recently have lacked chemical engineers who knew how to use synthetic rubber. Moreover, as we have pointed out earlier, they can buy natural rubber with sterling and other currencies, but they need dollars to pay for the synthetic product imported from the United States and Canada. Within Europe they can obtain practically no synthetic rubber. West Germany in 1957 was credited with only 11,600 tons; the United Kingdom produced an even smaller amount. In both countries, however, important new projects will come into production in 1958.

Problems of National Policy

As far as the domestic supply is concerned, the purposes of national rubber policy seem to have been satisfactorily attained. The manufacture of synthetic rubber set up in wartime under government ownership was transferred to private owners without interruption in production. Synthetic rubber plants now supply more than 60 percent of total domestic consumption of new rubber. The contrast with oil, lead and zinc is obvious. Dependence on foreign sources of supply for rubber has decreased. The new synthetic industry stands on its own feet; it asks for no tariff protection and no subsidies. Without raising prices over the level set under government ownership, the private owners have earned good profits, and in less than three years have doubled their productive capacity. As the result of continued research in rubber chemistry they have improved their products and have developed promising new ones. From the point of view of domestic policy, the principal remaining problem is to ensure the maintenance of competition among the new owners, a relatively few concerns which manufacture rubber and petroleum products.

In Southeast Asia and elsewhere, the prosperity of rubber producers in postwar years has been affected and will still be affected by U. S. policies. Countries exporting natural rubber are all economically underdeveloped; their people are poor, ill-fed, uneducated and afflicted with tropical diseases. The United States in the national interest has adopted a policy of aiding such countries to attain higher standards of living through greater economic efficiency.[30] On the political side we hope that economic progress will strengthen emerging democratic institutions, thus making these countries less vulnerable to Soviet penetration.

In the struggle between Russian Communism and the Western world, Southeast Asia occupies a critical position. Internal political institutions in Malaya, Indonesia and Indochina are in a fluid condition. In their foreign policy they are committed neither to the U.S.S.R. nor to the Free World. Rubber exports, the key to economic advance in both Malaya and Indonesia, provide the largest single source of foreign exchange and furnish a vital source of government revenue. Hence they and other rubber-exporting countries in Southeast Asia have viewed with apprehension the sudden growth in the United States of a great rubber industry. It is true that thus far their fears have not been realized. Because of the postwar expansion of total world demand (see Table 37), sales of natural rubber, although supplying a declining share of U. S. and world markets, have not actually fallen off. Estate owners have continued to earn liberal returns on their investments.

Available evidence seems to indicate that the American synthetic rubber industry does not threaten immediate injury to the growers of tree rubber. Their product has a market of its own; it has valuable characteristics not yet duplicated by any synthetic rubber produced on a commercial scale, or likely to be so produced in the immediate future. In products for which both the synthetic and natural rubber can be employed, the latter is tending to become more competitive on a price basis. Moreover, there are definite possibilities that, under pressure to hold mar-

30 In Indonesia, for example, we are engaged in providing technical assistance in agriculture, forestry and fisheries. From 1950 through 1956 the United States obligated $40.8 million for technical cooperation and development assistance programs in Indonesia and spent $29.6 million of these funds. In addition, the United States is a major contributor to the United Nations technical assistance program under which $260 million was obligated for expenditure in Indonesia in 1956.

Table 37

WORLD CONSUMPTION OF NEW RUBBER, NATURAL AND SYNTHETIC, 1937-39, 1945-1957

(in thousands of long tons)

Year	*United States*	*United Kingdom*	*Germany*[a]	*France*	*Japan*	*Canada*	*All other*[b,c]	*World total*[c]
1937–39 (av.)	524	115	90[c]	61[c]	[d]	29	239	1,058
1945	799	91	24[c]	21	20	42	131	1,128
1946	1,040	127	14	58	20	39	170	1,468
1947	1,123	156	16	74	17	61	288	1,735
1948	1,069	196	50	94	26	62	406	1,903
1949	989	187	68	99	35	56	453	1,888
1950	1,258	222	82	110	60	69	501	2,303
1951	1,214	238	97	128	59	71	521	2,328
1952	1,261	202	103	133	69	67	520	2,355
1953	1,338	224	118	128	91	73	558	2,530
1954	1,233	248	147	141	91	72	583	2,515
1955	1,530	267	173	154	92	85	644	2,945
1956	1,436	232	170	166	118	91	825	3,038
1957	1,469	239	176	184	145	88	832	3,133

[a] British zone, 1945-47; Bizone, 1948-49; Federal Republic since 1950.
[b] Data for the U.S.S.R. cover estimated net imports of natural rubber; they exclude consumption of synthetic rubber.
[c] Estimated.
[d] Included in "all other."
Source: International Rubber Study Group, U. S. Bureau of the Census

kets, the producers of natural rubber might reduce their price below the 23-cent level at which the principal type of synthetic rubber has sold since 1952. It is reliably reported that, on well-managed plantations employing advanced agricultural techniques, costs are now appreciably less than 23 cents. In Malaya replanting programs should bring on the market within a few years increasing supplies of low-cost rubber derived from high-yielding strains. The progress of replanting in Indonesia will await the establishment of more settled political conditions.

The Rubber Embargo

On grounds of national security, the United States in 1949 prohibited the export of rubber to the U.S.S.R. and its European satellites. To make the control effective Congress, in the Battle Act, sought to persuade this country's associates in the European Recovery Program to apply parallel restrictions. It is doubtful, however, whether these restrictions on East-West trade accomplished much in limiting Russia's rubber supply. The U.S.S.R., even before World War II, had developed its own synthetic rubber industry and later was able to secure supplementary supplies of natural rubber from the producing countries, either directly or by indirect routes.

In 1954, England and the United States relaxed their restrictions on East-West trade. In March, the United Kingdom announced that rubber could be freely exported from British ports to Russia and her East European satellites. Later, U. S. controls on exports of rubber to the Soviet bloc were relaxed. In 1956, the U. S. Department of Commerce issued licenses for the export of 170 tons of synthetic rubber to the Soviet bloc and, in 1957, 217 tons.

The United States prohibits exports of rubber to Communist China, in accordance with a complete embargo on all trade with that country imposed in December 1950. The United Nations in May 1951, on a motion of the United States, voted an embargo on strategic commodities, including rubber, and some 45 countries agreed to the action. The United States assumed major responsibility for checking on compliance, as part of its responsibility for the direction of military operations in Korea, and succeeded for a time in obtaining a high degree of cooperation from its allies. But after the United Kingdom, in early 1954, had permitted exports of rubber to the Soviet bloc, the United States was under pressure to agree to similar treatment of Communist China, for the British removal of the ban on rubber shipments to the U.S.S.R. opened a rather large loophole in the embargo, making it possible for the Chinese Communists to get all the rubber they needed by indirect trade, although at somewhat greater expense. An important source of direct supply had become available when Ceylon in October 1952 negotiated a barter deal for the annual delivery of 50,000 tons of rubber (half of its annual production) over a period of five years, in cxchange for Chinese rice.[31]

Malayan rubber growers complained that the embargo on rubber shipments to China unfairly discriminated against them and urged the British government to remove it. When Prime Minister Eden discussed the matter in Washington in early 1956 he found the United States unwilling to agree, but several months later the British government, acting on its own responsibility, lifted the embargo,[32] announcing that rubber could be exported to China from Malaya and Singapore, in reasonable quantities. After the British action the embargo crumbled rapidly as Indonesia, Thailand, Burma and Laos in quick succession lifted their prohibitions. From these sources and

[31] The Chinese are said to have offered to pay 37 cents a pound, approximately 10 cents above the October 1952 price. At this time Ceylon rejected an offer from the United States to buy its rubber at the world market price.

Communist China, in a new trade agreement negotiated in September 1957, agreed to buy 30,000 tons of rubber from Ceylon and to sell to that country 200,000 tons of rice. At the same time, China made a grant of 20 million Ceylon rupees, equivalent to about $4.5 million, to assist Ceylon in replanting unprofitable rubber land.

[32] In order that the break with U. S. policy might not be too obvious, the British action was described as a more liberal resort to the so-called "exceptions procedure." Under this procedure the sale of limited quantities of embargoed goods to China in exceptional circumstances was not considered a violation of the 1951 UN resolution.

Ceylon, China can obtain all the rubber its industries need. Hence the U. S. export prohibition is significant only as expressing continued disapproval of the Communist regime and its policies.

Stockpiling Policy

Stockpiling at present is probably the most controversial feature of national rubber policy. According to unofficial estimates, the government holds 1,200,000 tons of natural rubber as a reserve supply in case war or other emergencies should cut off imports, but the rubber stockpile, like all similar accumulations of essential raw materials, has been criticized as an anachronism in an atomic age. Wars fought with nuclear and thermonuclear weapons, some argue, will be too short to permit the processing of large stocks of materials. (See Chapter 3, pp. 48-52.)

The United States, however, may become involved in wars of considerable duration fought with conventional weapons. To sustain, during such conflicts, production of defense items, for example, tires for military vehicles, an emergency supply of natural rubber, or substitute material having identical characteristics, would be essential. For the present, synthetic-natural rubber is not being produced commercially; to bring it into quantity production would involve large investments in new plants and dangerous delay. But with synthetic production, plus the imports that would be available, plus the rubber which might be saved by restriction of nondefense uses, the government ought to be able to meet any probable emergency, *with a much smaller accumulation of natural rubber than it now holds.* It has been suggested that 300,000 tons would be adequate.

Stockpiling is a troublesome and expensive business. Rubber is a bulky commodity, requiring extensive storage space. It is flammable; hence fire protection must be provided. Because rubber deteriorates with age, the contents of the stockpile must be rotated periodically. To these and other costs of maintenance must be added, for accurate accounting, interest charges on an investment worth, at 1957 prices, over $800 million.

The disposal of several hundred thousand tons of rubber, without violently disturbing world markets, presents a formidable problem. Even rumors that the U. S. government might be considering reduction in its rubber holdings can depress prices in exporting countries.[33] Nevertheless, it ought to be possible, with careful management, to gradually dispose of some part of the stockpile without causing serious injury to producing countries. First, Congress would have to amend present legislation so as to facilitate the release to the market of materials held in the strategic stockpile, as recommended by the Special Stockpile Advisory Committee.[34] Then if the United States, in consultation with the producing countries, could set up, and rigidly adhere to, a schedule of amounts to be released, by months or quarters, market disturbances could be kept to a minimum. The timing of the disposal program would be important; it obviously should not be initiated in a declining market. Precedents for orderly disposal of government-held stocks may be found in the release to the market in 1944 and 1945 of several hundred million pounds of wool from the U. S. government's stockpile and in the sale, in 1947-50, of stocks of domestic wool which had been acquired by the Commodity Credit Corporation.

A factor of great significance, in the coming 10 to 20 years, to the well-being of countries exporting natural rubber will be the state of the United States economy. In prosperous years, U. S. imports, constituting about one-third of the world's total, rise in quantity and value; in recession years they fall. For example, in 1953, a fairly prosperous year, the United States paid $334 million for imports of

[33] The rubber market is sensitive even to the purchases and sales involved in rotation procedures. During the rubber shortage in late 1956, owing to the Suez crisis, the Rubber Manufacturers Association sponsored a plan which would have permitted delay in replacing rubber withdrawn from the stockpile. Importers of natural rubber objected that such action would constitute unwarranted government interference in the rubber market. They claimed that even a slight delay in replenishing the rubber in the nation's stockpile might be construed by the producing nations in the Far East as an unfriendly act. The ODM, whether for this or other reasons, rejected the industry's proposal.

[34] See Chapter 3, p. 53.

rubber; in 1954 the imports were valued at $265 million. Likewise, the value of rubber imports fell from $401 million in 1956 to about $350 million in 1957. Whatever success the United States can achieve in reducing the amplitude of cyclical variations in business activity will benefit suppliers of raw rubber and other materials, as well as ourselves.

The United States has wisely declined to take part in schemes for the stabilization of rubber prices through the creation of buffer stocks or other types of international commodity agreements. Such agreements the State Department has held to conflict with a basic objective of American foreign policy, viz., the expansion of international trade. The United States, nevertheless, is an active participant in agreements regulating import and export trade in wheat and sugar. Failure to take part in a rubber agreement is explainable not so much on grounds of principle as by the lack of any domestic producers of natural rubber who might benefit thereby, and by the strong opposition of fabricating interests.

Chapter 10

NATIONAL OIL POLICY

THE BLOCKING of the Suez Canal in November 1956 and the destruction of pumping stations on the oil pipelines crossing Syria threatened one of the major objectives of U. S. policy, to maintain an uninterrupted flow of oil from the Middle East to Western Europe. Oil furnishes about one-fifth of that area's total energy requirements, and 70 percent of that oil comes from Iran, Kuwait, Saudi Arabia and other Middle Eastern sources. Interruption of these supplies endangered the economic and military potential of countries allied with the United States in NATO. The history of the Eisenhower administration's handling of this crisis furnishes an instructive introduction to the study of national oil policy. It reveals the conflicts of objectives within government, and the conflicts of interest within the American oil industry, which have prevented the creation of an integrated national oil policy.

The first step in providing oil supplies for Western Europe was the organization, at government initiative, of the Middle East Emergency Committee, a group of 15 American oil companies with interests in foreign oil production and long-established markets in Europe and, in addition, one company whose interests were almost exclusively in the field of domestic production. To avoid the danger that the Department of Justice might later find that the Committee's activities had violated antitrust legislation it was necessary to obtain from the Department assurances of immunity on this score.

The Committee then made plans to increase by 500,000 barrels daily shipments of crude oil and refined products from U. S. Gulf ports to Europe, and to add 300,000 barrels to the daily shipments from those ports to U. S. East

Coast refineries, to compensate them for the loss of Middle East oil.

At this point, conflict of interest arose between the two major divisions of the American oil industry, the "international" companies, represented by the Middle East Emergency Committee, and the thousands of independent oil producers whose interests were concentrated in the domestic market. The independents declined to be represented on the Emergency Committee. They rejected, also, all unofficial appeals that they should agree to relaxation of restrictions imposed by state authorities on the output of crude oil. Instead, they proposed that shipments to Europe should be drawn from inventories, then at a high level, and that all Venezuelan oil then being imported into U. S. East Coast ports should be diverted to Europe. The international oil-importing companies declined to take this action, which would have deprived their East Coast refineries of the special types of crude oil not obtainable from domestic sources. Although Europe needed crude oil, the oil companies preferred to ship gasoline and other refined products.

The Suez crisis also revealed conflict between the federal government and the prorationing boards of oil-producing states, particularly the Texas Railroad Commission. To say that the state authorities were uncooperative would be an understatement. General Ernest O. Thompson, a veteran member of the Texas Commission, told the House Committee on Interstate and Foreign Commerce that in his opinion the Middle East oil crisis was largely manufactured by the newspapers, "just scareheads." The other members of the three-man board evidently shared his opinion. When Europe's need for more oil was most urgent, in late 1956 and early 1957, they refused to permit two large companies, subsidiaries of members of the MEEC, to expand their output. The Texas Railroad Commission, in fact, made no increase in its "allowables" until the middle of February 1957 (effective in March) when the emergency had nearly passed. But the international companies, by drawing down stocks and bringing in crude oil from areas as remote as Wyoming, were able in the months November 1956—March 1957 to ship an average of 245,000 barrels of crude oil daily to Europe, plus 220,000 barrels of gasoline and other petroleum products. With this supply and some Middle East oil obtained via still-functioning pipelines, Western Europe was able to weather the crisis without grave hardship.

In fairness to the Texas Railroad Commission, and other state bodies which followed its lead, it must be pointed out that the oil lift was the responsibility of the federal, not the state, government. It was initiated by the national Executive to promote objectives of its foreign policy. But neither the Department of the Interior, nor the Office of Defense Mobilization nor the President directly and officially requested the state authorities to permit increased oil production. Yet the President was fully armed with power, under the Connally Hot Oil Act, to enforce prompt compliance with his policy.

Oil policy has many ramifications. It must take account of state legislation restricting the output of domestic wells. It should be consistent with the objectives of American foreign policy, particularly in the oil-producing areas of Latin America and the Middle East. It must consider the interests of the major oil producers who have invested several billions of dollars abroad, and of thousands of independent oil producers whose capital in most cases is invested exclusively at home. The welfare of millions of American consumers of gasoline, kerosene, diesel oil and heavy fuel oil demands attention. The makers of oil policy, in their attempts to deal justly with Americans of this generation, have to consider whether they are prejudicing the interests of generations yet to come. When thinking about conservation of oil resources, they have to take account of the possibilities of discovery of new oil fields and technological progress in oil recovery. They have to consider the possibilities of production of petroleum from shale or coal, and of the development of synthetic substitutes.

A national policy dealing only with oil, it has been argued, is illogical since other sources of energy—coal, natural gas and hydroelectric power—compete with oil and, within limits, may be substituted for it. Hence, it has been said with some truth that there can be no reasonable oil policy except as part of a comprehensive national policy dealing with all forms of energy. Engineers have worked out the possibilities of substitution on the basis of British thermal units, but technical and cost factors, and consumers' preferences, substantially restrict, at least in the short run, the shifting from one fuel to another. Furthermore, conditions affecting supply and demand for each of the energy sources differ so widely that a unified policy would have to be couched in the most general terms. In this chapter, therefore, we shall concentrate on policy problems with respect to oil, keeping in mind, of course, the modifications which should be made in circumstances which permit substitution of other forms of energy.

Changing Conditions of Supply and Demand

Oil is an expendable, nonreplaceable resource. The United States, which consumes annually nearly 60 percent of the total Free World output of crude oil, has within its borders only 15 percent of the Free World's known oil reserves (i.e., oil recoverable in the present state of technology and under present conditions of costs and prices) and a smaller percentage of inferred reserves. During the last half century, Americans have frequently been warned that their oil resources were vanishing. In 1909, Dr. David T. Day of the Federal Geological Survey predicted a maximum recovery of 24½ billion barrels from fields known at the time.[1] In 1919, after the unprecedented consumption of gasoline and other petroleum products in World War I, it was estimated that the peak of American oil production would be reached within two years, and at the 1919 rate of production, American resources would be exhausted by 1936. Before that date, however, rich new oil fields were discovered in Texas and other Southwestern states, and in 1935 an exhaustive inquiry of the American Petroleum Institute found that American oil resources were in no imminent danger of depletion. In fact, the Institute's an-

[1] From fields known at the time and later discovered, the recovery of oil between 1909 and 1956 amounted to 53 billion barrels.

nual surveys have shown a steady increase in the estimates of "proved reserves," from 13.1 billion barrels in 1937 to 30.4 in 1957. These reserves represent oil actually known, as a result of drilling, to exist underground, recoverable under existing economic conditions and with existing technical procedures.[2]

World War II, with its huge consumption of motor fuel and other petroleum products, and later the Korean war and the subsequent rearmament drive, again aroused fears that our oil supplies would prove inadequate in a future emergency. A series of investigations were undertaken by Congressional committees, and oil was included in the studies by the Paley Commission in its searching inquiry into national resources of raw materials. The Commission warned against false interpretations of statistics on oil reserves:

> Public judgments of the prospects for future petroleum supplies have frequently been distorted because of popular misconceptions concerning the nature of proved reserves. Time after time the fact that proved reserves were equivalent to only about 12 to 15 years' production has come to the attention of publicists who have then sounded the alarm that the United States was about to run out of oil. Reserves must be considered not as the total reservoir from which all future production is to be drawn, but as the basis of operations, a sort of working inventory. Proved reserves are indeed like a reservoir, but a reservoir into which there is an inflow as well as an outflow. The fact that at any one time reserves are only a little more than a decade's outflow need not of itself be alarming if a steady inflow can be anticipated. The future position of United States oil production can accordingly be gaged not by the size of proved reserves but by the prospects for future discoveries relative to future demands on production.[3]

[2] Methods employed by the Institute in estimating reserves are described in the Bureau of Mines' *Mineral Facts and Problems* (1956), pp. 653-654. Such reserves are, of course, much less than the "potential reserves" (150 to 200 billion barrels) which geologists estimate may eventually be proved by discovery and drilling.

[3] *Resources for Freedom,* Report of the President's Materials Policy Commission (Washington: GPO, 1952), v. 3, *The Outlook for Energy Sources,* p. 5.

The accumulated total production of the two decades 1936-1956 was 36 billion. Nevertheless, at the end of the period proved reserves were 17 billion barrels greater than at the beginning. The explanation is found in the fairly steady year-by-year discovery of new oil, as well as in spectacular new discoveries, as in East Texas in 1930 and Illinois in 1937.

At some time, perhaps before the end of the present century, the production of oil from wells in the United States will begin to decline, but our oil resources may never be entirely exhausted. Before that time oil may be displaced by other sources of energy. The important fact, as the Tariff Commission pointed out, is the *rate* of disappearance.

> Even if we could know how much oil remains to be discovered and produced, the knowledge would be without much practical significance, if we did not also know when the oil would become available for use. A rate of discovery of 2 billion barrels annually over the next 25 years would have effects on the industry and the Nation vastly different from those of a rate of 1 billion or less a year for 50 years or more.[4]

All estimates of future availability of petroleum contain a large margin of error. Rates of discovery in the past have varied widely, upsetting predictions. Future increases in production and changes in rates of consumption are influenced by technological progress, by price trends and by the availability of substitute fuels. Furthermore, changes in government policy, restriction of imports by quota, for example, and limitations on the output of domestic wells are unpredictable factors. "Limitations of our domestic petroleum resources," the Paley Commission stated, "will exert upward pressures on real costs from now on. Experts generally agree that the real costs of crude oil discovery and development may rise considerably."[5] At another

[4] U. S. Tariff Commission, *Petroleum,* War Changes in Industry Series, Report no. 17 (Washington: GPO, 1946), p. 28.

[5] *Resources for Freedom,* cited, v. 1, *Foundations for Growth and Security,* p. 108. Comparisons of the trend of the price of crude oil with

place, the Paley report observed somewhat more cautiously:

> All in all, the available evidence gives some support to the argument that discovery and development of oil in the United States are becoming more costly, but this conclusion is not clearly established. It cannot be doubted, however, that at some time in the future, discovery in this country will become much more difficult, with attendant rises in cost, so that eventually alternatives to domestic crude oil production must be sought.[6]

The increasing depth of oil wells has often been cited as evidence of increasing costs. In 1925 the deepest oil-producing well in the United States was 7,591 feet. In 1956 the deepest well went down 21,000 feet. These data, however, are not conclusive. Between 1941 and 1956 contract drilling costs, which account for nearly 60 percent of total direct well costs, actually declined 7 percent for wells of comparable depth.[7] Improved recovery methods also checked the rise in the cost of "lifting"[8] oil as wells deepened. Finding and development, the major items in cost, are more apt to show an upward trend. In 1936, 21.5 percent of the total number of wells drilled yielded no oil; in 1946 the ratio had risen to 30.2 percent and in 1956 to

---

the general price level, affording a somewhat imperfect indication of variations in real costs, are shown below:

	Percent increase	
	Crude oil price	*Wholesale price index*
	(1947–49 = 100)	
1926 to 1956	48.4	75.2
1939 to 1956	173.2	127.3
1947–49 to 1956	18.3	13.9

Conclusions depend obviously on the selection of a base period. Over the long term it appears that oil prices have risen less steeply than the general price level, but in the short run, the years following World War II, oil prices rose faster.

[6] *Resources for Freedom,* v. 3, *The Outlook for Energy Sources,* cited, p. 6.

[7] See James R. Nelson, "Prices, Costs, and Conservation in Petroleum," *American Economic Review, Papers and Proceedings,* v. 48, no. 2 (May 1958), p. 509.

[8] The term refers to methods of bringing oil artificially to the surface, e.g., by injecting compressed air or gas or by mechanical pumping.

38.7. It is significant, however, that in the 20 years the percentage declined of exploratory wells (drilled outside known fields) that yielded no oil.

Rough estimates furnished to the Paley Commission showed a rise of about 50 percent in the real costs of finding and developing a *barrel of proved reserves* of crude oil between 1927-1930 and 1947-1950. But developments in reservoir engineering have improved oil recovery by 25 to 50 percent so that "for every barrel produced (as contrasted with discovered) the oil industry spends only very little more in constant dollars on finding and developing than in the past."[9]

Substitute fuels. Coal deposits in the United States may be rated as inexhaustible, within the time limits contemplated in this study. But the rapid progress made in recent years in substituting oil for coal makes a reversal of the process improbable. Electric power stations that maintain dual facilities could, in case of oil shortage, convert to coal, but for most consumers the substitution would be impractical because of capital expense and inconvenience.

Consumption of natural gas has shown rapid expansion. It has been widely substituted for fuel oil in residential and large heating installations and in power development, and in addition has special uses, for example, in the manufacture of carbon black. Reserves, estimated at nearly 240 trillion cubic feet, are approximately equal, on a heat-equivalent basis, to proved reserves of crude oil. The Paley Commission saw no prospect of declining supplies of natural gas before the end of the century. The Bureau of Mines is equally optimistic.

Rising costs of producing crude oil may bring about commercial production from oil-bearing shale in the near future, perhaps within the next decade or two. The Bureau of Mines has done much pioneering research in this field in laboratories and demonstration plants. The only known deposits of oil shale in the United States that

[9] *Resources for Freedom*, v. 3, *The Outlook for Energy Sources*, cited, p. 5.

would have commercial value, however, are in Colorado, Utah and Wyoming, at a great distance from the principal markets for liquid fuels. Transportation costs, therefore, will be a bar to large-scale development. Lack of adequate water supply will hamper large-scale refining operations. The Bureau of Mines has also experimented with the production of synthetic gasoline from coal by processes used commercially in Europe, but costs in this country at present are too high to permit competition with gasoline distilled from crude oil.

Long-range policy must consider the possibilities of supplementing our present fuel and energy resources with nuclear power. One expert in the field has said that within the next five or ten years power derived from nuclear reactors will be "barely competitive" with power generated from coal-burning plants and hydroelectric stations. If the prices of conventional fuel continue to rise the time span may be shortened, for it is probable that costs of nuclear power will decrease.[10] Nuclear power, when it is available commercially, will add to the total energy pool, but like coal will not replace petroleum products in special uses.

Within the time span considered in this book, i.e., the next 20 or 25 years, it seems probable that power generated from atomic fission will be able to compete with power supplied by hydro and steam generating plants, in locations where the latter is expensive. In September 1957, a Special Policy Committee of the National Planning Association on the Productive Uses of Nuclear Energy reported as follows on U. S. needs and programs:

Nuclear energy — as industrial process heat and electric power — is assumed to become competitive in the highest cost regions by 1965, and to decrease progressively in cost thereafter. On comparative cost considerations alone — and these may not be controlling — nuclear energy by 1980 is projected to supply

10 "Nuclear Power and Foreign Policy" by Henry DeWolf Smyth, *Foreign Affairs,* v. 35, no. 1 (October 1956), p. 9.

less than 10 percent of total energy consumption and more than 20 percent of total electrical power generation.[11]

In early 1958 a report of the Technical Appraisal Task Force on Nuclear Power to the directors of the Edison Electric Institute said:

> The Task Force believes that there is a good probability of reducing the cost of nuclear power sufficiently in the next ten years to make it competitive with power from fossil fuels in some parts of the United States. . . .[12]

The trend of demand. Against the uncertainties of the domestic supply of crude oil, the certainty of rising demand for refined products stands out in sharp contrast. Here is the crux of the oil problem. The American petroleum industry has developed over 5,000 products, six of which fill nearly 90 percent of the total demand. They are:

Gasoline, used for motor vehicles and motor boats, airplanes and farm machinery.
Kerosene, for household cooking, water-heating and small space-heating.
Distillate or light fuel oil, for diesel engines in trucks, buses and railway locomotives and also for heating of private homes.
Lubricants, oils and greases for industrial and automotive uses.
Residual fuel oil, for ships' bunkers, for generating electric power in large industrial plants and in public utilities, and for heating apartment houses and other large buildings.
Jet fuel, a relatively new product, a blend of low-grade gasoline with kerosene and distillate fuel oil.

The rising domestic consumption of petroleum products is shown in Table 38.

Improved refining techniques have made possible considerable variation in the proportions of the various joint products derived from crude oil. "If crude petroleum is subject to simple distillation alone, the various end products

[11] National Planning Association, *Productive Uses of Nuclear Energy* (Washington: Author, 1957), p. 16.
[12] "Status and Prospects of Nuclear Power . . . An Interim Survey," as quoted in the *New York Times*, March 16, 1958.

Table 38

U. S. DEMAND[a] FOR REFINED PETROLEUM PRODUCTS, 1939, 1946-1956

(in millions of barrels)

Year	*Gasoline*	*Distil-late*	*Residual*	*Lubri-cants*	*All Other*	*Total*
1939	556	132	314	24	205	1,231
1946	735	243	477	35	303	1,793
1947	795	298	519	36	342	1,995
1948	871	341	501	36	365	2,114
1949	914	329	496	33	346	2,110
1950	994	395	554	39	393	2,370
1951	1,090	447	564	42	427	2,578
1952	1,157	479	555	38	435	2,664
1953	1,206	488	560	40	481	2,775
1954	1,231	526	522	38	515	2,832
1955	1,334	581	557	43	573	3,088
1956	1,373	616	563	44	617	3,213

[a] Production plus imports less exports, adjusted for differences in inventories at beginning and end of year.
Source: U. S. Bureau of Mines

. . . are formed in virtually fixed proportions. By catalytic cracking processes, widely adopted since World War II, the middle distillates (kerosene and gas oil) can be converted into gasoline plus residual fuel oil. With additional equipment gasoline may be derived from residual oil. Consequently, the refiners can now choose an optimal product mix whereas formerly they were limited to a single optimal rate of total output."[13]

The variations in yield over the past 10 years reflect significant changes in demand. The substitution of diesel engines for steam locomotives on railroads has been in part responsible for the rise in distillate fuel oil from 16.6 percent in 1946 to 22.9 in 1956. This change is also responsible in part for the decline in the yield of residual fuel oil from 24.9 percent in 1946 to 14.7 percent in 1956. The total quantity of residual fuel oil consumed, however,

[13] Alan S. Manne, "Oil Refining: Yield Coefficients and Actual Prices," *Quarterly Journal of Economics,* v. 65, no. 3 (August 1951), p. 400.

gained 18 percent. Sales to western railroads fell off when diesel engines replaced oil-burning steam locomotives. But this loss was somewhat more than offset by increased consumption by public utilities, in power plants, and in large space-heating installations where residual fuel oil was substituted for coal.

The Trade Deficit

In terms of international oil trade the United States has become in postwar years a deficit country. (See Table 39.)

Table 39

U. S. TRADE IN CRUDE OIL AND REFINED PRODUCTS, 1939, 1946, 1956

	1939	*1946*	*1956*
		Quantity (in millions of barrels)	
Exports	179.6	136.5	123.7
Imports	52.4	144.6	533.7
Surplus of exports	127.2	—	—
Surplus of imports	—	8.1	410.0
		Value (millions of dollars)	
Exports	364.1	387.9	664.5
Imports	35.1	158.6	1,259.9
Surplus of exports	329.0	229.3	—
Surplus of imports	—	—	595.4

Source: U. S. Bureau of the Census

The causes of the decline (quantitatively) in shipments abroad are to be found in the rapid expansion of both United States consumption and of foreign production, especially in the Middle East. Furthermore, the scarcity of dollars in Western Europe caused a shift in purchases of crude oil from the Western Hemisphere to the Middle East. Exports from the United States now consist almost entirely (87 percent by value) of refined products, of which nearly one-fifth is high-priced aviation gasoline. Hence, the 1956 value of the exports, although the quantity had fallen, was considerably greater than in 1939 and 1946. (See Table 40.)

Table 40

U. S. EXPORTS OF CRUDE PETROLEUM AND PETROLEUM PRODUCTS, 1929, 1932, 1936-1956

(in millions of barrels)

Year	*Crude petroleum*	*Residual fuel oil*	*All other petroleum products*	*Total*
1929	26.4	[a]	126.4	152.8
1932	27.4	9.7	59.9	97.0
1936–40 (av.)	63.7	13.6	76.5	153.8
1941–45 (av.)	36.7	9.8	96.5	143.0
1946–50 (av.)	39.2	8.7	69.3	117.3
1951–55 (av.)	20.1	22.9	73.9	116.9
1951	28.6	24.1	75.9	128.6
1952	26.7	22.4	83.4	132.5
1953	19.9	19.9	78.5	118.4
1954	13.6	20.3	67.6	101.5
1955	11.5	27.5	64.3	103.3
1956	28.5	22.2	73.1	123.7

[a] Included in all other petroleum products.
Source: U. S. Bureau of the Census.

Measured in dollars, petroleum and its products, with a total value of $1,260 million, in 1956 ranked second (next to coffee) among American imports. In that year they constituted ten percent of all U. S. imports and almost 25 percent of all imports of crude and semimanufactured materials. In postwar years the imports have increased six times in value and three times in quantity.

Crude petroleum—350 million barrels valued at $829 million in 1956—constitutes the bulk of the imports. The balance consists almost exclusively of residual fuel oil. The growth of American industrial production and the quickening of business activity of all kinds stimulated imports of petroleum products. (See Table 41.) The same influences, of course, have caused the expansion of do-

Table 41

U. S. IMPORTS OF CRUDE PETROLEUM AND PETROLEUM PRODUCTS, 1929, 1932, 1936-1956

(in millions of barrels)

Year	*Crude petroleum*	*Residual[a] fuel oil*	*All other petroleum products*	*Total*
1929	78.9	20.5	9.1	108.5
1932	44.7	21.7	8.5	74.9
1936–40 (av.)	29.7	25.3	3.6	58.6
1941–45 (av.)	39.6	30.3	15.9	85.8
1946–50 (av.)	128.6	72.6	7.1	208.2
1951–55 (av.)	230.5	136.3	11.5	378.3
1951	177.5	121.8	8.6	308.0
1952	205.4	132.1	10.7	348.3
1953	233.0	139.6	7.6	380.2
1954	242.2	132.3	13.7	388.2
1955	294.3	155.8	16.9	466.9
1956	350.4	165.4	17.8	533.7

[a] Including topped crude in 1929, 1932, 1936-38.
Source: U. S. Bureau of the Census

mestic oil production. Chart O shows that the remarkably rapid growth of imports over the past 25 years outstripped domestic production. In prewar years imports were 4.7 percent of domestic production. The ratio in 1956 was 20.4 percent. (See Table 42.)

Sources of Imports

Western Hemisphere countries, principally Venezuela, in 1946 supplied 98 percent of U. S. imports of petroleum and its products; 10 years later, because of the rapid increase in receipts of Middle East oil, the percentage share had fallen to less than 80. In 1956 Venezuela,[14] the world's largest exporter of crude petroleum, alone supplied 175 million barrels of crude oil and 147 million barrels of residual oil out of total U. S. imports of these products of

[14] Large quantities of petroleum products refined from Venezuelan crude oil are exported from the port of Aruba in the Dutch West Indies. Hence, in this chapter, imports into the United States from that colony are added to those received directly from Venezuela.

CHART O

U. S. PRODUCTION OF CRUDE PETROLEUM AND IMPORTS AND EXPORTS OF PETROLEUM AND PRODUCTS, 1929-1956

(in millions of barrels)

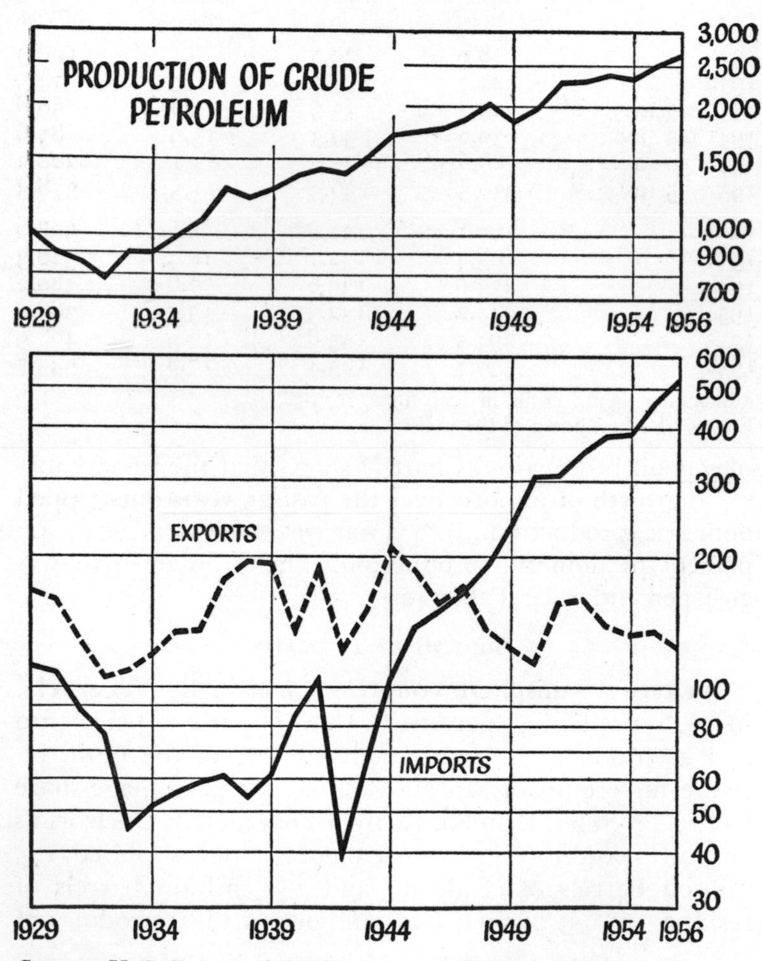

Source: U. S. Bureau of the Census, U. S. Bureau of Mines

Table 42

U. S. IMPORTS OF PETROLEUM AS A PROPORTION OF DOMESTIC PRODUCTION, 1929, 1932, 1936-1956

(in percent)

Year	*Ratio of imports of crude oil to production of crude oil*	*Ratio of imports of residual oil to production of crude oil*	*Ratio of all petroleum imports to production of crude oil*
1929	7.8	2.0	10.8
1932	5.7	2.8	9.5
1936–40 (av.)	2.4	2.0	4.7
1941–45 (av.)	2.6	2.0	5.6
1946–50 (av.)	6.8	3.8	11.0
1951–55 (av.)	9.9	5.8	16.2
1951	7.9	5.4	13.7
1952	9.0	5.8	15.2
1953	9.9	5.9	16.1
1954	10.5	5.7	16.8
1955	11.8	6.3	18.8
1956	13.4	6.3	20.4

Source: U. S. Bureau of Mines, U. S. Bureau of the Census

350 million and 165 million barrels respectively. (See Table 43.) Venezuela's production is about 2.5 million barrels daily (the U. S. figure is roughly 7.0 million). Known reserves are reported to be 15 billion barrels, a figure which undoubtedly will be increased as reservoirs are found in the extensive new areas opened in 1956 for exploration and development.

Residual fuel oil, used principally in ships' bunkers and large heating installations, is imported almost exclusively from Venezuela and from offshore islands in the Netherlands West Indies, where large refineries treat Venezuelan crude. U. S. imports of this oil from all sources rose from 77 million barrels in 1949 to 165 million in 1956, valued at $366 million.

Foreign Production

The competition of Venezuelan oil in American markets depends upon advantages in transportation costs, in the

Table 43

U. S. IMPORTS OF CRUDE PETROLEUM AND PETROLEUM PRODUCTS, BY COUNTRIES, 1946, 1956

(in thousands of barrels)

Country of origin	*Year*	*Crude petroleum*	*Residual fuel oil*	*All other*	*Total*
Canada	1946	—	72	157	229
	1956	43,228	603	1,663	45,494
Venezuela and N.W.I.	1946	74,362	46,028	5,316	125,706
	1956	174,650	146,698	14,779	336,127
Other Western Hemisphere	1946	13,029	1,428	1,964	16,421
	1956	16,652	16,410	637	33,699
Total, Western Hemisphere	1946	87,391	47,528	7,437	142,356
	1956	234,530	163,711	17,079	415,320
Middle East	1946	115	3	2,077	2,195
	1956	102,700	1,697	724	105,121
Other Eastern Hemisphere	1946	—	1	—	1
	1956	13,213	—	38	13,251
Total, Eastern Hemisphere	1946	115	4	2,077	2,196
	1956	115,913	1,697	762	118,372
Total, all countries	1946	87,506	47,532	9,514	144,552
	1956	350,443	165,408	17,841	533,692

Source: U. S. Bureau of the Census

quality of the product and in the yield of oil wells. The distance from ports in northern South America to the refineries at Philadelphia and New York (1,900 miles) is practically the same as from United States ports on the Gulf of Mexico. Much of the Venezuelan crude is of heavier gravity than the average domestic product and hence more suitable for producing residual fuel oil. But the domestic demand in Venezuela for gasoline and distillates has increased faster than the demand for residual oil; hence, the need to find export markets for this product.

The average well in Venezuela yields about 220 barrels per day. In Texas the average is 20 barrels, in Louisiana 48 and in the entire United States 13-14 barrels, although several hundred thousand "stripper"[15] wells average only

[15] "The term 'stripper wells' has been used in the petroleum industry for many years in a more or less generic sense without specific definition.

3 barrels. In part, the lower average production of American wells is the result of closer spacing.

Venezuela's ability to export petroleum and its products to the United States is not the result of low wage rates. The Creole Petroleum Corporation, one of the largest Venezuelan producers, under a three-year collective wage contract, 1953-1956, paid a minimum of $3,287 per year to ordinary labor. The annual take-home pay of a skilled workman was $5,896.[16] Moreover, the average worker in the Venezuelan oil industry was said to receive in cash, subsistence and other benefits nearly three times his basic wage. On this basis, the cost to the Creole Corporation of its lowest paid workers was estimated at $18 per day and for foremen $40.[17] In the United States the basic wages paid by the Standard Oil Company to hourly rated employees averaged $2.50 per hour.

Middle East Oil

The world's largest reserves of oil, 70 percent of the Free World's total, are centered in the area surrounding the Persian Gulf, chiefly in Iran, Iraq, Saudi Arabia, and the states of Kuwait, Qatar and Bahrein. In 1946 these Middle East countries supplied about 2 million barrels, less than one-half of one percent of total United States imports. Ten years later, the imports of Middle East oil were 105 million barrels, 20 percent of the United States total.

(Some engineers contend that a 'stripper' well is not subject to exact definition.) In the early days of the industry a stripper well was one through which the last remnant of recoverable oil was being 'stripped' from the producing sand." The Bureau of Mines uses the term to denote marginal wells, "those in which the value of the oil produced approaches the cost of production, having only a small margin of profit." See U. S. Bureau of Mines, *Mineral Facts and Problems,* Bulletin 556 (Washington: GPO, 1956), p. 633.

16 Statement of Harold W. Haight, president of the Creole Petroleum Corporation, in *Trade Agreements Extension,* Hearings before the House Ways and Means Committee, 84th Cong., 1st sess., on H.R. 1 (Washington: GPO, 1955), p. 450.

17 Wayne C. Taylor and John Lindeman, *The Creole Petroleum Corporation in Venezuela, A Case Study in United States Business Performance Abroad* (Washington: National Planning Association, 1955), p. 70.

Middle East oil finds its principal market in Western Europe. In selling to the United States, transportation costs are a handicap, for the distance from the Persian Gulf to U. S. East Coast ports, via Suez, is 8,500 miles, 6,600 miles farther than from Venezuela and ports on the Gulf of Mexico. Wages in the Middle East have risen steeply since World War II, but are still far below United States levels. In Saudi Arabia, the minimum daily wage in 1956 was $1.73, but, in addition, the oil companies made large outlays for supplemental benefits, for health and education and for many other services provided in the United States at government expense. Moreover, a large proportion of the labor force, as high as 30 percent in Saudi Arabia, consists of engineers and other technical personnel of nonlocal origin whose pay approximates American standards. The decisive factor, however, in Middle East competition in the American market is not labor costs but the high yield of its wells, which are said to average about 5,000 barrels daily.

At present, practically all the foreign oil brought into the United States is imported by a relatively few (25-30) companies who have large investments in domestic oil wells, refineries, transportation and marketing facilities, in Venezuela and Canada as well as in the Middle East. The inflow of foreign oil is therefore affected by factors not related to differences between foreign and domestic costs of production. As producers of crude oil in the United States, the importing companies are interested in supporting its price. But they also purchase crude oil for their domestic refineries from independent producers, and in these operations find low prices advantageous. Under such conditions the determination of the amount of imports which will maximize net profits poses a complex problem of economic calculation.

The American Oil Industry

The American petroleum industry in 1956 gave employment to over 2 million persons. Its gross assets had an estimated value of more than $50 billion. Some 18,000 firms were engaged in production (including exploration and drilling for oil), about 500 in refining crude oil and in manufacturing lubricants and greases. Transportation of the crude oil and its products occupied 1,400 firms. There were 30,000 wholesale distributors and 188,000 retail outlets (service stations).

The industry's wells are scattered over 28 states. Five states (Texas, California, Louisiana, Oklahoma and Kansas) supplied 80 percent of the 1956 output; Texas alone supplied 42 percent. The bulk of production came from three principal regions, the Gulf of Mexico, Mid-Continent and California. Each of these regions has a preferential, but not a monopoly, position in the three chief areas of consumption. The geographical distribution of domestic oil has been described as follows: "Oil flows from the producing areas in three main streams—from the ports of the Gulf of Mexico by sea to the Eastern seaboard; from the Mid-Continent area of Kansas, Oklahoma and Northern Texas north by pipeline and rail to the great industrial and population centers of the northern Middle West; from the California fields to West Coast and transpacific markets."[18]

Imported crude oil is refined on the East Coast, where it constitutes 60 percent of the supply, competing with the domestic crude. The refined products are marketed on the East Coast and also in the Mid-Continent area. Oil imported into West Coast ports supplies about 30 percent of consumption in the Pacific Coast states.

Producers of petroleum fall into two groups whose interests are to a considerable extent divergent and whose views on national policy, in consequence, sometimes conflict. There are some 35 large integrated companies with operations covering all branches of the industry, from exploration and discovery of crude oil to retail distribution of gasoline and other refined products. They produce about 58 percent of the total Free World's output and refine about 65 percent. Included in this group are five major

[18] Eugene V. Rostow, *A National Policy for the Oil Industry* (New Haven: Yale University Press, 1948), p. 9.

companies[19] who have made large investments in oil production, refining, transportation and marketing in foreign countries. In 1955 about two-thirds of their output was derived from their foreign wells, and about 90 percent of their proved reserves are located abroad. Imports from their foreign wells and refineries constitute the bulk of United States oil imports. These American companies are linked with two great foreign oil groups, Royal Dutch Shell and British Petroleum, through joint holdings in subsidiaries and by agreements for the purchase and sale of crude oil and refined products, and for the use of patent rights. In 1955 the seven companies were said to control nearly 90 percent of all foreign oil. Standard Oil of New Jersey is the largest American company. Seventy-six percent of the 1954 production of its affiliated companies originated in foreign countries. Two-thirds of their output of gasoline and other petroleum products were refined abroad. About 60 percent of the output of its foreign refineries was marketed outside the United States.

The Independent Producers

The second division of the American oil industry, the independent producers, embraces some 18,000 units. Among them are companies and individuals who operate on a large scale, with investments in foreign countries as well as in the United States, but the majority are small enterprises with no interests outside the country. The small operator finds it easy to get started as an oil producer. He needs practically no capital; he pays for drilling and other expenses with shares in the lease. But, because of the speculative nature of the business, the mortality rate among small producers is high. Yet most of the drilling for oil in the United States has been done by small and medium-sized operators. Their activities now supply two-fifths of total United States production.

There are many sellers of crude oil but only a small number of buyers, the companies who own pipelines and

[19] Socony-Mobil Oil, Standard Oil of California, Standard Oil of New Jersey, The Texas Company and Gulf Oil.

refineries. Hence there arises a conflict of interest between the independents and the integrated companies. Yet each group needs the other. An experienced oil man has described the interrelation of independents and integrated companies as follows:

> The American petroleum industry is made up of a number of rather large corporations. Some have foreign oil supplies and some do not. Each of these companies . . . is the nucleus for an oil finding effort. Nearly all independents' operations are in an orbit around one or more of these companies. The so-called independent frequently looks to these companies as a source for farm-out leases, for some financing, and most importantly for market outlets. In a way, they [i.e., the independents] are part-time, extra hands for the companies. They can move fast, make decisions quickly. Independents are, in effect, usually one-generation oil companies. But the results of their activities, particularly in oil finding, are eventually merged into bigger and better known perpetuated corporations and become a substantial part of the domestic industry. These independent operators drill about 85 per cent of all the wells that are drilled in this country and they operate in a very wide range of skillfulness. Some are better at promoting money than they are in actually finding oil. All together they make a lot of mistakes, drill a lot of wells that better informed operators or well-equipped companies would not touch. But the nature of oil finding is such that it takes efforts on a wide scale to locate what we have. Many of our best fields have been found or developed by independents who didn't "know any better."[20]

The State of the Industry

Judged by aggregate figures, the American oil industry is in a flourishing condition. The rising level of operations in the past 10 years is shown on page 306.

The earnings of the gas and oil producing companies are among the highest to be found in any manufacturing or mining industry. They have been sufficient to supply large annual investments of new capital. But wide variations in profits are to found among the firms that comprise the oil industry, and also among producing areas. Examin-

[20] Information supplied by Harry W. Bass, president of the Wilcox Trend Oil Company, Dallas, Texas.

	1946	*1956*
Output of crude oil (million barrels)	1,734	2,617
Wholesale value of refined products (million dollars)	3,950	11,603[a]
Employment, crude petroleum and natural gas (thousands)	220	330
Producing oil wells drilled	16,067	30,528
Proved reserves (billion barrels end of year)	20.9	30.4

[a] 1955.

ation of the trend in crude oil output by states shows that in some areas production declined, and among those which gained there was a wide variation above and below the national average.

Comparison of 1956 with 1946 output gives the following results:

	Percent
National increase in production	51
States showing increase in production:	
Colorado	413
Wyoming	168
Montana	145
New Mexico	139
Louisiana	107
Indiana	71
Mississippi	67
Oklahoma	60
Texas	46
Kansas	27
California	12
Illinois	9
States showing decrease in production:	
New York	43
Pennsylvania	37
Michigan	36
West Virginia	16

Oil Policies, State and Federal

Measures which constitute national oil policy may be grouped under these headings:

(1) Tax incentives, land laws and other federal legislation designed to promote oil production;

(2) Restrictions on production imposed by state governments, with federal cooperation;
(3) Activities of the federal government designed to assist American companies to develop oil reserves in foreign countries.

Federal legislation designed to promote the expansion of domestic oil production includes the statistical and scientific services of the Department of the Interior, especially the Bureau of Mines, and also special provisions of tax laws. The principal item in this category is the percentage depletion allowance, authorized in the Revenue Act of 1926, which has been discussed in Chapter 2. The Act authorized oil and gas companies to deduct from net taxable income a tax credit amounting to 27½ percent of gross sales (but not to exceed 50 percent of net revenue) on account of depletion of natural resources.[21] By choosing percentage depletion rather than the alternate method of cost depletion, oil producers have been able substantially to reduce their net taxable incomes.

In the past 30 years the privilege of computing the depletion allowance at the rate of 27½ percent on gross sales has been equivalent to granting the owners of oil wells a subsidy whose value has increased with the rising price of oil (see Chart P) and with rising rates of the federal tax on the income of corporations.

Restriction of Oil Production by State Governments

Tax incentives, designed to stimulate oil production, contrast strangely with restrictions on production imposed by state governments. Each month the U. S. Bureau of Mines estimates the market demand, domestic and export, for gasoline and for crude oil. The Bureau's estimates, broken down by states, are used, together with other market data, by state authorities in fixing the quotas of allowable production for oil wells. A well-known oil man described the process as follows:

21 An act of 1951 permitted producers of other mineral products to calculate depletion by the percentage method, but at lower rates.

CHART P

U. S. AVERAGE PRICE OF CRUDE PETROLEUM AT WELL AND WHOLESALE PRICES OF ALL COMMODITIES, 1929-1957
(index numbers, 1947-49 = 100)

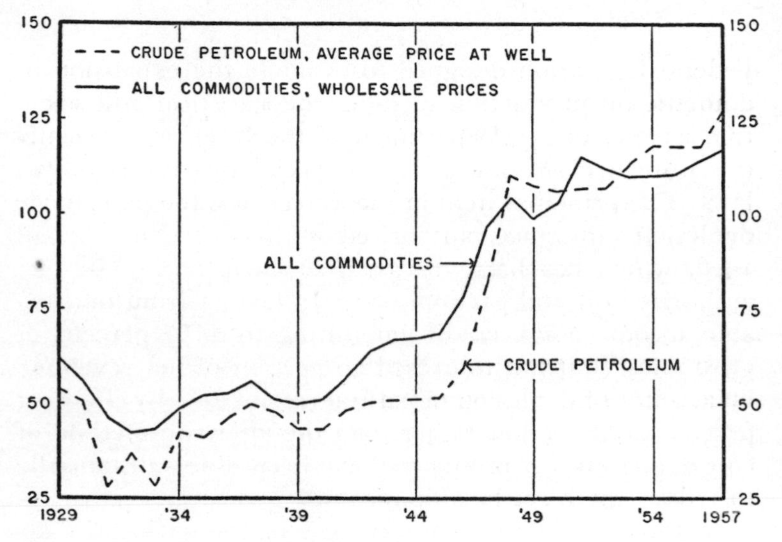

Source: U. S. Bureau of Labor Statistics
U. S. Bureau of Mines

The proration mechanism is provided with advisory estimates of demand subdivided into State allocations, prepared monthly by the U. S. Bureau of Mines. These quotas are viewed as evidence of demand by the administrative bodies in the States and serve a useful purpose as a check on the quotas determined in the States by a summation and adjustment of buyers' nominations. The State quotas, accordingly, do not match precisely the advisory figures, although there is a general tendency toward approximate conformance. . . . These estimates are welcomed by the State administrative bodies and constitute a comparison for the market demand level which the proration mechanism seeks to approximate with supply.[22]

The Bureau of Mines persistently denies that its advisory estimates have anything to do with oil prices. In effect,

[22] Statement of Joseph E. Pogue, in *Investigation of Concentration of Economic Power,* Hearings before the Temporary National Economic Committee, 76th Cong., 2d sess. (Washington: GPO, 1940), pt. 14, sec. 1, p. 7448.

however, they constitute predictions of how much oil can be sold at the prevailing price. The Bureau's allocations to the states actually become production quotas.

Texas, the largest producing state, rigidly enforces the "allowables" fixed by its Railroad Commission.[23] Texas, Louisiana, Oklahoma, New Mexico, Arkansas, Kansas and North Dakota issue monthly proration orders "to adjust production to market demand." Taken together, these states in 1956 produced nearly three-fourths of the national total. In California, a committee of the oil industry each month sets the maximum production for the state and divides it among oil wells.

Illinois, a large producing state, places no restrictions on oil production. In certain other states, compliance with prorationing is voluntary, but the over-all result is substantially to restrict production of crude oil. Spare capacity, which in 1955 was "shut in" for lack of a market, would have provided, temporarily, an additional output of 2 million barrels daily, nearly 30 percent of actual production.[24] According to a later estimate, 1957 productive capacity was 3 million barrels a day above actual production.

Conservation and Price Control

Price support was the objective of the earliest state legislation and administrative measures that restricted oil production. (An Oklahoma statute of 1914 forbade producers to take more oil from their wells than could be sold at 65 cents a barrel.) When they were declared unconstitutional by federal courts, the state legislatures introduced prorationing, thus sanctifying price control by combining with it the conservation motive. Until the late 1920's, oil wells

[23] The process of prorationing was described by General Ernest O. Thompson, a member of the Commission, in *Petroleum Survey,* Hearings before the House Committee on Interstate and Foreign Commerce, 85th Cong., 1st sess. (Washington: GPO, 1957), especially p. 217.

[24] This figure was cited by spokesmen for both the independent producers and the integrated companies. See *Trade Agreements Extension,* Hearings before the Senate Finance Committee, 84th Cong., 1st sess., on H.R. 1 (Washington: GPO, 1955), pp. 1785, 1913.

were producing "wide open," and much natural gas was either blown into the air or burned (flared). Gusher wells spread great pools of oil over surrounding territory before they could be capped. Much inert oil also was left in the ground and could not be recovered. The Texas Oil Conservation Act of 1919 provided that gas and oil should not be produced in such a way as to constitute waste. The administration of the act was assigned to the Texas Railroad Commission with authority to supervise the spacing of wells. Legislation similarly stressing conservation was enacted by Louisiana in 1926.

The large annual increases in crude oil production following the discovery of new oil fields in California in the early 1920's, in Oklahoma in 1926 and in Texas in 1930, were responsible for a strong downward trend in prices. Shrinking demand for refined products, caused by the business collapse, depressed crude oil prices still further. When the bottom was reached in 1931 the United States average price of crude oil was 65 cents a barrel, about 35 percent of the 1926 price. Texas crude, at this time, was selling for 13 cents. In this situation the federal government intervened. In 1932 the U. S. Supreme Court upheld the state prorationing laws. In the Connally Act Congress prohibited the interstate movement of "hot oil," produced in violation of state laws.[25] The federal government also has blessed with its approval the Interstate Compact to conserve oil which coordinates the restrictive legislation of 30 oil-producing states.

Prorationing regulations, if they are to be 100 percent effective as conservation[26] measures, should adjust the flow of oil from each field according to its MER, its maximum efficient rate of production. If unrestricted, the flow would be determined, in primary recovery, by the pressure exerted by underground water or gas on the oil-bearing strata. By limiting the flow, it is theoretically possible to

[25] Enacted in 1935, for a period of two years, this legislation has been extended periodically. The latest extension, in 1955, was for a period of four years.

[26] Conservation is used here in the physical sense, without reference to the probable future value of the oil.

maintain the pressure, so as to obtain from the field the maximum amount it can yield, i.e., reduce to a minimum the unrecoverable residue. This is the theory of prorationing, but the practice shows considerable divergence.

In the first place, the MER is not an exact figure, but only a rough approximation, subject to error in the order of 10 to 20 percent. Secondly, MER's are fixed in relation to the quantity of oil recoverable by primary operations, which leave in the ground up to a third of the oil. But by water flooding, and other secondary operations, additional amounts may be recovered, and still further recovery may be possible by tertiary operations, which are still in an experimental stage. Thirdly, state regulatory bodies do not base their prorationing orders exclusively on calculation of the maximum rates of recovery. They take into consideration, also, the market for crude oil. If demand is sluggish, the "allowables" will be fixed below the calculated MER.

"Price 'stabilization'," wrote Myron Watkins, "is a thinly veiled objective of the institution of oil proration, and in fact, as it has developed in the several state jurisdictions, it may be stated unreservedly to have been everywhere the dominant desideratum."[27] Comments in the daily press and in trade journals confirm Dr. Watkins' observation. The *Oil and Gas Journal* complained editorially, July 2, 1956, that crude oil was "in seriously long supply." The situation, it said, could not be corrected "unless the prorating states simultaneously curtail to actual market demand." The same publication, on July 9, 1956, accused the Oklahoma Corporation Commission, the prorationing authority, of concentrating its political sympathy on oil producers, ignoring market demand, in order to force purchasers to take more crude than they wanted. The Texas Railroad Commission, on February 20, 1958, cut the allowable oil production for March to the equivalent of 9 days' production. The cutback followed

[27] "Scarce Raw Materials: An Analysis and a Proposal," *American Economic Review*, v. 34, no. 2 (June 1944), p. 254. See also Eugene V. Rostow, *A National Policy for the Oil Industry*, cited, Ch. 5, and Clair Wilcox, *Public Policies toward Business* (Chicago: Irwin, 1955), p. 477.

requests from both producers and purchasers that output be reduced to shrink the industry's excessive stocks. "The Texas Railroad Commission," said W. C. Whaley, president of the Sunray Mid-Continent Oil Company, "has met the challenge of too much oil by reducing allowables in Texas. . . ."[28]

Despite the predominant emphasis on price control, prorationing must be credited with real achievement in preventing physical waste and in increasing the total amount of oil which can be recovered from a given field. But even with the most scrupulous attention to the MER, real conservation is impossible as long as the "law of capture" permits each landowner to regulate his drilling so as to get all the oil possible from the underlying reservoir. The remedy is the "unitization" of each oil field, its exploitation under common management. In some states oil producers have entered into voluntary unitization agreements; in general they are not compulsory.

Import-Excise Taxes

The restriction of oil production logically led to demands for the restriction of imports. The transition in U. S. tariff policies from free trade in oil to a restrictive policy has a long history. Voluntary quotas were tried first. In 1930, at the request of the Secretary of Commerce, the principal U. S. companies operating in Venezuela cut their production by about one-third, and reduced their imports of crude oil and gasoline. When the resulting decline in imports into the United States did not satisfy the independent producers, they sponsored legislation which would have limited imports to less than one-fifth the amounts then entering. Congress rejected this proposal, but instead imposed import taxes.

Until 1932, petroleum and refined products entered the United States free of duty. The Revenue Act of that year imposed a "tax" of ½ cent a gallon (21 cents a barrel of 42 gallons) on imports of crude petroleum, residual fuel oil and distillate fuel oil (diesel oil). The tax on im-

28 Quoted in *New York Times,* February 21, 1958.

ported gasoline was 2½ cents per gallon and on lubricating oil 4 cents. Compared with current import prices—crude was then selling for 64 cents a barrel and gasoline at 3.6 cents a gallon—the taxes were substantial, amounting to 33 percent of the foreign value of crude petroleum and 70 percent of the foreign value of gasoline.

The 1939 trade agreement with Venezuela imposed a tariff quota on crude oil and fuel oils. The agreement reduced the import taxes by 50 percent, but the reduction applied in any year only to a quota of imports equal to 5 percent of the quantity of crude oil processed in American refineries in the previous year. Imports in excess of that amount remained dutiable at the 1932 rate of one-half cent per gallon.

The quota limitation was removed in the 1943 trade agreement with Mexico, so that during the life of this agreement all imports of crude and fuel oils took the one-quarter cent rate. With the termination of the Mexican agreement in 1950, all imports were again taxed at the rates provided in the 1939 agreement with Venezuela. A second agreement (1952) with that country eliminated the quota restriction.[29] At the same time the taxes on imports of crude and fuel oil below 25 degrees API gravity were reduced to 1/8 cent a gallon (5.25 cents per barrel). This change was intended to benefit Venezuela, the country from which the heavier oils are principally imported. Table 44 summarizes the changes in oil import taxes in the years 1932-1957.

The NRA code for the petroleum industry authorized the President to fix quotas on petroleum imports. Under this legislation imports were limited to about 4.5 percent of domestic consumption. For several years after 1935, when the National Recovery Act was declared unconstitutional, the major companies voluntarily kept their im-

[29] This action of President Truman disregarded a finding of the Tariff Commission. The Commission had held that removal of the quota would violate the peril-point provision of the 1951 Trade Agreements Extension Act (Sec. 3a). See U. S. Tariff Commission, *Report to the President . . . with Respect to Certain Petroleum Products* (Washington: Author, 1952).

Table 44

U. S. IMPORT-EXCISE TAXES ON CRUDE PETROLEUM AND PETROLEUM PRODUCTS

(in cents per gallon)

	Act of 1930	*Revenue Act of 1932*	*As of 1945*	*As of 1948*	*As of 1957*
Crude petroleum:					
Testing under 25 degrees API	Free	½	¼	¼	⅛
Testing 25 degrees API or more	Free	½	¼	¼	¼
Gasoline	Free	2½	2½	1¼	1¼
Distillate fuel oil					
Testing under 25 degrees API	Free	½	¼	¼	⅛
Testing 25 degrees API or more	Free	½	¼	¼	¼
Lubricating oils	Free	4	4	2	2
Residual fuel oil:					
Testing under 25 degrees API	Free	½	¼	¼	⅛
Testing 25 degrees API or more	Free	½	¼	¼	¼

Note: All crude petroleum and products were tax-exempt when imported for government use and all refined products when purchased for supplies of vessels and aircraft.

ports at about this ratio,[30] but in postwar years it has been greatly exceeded. (See Table 42.)

The import taxes imposed by the Act of 1932 affected principally refined products, and imports of gasoline soon became insignificant. For a number of years, imports of residual fuel oil for the most part entered free of tax as bunker oil for merchant vessels. Later, with the increase in total imports of residual oil, the exemption became less significant. In 1956, out of total imports of 165 million barrels, 32 million entered free of tax on this account. Imports of residual oil for government use are not taxable.

On imports of crude oil the impact of the tax was lessened by the upward trend of oil prices and the corresponding fall in the *ad valorem* equivalent of the tax. When imposed, the one-half cent rate was 33 percent of foreign value. In 1939 it was 30 percent; in 1946 the one-fourth

30 U. S. Tariff Commission, *Petroleum,* War Changes in Industry Series (1946), cited, pp. 76-77.

cent rate was 9 percent, and 10 years later it was less than 5 percent.

During World War II, the increased imports, as well as the enlarged output of domestic wells, were readily absorbed in expanded consumption. This situation changed abruptly after the war. Imports of crude oil which had averaged less than 40 million barrels in 1941-1945 rose to 129 million in 1946-1950, and to 265 million in 1952-1956. In this period, imports increased 6½ times,

Table 45

U. S. PRODUCTION OF CRUDE PETROLEUM,[a]
1929, 1932, 1936-1956
(in millions of barrels)

Year	*Production*	*Year*	*Production*
1929	1,007	1951	2,248
1932	785	1952	2,290
1936–40 (av.)	1,242	1953	2,357
1941–45 (av.)	1,537	1954	2,315
1946–50 (av.)	1,885	1955	2,484
1951–55 (av.)	2,339	1956	2,617

[a] Excluding production of natural gas liquids, amounting to approximately 10 percent of crude oil production.
Source: U. S. Bureau of Mines

but domestic production rose by less than 60 percent. (See Tables 41 and 45 and Chart Q.) These changes brought demands by spokesmen for the independent oil producers for quantitative restrictions on imports. Quotas, they believed, would exert a more positive effect on imports than customs duties and could perhaps be made a means of discriminatory action against imports from the Middle East. They asked that a "fair relationship" be established between imports and domestic production. In order that both share *pro rata* in the growth of the American market, they asked that imports be restricted to a fixed percentage of domestic production.

CHART Q

U. S. PRODUCTION OF CRUDE PETROLEUM, NET EXPORTS, NET IMPORTS AND SUPPLY OF PETROLEUM AND PRODUCTS, 1929-1956
(in millions of barrels)

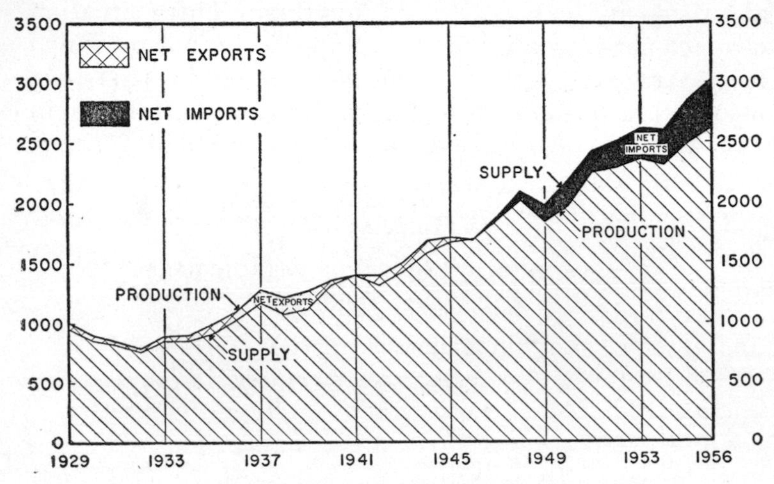

Source: U. S. Bureau of the Census, U. S. Bureau of Mines

Senator Neely's Amendment

An amendment offered by Senator Neely of West Virginia to the 1955 Trade Agreements Extension Act,[31] which was strongly supported by the bituminous coal industry as well as by independent oil producers, would have limited imports of oil to 10 percent of domestic consumption. The administration strongly opposed import quotas and was able to secure the adoption of a compromise. An amendment, sponsored by the administration (Section 7 of the Trade Agreements Extension Act of 1955), gave the President discretionary authority to "adjust" the imports when he finds that such imports are threatening to *impair the national security.* Before taking such action he is to be advised by the Office of Defense Mobilization. The "adjustment provision," it was gener-

[31] For text, see *Trade Agreements Extension,* House Hearings (1955), cited, p. 1850.

ally understood, referred particularly to imports of oil, although it did not specifically mention that commodity.

During the debate on Senator Neely's proposal, the President's Advisory Committee on Energy Supplies and Resources Policy released a report recommending that the 1954 ratio of imports of crude and residual fuel oil to domestic production (about 10 percent) should be adopted as the rule for restricting future imports. The Committee believed that if the imports of crude and residual oils "should exceed significantly the respective proportions that these imports of oils bore to the production of domestic crude oil in 1954, the domestic fuels situation could be so impaired as to endanger the orderly industrial growth which assures the military and civilian supplies and reserves that are necessary to the national defense. There would be an inadequate incentive for exploration and the discovery of new sources of supply."[32] Voluntary action by importers was recommended to keep imports at 1954 levels.[33] "The committee believes," the report stated, "that every effort should be made and will be made to avoid the necessity of governmental intervention." But, if this policy should prove unsuccessful, the government should enforce the limitation.

"Voluntary" Restrictions on Imports

As soon as the new legislation became effective, independent oil producers demanded that the ODM take action. This agency within a few months found that imports of some companies were excessive and called for voluntary restriction. When they failed to comply, Dr. Arthur S. Flemming, the Director, on October 29, 1955, requested importing companies to reduce by seven percent the amount of oil they were planning to bring in, in the

[32] *Report on Energy Supplies and Resources Policy,* White House press release of February 26, 1955, p. 3.

[33] The suggestion that restriction might be accomplished by voluntary action had been made earlier by Secretary of the Interior Douglas McKay. See National Petroleum Council, *Minutes of Meeting . . . May 28, 1953* (Washington, 1953), Statement of Hon. Douglas McKay, p. 14.

period April 1-December 31.[34] This order did not require any reduction in imports from Venezuela or from Canada. These, and other Western Hemisphere countries, were considered within the United States defense orbit. Imports of crude oil into West Coast ports, *from all sources,* were later exempted, and also residual oil for fueling ships at United States ports, and for military use. These exemptions, covering more than 75 percent of all imports scheduled for 1956, marked a significant departure from the formula proposed earlier by the President's Advisory Committee, and drew strong criticism from spokesmen for the independent oil producers and from Congressmen from oil-producing states. They pressed for compulsory limitation of imports to 10 percent of domestic production, the 1954 ratio.

Importing companies opposed legal quotas as undesirable extensions of government control over the oil industry. The administration also was reluctant to take the action which Congress had authorized. In the first place, the voluntary system, with all its defects and leakages, was perhaps more effective than it seemed. Although all the companies did not reduce their imports to the full extent of the government's request, the majority, nevertheless, exercised some restraint. Importing companies were sensitive to "industry opinion" and were eager to retain the good will of the independent producers. Hence, although total imports continued to rise, the increase probably would have been larger had there been no attempt at restriction.

Secondly, resort to compulsion would have forced government to set up additional administrative machinery, and to accept clear responsibility for its operation, or failure to operate. Compulsory quotas, moreover, would constitute a sharp break with traditional trade policy,[35]

[34] The request was later withdrawn since imports for April-October were already entered and part of November imports were on the way.

[35] "Absolute" quotas had been imposed on cotton and certain dairy products as authorized by Sec. 22 of the Agricultural Act of 1933. "Tariff" quotas, setting limits on the quantities of certain commodities which might enter at reduced rates of duty, had been used more frequently. Such a quota had been fixed on oil in the 1939 trade agreement with Venezuela.

and would expose the United States to the charge of inconsistency, because of our frequent denunciation of quantitative restrictions applied by other countries. Oil-exporting countries might even charge the United States with violation of obligations undertaken in the General Agreement on Tariffs and Trade. The Agreement, it is true, permits quantitative restrictions, if imposed for reasons of national security, or for the conservation of national resources, but the United States might find some difficulty in stretching the language so as to cover its quantitative restrictions on oil imports. Hence, it was not until the fall of 1956 that the ODM set in motion the machinery which Congress had provided more than a year earlier in Section 7 of the Trade Agreements Act of 1955.

In October 1956, the ODM announced that the amounts of oil which the importing companies were planning to bring in would constitute a threat to the national security. The blocking of the Suez Canal, however, eliminated temporarily the need for enforcing import restrictions. Imports from the Middle East fell off and also from Venezuela, large supplies of oil from that country having been directed to Western Europe.

Shortly after the Canal was reopened, in 1957, the ODM again reported that imports threatened national security. The President thereupon appointed a Special Committee to Investigate Crude Oil Imports, which reported: "... if we are to have enough oil to meet our national security needs, there must be a limitation on imports that will insure a proper balance between imports and domestic production."[36] The Committee did not recommend that the President, using the power delegated by Congress, should compel the oil companies to reduce their imports. Instead, it advised him to make another attempt to accomplish restriction by voluntary action. Accordingly, he again called upon the major oil-importing companies to cut imports of crude oil "voluntarily" to specified levels, or face formal action.

36 Report of the Special Committee to Investigate Crude Oil Imports (Washington: Department of Commerce, July 29, 1957), p. 5.

Thus the oil controversy in July 1957 was in about the same situation as in June 1955. After two years of persuasion, investigation and threats of legal action, the government was still attempting to make its omelet without breaking any eggs. However, one step had been taken in the direction of compulsion. In the new scheme, announced at the end of July 1957, for the first time a quota was "recommended" to each importing company. Seven major companies were requested to reduce their imports about 10 percent from the 1954-56 level. Ten of the 15 "new" importers, companies which had begun to buy crude oil abroad within the three previous years, were allowed to increase their imports, but not as much as they had planned. Five companies importing from Canada were allowed to keep to scheduled imports. A liberalizing feature of the new plan was the increase in the allowable over-all ratio of imports to domestic production from 10.3 to 12 percent in the area east of the Rocky Mountains (Districts I to IV). In the Pacific Coast area (District V), the permitted ratio was 29.8 percent. No restrictions were imposed on imports of residual fuel oil.

But the new plan did not prove any more successful than its predecessors. Importing companies were dissatisfied and asked for higher allocations. One large company flatly refused to accept its quota. Others found ways to evade the restrictions. Companies with refineries on both coasts were able to maintain their volume of imports by directing shipments to the West Coast where no restrictions had been imposed. Some companies, instead of importing crude from the Caribbean area, brought in refined products, principally heavy fuel oil which had not been subjected to restriction. Independent producers complained of continuing high volume of imports and demanded that the loophole in the new plan which allowed unrestricted imports into the West Coast should be plugged. The President complied in an order dated December 24, 1957.

Repercussions in Canada

The repercussions in Canada, the country principally affected by the new ruling,[37] were prompt and forceful. Bruce Hutchison, the Canadian correspondent for the *Christian Science Monitor,* wrote on January 10, 1958: "No recent event has so gravely damaged good American-Canadian relations. . . ." In a widely syndicated newspaper article, Lester Pearson, one of the most eminent and respected figures in Canadian political life and a good friend of the United States, denounced the President's action. He branded as "nonsense" the argument that restrictions on imports of Canadian oil were necessary for U. S. national defense. "Oil in Alberta," he wrote, "is as safe from hostile interference, and as available for United States use, as oil in Oklahoma."[38] Rejection of this self-evident truth, he asserted, was inconsistent with the United States-sponsored doctrine of economic cooperation in the NATO treaty.

In a formal statement, Donald Fleming, Canadian Minister of Finance, denied that the limitation of oil coming from Canada had any justification either on economic or defense grounds. In a strong protest note sent to Washington on January 15, 1958, the Canadian government called attention to Canadian imports of American petroleum and products which in 1956 were valued at more than $100 million. "Surely it is unwise," the note said, "to jeopardize this two-way trade which works to the benefit of both countries."[39] The note again urged that the United States should reconsider its oil import program and remove the limitations imposed on imports from Canada. In reply the Department of State asserted that imports were threatening

[37] In 1956, practically 100 percent of Canada's exports of crude oil (42,600,000 out of 42,900,000 barrels) was shipped to the United States. The bulk of these exports entered West Coast ports.

[38] As quoted in *Christian Science Monitor,* January 10, 1958.

[39] Canadian Embassy Note no. 30 to the Department of State, January 15, 1958.

to impair the domestic oil industry on the West Coast. The Department claimed that the effect of the restrictions on the Canadian oil industry would not be serious, but the note made no attempt to refute the argument that the President's action had disregarded the principle of collective security.

United States Policy with Respect to Foreign Investments of American Oil Companies

In the past half century, American corporations have invested over $7 billion in the exploration, discovery and production of crude oil in foreign countries—in refineries, pipelines and other methods of transportation and in facilities for the market distribution of gasoline and other refined products. These investments constitute about a third of all direct investments of American firms in foreign countries.

Thirty-three American oil companies produce about 58 percent of the Free World's oil and refine about 65 percent. A group of five "major" oil companies (Socony-Mobil Oil, Standard Oil of California, the Texas Company, Gulf and Standard Oil of New Jersey) hold, under lease or concessions from foreign governments, more than one-half of the world's oil reserves outside of Soviet Russia. The largest recent gains in foreign drilling by American firms have taken place in Canada, where as many as 100 companies are at work.

In recent years, a number of the independent American companies, including such well-known firms as Sun, Tidewater and Atlantic, have begun exploration and production of oil outside of the United States. "Today," the *Oil Forum* reported in March 1957, "over 150 American independent oil operators are working in some 32 countries of the world, some just looking, others carrying out exploration and development, and others who are producing."

The 1956 value of all direct investments of American companies in petroleum in foreign countries is shown below:

U. S. DIRECT OIL INVESTMENTS ABROAD, 1956

(in millions of dollars)

World total	*7,244*
Canada	1,752
Venezuela	1,411
Other Latin American countries	816
Western Europe	994
All other	2,271

Source: U. S. Department of Commerce

Large-scale investments in foreign countries date from World War I, which created an unprecedented military demand for motor fuel. Civilian demand was increasing, and at the same time oil experts viewed pessimistically the outlook for expansion of domestic production. American companies which had built up a large export trade in kerosene and other refined products were looking abroad for ample supplies of low-cost crude oil to supplement the output of their domestic wells.

Oil companies, as well as many other types of American business firms which have invested abroad, have benefited from various types of government aid. These have included tax incentives[40] and insurance against inability to convert into dollars earnings in foreign currencies, and against loss from expropriation or confiscation. Furthermore, American firms investing capital abroad, in branch factories and many other types of enterprises, receive as a matter of course diplomatic support when they become involved in controversies with governments of countries where their enterprises are situated. Usually such controversies involve no major problem of foreign relations. But the American oil industry went abroad under conditions which led to extraordinary measures of government intervention on its behalf. (1) In foreign countries, subsoil deposits of petroleum and other minerals are uniformly the property of the state, not of the owner of the land under which they are found. Hence, American firms, in securing concessions, have had to deal with governments, not with private indi-

[40] The 27½-percent depletion allowance may be applied to income from foreign oil production.

viduals. (2) The richest oil deposits are found in underdeveloped countries whose governments were often weak and inefficient, sometimes venal. (3) In the Middle East, American companies were at a disadvantage in competing with British, Dutch and French concerns for economic opportunities, since the latter were in reality not private enterprises but were to a large extent government-owned. (4) In the period of intense international struggle over oil in the early 1920's, the richest oil-bearing areas in the Middle East were colonies, dependencies, protectorates or mandates of Great Britain, France or the Netherlands. These "colonial" powers made use of their legal position and influence to secure for their nationals exclusive opportunities for exploiting oil, and other natural resources, in the areas over which they exercised political control.

U. S. Demands Open Door Policy

Against this attitude, the United States government protested, demanding an Open Door policy which would allow foreign firms of whatever nationality equal access to the raw materials of the world. The public interest, as interpreted by spokesmen for the Department of State, required "large-scale expansion of holdings in foreign oil reserves by United States nationals." The Department, therefore, "actively supported the efforts of United States petroleum interests to secure and to consolidate concessions abroad."[41] The Department of State protested vigorously in the early 1920's, when American companies complained that they were being excluded from opportunities to acquire oil concessions in the Middle East and in the Netherlands East Indies. It bluntly warned the British, Dutch and French governments that "refusal to share opportunity would be regarded as unfriendly and cause the American government to strike back."[42] This was not empty talk. The

[41] Quoted from statement of Charles Rayner, Petroleum Adviser, Department of State, at Hearings before a Special Committee Investigating Petroleum Resources, U. S. Senate, 79th Cong., 1st sess., pursuant to S. Res. 36 (Washington: GPO, 1945), June 27 and 28, 1945, p. 1.

[42] Herbert Feis, *Petroleum and American Foreign Policy,* Commodity Policy Studies no. 3 (Food Research Institute, Stanford University, March 1944), p. 6.

United States government took steps to prevent the Royal Dutch Shell Company from obtaining further leases on its public lands. The threat of retaliation forced the government of the Netherlands to grant concessions to American companies in its Far Eastern colonies. In 1930, the State Department successfully invoked the Open Door policy in Kuwait, enabling American companies to secure concessions in a rich oil-producing area from which they had been excluded. Somewhat earlier, the Department had secured for American firms participation in the Iraq Petroleum Company, after prolonged negotiations with Great Britain, the mandatory power.

Thus, with government backing, American companies had obtained by 1940 a 23.75-percent share in the Iraq Petroleum Company, one-half ownership in the Kuwait Oil Company and, in addition, exclusive rights in the Bahrein archipelago and in Saudi Arabia. A 1957 estimate assigns 55 percent of Middle East reserves to the control of American companies.

Government Takes the Initiative

In the 20-year period of struggle for American participation in the development of the oil resources of the Middle East, which began after World War I, the United States government, not the oil companies, usually took the initiative. The government's policy, motivated by economic and, particularly after World War II, by strategic considerations, received strong support in public opinion. It was widely believed that domestic oil resources were rapidly approaching exhaustion and that, unless American firms secured rights in oil fields abroad, the country would be "at the mercy" of the foreigners who had got there first. The big oil companies were at first reluctant to take advantage of the opportunities in the Middle East which their government was striving to obtain for them. Too close an association with government, they feared, might lead to supervision and control. They successfully opposed several plans for the investment of government funds in production and transportation of Middle Eastern oil.

The government's hard-fought struggle to establish the Open Door policy in the Middle East achieved only partial success. When, during the interwar years, oil surpluses appeared in world oil markets in place of shortages, the American companies found that they were better able to secure participation in the exploitation of Middle East oil through agreements with foreign companies than through diplomatic channels. The State Department, however, did not relax its activities. In the Anglo-American Treaty, submitted to the Senate in 1944, and again in revised form in the following year, it went beyond the policy of protecting and expanding the foreign oil investments of American companies. The proposed agreement contained principles governing the behavior of producing and consuming countries so as to avoid monopoly and discrimination, and to make adequate supplies of petroleum accessible to nationals of all countries on a competitive and nondiscriminative basis. Producing countries were to respect, and refrain from interfering with, valid concession contracts. In revised form, the treaty was approved by the Senate Committee on Foreign Relations on July 1, 1947 and sent to the Senate but was never brought to a vote. Support by the Department of the Interior, by the armed services and by the major oil companies was not able to overcome the opposition of the independent oil producers "who argued that the new agreement was the first step toward placing the American oil industry under the control of an international body. . . ."[43]

Mounting tension with the Soviet Union after World War II led the United States government again to encourage American firms to expand their foreign operations, so as to assure continued access to foreign supplies, and to deny them to the U.S.S.R. Fear of the expansion of Russian economic and political power played a large part in the State Department's efforts from 1951 to 1953 to bring about a settlement of the dispute over the nationalization of the Iranian oil industry. Only after considerable urging

[43] Benjamin Shwadran, *The Middle East, Oil and the Great Powers* (New York: Praeger, 1955), p. 331.

by the Department of State, and a guarantee by the Department of Justice of immunity from antitrust prosecution, five major American companies and nine smaller enterprises joined with three European companies in the international consortium which undertook to market Iranian oil.

In recent years the Federal Trade Commission and the Department of Justice have questioned the legality of agreements between American and foreign oil companies. In December 1949, the Commission began an investigation of an alleged international cartel in the petroleum industry. Its staff report, submitted to a Congressional committee and to the Department of Justice in August 1952, was the basis for an antitrust suit. In it the government charged, *inter alia,* that the five major integrated companies had improperly regulated imports into the United States, thereby maintaining unduly high prices in the American market. A year later (1953) the grand jury investigation was dropped. Civil proceedings against the companies were initiated, but the inconsistency between foreign and domestic policies brought these proceedings to a halt. To forward the objectives of American policy in the Middle East, the State Department encouraged 16 American companies to join in the oil lift to Europe. In this case, the Department of Justice again found it necessary to give the participating companies informal assurance of immunity from prosecution under laws forbidding combination in restraint of foreign trade.

On these occasions, the Attorney General refrained from vetoing the plans of the Secretary of State, but the latent conflict remains between antitrust policy and certain aspects of foreign policy. On this matter Professor Mason has written: "The time has almost come for the United States Government to treat the problem of Middle Eastern oil as something more than a business matter to be handled by the oil companies with no other interposition—if I may use a Southern word—than prosecution under the antitrust laws. I do not pretend to know whether the antitrust laws have in fact been violated, but I must say that the current so-called cartel case seems to me to be magnificent in its irrelevance to any important interests the United States has in that part of the world."[44]

The Reform of National Oil Policy

In the next 20 or 25 years this country, unless government intervenes, will become increasingly dependent on foreign countries for its supply of oil; the Paley Commission estimated that in the 25 years 1950-1975 the United States demand for petroleum products would double, rising from 2,375 to almost 5,000 million barrels, but before 1975 the United States will probably reach the peak of its oil production, with an output of about 4,100 million barrels.[45] According to these estimates, the gap to be filled by imports in 1975 would be about 900 million barrels. The Chase Manhattan Bank in 1957 predicted[46] that domestic demand would grow at the rate of 5 percent per year, reaching in 1966 an annual level of 5.2 billion barrels. Production in the United States, the bank estimated, would rise more slowly, reaching only 3.5 billion barrels at the end of the 10-year period. Accordingly, the gap to be filled by imports in 1966 would be 1.75 billion barrels, a figure almost twice the imports which the Paley Commission had forecast for 1975. In Europe, and elsewhere in the Free World, demand for petroleum products will probably increase in the next 20-25 years even more rapidly than in the United States. The Paley Commission estimated a three-fold increase in Europe and a possible four-fold increase in other Free World areas. Thus the total demand of the Free World (excluding the United States) would rise from the 1950 level of 1,275 million barrels to 4,780 million in 1975.

[44] "Emerging Requirements for an Expanding World Economy," by Edward S. Mason, in *The Changing Environment of International Relations* (Washington: Brookings Institution, 1956), p. 83.

[45] *Resources for Freedom,* v. 3, *The Outlook for Energy Sources,* cited, pp. 4, 10.

[46] *Future Growth of the World Petroleum Industry,* by Kenneth E. Hill, Harold D. Hammar and John G. Winger (New York: Chase Manhattan Bank, 1957), pp. 22-26.

The Paley Commission's conclusion regarding future supplies of oil, which was supported by later studies of the Chase Bank, was that the task of U. S. policy in meeting peacetime demands for liquid fuel did not appear formidable. Looking at the whole energy situation, a member of the Commission wrote: "When full account is taken of the substitutabilities of coal, petroleum, natural gas and hydroelectric power, and the flexibility of conversion of one energy source into another, there are no overwhelming technical obstacles to the satisfaction of projected energy requirements at real costs that—if not declining—at least need not rise very much."[47] This was written in 1952. Later experience in the development of nuclear energy, as a source of heat for industrial processes and of electric power, have reinforced the optimistic conclusion. By 1980 nuclear energy, according to a 1957 study of the National Planning Association, may supply more than 20 percent of all electric power generated in the United States. "The introduction of nuclear energy on this scale will affect mainly the expansion of markets for coal and oil, taking about 15 percent and 7 percent respectively, though the total demand for each then will be much greater than at present. . . . Already the influence of nuclear energy is not unlike the potential supplies of fluid fuel that would become economically recoverable from shale at moderate increases over present prices."[48]

Oil and Defense

National security, not economic advantage, today is the critical factor in oil policy. Does the increasing depend-

47 "An American View of Raw-Material Problems" by Edward S. Mason, in the *Journal of Industrial Economics,* v. 1, no. 1 (November 1952). Reprinted in *Economic Concentration and the Monopoly Problem,* Harvard Economic Studies (Cambridge: Harvard University Press, 1957), pp. 265-266.

48 *Productive Uses of Nuclear Energy,* cited, p. 16. For discussion of the costs of generating electricity in nuclear power stations and in conventional plants, see Walter H. Zinn, "An Appraisal of the United States Nuclear Power Program" in *Atoms for Power,* a report of the American Assembly (New York: Columbia University Press, 1957), pp. 80-99.

ence of the United States on foreign countries for its supply of oil threaten national security?

Whether or not the United States will have adequate supplies of oil in a future war depends on what kind of war we shall be fighting. In a war of a few weeks' duration, fought with atomic or hydrogen bombs, there would be no opportunity for expanding domestic production of crude oil, or for increasing imports. We would have to rely on stocks in being and on current domestic production which would probably exceed the capacity of the refineries that remained intact. But a prolonged conflict fought with conventional weapons would require continuous large supplies of oil. Describing the situation in World War II, Secretary Ickes said:

> Without petroleum products the machinery in the factories producing war materials would have ground to a dissonant halt. Our ships could not have carried supplies of arms and of men to the theaters of war. Our rifles and our heavy artillery would have been useless. Our motorized transportation would have been so much high-class junk. Our airplanes would have had no option except to sit on the ground like so many tame ducks.[49]

In 1948 Admiral Nimitz said: "Oil is the life's blood of our Navy, Air Force and mechanized Army." General Spaatz, in less colorful language, told a House committee: "Oil is the essential ingredient of modern warfare. Even supermodern atomic weapons amount to nothing unless the means of delivery are fueled with oil." Ballistic missiles developed in the succeeding decade employ other types of fuel, but it seems improbable that they will replace strategic bombers within the time period contemplated in this study.

The continued functioning of the civilian economy, essential to any war effort, is dependent on oil. It furnishes more than one-third of the country's total supply of energy and, in addition, is an important industrial raw material. With the development of the petrochemical industry, oil

49 U. S. House, Special Subcommittee on Petroleum of the Committee on Armed Services, *Petroleum for National Defense,* Hearings, 80th Cong., 2d sess. (Washington: GPO, 1948), p. 759.

has become the chief source of toluene (a basic component of TNT) and also one of the principal sources of butadiene and other components of synthetic rubber.

In a prolonged conflict, or for a series of brush-fire wars, the country would have to rely for its oil supplies on imports and on domestic production. Stockpiling of oil in the conventional manner is impractical. A 1946 report of the U. S. Tariff Commission said:

> Sufficient storage tanks to hold the enormous quantities [of oil] required for even a relatively short war would involve very great investment; moreover, both crude petroleum and its refined products deteriorate materially during prolonged storage. Vulnerability of oil-tank "farms" to enemy action is another objection to extensive stockpiling. The most efficient and economical way to keep a reserve of petroleum is to keep it in the ground where nature has put it.[50]

The Commission suggested that the government maintain as an "underground stockpile" areas containing semi-proved reserves where productive wells could be drilled quickly. Certain pools, or parts of pools which have already been opened up, might be set aside as government-owned reserves. Alternatively, the government might acquire all or part of selected pools hereafter discovered. Such oil reserves, however, would not be available immediately, but only after wells had been drilled.

Imports in 1956 supplied 534 million barrels of oil, about 17 percent of total U. S. consumption. In a war emergency, according to military authorities, we could not rely on oil from the Middle East. The blocking of the Suez Canal and the sabotage of pipelines in Syria showed the unreliability of this source of supply. But the loss of oil from this source, which supplies only 3 or 4 percent of consumption, could easily be offset by restrictions on civilian uses.

On the wartime importance of Middle East oil, John Campbell has written:

50 *Petroleum,* War Changes in Industry Series (1946), cited, p. 41.

In a limited war it could be tremendously useful if the installations were held more or less intact. In a general war of any duration it is at least open to grave doubt whether the oil would be available to anybody. Even if the Western powers could hold the Middle East for an extended period, the oil installations and pipelines would be primary targets for missiles, bombing and sabotage. If it be assumed that Soviet forces could overrun the Middle East, the chances that they would find the installations intact would be minimal, and even if they did they could not get the oil over the mountains into the Soviet Union.[51]

In a war emergency the United States would have to rely for its supply of foreign oil on imports from Western Hemisphere countries. There are important possibilities of enlarging imports from Canada which amounted to less than 50 million barrels in 1956. The total Canadian output (183 million barrels in 1956), it has been predicted, will rise within 10 years to 475 million barrels annually. Venezuela's oil production, 900 million barrels in 1956, is also due for rapid expansion; an output of 1,640 million barrels is predicted for 1966. In the event that war should prevent shipments of Venezuelan oil to Europe, all of the exports would seek markets in the United States. How much of this oil would actually arrive in U. S. ports would depend on the number of tankers available and on the ability of the U. S. Navy to protect them against the attacks of hostile submarines.

Whatever losses were suffered in imported oil would have to be made up (1) by expanding domestic production and (2) by restricting nonessential civilian consumption of gasoline and lubricants in highway and air transport. (A reduction of only 15 percent from the 1956 use of gasoline in highway transport would have compensated for the loss of one-third of all the oil imported that year.) Domestic production of crude oil could be quickly expanded by perhaps as much as a million barrels daily with little new investment by drilling wells in fields already explored but not developed. Moreover, in wartime the

[51] *Defense of the Middle East* by John C. Campbell (New York: Council on Foreign Relations, 1958), p. 229.

federal government could insist, as it was unwilling to do in the Suez crisis, that state prorationing authorities should relax at once their restrictions on the output of crude oil. If necessary all restrictions could be removed, even at the risk of diminishing the total eventual recovery of oil from the prorationed fields. By this means 2 or 3 million barrels daily of crude oil could be added temporarily to the domestic supply.

The bottleneck in wartime, if we can judge from the experience of World War II, would appear not in production, nor in refining, but in transportation — in pipelines and more especially in the supply of tankers available for overseas transport. Great quantities of gasoline and fuel oil, to be used by airplanes, ships and mechanized equipment, would have to be moved from the wells, whether in South America, the Middle East or Texas, to the various theaters of operation, which we assume will not be in the United States. To maintain excess capacity in pipelines and refineries would not be prohibitively expensive. But tankers present a more difficult problem. To keep a fleet of several hundred large vessels in stand-by condition, dispersed so as not to invite aerial bombing or submarine attack, would be costly. A still greater obstacle would be the difficulty in rapidly mobilizing competent crews.

For wartime supplies of oil for consumption within the United States, reliance would have to be placed on the output of domestic wells and refineries. Hence it should be the aim of national policy in peacetime to maintain the industry in vigorous condition, capable of rapid expansion in a war emergency. As far as can be judged from readily available sources, the American oil industry taken as a whole is prosperous. Output of crude oil from domestic wells increased by 50 percent in the years 1946-1956 and employment in the industry gained in the same proportion. The number of producing wells drilled in 1956 was 30,000 as against 16,000 ten years earlier. Proved reserves of oil were 50 percent higher at the end of the postwar decade than at the beginning. Meanwhile, the price of crude oil rose by 98 percent, from $1.41 to $2.77 per barrel. The financial reports of the largest companies, many of which derive their profits principally from foreign operations, show earnings as high as those of any American industry. Comparable data are not available for the thousands of independent oil companies, most of which do not publish annual reports. Such general evidence as is available, however, does not indicate that this section of the industry has suffered a postwar depression. It is perhaps significant that President Eisenhower, when he announced that imports of oil threatened to injure the domestic industry, did not support his decision by the publication of economic data of any sort.

Oil producers now receive *indirectly* substantial subsidies from the federal government in the form of tax favors (the percentage depletion allowance) and tariff protection. Federal cooperation, also, makes possible the prorationing procedures of state governments which support the price of crude oil. These measures deserve more serious, objective study than has yet been given them, to determine how far they are needed to maintain an adequate mobilization base in the oil industry, and how far they impose an unnecessary burden on taxpayers and on the consumers of petroleum products.

* * * *

Secretary Ickes was right; the United States has no oil policy. Instead we have an assortment of federal and state laws and administrative decisions, often conflicting in their objectives, and adopted for the most part to satisfy insistent special and local interests rather than in pursuit of a clearly defined national interest. Congress in income tax legislation has provided strong incentives to increase the output of oil, but state regulatory bodies have pursued a contrary policy of restricting output. The federal government supports the restrictive policies but refuses to accept responsibility for them. U. S. national authorities in the past encouraged American oil companies to invest large sums in foreign oil production, and in the Middle East, particularly, has intervened actively to obtain for them the necessary concessions. Yet the President, in the name of national security, has imposed restrictions on the import of foreign oil into the United States. The State Department in order to forward objectives of foreign policy has encouraged American international oil companies to act in cooperation with British, Dutch and other foreign companies. But such activities might be punished as violating antitrust legislation, unless they received in advance the blessing of the Department of Justice. The conflict of aims confuses the thinking of laymen, preventing the formation of intelligent public opinion on questions of oil policy, and it prevents the oil industry from making its maximum contribution to the national welfare and to national strength.

The United States needs a truly national oil policy which will deal with the relation of government, federal and state, to the oil industry, not piecemeal but as a whole. The task of framing such an integrated policy should not be entrusted to a Congressional committee or to a group of administrative officials but rather to a nonofficial body of the highest competence, animated only by the ideals of public service. Its report might serve as a landmark in national policy on raw materials.

Chapter 11

THE REFORM OF NATIONAL POLICY

I

JUDGED by accomplishment in times of national emergency, American policies dealing with raw materials attained considerable success. The emergency measures adopted during World War II and in the Korean conflict provided the metals, the oil, and the textile fibers needed to sustain defense production and to make victory possible. This result, moreover, was accomplished without imposing drastic restrictions on the use of fuels and raw materials in producing goods for civilian consumption. The creation, during World War II, of a great new industry for the production of synthetic rubber and its successful operation and technical progress under government ownership were remarkable achievements. The transfer, after the war, of the plants to private owners, who thereafter successfully operated them without tariff protection, subsidy or other form of government assistance, was a further indication of the success of the government's rubber policy. The development of uranium production with government subsidy, and with government monopoly of supply, was another major accomplishment. Government participation in nickel mining in Cuba resulted in valuable additions to the wartime supply of a critically important metal, although the postwar history of the nickel venture was disappointing.

In the years 1947-1956 industrial production increased nearly 50 percent without encountering, except during the Korean conflict, serious shortages of raw materials. The unprecedented upswing in the national economy in this decade, however, may have been hampered rather than assisted by Congressional and Executive activities in the field of raw materials supply. For optimum economic growth, the nation's industries should be able to obtain their raw materials supplies at minimum real cost. This principle, however, as earlier chapters have shown, was disregarded. Concealed subsidies to domestic producers of oil and metals in the form of depletion allowances reduced the federal revenue and, like all systems of preferential taxation, tended to divert labor and capital away from unsubsidized industries, thus raising their costs.

The protection against foreign competition which the tariff afforded to raw materials producers was insignificant in most cases. Raw materials as a general rule entered free of duty, and on the dutiable items the rates were low. Only on wool and on a few metals were they high enough to raise appreciably prices in American markets. At the end of the decade, however, so-called voluntary restrictions on oil imports constituted a substantive violation of the minimum-cost principle. By limiting the supplies of low-cost oil that might be obtained from Venezuela, Canada and the Middle East, the restrictions forced larger use of the more expensive domestic product.

Preferences accorded in government purchasing to commodities fabricated from domestic materials, in accordance with the Buy American Act, furnish a further example, in a limited area, of uneconomic raw materials policies. In the stockpiling program, the misuse of purchases of strategic materials, as a means of subsidizing domestic producers of lead and zinc and other materials, added needlessly to the costs of the undertaking. Failure to take account of technological change, which had developed synthetic substitutes, resulted in unnecessarily large accumulations of certain materials, notably wool and rubber.

The coordination of raw materials policies with foreign policy was far from perfect. In some instances, notably the embargo on shipments of strategic materials to the Soviet bloc and the prohibition on all exports to Red China, the policies were in agreement; more often, however, they were in conflict. One of the repeatedly emphasized objectives of American foreign policy was to preserve good relations with countries in the Western Hemisphere, and to prevent, in Latin America particularly, penetration by Soviet influence. To avoid giving offense to Mexico, Peru and Canada, President Eisenhower resisted for four years strong pressures from domestic producers to raise import duties on lead and zinc. But in 1955, when he imposed quantitative restrictions on imports of oil, he threatened Venezuela's principal export industry. His action added fuel to the smoldering resentment in that country at other aspects of American economic policy, and contributed to the explosion of anti-American feeling that greeted Vice President Nixon in May 1958 at Caracas. The reaction in Canada, also an exporter of oil to American markets, was less spectacular, but it may have been equally profound. Canadians, like many Americans, could not understand how shipments of oil from Alberta into West Coast ports in the United States could endanger American security. In fact, the President's justification of the restrictions on grounds of national defense seemed to disregard the geographic situation, the economic conditions and the political arrangements which guarantee that all Canadian fuels and raw materials will be available to the United States in time of crisis. If the principle of collective, especially continental, security has any meaning, it should have been applied in this case.

In general, the measures affecting raw materials undertaken in the first postwar decade displayed virtues and defects characteristic of American democracy. When facing an emergency, the federal government accomplished prodigies of improvisation. It mobilized economic and technological resources, accumulated vast stores of strategic materials and, by purchase contracts, tax incentives and loans, greatly stimulated production at home and abroad. These measures were expensive, but they produced results, the dominant consideration in wartime. In times of peace, however, or near-peace, it is legitimate to require that results be obtained as far as possible at minimum costs. Raw materials policies failed to meet this test.

The preceding chapters, especially the studies of particular materials (Chapters 4 to 10), have shown that Congress and the President often failed to adapt measures affecting supplies of raw materials to the changed economic conditions which had made the country increasingly dependent on foreign sources. They failed, also, to bring raw materials policies into agreement with the changed position of the United States in world affairs and with the new objectives of American foreign policy.

These failures are to be attributed neither to ignorance nor to stupidity, but rather to certain characteristic defects of the democratic process which afflict national policy in many areas. First, the dead weight of tradition slows the adaptation of policies to changed economic conditions. Most Congressmen and Senators are acquainted, at least in broad outline, with the facts of export and import trade. Most of them, it may be assumed, know that domestic mines cannot provide substantially increased supplies of manganese, tungsten, lead and zinc except at costs which would prove burdensome to fabricating industries. Their speeches and their votes, however, indicate that many of them still cherish the delusion of national self-sufficiency. Likewise, it may be assumed that legislators know that the United States in its conflict with international communism needs the support, diplomatic, economic and military, of allied countries in the Free World, and that it is striving to prevent the spread of Soviet influence among the uncommitted nations. Yet Congressional debates often display attitudes on foreign policy which would be more relevant to the situation of the United States in international affairs in 1890 than to its present difficulties and responsibilities.

More important than tradition in explaining failure to bring policy into harmony with changing national interest are the pressures brought by special and local interests, by miners, oil producers, wool growers and others. But these pressures, in fairness it must be remarked, have not been confined to measures affecting the supply of raw materials. The triumphs of well-organized special interests over the national interest are all too familiar in American history.

II

New policy should not be designed only to remedy old errors. If it is to fit the needs of the next 20 to 25 years, Congress and the President should endeavor to anticipate the economic, technological and political changes which will modify the conditions of supply and demand for raw materials in this country and in the Free World. Should American policy be based on the anticipation of world-wide shortages, or of surpluses? What measures would be appropriate to protect the national interest in either case?

First, it must be recognized that wars and the threat of wars can upset predictions based on economic reasoning. Hence certain assumptions are necessary on the probable state of international relations. In Chapter 3 we considered three alternatives: (1) an all-out atomic war, (2) a third world war, i.e., a prolonged struggle fought with conventional weapons, after the model of World War II, and (3) the continuance of the present state of tension between the United States and the Soviet Union. An all-out war fought with nuclear weapons, if we are to believe military experts, would create such disaster as to render useless present calculations of trends in demand for industrial materials. Our political leaders, however, encourage us to believe that the occurrence of such a catastrophe is not probable. It now appears equally improbable that in the next 20 or 25 years the United States will engage in a protracted military conflict of world-wide scope requiring full-scale industrial mobilization. If, however, such a war should be fought, we might expect that the military demand for certain materials would absorb practically the entire available supply, leaving only a bare minimum for essential civilian needs, and making necessary extraordinary programs of substitution and conservation. As things stand now, the continuance of the present state of no peace-no war, punctuated perhaps by armed conflicts of limited scope and duration, seems the most probable of the three alternatives; hence, this assumption will underlie the following examination of the probable trends in demand and supply.

Comparisons between rapidly expanding growth in future demand—based on projections of population increase—with supposedly inflexible supplies of materials often have given rise to fears of long-run shortages. Metals and minerals are nonrenewable resources. As the richest veins of ore are worked out and the most productive oil fields are drained, real costs, it is argued, will rise. Demand for fuels and the basic materials seems to be subject to no comparable limitation, since human wants, except for food, are indefinitely expansible. Thus, it is said, the collision of dynamic demand with the relatively static conditions of supply portends scarcity. But examination of the actual trends in supply and demand show that the a priori reasoning which led to this pessimistic conclusion was based on questionable assumptions.

The Probable Trends in Demand

Although the increase of U. S. population may not continue at the amazing rate recorded in 1940-1950, the next 25 years will still bring significant gains. Elsewhere in the Free World, experts predict accelerated rates of increase. But in industrialized countries the demand for raw materials does not expand in proportion to the growth in population, because of changes in the way people spend their incomes. With rising standards of living, they devote relatively less of their incomes to commodities, and more to intangibles, education and the arts, recreation, medical care, beauty treatments, and other items in which wages rather than materials are the principal costs. In the next 25 years, the changing age grouping of the population, the increasing proportion of older people, will probably reinforce this trend.

We may expect, also, that structural changes in industry will cause the consumption of raw materials to rise more slowly than the index of industrial production. An increasing proportion of American industrial output will consist of highly fabricated products, automobiles and airplanes, typewriters, accounting and calculating machines, radio and television apparatus, and other products in which materials make up a less important element of cost than labor. For these reasons a relatively smaller expenditure on materials will be needed to sustain the expected rise in gross national product. Reasoning in this way, the Paley Commission estimated that in the United States a doubling of the total output of goods and services in the period 1950-1975 would require only a 50 to 60 percent increase in supplies of materials.[1]

Defense production will show the same sort of change. U. S. expenditures for military hardware (if we assume no significant relaxation in U. S.-Soviet tension) will increase, but probably without a proportionate increase, tonnagewise, in the demand for metals. Ballistic missiles and their accessories are highly fabricated products that require heavy inputs of labor relative to materials. In respect to consumption of metals, they may have the same relation to the airplane, which they will partially displace, as the plane had to the destroyer and the battleship. Moreover, the new weapons, it appears, will not require greatly increased quantities of any single material. In addition to aluminum and titanium, it has been reported that they will use alloy steels containing chromium, nickel, molybdenum, vanadium, columbium, cobalt and tungsten.

Rising standards of living in the industrialized countries of Western Europe and in Canada, Australia, New Zealand and Japan will add to the drain on the supplies of materials available to the Free World. Patterns of consumption in these countries, however, are similar to those of the United States, and probably will become increasingly so; hence the growth of their materials consumption, relative to gross national product, will presumably resemble ours.

[1] President's Materials Policy Commission, *Resources for Freedom* (Washington: GPO, 1952), v. 1, *Foundations for Growth and Security*, p. 59.

The Outlook for Supply

Agricultural production, including food and raw materials, economists have traditionally stated, is subject to the Law of Diminishing Returns. After a certain stage in production had been reached, further increments of output, *other conditions remaining constant,* could be obtained only at the expense of disproportionately large inputs of other economic factors. But in the next 20 to 25 years the real costs of rubber, wool and other raw materials of agricultural origin may not in fact rise because of changes in "other conditions," technological advance in seed selection, for example, and in the breeding of animals. Economies of scale, in some instances, may accompany expansion in the size of productive units.

As regards metals and other mineral resources, the outlook for expansion of supplies from *domestic sources in the United States* is not promising. The declining yield of the older oil fields, the need of drilling ever deeper wells, and other circumstances are indications of the progressive exhaustion of our petroleum reserves. It seems improbable that, within the next 20 or 25 years, the discovery of new oil fields will greatly change the present supply situation. We may expect, however, that technological advance will make possible further economies in the extraction of coal and oil, thus stretching out the life of our fuel resources. Within the near future, moreover, atomic energy will supplement fuel oil in the heating of homes, offices and public buildings, and in the generation of power for public utilities and manufacturing. For highway and air transport we shall continue to depend on petroleum, but redesign of internal combustion engines, for example, the introduction of fuel injection systems, will bring economies in fuel consumption. Increasing traffic congestion, and perhaps a greater reverence for life, may check the trend toward heavier and faster cars.

Geologists do not expect to uncover, at any time in the near future, new deposits of ferrous or nonferrous ores in the United States as rich and as easily accessible as those exploited in the past 50 years. "The mineral frontier, which seemed endless in its capacity to yield new sources of raw materials, has all but disappeared insofar as new deposits are concerned."[2] The country has been so thoroughly combed by prospectors that surface outcroppings cannot be expected to yield large new supplies. New methods of exploration, it is true, may reveal the existence of hidden deposits, although no one can now foretell how large they will be or whether they can be worked at a profit. New and more economical processes of milling, concentration and refining, however, will probably make possible the more extensive use of low-grade ores.

The outlook for supply is not uniform for all metals. For two light metals, magnesium and titanium, which have come into greatly increased use in postwar years, domestic reserves appear adequate for the foreseeable future demands. Whether or not the refined metals can be produced at a cost low enough to stimulate widespread use will depend on the availability of large supplies of cheap electrical energy. Electric power may also prove a limiting factor in the future expansion of aluminum production.

At the end of World War II, a trained observer predicted that the "potential effect of substitutes on the mineral position of the United States may be regarded as of minor importance." He foresaw no likelihood that plastics would to any significant degree serve to replace metals.[3] But the following decade witnessed the development of an enormous new industry, the production of polymeric materials. Utilizing a few readily available substances, coal and

2 Howard A. Meyerhoff, "What Is Involved in Metals Conservation Today?" *Annals of the American Academy of Political and Social Science,* v. 281 (May 1952), p. 40. "The pick-and-shovel prospector will soon strike pay dirt only in western movies." J. Frederic Dewhurst and Associates, *America's Needs and Resources* (New York: Twentieth Century Fund, 1955), p. 759.

3 "Plastics provide substitutes for some mineral products, but as yet offer no likelihood of being put to major use; their ultimate significance as replacements for minerals probably will be small." Elmer Walter Pehrson, "Our Mineral Resources and Security," *Foreign Affairs,* v. 23, no. 4 (July 1945), p. 654.

oil, water and, in lesser amounts, chlorine, silicon and fluorine, the chemical industry has produced cheap and effective substitutes for nonferrous metals, for iron and for natural rubber, wood, glass, cotton and wool.

American industries have made great strides in postwar years in economies in the use of minerals, in utilizing a greater variety of resources, as well as in the techniques of exploration and discovery, in mining and processing metals.[4] There seems good reason to expect that, granted a continued high level of demand and continued research by private firms and government agencies, this progress will continue. Industrial engineers will increasingly exercise their ingenuity in substituting for copper, lead and zinc, as the latter become scarcer, the more abundant light metals, aluminum, magnesium, silicon and titanium.

But even under the most favorable assumptions regarding technological advance, the outlook for the United States, *if the country had to depend exclusively on its own resources,* would be grim. Attempts to achieve self-sufficiency could result only in lower standards of living and a decline in national power. But if we enlarge the scope of our inquiry, and compare the potential raw materials supplies of the Free World with prospective demand, we are confronted with a much different situation. A century of rapid industrial expansion and the demands of two world wars have greatly depleted the formerly abundant mineral resources of the United States. But in the underdeveloped countries, in Latin America, Africa and Southeast Asia, vast supplies still await exploitation. In Canada, new discoveries and the rapid development of mineral industries, uranium, iron ore, oil, nickel and other nonferrous metals, have revealed large possibilities of low-cost expansion.[5] The enlargement of production of oil in

[4] For a good description, see J. Frederic Dewhurst and Associates, *America's Needs and Resources,* cited, pp. 757-760. Also, President's Materials Policy Commission, cited, v. 4, *The Promise of Technology.*

[5] The history of the Creighton mine of the International Nickel Company affords an excellent illustration. According to the president of the company: "That mine was to all intents and purposes to be abandoned in the early 1930's. It's number was up. We were putting it to bed, and it

Venezuela, the Middle East and in Africa, of copper in Chile and in Rhodesia and nonferrous metals in Mexico and in South America, all give promise of abundant supplies at no increase in real costs.

Fear has sometimes been expressed that, as industrialization progresses in the underdeveloped countries, their consumption of domestically produced materials will cut into the supplies available for consuming countries in the United States and Western Europe. This is a possible but not a necessary consequence. Industrialization need not check the expansion of raw materials production, for the two kinds of economic activity may supplement rather than conflict with each other. But even if industrialization should absorb some of the materials which otherwise would have been exported, the resulting decrease in the next 20 years in the supplies available to industrialized economies could not be large. The underdeveloped countries now account for less than 20 percent of the total Free World demand for materials. Even a very high rate of industrialization would not make a large absolute increase in the quantities of materials they consume.

Political Obstacles

The available evidence does not indicate that in the next 20 or 25 years world-wide shortages of fuels or industrial materials will be inevitable. It will be physically possible to obtain metals, fibers and other materials in quantities sufficient to satisfy the Free World's requirements at real costs which will not exert downward pressures on the standards of living in industrial countries.

But the great unsolved problems of raw materials supplies for the United States and other countries in the Free World are not exclusively, or primarily, matters of geology or economics. They lie rather in the realm of politics. The pertinent question is not, "Will the supplies physi-

---

was disappearing. . . . Today the Creighton mine is the greatest source of nickel in the world." Statement of Henry S. Wingate in *Supply and Distribution of Nickel,* Hearings before the Senate Select Committee on Small Business, 84th Cong., 2d sess. (Washington: GPO, 1956), p. 153.

cally present in the countries of the Free World be adequate?" Instead, we must ask ourselves, "On what terms will the nations within whose domains the ore deposits and the oil wells are found allow them to be exploited by American or other investors?" Will they permit the products of extractive industries to be freely produced and exported, or will they impose onerous restrictions? Will their legislation and administrative regulations provide a "climate" favorable to the inflow of capital, equipment, technology and management skills? The answers to these questions will determine whether foreign investors, principally American, will provide the capital necessary for adequate production of materials in the underdeveloped countries.

There is no need to describe here in detail the obstacles which supplying countries have put in the way of foreign investors desiring to develop raw materials. They include threats of nationalization and other measures which render uncertain the legal status of ownership, demands for increasing shares of the profits of the enterprises, requirements for extensive local participation in management, import and export controls, restrictions on the repatriation of earnings and capital.[6]

The difficulties do not lie primarily in the obvious conflict of interest between foreign investors and the governments of source countries over the division of profits of minerals development. No doubt these governments are showing themselves to be increasingly hard bargainers and no doubt occasionally the terms offered are such as to discourage investment. But the principal difficulties are concerned with doubts whether bargains once made will be kept, and with limitations that source countries seek to impose on the control and management of foreign enterprises within their borders. Oil companies can live with a "50-50" division of earnings; it is questionable whether they can live — or at least expand — under the threat of overt or "creeping" expropriation.[7]

[6] A rather full discussion of these measures will be found in the Paley report, v. 1, cited, pp. 63-67. See also Edward S. Mason, "Raw Materials, Rearmament, and Economics," *Quarterly Journal of Economics,* v. 66, no. 3 (August 1952), pp. 337-338.

[7] Mason, same.

The policies referred to spring from many causes, but all in greater or lesser degree are related to what Adlai Stevenson has called "the revolution of rising expectations."[8] The underdeveloped countries, the principal source of primary products, have become increasingly aware of the great, and widening, gap that separates their poverty from the prosperity of the Western world. Their weakness, political as well as economic, they attribute to specialization in basic industries which have been owned and operated by foreigners. Industrialization, they believe, would not only raise the productivity of labor; by diversifying occupations it would render their economies less vulnerable to alternations of prosperity and depression originating in the industrialized countries, principally the United States. The leaders of the new, self-conscious nationalism demand control of the management of basic industries. They insist that a larger share of the earnings be retained for the benefit of the native economy. Conservation is another objective. Crude oil, copper ore and other metals are nonrenewable national assets. On these resources the industrialization programs of the future will be built. Hence, they should not be alienated, i.e., disposed of to foreign countries, except under strict surveillance.

Economic factors furnish only partial motivation for nationalistic policies. Industrialization, it is believed, would enhance national prestige. The underdeveloped countries which have recently gained political independence now want to attain what they call "economic independence." But this, they believe, is impossible as long as the control of vital industries is in the hands of foreigners.

The Reform of Policy

The realities of world politics, as well as humanitarian and economic considerations, require that the United

[8] Gunnar Myrdal, borrowing a term originally used to describe the religious revival in the American colonies (*c.* 1750), calls the demands of the poverty-stricken nations for economic development, as well as for national independence, "the Great Awakening." *Rich Lands and Poor* (New York: Harper, 1957), p. 7.

States give especial attention to the effects of its raw materials policies on its relations with underdeveloped countries. We might first consider Canada, a country which furnishes a larger proportion than any other of the basic materials imported for the use of American industries: 100 percent of pulpwood, 94 percent of newsprint paper, 80 percent of nickel, 55 percent of titanium ore, 45 percent of iron ore, 36 percent of zinc, 20 percent of copper and 12 percent of oil. In postwar years our dependence on our northern neighbor for industrial materials has significantly increased.

Canada, because of its rapid strides in manufacturing and the high standard of living of its people, is not usually classified among underdeveloped countries. Yet it displays some of their characteristic attitudes and policies. Although predominantly a producer of raw materials, with rich resources far from being fully exploited, rapid industrialization is a prime objective of public policy. Moreover, Canadian attitudes toward foreign investors show a strong strain of nationalism. Canadians put a high premium on economic independence. They are unwilling to become "a mere satellite of the United States," but this, they fear, may result from the closeness of their economic relations with their great neighbor to the south. Noting that 73 percent of Canada's imports came from the United States and that 60 percent of her exports were sold there, a Canadian Minister of Finance remarked: "To a disquieting degree Canada has placed her trading eggs in one basket." [9]

An even greater source of anxiety is the rapid influx of American capital on an equity, not a loan, basis, which means the ownership and management of Canadian industries by citizens of the United States. Approximately two-thirds of the oil and mining development in Canada is controlled by American capital. Foreign-controlled companies have "a dominating influence" in the production of oil and gas, nickel, iron ore, aluminum, synthetic rubber, pulp and paper. The fear is occasionally expressed that

[9] Donald M. Fleming, address before the Canadian Society of New York, November 1, 1957.

American business interests may exercise undue control on Canadian legislation. "The extreme Canadian nationalist today," writes G. V. Ferguson, "must regard the prairie oil lobby in Ottawa as a Trojan horse inside the walls of the capital, whose belly is filled with oil experts from Texas." [10]

American tariff restrictions on industrial materials have long been a source of irritation to lumbering, mining and oil interests north of the border. The persistent attempts, since 1953, of American producers to obtain higher import duties on lead and zinc threatened an important section of the Canadian mining industry. (Canada's exports of lead and zinc to the United States in 1956 were 61 percent, by value, of her total exports of these metals and 37 percent of the value of production.) President Eisenhower's decision, December 24, 1957, to impose quota restrictions on imports of Canadian oil [11] aroused bitter protest. (See Chapter 10, pp. 321-322.)

Suggestions have occasionally been made in Canada that restrictions should be laid on exports of fuels and industrial materials, either to bring pressure on the United States to relax tariff barriers, or to promote industrial development in Canada. British Columbia in 1957 imposed a tax of 25 to 50 cents a ton on iron ore mined for export. The stated purpose of the tax was not to produce revenue but rather to encourage the establishment of a steel industry in the province.[12] But a Royal Commission

[10] "Likely Trends in Canadian-American Political Relations," *Canadian Journal of Economics and Political Science*, v. 22, no. 4 (November 1956), p. 442.

[11] Canadian oil is exported principally to Pacific Coast markets. Imports into this area had hitherto been continuously exempted from the so-called voluntary restrictions dating from October 1955. The President's action cancelled this exemption.

[12] Regulations of the provinces and territories of Canada restrict the exportation of unrefined metal-bearing ores. Saskatchewan, Quebec and New Brunswick require all ore mined within their borders, except as otherwise may be permitted by the Minister of Mines or by the Lieutenant-Governor in Council, to be also refined within their borders. British Columbia, Alberta, Nova Scotia, Newfoundland and the Yukon Territory have no such requirement, but Ontario and Manitoba require that ore mined under their jurisdiction, except as otherwise may be permitted by

called attention to the probability that export restrictions, by increasing the costs of the final product, would make the development of the resource less attractive. It cautiously concluded that, "There may be sound arguments and better opportunities for refining a greater percentage of certain metals—for example, nickel, lead, zinc, titanium and perhaps uranium—prior to export, but each situation requires careful study on an individual basis before any such conclusion would be justified." [13]

In March 1953 the Canadian Minister of Trade and Commerce announced that no permits for the export of natural gas would be granted until it was clear that "there can be no economic use, present or future, for that natural gas within Canada." [14] But within a few years changed conditions seemed to warrant a modification of this policy, and temporary permits were granted for the export of gas to metal-processing plants in Montana. In 1956, a project took shape for a 2,200-mile pipeline to carry gas from the newly developed oil and gas fields in southern Alberta to industrial areas in Ontario and Quebec. Whether or not the new Conservative government would permit some of the gas to be diverted to American cities in the Middle West was undecided at the end of 1957. The decision will probably depend on the report of a Royal Commission appointed to investigate the Canadian gas and oil industries.

It is ironical that, while Canadian policy was tending toward restriction, American policy was moving toward facilitating imports of gas. On November 15, 1957, the U. S. Federal Power Commission, which had hitherto

---

the Lieutenant-Governor in Council, must be refined in Canada. The Northwest Territories have the same requirement as Manitoba and Ontario except that they have no authority to enable special permission to be granted by the Governor General in Council for the export of certain unrefined ores and that unrefined iron ores produced in excess of smelter requirements may be shipped from islands in Hudson Bay.

[13] Royal Commission on Canada's Economic Prospects, *Preliminary Report* (Ottawa: Queen's Printer, 1956), p. 48.

[14] Canadian Department of External Affairs, *Government Policy in the Canadian Petroleum Industry,* Reference Papers, no. 96 (Ottawa, June 1957), p. 12.

refused to approve the construction of any pipeline which would depend entirely on sources of supply in Canada, reversed its position.

The Congress of the United States and the Executive, too, have been accustomed to assume that Canadians would see eye to eye with us in matters of foreign policy. In the past, this assumption, although it irritated our neighbors across the border, has generally proved well founded. But with the rising sense of national power, Canada is adopting a more independent attitude, for example, in debates and votes in the United Nations and in NATO. The United States needs Canada's support. It may not be readily forthcoming unless our policies on basic materials recognize the identity of interests—Canada's and ours—in collective security and in the expansion of trade.

Competition with the U.S.S.R.

In the conflict between the United States and the Soviet Union, underdeveloped countries in Latin America, in the Middle East and in Southeast Asia, the Free World's principal sources of industrial materials, occupy a critical position. To aid them in overcoming poverty and the attendant evils of disease and ignorance, we have been extending economic aid running into billions of dollars. Consistent with this program are governmental activities that facilitate the investment of American capital in the underdeveloped countries. The bulk of these investments looks toward the expansion of production and exports of oil, minerals and other industrial materials, thereby adding to the supplies available to the United States and its allies for defense production, as well as for the growth of their economies.

Lenin and Stalin taught that the underdeveloped countries were steppingstones, first to the domination of Europe and ultimately of the world. In accordance with this doctrine, the U.S.S.R. has been trying to win them over by subversion, by propaganda and by economic aid. Until a few years ago Americans would not have taken seriously Russian competition in the field of economic assistance.

But, as the result of rapid advances in industrial production, Russia is now able to export machinery and heavy equipment, to provide engineering services and capital loans. Moreover, Russia purchases from the recipients of her aid foodstuffs and raw materials, including soybeans, copper, lead, rubber and cotton.

Thus far the United States has surpassed the Soviet bloc in financing economic development. Professor Joseph Berliner has estimated that the total dollar equivalent of the credit agreements made by the U.S.S.R. with underdeveloped countries in the years 1953-1957 was $1,227 million. In addition, satellite countries, principally Czechoslovakia, gave credits of $534 million. Most of the credits from the Soviet bloc went to South and Southeast Asia. In a single year (fiscal 1957) total aid from the United States to underdeveloped countries (new credits and gross grants) amounted to $1,628 million.[15]

But the underdeveloped countries want trade as well as aid; they want expanded markets for their primary products. In this respect, as an importer of raw materials, the United States occupies a far stronger position than the U.S.S.R. Incomplete statistics of exports of 23 underdeveloped countries to the Soviet Union, to the Soviet bloc and to the United States in 1955 are shown below:

	To the U.S.S.R.	*To the Soviet bloc*	*To the United States*
	(in millions of United States dollars)		
From Africa and the Middle East	45.6	250.9	288.4
From Southeast Asia	47.8	205.3	711.5
From Latin America	31.1	100.7	1,360.9
From Yugoslavia	41.6	77.4	30.8
Total	166.1	634.3	2,391.6

Note: Included in the total for Africa and the Middle East are incomplete figures for the Sudan and Syria. Likewise in the totals for Latin America are included incomplete figures for the trade of Argentina.
Source: U. S. Bureau of Foreign Commerce

The trade figures show that for each of the three regions the United States furnished a far larger market than the

[15] Total nonmilitary aid to all countries amounted to $2,213 million.

U.S.S.R. Analysis by countries, however, discloses that in certain critical areas sales to the members of the Soviet bloc have either exceeded sales to the United States or have furnished close competition. In 1956 Egypt sold goods valued at $139 million to the Soviet bloc (including $16 million to the U.S.S.R.) and only $15 million to the United States. Pakistan's sales were: to the Soviet bloc, $20 million, almost nothing to the U.S.S.R., and to the United States, $37 million. Turkey sold to the Soviet bloc goods valued at $60 million, including $6.6 million to the U.S.S.R., and to the United States, $68 million.[16]

The concentration of Soviet imports on certain products of particular interest to the exporting countries appears to indicate political motivation. Russian buying of Egyptian cotton affords an illustration. In 1955 Communist countries bought 401,000 bales of Egyptian cotton, 31.5 percent of all exports of that commodity; in 1956 they purchased 450,000 bales, 41.8 percent of the total. The increase in Russian imports of wool from Uruguay, directly and via the Netherlands, has to a small extent compensated that country for the drastic decline in sales to the United States.

The U.S.S.R. with its monopoly of foreign trade can use imports as a vehicle of political penetration, but for the United States this kind of trade policy is impossible. Now that stockpile goals have been so largely attained, the government's purchases of strategic materials from abroad are inconsiderable. Importing, as long as we are not at war, will be conducted by private business firms and motivated by economic rather than political considerations.

Trade Policy

The government of the United States has at its disposal means of influencing trade in raw materials to the advantage of the economies of the underdeveloped countries, and its own as well. To invitations to join in agreements to

[16] The figures in this paragraph were compiled by Joseph S. Berliner from data published by the U. S. Bureau of Foreign Commerce. They appear in his book, *Soviet Economic Aid: The New Aid and Trade Policy in Underdeveloped Countries,* published for the Council on Foreign Relations.

iron out short-term fluctuations in raw materials prices, this country, except in the cases of wheat and sugar, has turned a deaf ear. This negative attitude we should maintain. It is founded on the belief that the somewhat uncertain benefits which buffer stock schemes might confer on exporters of raw materials would be more than offset by the losses which importing countries, chiefly the United States, would sustain because of the restraints and rigidities which attempts at price stabilization would introduce in international trade.

Underdeveloped countries suffer when business recessions in the United States cause contraction in imports of raw materials. Hence in their interests, as well as our own, we should endeavor, through appropriate credit and fiscal policies, to forestall incipient depressions and, if they nevertheless occur, to moderate their severity and to shorten their term.

We turn now to the consideration of tariff policy. From the point of view of economic advantage, in order to obtain adequate supplies of raw materials at minimum real costs, a rational national policy would remove all import duties, taxes and quotas so that supplies of raw materials from foreign countries would enter free of all restrictions. The immediate result of this sweeping action would be psychological rather than economic. It would replenish the sadly depleted reservoir of good will toward the United States, but without conferring great material benefits on the exporting countries, and without causing great losses to producers of raw materials in the United States. About half of the materials imported into this country already enter free of duty, and the remainder, with only a few exceptions, pay low or moderate rates.[17] For this reason, and because the demand for basic commodities appears to be inelastic with respect to price changes, we should not ex-

[17] This situation, it should be remembered, is largely fortuitous, having resulted from rising prices of basic commodities in world markets rather than from reduction of U. S. import duties. Should the present downward trend in prices continue, the duties, which are levied on a specific basis, not as a percentage of value, would automatically become more burdensome.

pect tariff reduction to bring greatly increased imports. By the same token, the resulting displacement of American labor and capital would be minimal. If the new policy were inaugurated in a period of full employment, and accompanied by measures to facilitate economic adjustment, serious hardship could be avoided.

Complete free trade in raw materials is the goal which American policy should strive to attain, but in terms of today's practical politics it is a chimera. The opposition of a bloc of Senators from eight Western states would be sufficient to kill legislation of this sort. They represent the "heart of the West," the sparsely populated, semiarid area lying between the Great Plains and the Pacific slope, where mining, oil production and sheep and cattle raising are the predominant occupations. If represented in Congress only in proportion to their population, the eight states would have little influence on national policy, but their sixteen Senators wield power sufficient to defeat measures thought to be injurious to their constituents.

In the national interest, nevertheless, the Eisenhower administration, and its successors, should persist in efforts to bring about freer conditions of trade, boldly utilizing the power delegated by Congress to reduce import duties by multilateral agreements. It should set its face against attempts to impose further restrictions on imports of raw materials, whether by higher duties or by quotas. The claims of domestic industries that they are essential to national defense, and that therefore the government should restrict competing imports, should be rigidly scrutinized in order to determine (1) whether imports actually have caused injury or threaten injury, and (2) if injury is real or imminent, whether the remedy sought would be appropriate.

Congress, in an amendment to the 1955 Trade Agreements Extension Act, gave the President authority to take such action as he deems necessary to "adjust" (i.e., to restrict) the imports of any commodity when he finds that such imports are threatening to impair the national security.[18] The amendment, hastily improvised at the end of the legislative session to appease coal and oil interests who were demanding quotas on imports of petroleum, was loosely drawn. It set up no procedure, required no publication of results of investigations and imposed no limits on the President's powers to "adjust" the imports. But the investigations made by the Office of Defense Mobilization and by the President in the administration of the amendment, nevertheless, should be exhaustive, and proof that essential industries actually have suffered injury from imports should be given full publicity.

The basic question is how large an oil industry, or a lead and zinc industry, etc., does the country need. The ODM should be required to furnish a quantitative answer. When it has determined that national security requires the domestic production of X millions of barrels of oil daily, or Y tons of manganese a year, the next question is "what methods shall government employ to get the desired result?" Restriction of imports has proved a clumsy and expensive means of stimulating production. The payment of subsidies directly to producers on a predetermined maximum output would have many advantages. The cost to the U. S. Treasury would be known, and specific performance could be required of the recipients.

In 1954 Congress, at President Eisenhower's suggestion, introduced a subsidy plan for wool growers in the form of "incentive payments." (See Chapter 8, pp. 234-240.) Four

[18] Sec. 7 (b), *Public Law* no. 86, 84th Cong., 1st sess., approved June 21, 1955. The paragraph reads as follows:

> In order to further the policy and purpose of this section, whenever the Director of the Office of Defense Mobilization has reason to believe that any article is being imported into the United States in such quantities as to threaten to impair the national security, he shall so advise the President, and if the President agrees that there is reason for such belief, the President shall cause an immediate investigation to be made to determine the facts. If, on the basis of such investigation, and the report to him of the findings and recommendations made in connection therewith, the President finds that the article is being imported into the United States in such quantities as to threaten to impair the national security, he shall take such action as he deems necessary to adjust the imports of such article to a level that will not threaten to impair the national security.

years later the Eisenhower administration proposed a more general use of subsidies in the Domestic Minerals Stabilization Plan which Secretary of the Interior Seaton presented to Congress, April 28, 1958. The Plan called for "stabilization payments" to domestic producers of five minerals: copper,[19] lead, zinc, acid-grade fluorspar and tungsten. For each mineral the payments would be equal to the difference between the stabilization price and the price obtained by producers in the American market. The proposed prices and the maximum amounts of the various commodities on which subsidies would be paid, with comparative data for 1957, are shown below:

	Proposed Stabilization Price		*Average Price in 1957*	*Maximum Output on Which Subsidy Would Be Paid*		*Output in 1957 (preliminary)*
				(in thousands)		
Copper	27.50	cents per lb.	29.58	1,000	tons	1,075
Lead	14.75	cents per lb.	14.66	350	tons	334
Zinc	12.75	cents per lb.	11.44	550	tons	520
Fluorspar (acid-grade)	48	$ per short-ton	51	180	tons	187
Tungsten	36	$ per short-ton unit	19	375	short-ton units	377

The Plan, the Secretary explained, was designed to provide temporary assistance to the distressed mining industries, pending the expected upswing in the general economy. He did not state, however, that when this occurred the subsidy would be discontinued. Congress was asked to authorize annual stabilization payments over a period of five years. The cost of the Plan, estimated at about $160

[19] Copper was later dropped from the list.

million for the first year, was expected to diminish with economic recovery and rising market prices.

The prospective beneficiaries, the domestic mining industries, expressed their opposition promptly and forcefully. Lead and zinc producers found the payments inadequate. They, and others, rejected subsidy payments as humiliating—"the mining industry doesn't want to live on handouts." They preferred tariff protection, not only because it was a more respectable form of assistance, but also because it gave more promise of being permanent. Congress, even if it authorized a Five-year Plan, would have to make annual appropriations. The hearings and debates which took place on these occasions might afford critics of the Plan a chance to defeat it. An official of a large copper mining company is reported to have said that he could not imagine the United States taxpayer making stabilization payments to Kennecott, Anaconda and Phelps Dodge.[20]

As originally presented, the Seaton Plan provided for a flat subsidy to all producers, making no distinction between high-cost and low-cost firms. To remedy this defect an amendment, accepted by the administration, would grant larger benefits to firms with an annual output of less than 2,000 tons.

Like the incentive payments to wool growers, the proposed subsidies to mining industries supplement tariff protection; they do not replace import duties. In time, however, it seems probable that the tariff may become relatively insignificant. Its benefits will be received only indirectly and will probably continue to provide a smaller share of the income of the beneficiaries than will the direct payments.

The Seaton Plan should be regarded as a significant forward step in American policy affecting raw materials. It will be exposed to the danger that log-rolling tactics, familiar in tariff legislation, will extend its benefits to undeserving industries, and that the scale of payments will

[20] *New York Times,* May 4, 1958.

be progressively raised so that in the subsidized industries the margin of production will be unnecessarily extended. If, however, we assume equally honest and public-spirited legislators and administrators, subsidies have two advantages when compared with import duties. First, as we have already pointed out, their cost is much more easily ascertainable and the burden is more equitably distributed. Subsidies, moreover, have this important additional merit, that unless applied so extravagantly as to substantially increase domestic production, they do not interfere with international trade and, unlike import duties, are not regarded by exporting countries as injurious to their interests.

Government assistance to producers of nonrenewable resources, whether by tax incentives, stockpile purchases, tariff protection or subsidies, tends to hasten their depletion and thus raises the conservation issue. The question is: Has government an obligation to regulate the rate of exploitation of natural resources, to prevent waste and to preserve the resources for the use of succeeding generations? A significant answer requires that physical waste be distinguished from economic waste. In mining, for example, much ore is left in the ground which may never be recoverable because at prevailing prices its market value would not cover the cost of bringing it to the surface. In a system of free enterprise, a certain amount of physical waste seems unavoidable, although government can reduce it by the dissemination of the results of research and advances in engineering. Public authorities, through appropriate regulation of production, as for example by compulsory unitization of oil fields, may prevent or at least reduce economic waste, i.e., the loss of resources which are actually worth more than the cost of recovering them.

Frequently the term "conservation" is not used to denote the most efficient use of resources, either in the physical or the economic sense. It means rather non-use. This "hair-shirt philosophy," prominent in the conservation movement of fifty years ago, has now lost much of its appeal. Economists, political scientists and intelligent and well-informed laymen no longer stress the community's obligation to abstain from consumption of nonrenewable resources, in order that they may be "conserved" for future generations. This change of attitude does not imply deterioration of moral fiber or ethical standards. All of us probably feel as deeply as did our parents a responsibility for the welfare of those who come after us. We differ only in doubting whether the best way to give them a good inheritance is to preserve in the ground certain minerals and sources of energy. It would better serve the interests of our successors, we believe, to transmit other types of capital assets, efficient industrial plant, for example, and a highly productive economic system. For this change in attitude toward conservation the rapid technological advances of the past half century are largely responsible. The development of new methods of discovering hidden ore reserves and of more economical methods of processing low-grade ores has, in effect, expanded our natural resources. Elsewhere in the Free World, surprising new discoveries have enlarged proven reserves of some materials—oil, copper and nickel—at a rate much faster than the rate of depletion. Necessity still proves to be the mother of invention. Whenever real costs have begun to rise scientists and engineers have succeeded in providing synthetic substitutes for natural products, and have found means of replacing scarce metals with those which are more abundant. In view of these possibilities it would be false economy to limit the present generation in its use of resources which might prove to have had more value to them than to their children.

Policies of non-use, although bad economics, may nevertheless find some justification on grounds of national security. In an emergency, our reserve supply of "shut-in" oil might prove a valuable asset. Even high-cost tungsten from marginal mines in a Western state would be worth having if supplies from abroad were cut off. But caution, nevertheless, should be observed in the payment of subsidies to producers of nonrenewable resources, in order to guard against too rapid depletion. The payments should aim at the maintenance of a going industry of dimensions adequate for a mobilization base; they should not aim at encouraging unlimited expansion.

* * * *

Secretary Ickes in 1942 told a Congressional committee that the United States had no oil policy. By that he meant that he had been unable to find in any one place a condensed description of statutes and regulations affecting production and trade in petrolum and its products, or any authoritative statement of underlying purposes. The Secretary, were he alive today, would be equally frustrated should he search for an authoritative statement of over-all policy on industrial materials. National policy in this field is the product of almost two centuries of undisciplined growth. It consists of a variety of statutes and administrative regulations adopted to deal *ad hoc* with the needs of the moment. It retains the remnants of measures employed to cope with conditions which no longer exist. It bears the marks left by pressures exerted by special and local interests, as well as the impress of national emergencies.

It is high time that the President and the Congress should take an all-inclusive view of raw materials policy, instead of dealing with commodities separately in response to the pressures of the moment. Their purpose should be to make sure that measures regulating trade in raw materials reinforce rather than obstruct the aims of foreign economic policy. Raw materials policy should supplement and not work at cross purposes with loans, grants and technical assistance to underdeveloped countries; it should be consistent also with the measures advocated by the United States in the International Bank and the International Monetary Fund. Only a unified raw materials policy, integrated with foreign economic policy, can further the objectives of the United States in its international relations—the betterment of living conditions for all peoples and the establishment of peace with justice.

National strength depends upon the best use of all kinds of national resources, the services of scientists and engineers, the initiative of businessmen, as well as reserves of oils and metals. Import restrictions and stockpile purchases which perpetuate production from high-cost mines or from depleted oil fields weaken rather than strengthen the national economy. They weaken also the system of free enterprise and the efficient functioning of democratic institutions. Every new measure of government aid eventually brings government regulation and provides the camel of government control with more ample accommodations in the tent of private enterprise. Furthermore, the lobbying and vote-swapping which accompany the extension of government assistance to producers of raw materials bring discredit on democratic institutions. It is doubtful whether government assistance provided under such conditions actually promotes national security.

Policy makers, in the years which lie ahead, must interpret "national security" in the broadest sense. They must by their acts recognize that the strength of the American economy, and our defense potential, depend on the effective functioning of the economies of our allies in the Free World. They must act in the belief that for the United States there is no national security outside the framework of collective security.

APPENDICES

APPENDIX A

Table A

U. S. IMPORTS OF CERTAIN INDUSTRIAL MATERIALS: PROPORTIONS SUPPLIED BY PRODUCING COUNTRIES OR AREAS, 1956

(as percent of total quantities imported)

Material	*Canada*	*Mexico*	*Total Western Hemi-sphere*	*Europe*	*Africa*	*Middle East*	*India*	*Southeast Asia*	*Australia*	*All Other*
Aluminum[a]	85.0	—	85.0	14.3	—	—	—	—	—	.7
Antimony[b]	1.8	34.4	53.1	31.0	15.5	.4	—	—	—	—
Asbestos[c]	92.1	—	92.1	.6	6.8	—	—	—	.5	—
Bauxite[d]	—	—	99.5	—	.5	—	—	—	—	—
Beryl[e]	—	21.1	39.9	1.9	30.8	—	27.2	—	—	.1
Bismuth	5.4	13.7	54.0	46.0	—	—	—	—	—	—
Cadmium[f]	20.2	31.4	52.2	31.5	10.5	—	—	—	—	5.8[g]
Chromium[h]	—	—	2.1	1.0	39.8	26.9	1.9[i]	25.6	—	2.7
Cobalt[j]	8.5	—	8.5	15.2	76.3	—	—	—	—	—
Columbium[k]	—	—	2.9	9.9	78.0	—	—	9.2	—	—[l]
Copper[m]	19.7	9.5	80.3	2.8	10.6	1.0	—	2.0	3.2	.1
Fluorspar[n]	7.2	65.0	72.2	27.8	—	—	—	—	—	—
Iron[o]	45.1	.4	92.0	3.3	4.6	—	—	—	—	—[l]
Lead[p]	9.8	18.4	54.8	10.6	9.0	—	—	.5	25.1	—[l]
Manganese[q]	—	8.0	28.6	.2	42.4	.2	28.3	.3	—	.1
Mercury	.2	24.3	25.3	74.6	—	.1	—	—	—	—

See footnotes at end of table.

Table A (continued)

U. S. IMPORTS OF CERTAIN INDUSTRIAL MATERIALS: PROPORTIONS SUPPLIED BY PRODUCING COUNTRIES OR AREAS, 1956

(as percent of total quantities imported)

Material	*Canada*	*Mexico*	*Total Western Hemi-sphere*	*Europe*	*Africa*	*Middle East*	*India*	*Southeast Asia*	*Australia*	*All Other*
Nickel[r]	79.3	—	90.0	9.4	—	—	—[1]	—	—	.6
Petroleum, crude	12.3	1.7	66.9	—	—	29.3	—	3.8	—	—
Platinum group metals[s]	27.8	—[1]	31.2	68.6	—	—[1]	—	—	—[1]	.1
Rubber, crude natural	—	—	.4	—	9.2	—	—	90.3	—	.1
Tantalum[t]	—	—	12.1	.5	79.0	—	—	—	8.3	—
Tin[u]	.3	.2	11.7	23.5	1.5	—	—	63.2	.1	—
Titanium ore:										
Ilmenite	54.7	—	54.7	—[1]	—	—	37.2	8.0	.1	—
Rutile	—	.1	.1	—[1]	—	—	—	—	99.9	—
Tungsten[v]	7.9	3.2	57.2	9.3	5.0	—	—	4.7	8.9	14.9[w]
Vanadium[x]	—	—	100.0	—	—	—	—	—	—	—
Wool,[y] total	.1	—	32.3	7.0	5.5	11.5	10.1[i]	—	16.9	16.7[z]
Apparel	.3	—	25.8	2.5	12.3	—	—	—	40.3	19.1[z]
Zinc[aa]	36.3	29.7	83.2	9.8	3.0	—[1]	—	.1	3.2	.7
Zirconium[bb]	1.0	—	2.0	.5	—	—	—	—	97.4	—[1]

See footnotes at end of table.

Table A (continued)

U. S. IMPORTS OF CERTAIN INDUSTRIAL MATERIALS: PROPORTIONS SUPPLIED BY PRODUCING COUNTRIES OR AREAS, 1956

Note: A large proportion of the materials imported from Europe were refined there from the raw products produced elsewhere. Import statistics show only country of shipment to the United States, not country of origin. Hence, particularly for antimony, bismuth, cadmium, the platinum group metals and tin, this table does not accurately reflect the sources of U. S. supplies.

[a] Crude aluminum metal and alloys (incl. pigs, ingots and wire bars) and plates, sheets, bars, etc.
[b] Antimony ore, needle or liquated antimony, and regulus or metal.
[c] Crude asbestos (chrysotile and blue) and fiber (textile, shingle, other).
[d] Crude and calcined bauxite.
[e] Beryl or beryllium ore.
[f] Cadmium metal and flue dust. Import statistics for cadmium do not show the total supply available from imports. About 60 percent of the cadmium of foreign origin is obtained from imported zinc ores and concentrates, whose cadmium content is not reported separately.
[g] Entirely from Japan.
[h] Chemical, metallurgical and refractory grade chrome ore and metal. Ferrochrome is excluded.
[i] India and Pakistan.
[j] Cobalt ore, concentrates and metal.
[k] Columbium ore and concentrates.
[l] Less than 1/10th of one percent.
[m] Copper ore and concentrates, regulus, refined and unrefined pigs, ingots, bars, etc., and composition metal.
[n] Fluorspar containing over 97 percent calcium fluoride and not over 97 percent calcium fluoride.
[o] Iron ore, excluding granular or sponge iron and pig iron.
[p] Lead in lead ores not recoverable, ore, flue dust and matte, bullion, pigs and bars, and type metal.
[q] Ore with over 10 percent manganese content. Ferromanganese is excluded.
[r] Nickel ore and matte, nickel-containing material imported for recovery of metal, oxide, pigs, ingots, etc., bars, rods, plates, etc.

Table A (continued)

U. S. IMPORTS OF CERTAIN INDUSTRIAL MATERIALS: PROPORTIONS SUPPLIED BY PRODUCING COUNTRIES OR AREAS, 1956

[s] Platinum, iridium, osmium, osirisium, palladium, rhodium, ruthenium.
[t] Tantalum ore.
[u] Tin ore, and pigs, bars, blocks, etc.
[v] Tungsten ore and concentrates, and metal, carbides and combinations. Ferrotungsten is excluded.
[w] Chiefly from Korea.
[x] Vanadium ore and concentrates.
[y] Carpet and apparel wool, excluding hair of cashmere and angora goats, camel, alpaca, llama and vicuna hair.
[z] Chiefly from New Zealand.
[aa] Zinc-bearing ores (incl. zinc not recoverable), dross and skimmings, and blocks, pigs and slabs.
[bb] Zirconium ore.
Source: U. S. Bureau of the Census.

Table B

EXPORTS OF INDUSTRIAL MATERIALS FROM PRODUCING COUNTRIES, TOTAL AND TO THE UNITED STATES

Exporting Country, Year and Commodity	*Total Exports*	*Exports to United States*	*Percent to United States*
	(in thousands of U. S. dollars)		
Canada (1955):			
All commodities	4,339,160	2,647,185	61.0
Newsprint	674,800	586,072	86.9
Planks and boards	390,476	277,088	71.0
Woodpulp	301,288	236,930	78.6
Nickel	218,052	147,783	67.8
Aluminum (primary)	200,309	77,149	38.5
Copper	111,119	49,477	44.5
Iron ore	101,152	80,782	79.9
Asbestos	96,074	53,964	56.2
Zinc	71,035	47,966	67.5
Petroleum, crude	36,736	36,736	100.0
Lead	22,381	8,864	39.6
Latin America			
Argentina (1953):			
All commodities	1,147,439	217,500	19.0
Wool	167,511	62,902	37.6
Bolivia (1955):			
All commodities	100,645	61,007	60.6
Tin, all forms	57,066	23,457	41.1
Tungsten	15,674	15,674	100.0
Lead	6,218	6,054	97.4
Zinc ore	5,727	5,662	98.9
Copper ore	1,905	1,891	99.3
Antimony ore	1,887	1,722	91.3
Brazil (1955):			
All commodities	1,423,246	601,611	42.3
Iron ore	29,966	12,689	42.3
Sisal and similar fibers	11,291	6,400	56.7
Manganese ore	5,378	5,001	93.0
Chile (1954):			
All commodities	403,211	187,150	46.4
Copper	151,133	67,069	44.4
Nitrates	67,502	28,868	42.8
Iron ore	7,883	7,353	93.3

Table B (continued)

EXPORTS OF INDUSTRIAL MATERIALS FROM PRODUCING COUNTRIES, TOTAL AND TO THE UNITED STATES

Exporting Country, Year and Commodity	*Total Exports*	*Exports to United States*	*Percent to United States*
	(in thousands of U. S. dollars)		
Mexico (1954):			
All commodities	658,502	395,172	60.0
Lead, refined	53,975	16,884	31.3
Petroleum, crude, and fuel oil	39,534	33,576	84.9
Copper	29,543	23,975	81.2
Zinc, refined	7,834	2,108	26.9
Peru (1954):			
All commodities	247,622	88,163	35.6
Lead	27,556	16,127	58.5
Copper	17,463	10,722	61.4
Iron ore	12,925	7,235	56.0
Zinc	9,352	6,476	69.2
Wool, alpaca	5,752	3,620	62.9
Petroleum, crude	5,005	1,604	32.0
Tungsten	2,404	2,394	99.6
Uruguay (1953):			
All commodities	269,816	49,983	18.5
Wool	165,059	38,783	23.5
Venezuela (1954):[a]			
All commodities	1,689,806	502,700	29.7
Petroleum and products	1,593,092	412,200	25.9
Africa			
Belgian Congo (1955):			
All commodities	467,840	75,320	16.1
Copper	160,814	7,954	4.9
Tin	28,824	2,660	9.2
Zinc	11,220	3,078	27.4
Manganese ore	6,404	4,428	69.1
Tungsten	4,776	2,966	62.1
Egypt (1955):			
All commodities	393,219	25,945	7.4
Cotton	308,559	22,720	6.6

See footnotes at end of table.

Table B (continued)

EXPORTS OF INDUSTRIAL MATERIALS FROM PRODUCING COUNTRIES, TOTAL AND TO THE UNITED STATES

Exporting Country, Year and Commodity	*Total Exports*	*Exports to United States*	*Percent to United States*
	(in thousands of U. S. dollars)		
Rhodesia and Nyasaland (1955):			
All commodities	483,795	62,463	12.9
Copper	311,020	53,255	17.1
Asbestos	20,823	2,080	10.0
Chrome	7,842	4,896	62.4
Union of South Africa (1955):			
All commodities	1,030,806	95,478	9.3
Wool	165,016	20,852	12.6
Lead	29,500	8,360	28.3
Copper	28,900	7,018	24.3
Asbestos	23,527	4,745	20.2
Manganese ore	8,791	5,046	57.4
Asia			
India (1955):[b]			
All commodities	1,254,594	184,167	14.7
Jute burlaps	124,077	60,623	49.3
Manganese ore	22,519	8,522	37.8
Wool	20,431	8,244	40.4
Mica	17,580	7,580	43.1
Shellac	15,295	2,679	17.5
Indonesia (1955):			
All commodities	931,415	163,629	17.6
Rubber, crude	429,913	121,047	28.2
Tin, ore, slag and ash	59,488	13,780	23.2
Petroleum, crude	42,447	19,866	46.8
Malaya (1955):			
All commodities	1,316,778	234,074	17.8
Rubber, crude	761,106	139,929	18.4
Tin	141,467	86,352	61.0

See footnotes at end of table.

Table B (continued)

EXPORTS OF INDUSTRIAL MATERIALS FROM PRODUCING COUNTRIES, TOTAL AND TO THE UNITED STATES

Exporting Country, Year and Commodity	*Total Exports*	*Exports to United States*	*Percent to United States*
	(in thousands of U. S. dollars)		
Oceania			
Australia (1955):			
All commodities	1,734,127	117,831	6.8
Wool	1,046,305	62,930	6.0
Lead, refined	38,488	15,123	39.3
New Zealand (1954):			
All commodities	684,505	39,421	5.8
Wool	247,624	17,919	7.2

Note: The data in this table have been compiled from official sources of the exporting countries. Thus exports to the United States may differ from official U. S. statistics of imports.

[a] Half of Venezuela's crude petroleum exports is shipped to the Netherlands Antilles, where it is refined. All of the U. S. imports of refined products from the Netherlands Antilles are thus originally Venezuelan oil.

[b] Fiscal year April 1, 1955—March 31, 1956.

Source: U. S. Bureau of Foreign Commerce, World Trade Information Service; United Nations, *Commodity Trade Statistics, Yearbook of International Trade Statistics;* U. S. Bureau of Mines, *Mineral Trade Notes.*

APPENDIX B

The following persons assisted the author in the preparation of this volume, by advice and information and in other ways. None of them, however, bears any responsibility for the accuracy of the facts as presented by the author or for his conclusions. A number of these persons also served as discussion leaders at meetings of the Council's study group; their names are marked by asterisks.

Oil

* Bass, Harry W.—Wilcox Trend Oil Company (Dallas)
Duce, James Terry—Arabian American Oil Company (New York City)
Levorsen, A. I.—geologist (Tulsa)
Mueller, Gilbert—Argo Oil Company (Denver)
Schultz, P. R.—Blackwell Oil and Gas Company (Tulsa)
Sherry, William J.—oil producer (Tulsa)
Smyth, Virginia M.—American Petroleum Institute (New York City)
* Swensrud, Sidney A.—Gulf Oil Corporation (Pittsburgh)
* Wilson, Robert E.—Standard Oil Company of Indiana (Chicago)

Lead and Zinc

Ankeny, Marling J.—U. S. Bureau of Mines (Washington, D. C.)
East, J. H., Jr.—U. S. Bureau of Mines (Denver)
Greene, Kenneth W.—Electric Storage Battery Company (Philadelphia)
Harrison, Harry—American Smelting and Refining Company (Denver)
* Hendricks, Robert—Consolidated Mining and Smelting Coming of Canada, Ltd. (Montreal)
* Herres, Otto—Combined Metals Reduction Company (Salt Lake City)
Morgan, John D., Jr.—consulting mining engineer (Washington, D. C.)

Mulock, F. S.—United States Smelting, Refining and Mining Company (Boston)
Rosenbaum, Joseph—U. S. Bureau of Mines (Denver)
Snyder, Edward H.—Combined Metals Reduction Company (Salt Lake City)
* Strauss, Simon D.—American Smelting and Refining Company (New York City)
Swent, J. W.—Triumph Mine (Hailey, Idaho)

Copper

Barker, Robert R.—William A. M. Burden Company (New York City)
* Getzin, Edmund E.—U. S. Department of State (Washington, D. C.)
Green, F. C.—Kennecott Copper Company (Salt Lake City)
Hills, Robert C.—Freeport Sulphur Company (New York City)
Hochschild, Walter—American Metal Climax, Inc. (New York City)
Prain, Sir Ronald—Rhodesian Selection Trust, Ltd. (London)
* Vuillequez, Jean—American Metal Climax, Inc. (New York City)
Weed, Clyde E.—The Anaconda Company (New York City)
Wight, Charles A.—Freeport Sulphur Company (New York City)
Zender, Austin R.—Bridgeport Brass Company

Nickel and Materials for the Iron and Steel Industry

Fuller, Margaret H.—American Iron and Steel Institute (New York City)
Jeffries, Zay—General Electric Company (Pittsburgh)
Sullivan, John—Battelle Memorial Institute (Columbus, Ohio)
Wildman, Anthony J.—International Nickel Company, Inc. (New York City)
Williams, Clyde—Clyde Williams & Company (Columbus, Ohio)
Wingate, Henry S.—International Nickel Company, Ltd. (Copper Cliff, Ontario)

Wool

Archabal, Fidel—The Top Company, Inc. (Boston)
Barkin, Solomon—Textile Workers Union of America (New York City)

Breckenridge, J. H.—wool grower (Twin Falls, Idaho)
Brown, Glen F.—National Association of Wool Manufacturers (New York City)
Butland, Ralph A.—John P. Maguire & Company, Inc. (New York City)
Jackendoff, Ruth—The Wool Bureau, Inc. (New York City)
Johnston, Alexander—University of Wyoming (Laramie)
Jones, J. C.—American Sheep Producers Council (Denver)
Judd, David E.—National Wool Marketing Association (Boston)
Phillips, Reed—U. S. Department of Agriculture (Washington, D. C.)
* Richards, Preston—U. S. Department of Agriculture (Washington, D. C.)
Tinker, Arthur—business consultant (New York City)
Warner, Harry B.—B. F. Goodrich Chemical Company (Cleveland)
Wilkinson, Edwin—National Association of Wool Manufacturers (New York City)
Winder, G. Norman—American Sheep Producers Council (Denver)

Rubber

* Armstrong, Willis C.—U. S. Department of State (Washington, D. C.)
Bugbee, H. C.—Natural Rubber Bureau (Washington, D. C.)
Cake, Wallace E.—United States Rubber Company (New York City)
Carson, Dean E.—B. F. Goodrich Company (Akron)
Collyer, John L.—B. F. Goodrich Company (Akron)
Humphreys, H. E., Jr.—United States Rubber Company (New York City)
Jiskoot, Lodewyk J.—Imperial Commodities Corporation (New York City)
Ormsby, Ross R.—Rubber Manufacturers Association, Inc. (New York City)
Reilly, Robert D.—Imperial Commodities Corporation (New York City)
Roberts, J. C.—Firestone Tire and Rubber Company (Akron)
Sears, W. J.—Rubber Manufacturers Association, Inc. (Washington, D. C.)
* Spencer, Leland E.—Goodyear Tire and Rubber Company (Akron)

General

Bent, Donn N.—U. S. Tariff Commission (Washington, D. C.)
Brokaw, Charles E.—U. S. Department of Commerce (Denver)
Cavanaugh, Eleanor S.—Standard & Poor's Corporation (New York City)
Gray, Gordon—Office of Defense Mobilization (Washington, D. C.)
Kretchman, H. F.—*Salt Lake Tribune* (Salt Lake City)
McGee, Gale—University of Wyoming (Laramie)
McHendrie, Douglas—Grant, Shafroth and Toll (Denver)
Morris, W. E., Jr.—University of Tulsa
Ritchie, A. E.—Minister, Canadian Embassy (Washington, D. C.)
Wall, Hugo—University of Wichita
Walther, A. A. (Boise)

SELECTED BIBLIOGRAPHY

I. STOCKPILING

DeMille, John B. *Strategic Minerals: A Summary of Uses, World Output, Stockpiles, Procurement.* New York: McGraw-Hill, 1947. 626 p.

Mendershausen, Horst. "Stockpiling Materials for Security." In U. S. President's Materials Policy Commission, *Resources for Freedom.* Washington: GPO, 1952. v. 5, pp. 137-149.

Patterson, Gardner, and others. *Survey of United States International Finance 1952.* Princeton: Princeton University Press, 1953. Pp. 214-221.

———. *Survey of United States International Finance 1953.* Princeton: Princeton University Press, 1954. Pp. 253-259.

U. S. House. Committee on Military Affairs. *Strategic and Critical Raw Materials.* Hearings, 76th Cong., 1st sess. Washington: GPO, 1939. 232 p.

———. Committee on Public Lands. Subcommittee on Mines and Mining. *Stock Piling of Strategic and Critical Materials and Metals.* Hearings, 80th Cong., 1st sess. Washington: GPO, 1947. 190 p.

———. ———. ———. *Strategic and Critical Minerals and Metals.* Hearings, 80th Cong., 2d sess. Washington: GPO, 1948. Pt. 5, *Stockpiling,* [621] p.

U. S. Office of Defense Mobilization. *Stockpile Report to the Congress.* Washington: Author, semiannual.

U. S. President. Announcement of "long-term" mineral stockpile objectives. White House press release, March 26, 1954.

U. S. Senate. Committee on Armed Services. *National Stockpile.* Hearings before Subcommittee, 85th Cong., 1st sess. Washington: GPO, 1957. 52 p.

———. Committee on Interior and Insular Affairs. *Defense Minerals Policy.* Hearings, 82d Cong., 2d sess. Washington: GPO, 1952. 226 p.

———. ———. Subcommittee on Minerals, Materials and Fuels Economics. *Stockpile and Accessibility of Strategic and Critical Materials to the United States in Time of War.* Hearings, 83rd Cong., on S. Res. 143. Washington: GPO, 1953, 1954. 12 pts.

———. ———. ———. *Accessibility of Strategic and Critical Materials to the United States in Time of War and for Our Expanding Economy.* Report no. 1627, 83rd Cong., 2d sess., pursuant to S. Res. 143. Washington: GPO, 1954. 415 p.

———. Committee on Military Affairs. *Strategic and Critical Materials.* Hearings before Subcommittee, 77th Cong., 1st sess. Washington: GPO, 1941. 307 p.

———. ———. Subcommittee on Surplus Property. *Stock-Piling.* Hearings, 79th Cong., 1st sess., on S. 752. Washington: GPO, 1945. 76 p.

U. S. Special Stockpile Advisory Committee. *Stockpiling for Defense in the Nuclear Age.* A Report to the Director of the Office of Defense Mobilization. Washington: Author, 1958. 20 p.

II. TAX INCENTIVES

Barlow, E. R., and Ira T. Wender. *United States Tax Incentives to Direct Private Foreign Investment.* Cambridge: Harvard Law School, 1954. 60 p.

Blakey, Roy G., and Gladys C. Blakey. "Revenue Act of 1932," *American Economic Review,* v. 22, no. 4 (December 1932), pp. 620-640.

Eldridge, Douglas H. "Tax Incentives for Mineral Enterprise," *Journal of Political Economy,* v. 58, no. 3 (June 1950), pp. 222-240.

Fernald, Henry B. "Distinctive Tax Treatment of Income from Mineral Extraction." Paper submitted to the Joint Committee on the Economic Report, in *Federal Tax Policy for Economic Growth and Stability.* 84th Cong., 1st sess. Washington: GPO, 1956. Pp. 419-429.

Harberger, Arnold C. "The Taxation of Mineral Industries." Paper submitted to the Joint Committee on the Economic Report, in *Federal Tax Policy for Economic Growth and Stability.* 84th Cong., 1st sess. Washington: GPO, 1956. Pp. 439-449.

Oakes, Eugene E. "Incentives for Minerals Industries." In U. S. President's Materials Policy Commission, *Resources for Freedom.* Washington: GPO, 1952. v. 5, pp. 10-25.

United Nations. Department of Economic Affairs. *United States Income Taxation of Private United States Investment in Latin America.* 1953.XVI.1. New York: Author, 1953. 80 p.

U. S. Commission on Foreign Economic Policy. *Staff Papers.* Washington: GPO, 1954. Pp. 98-126.

U. S. Congress. Joint Committee on the Economic Report. *Federal Tax Policy for Economic Growth and Stability.* Hearings before Subcommittee, 84th Cong., 1st sess., pursuant to Sec. 5 (a) of *Public Law* no. 304, 79th Cong. Washington: GPO, 1956. 708 p.

———. ———. *Federal Tax Policy for Economic Growth and Stability.* Papers submitted by panelists appearing before the Subcommittee on Tax Policy. 84th Cong., 1st sess. Washington: GPO, 1956. 930 p.

———. ———. *Federal Tax Policy for Economic Growth and Stability.* Report, 84th Cong., 2d sess. Washington: GPO, 1956. 16 p.

U. S. National Resources Board. *A Report on National Planning and Public Works in Relation to Natural Resources . . . .* Washington: Author, 1934. Pt. 4, *Report of the Planning Committee for Mineral Policy,* [60] p.

III. TRADE CONTROLS

Knorr, Klaus. "Import Restrictions and National Security: A Problem in American Policy." In U. S. House, Committee on Ways and Means, Subcommittee on Foreign Trade Policy, *Foreign Trade Policy,* Compendium of papers collected by the staff. Washington: GPO, 1957. Pp. 649-661.

Mason, Edward S. *Controlling World Trade: Cartels and Commodity Agreements.* New York: McGraw-Hill, 1946. 289 p.

Stocking, George W., and Myron W. Watkins. *Cartels in Action: Case Studies in International Business Diplomacy.* New York: Twentieth Century Fund, 1946. 533 p.

U. S. House. Committee on Banking and Currency. *Export Control Act of 1949*. Hearings, 81st Cong., 1st sess., on H. R. 1661. Washington: GPO, 1949. 181 p.

———. ———. *Regulation of Exports*. Hearings, 84th Cong., 2d sess., on H. R. 9052. Washington: GPO, 1956. 182 p.

U. S. Department of Commerce. *Export Control*. Quarterly Reports by the Secretary of Commerce. Washington: GPO, various years.

U. S. Mutual Defense Assistance Control Act Administrator. *East-West Trade Developments 1956-1957*. Tenth Report to Congress on Operations under the Mutual Defense Assistance Control Act of 1951. Washington: GPO: 1958. 62 p.

———. *The Strategic Trade Control System 1948-1956*. Ninth Report to Congress on Operations under the Mutual Defense Assistance Control Act of 1951. Washington: GPO, 1957. 115 p.

U. S. Senate. Committee on Banking and Currency. *Extension of Export Control Act of 1949*. Hearings before Subcommittee, 84th Cong., 2d sess., on S. 3238. Washington: GPO, 1956. 148 p.

———. ———. *Extension of Export Controls*. Hearings before Subcommittee, 81st Cong., 1st sess., on S. 548. Washington: GPO, 1949. 234 p.

IV. COMMODITIES

Copper, lead, zinc

"Adventure in Copper," *Economist*, v. 77 (November 26, 1955), pp. 765-767.

American Bureau of Metal Statistics. *Yearbook of the American Bureau of Metal Statistics*. New York: Author, annual.

Fletcher, Andrew. "Why a Healthy Domestic Mining Industry Will Benefit: the United States and the Metal Consumer as Well as the Metal Producer," *Engineering and Mining Journal*, v. 157, no. 3 (March 1956), pp. 75-79.

Gates, W. B., Jr. *Michigan Copper and Boston Dollars: An Economic History of the Michigan Copper Mining Industry*. Cambridge: Harvard University Press, 1951. 301 p.

Ramsey, Robert H. "Outlook for Nonferrous Metals," *Conference Board Business Record*, v. 12, no. 10 (October 1955), pp. 382-385.

Strauss, Simon D. "The Metals Outlook: Lead and Zinc," *Conference Board Business Record*, v. 13, no. 3 (March 1956), pp. 124-126.

Taussig, Frank W. *Some Aspects of the Tariff Question*. 2d ed. Cambridge: Harvard University Press, 1924. Ch. 11, "Copper," pp. 161-170.

United Nations. Department of Economic and Social Affairs. *Non-ferrous Metals in Under-developed Countries*. 1955.II.B.3. New York: Author, 1956. 129 p.

U. S. Bureau of Foreign Commerce. *Investment in Federation of Rhodesia and Nyasaland*. Washington: GPO, 1956. 158 p.

U. S. Bureau of Mines. *Mineral Industry Surveys* [for copper, lead and zinc]. Washington: Author, various years.

U. S. Federal Trade Commission. *The Copper Industry*. Washington: GPO, 1947. 420 p.

U. S. House. Committee on Public Lands. Subcommittee on Mines and

Mining. *Strategic and Critical Minerals and Metals.* Hearings, 80th Cong., 2d sess. Washington: GPO, 1948. Pt. 3, *Copper,* pp. 667-877.

———. Committee on Ways and Means. *Lead and Zinc.* Hearings, 85th Cong., 1st sess. Washington: GPO, 1957. 355 p.

U. S. President. Letter rejecting U. S. Tariff Commission's recommendations in the lead and zinc investigation. White House press release, August 20, 1954.

U. S. Senate. *Lead and Zinc Industries.* Report of the U. S. Tariff Commission under Sec. 332 of the Tariff Act of 1930 pursuant to a resolution of the Senate Committee on Finance of July 27, 1953. Senate Doc. no. 119, 83rd Cong., 2d sess. Washington: GPO, 1954. 356 p.

———. Committee on Finance. *Copper Import Tax Suspension.* Hearings, 83rd Cong., 1st sess., on H. R. 568. Washington: GPO, 1953. 73 p.

———. ———. *Import Tax on Lead and Zinc.* Hearings, 85th Cong., 1st sess., on S. 2376. Washington: GPO, 1957. 311 p.

———. ———. *Suspension of Import Duty on Copper.* Hearings, 84th Cong., 1st sess., on H. R. 5695. Washington: GPO, 1955. 33 p.

U. S. Tariff Commission. *Lead and Zinc.* Report to the President on Escape-clause Investigation no. 27. Washington: Author, 1954. 33 p. + statistical appendix.

———. *Lead and Zinc Industries.* See U. S. Senate, *Lead and Zinc Industries.*

———. *Summaries of Tariff Information.* Washington: GPO, 1948. v. 3, pt. 5, *Metals and Manufactures,* copper, pp. 42-56b; lead, pp. 134-152; zinc, pp. 155-176.

"What Price for Copper," *Economist,* v. 183 (June 8, 1957), pp. 905-907.

Materials for the iron and steel industry

Buck, W. Keith. *Iron Ore in Canada.* Reference Paper no. 81 of the Information Division, Department of External Affairs, Ottawa, March 28, 1956. 5 p.

Canada. Royal Commission on Canada's Economic Prospects. *The Canadian Primary Iron and Steel Industry,* prepared by Lucy Morgan. Ottawa: Queen's Printer, 1956. 104 p.

European Coal and Steel Community. High Authority. *Fifth General Report on the Activities of the Community* (April 9, 1956 to April 13, 1957). Luxembourg: Author, 1957. 358 p.

———. ———. Information Service. *Press Communique.* Luxembourg, July 12, 1957. 1 p. (On the purchase of iron and steel scrap.)

———. ———. ———. *Press Release.* Luxembourg, June 18, 1957. 1 p. (On the limitation of imports of iron and steel scrap.)

Kalijarvi, Thorsten V. (Assistant Secretary of State for Economic Affairs). Statement before the House Select Committee on Small Business, June 21, 1957, on iron and steel scrap. Reprinted as a Department of State press release, June 21, 1957. 17 p.

U. S. Bureau of Mines (in cooperation with the Geological Survey). *Manganese.* Materials Survey compiled for the National Security Resources Board. Washington: GPO, 1952. [646] p.

———. *Mineral Industry Surveys* [for fluorspar, iron and steel scrap, manganese, tungsten]. Washington: Author, various years.

U. S. Department of Commerce. *Report on Iron and Steel Scrap.* See U. S.

House, Committee on Banking and Currency, *Report . . . by the Department of Commerce.*

————. Business and Defense Services Administration. *Tungsten.* Materials Survey compiled for the Office of Defense Mobilization. Washington: GPO, 1956. [114] p.

U. S. House. Committee on Banking and Currency. *Report on Iron and Steel Scrap by the Department of Commerce.* Committee Print, 85th Cong., pursuant to *Public Law* no. 631, 84th Cong. Washington: GPO, 1957. 94 p.

————. Committee on Government Operations. *Investigation of United States Government Contracts for Purchase of Tungsten in Thailand.* Hearings before Subcommittee, 83rd Cong., 1st sess. Washington: GPO, 1954. 394 p.

————. Committee on Public Lands. Subcommittee on Mines and Mining. *Strategic and Critical Minerals and Metals.* Hearings, 80th Cong., 2d sess. Washington: GPO, 1948. Pt. 1, *Manganese,* pp. 1-497; pt. 4, *Tungsten,* pp. 879-895.

————. Select Committee on Small Business. *Small-Business Problems Relating to Iron and Steel Scrap.* Hearings, 85th Cong., 1st sess., pursuant to H. Res. 56. Washington: GPO, 1957. 427 p.

U. S. Senate. Committee on Armed Services. Preparedness Subcommittee. *Investigation of the Preparedness Program.* 82d Cong., 1st sess. Washington: GPO, 1951. Twenty-seventh Report, *Tungsten,* 55 p.

U. S. Tariff Commission. *Acid Grade Fluorspar.* Report to the President on Escape-clause Investigation no. 42. Washington: Author, 1956. 58 p. + statistical appendix.

————. *Fluorspar.* Report on investigation conducted pursuant to resolution of the Senate Committee on Finance. Washington: Author, 1955. 141 p.

————. *Summaries of Tariff Information.* Washington: GPO, 1948. v. 2, pt. 1, *Earths, Earthenware and Glassware,* fluorspar, pp. 75-79. v. 3, pt. 1, *Metals and Manufactures,* iron and steel scrap, pp. 11-14; manganese ore, pp. 21-29; tungsten ore, pp. 32-35. v. 16, pt. 3 (1950), *Free List,* iron ore, pp. 159-162.

Voskuil, Walter H. "The Strategic Position of Iron Ore in the Economy of the Atlantic Basin Nations," *Illinois Engineer* (November 1956).

Wansbrough, V. C. "Implications of Canadian Iron Ore Production," *Canadian Journal of Economics and Political Science,* v. 16, no. 3 (August 1950), pp. 334-339.

Nickel

Canada. Department of Mines and Technical Surveys. *Nickel in Canada.* Memorandum Series no. 130. Ottawa: Queen's Printer, 1955. 53 p.

Director, Herman B., and Associates. *Nickel Handbook and Commercial Outlook for 1957.* Washington: Author, 1956. [75] p.

Hall, Albert M. *Nickel in Iron and Steel.* New York: Wiley, 1954. 595 p.

"Inco Cut Out," *Economist,* v. 84 (July 20, 1957), p. 218.

"Inco's Novel Problem, Competition," *Fortune,* v. 55, no. 5 (May 1957), pp. 128-133, 192-200.

International Nickel Company of Canada, Ltd. *The Nickel Industry in*

Canada. A presentation to the Royal Commission on Canada's Economic Prospects. Toronto: Author, 1956. 61 p.

Main, O. W. *The Canadian Nickel Industry: A Study in Market Control and Public Policy*. Canadian Studies in Economics no. 4. Toronto: University of Toronto Press, 1955. 168 p.

Skelton, Alex. "Nickel." In William Y. Elliott and others, *International Control in the Non-ferrous Metals*. New York: Macmillan, 1937. Pp. 109-209.

Staley, Eugene. *Raw Materials in Peace and War*. New York: Council on Foreign Relations, 1937. Pp. 276-281.

Townsend, John R. *Summary of the Report of the Nickel Situation* [to the Office of Defense Mobilization]. In U. S. Congress, Joint Committee on Defense Production, *Study of Supply and Distribution of Nickel. Defense Production Act Progress Report no. 36*. 85th Cong., 1st sess. Washington: GPO, 1957. Pp. 103-106.

U. S. Bureau of Mines. *Mineral Industry Surveys*. Washington: Author, various years.

———— (with the cooperation of the Geological Survey). *Nickel*. Materials Survey compiled for the National Security Resources Board. Washington: GPO, 1952. [296] p.

————. *Nickel-Cobalt Resources of Cuba,* prepared by W. D. McMillan and H. W. Davis. Washington: Author, 1955. 86 p.

U. S. Commission on Organization of the Executive Branch of the Government. *Staff Study on Business Enterprises Outside of the Department of Defense*. Washington: Author, 1955. Ch. 15, "Nicaro—The Government's Nickel Plant," pp. 81-85.

U. S. Congress. Joint Committee on Defense Production. *Defense Production Act Progress Report No. 33*. Hearing, 84th Cong., 1st sess. Washington: GPO, 1955. 285 p.

————. ————. *Study of Supply and Distribution of Nickel. Defense Production Act Progress Report No. 36*. 85th Cong., 1st sess. Washington: GPO, 1957. 109 p.

————. ————. *Supplementary Report to Study of Supply and Distribution of Nickel,* by the Secretary of Commerce. *Defense Production Act Progress Report No. 37*. 85th Cong., 1st sess. Washington: GPO, 1957. 5 p.

U. S. Department of Commerce. Business and Defense Services Administration. *Interim Report on Nickel to the Senate and the House of Representatives of the United States*. Washington: Author, 1956. 25 p. + appendices.

————. ————. *Review of Nickel in the United States, 1946-1956,* prepared by Herman B. Director. Washington: GPO. 1955. 41 p.

U. S. Department of Justice. *Report of the Attorney General,* pursuant to Sec. 708 (e) of the Defense Production Act of 1950, as amended. Washington: Author, 1957. 100 p.

U. S. House. Committee on Government Operations. *Inquiry into the Expansion and Operation by General Services Administration of the Government Nickel Plant at Nicaro, Cuba*. Hearings before Subcommittee, 84th Cong., 2d sess. Washington: GPO, 1956, 1957. 2 pts., 618 p.

U. S. House. Committee on Government Operations. *Inquiry into the Expansion and Operation by General Services Administration of the Government Nickel Plant at Nicaro, Cuba.* Report no. 2390, 84th Cong., 2d sess. Washington: GPO, 1956. 46 p

U. S. Senate. Committee on the Armed Services. Preparedness Investigating Subcommittee. *Investigation of the Preparedness Program.* 85th Cong., 1st sess. Washington: GPO, 1957. Eleventh Report, *Nickel,* 35 p.

———. ———. Preparedness Subcommittee. *Investigation of the Preparedness Program.* 82d Cong., 1st sess. Washington: GPO, 1951. Fourth Report, *Nickel,* 27 p.

———. Select Committee on Small Business. *Supply and Distribution of Nickel.* Hearings, 84th Cong., 2d sess. Washington: GPO, 1956. 196 p.

———. ———. *Supply and Distribution of Nickel.* Report, 84th Cong., 2d sess. Washington: GPO, 1956. 33 p.

U. S. Tariff Commission. *Summaries of Tariff Information.* Washington: GPO, 1948. v. 3, pt. 5, *Metals and Manufactures,* nickel, pp. 114-120.

Oil

American Bar Association. *Legal History of Conservation of Oil and Gas. A Symposium.* Chicago: Author, 1939. 302 p.

American Petroleum Institute. *Petroleum Facts and Figures.* New York: Author, annual.

Campbell, John C. *Defense of the Middle East.* New York: Harper, for the Council on Foreign Relations, 1958. 392 p.

Canada. Department of External Affairs. *Government Policy in the Canadian Petroleum Industry,* by R. B. Toombs. Reference Papers, no. 96. Ottawa, June 1957. 13 p.

Chase Manhattan Bank. Petroleum Department. *Annual Financial Analysis of the Petroleum Industry,* by Frederick G. Coqueron and others. New York: Author, various years.

———. ———. *Future Growth and Financial Requirements of the World Petroleum Industry,* by Joseph E. Pogue and others. New York: Author, 1956. 39 p.

———. ———. *Future Growth of the World Petroleum Industry,* by Kenneth E. Hill, Harold D. Hammar and John G. Winger. New York: Author, 1957. 44 p.

———. ———. *Investment Patterns in the World Petroleum Industry,* by Frederick G. Coqueron and Joseph E. Pogue. New York: Author, 1956. 55 p.

Connelly, William L. *The Oil Business as I Saw It: Half a Century with Sinclair.* Norman: University of Oklahoma Press, 1954. 177 p.

"Critical Hurdle for U. S. Imports," *Petroleum Press Service,* v. 24, no. 6 (June 1957), pp. 202-206.

DeGolyer and MacNaughton. *Twentieth Century Petroleum Statistics.* Dallas, Texas: Author, annual.

Eakens, Robert H. S. "Oil Imports and the U. S. Economy," *Department of State Bulletin,* v. 27 (November 10, 1952), pp. 733-735.

Feis, Herbert. "Order in Oil," *Foreign Affairs,* v. 22, no. 4 (July 1944), pp. 616-626.

Feis, Herbert. *Petroleum and American Foreign Policy*. Commodity Policy Studies no. 3, Food Research Institute. Stanford: Stanford University Press, 1944. 62 p.

International Petroleum Trade. Monthly journal, by the U. S. Bureau of Mines.

Longrigg, Stephen Hemsley. *Oil in the Middle East: Its Discovery and Development*. London: Oxford University Press, 1954. 305 p.

Manne, Alan S. "Oil Refining: Yield Coefficients and Actual Prices," *Quarterly Journal of Economics*, v. 65, no. 3 (August 1951), pp. 400-416.

Mikesell, Raymond F., and Hollis B. Chenery. *Arabian Oil: America's Stake in the Middle East*. Chapel Hill: University of North Carolina Press, 1949. 201 p.

Murphy, Blakely M., ed. *Conservation of Oil and Gas: A Legal History, 1948*. Chicago: American Bar Association, 1949. 754 p.

Nakasian, Samuel. "The Security of Foreign Petroleum Resources," *Political Science Quarterly*, v. 68, no. 2 (June 1953), pp. 181-202.

National Planning Association. *Productive Uses of Nuclear Energy*. Report of a Special Policy Committee on the Productive Uses of Nuclear Energy. Washington: Author, 1957. 62 p.

———. *The Creole Petroleum Corporation in Venezuela*. See Wayne C. Taylor and John Lindeman.

Nelson, James R. "Prices, Costs, and Conservation in Petroleum," *American Economic Review, Papers and Proceedings*, v. 48, no. 2 (May 1958), pp. 502-515.

Oil and Gas Journal. Weekly journal.

Petroleum Press Service. Monthly journal.

Rostow, Eugene V. *A National Policy for the Oil Industry*. New Haven: Yale University Press, 1948. 173 p.

Sharp, Roger R. "America's Stake in World Petroleum," *Harvard Business Review*, v. 28, no. 5 (September 1950), pp. 25-41.

Shwadran, Benjamin. *The Middle East, Oil and the Great Powers*. New York: Praeger, 1955. 500 p.

———. "Oil in the Middle East Crisis," *Middle Eastern Affairs*, v. 8, no. 4 (April 1957), pp. 126-134.

Struth, Henry J., ed. *World Petroleum Report*. New York: Palmer Publications, 1955. 488 p.

Taylor, Wayne C., and John Lindeman. *The Creole Petroleum Corporation in Venezuela*. Case Study in United States Business Performance Abroad. Washington: National Planning Association, 1955. 106 p.

U. S. Bureau of Mines. "Crude Petroleum and Petroleum Products," *Mineral Industry Surveys*. Washington: Author, various years.

U. S. Federal Trade Commission. *The International Petroleum Cartel*. See U. S. Senate, Select Committee on Small Business.

U. S. House. Committee on the Armed Services. Special Subcommittee on Petroleum. *Petroleum for National Defense*. Hearings, 80th Cong., 2d sess., pursuant to H. R. 141 and H. R. 447. Washington: GPO, 1948. 917 p.

———. ———. ———. *Report of Investigation of Petroleum in Relation to National Defense*. 80th Cong., 2d sess. Washington: GPO, 1948. 24 p.

U. S. House. Committee on Interstate and Foreign Commerce. *Petroleum Survey*. Hearings, 85th Cong., 1st sess. Washington: GPO, 1957. 505 p.

———. ———. *Petroleum Survey*. Preliminary Report, 85th Cong., 1st sess. Washington: GPO, 1957. 48 p.

U. S. Senate. Committee on the Judiciary. Subcommittee on Antitrust and Monopoly. *Petroleum, the Antitrust Laws and Government Policies*. Report, 85th Cong., 1st sess., on S. Res. 57. Washington: GPO, 1957. 164 p.

———. Select Committee on Small Business. *The International Petroleum Cartel*, Staff Report submitted by the U. S. Federal Trade Commission. 82d Cong., 2d sess. Washington: GPO, 1952. 378 p.

———. Special Committee Investigating Petroleum Resources. *Investigation of Petroleum Resources*. Hearings, 79th Cong., 1st and 2d sess., pursuant to S. Res. 36. Washington: GPO, 1945, 1946. 7 v.

———. ———. *Investigation of Petroleum Resources in Relation to the National Welfare*. Report no. 9, 80th Cong., 1st sess., pursuant to S. Res. 36 — 79th Cong. Washington: GPO, 1947. 59 p.

U. S. Special Committee to Investigate Crude Oil Imports. *Petroleum Imports*. Washington: U. S. Department of Commerce, 1957. 15 p. + appendix.

U. S. Tariff Commission. *Petroleum*. War Changes in Industry Series, Report no. 17. Washington: GPO, 1946. 152 p.

———. *Report to the President under Section 3 of the Trade Agreements Extension Act of 1951 (Public Law 50, 82d Congress) with Respect to Certain Petroleum Products included in the President's List of August 29, 1951, Specifying Articles Imported into the United States Which Were to Be Considered in Trade Agreement Negotiations with Venezuela*. Washington: Author, 1952. 49 p. + supplementary statements.

———. *Summaries of Tariff Information*. Washington: GPO, 1948. v. 1, pt. 6, *Crude Petroleum and Products*. 43 p.

World Oil. Monthly journal.

Rubber

Bauer, Peter T. "Malayan Rubber Policy," *Political Science Quarterly*, v. 72, no. 1 (March 1957), pp. 83-99.

———. *The Rubber Industry: A Study in Competition and Monopoly*. Cambridge: Harvard University Press, 1948. 404 p.

Chemical and Rubber. Monthly journal, by the U. S. Department of Commerce.

Collyer, John L. *National Security in Rubber*. Rubber Studies Series no. 16. Akron: B. F. Goodrich Company, 1956. 22 p.

Fisher, Harry L. "Rubber," *Scientific American*, v. 195, no. 5 (November 1956), pp. 32+, 74-84+.

International Rubber Study Group. *Summary of Proceedings of the Twelfth Meeting*. Monrovia, 17th-21st October, 1955, with Short Review of First Eleven Meetings. 128 p.

Knorr, Klaus. *Rubber After the War*. War-Peace Pamphlets no. 4, Food Research Institute. Stanford: Stanford University Press, 1944. 46 p.

———. *World Rubber and Its Regulation*. Stanford: Stanford University Press, 1945. 265 p.

National Planning Association. *The Firestone Operations in Liberia.* See Wayne C. Taylor.

Natural Rubber News. Monthly journal, by the Natural Rubber Bureau.

Peaslee, Amos J. *International Governmental Organizations.* The Hague: Nijhoff, 1956. v. 2, pp. 332-337.

Rippy, J. Fred. "Some Rubber-Planting Fiascos in Tropical America," *Inter-American Economic Affairs,* v. 10, no. 1 (Summer 1956), pp. 3-24.

Rubber Age. Monthly journal.

Rubber Statistical Bulletin. Monthly journal, by the Secretariat of the International Rubber Study Group.

Rubber World. Monthly journal.

"Rubber's Bulging Money Bags," *Economist,* v. 81 (November 3, 1956), pp. 437-439.

Saunders, D. A. "The New Bounce in Rubber," *Fortune,* v. 54, no. 2 (August 1956), pp. 96-99, 153.

Solo, Robert. "The New Threat of Synthetic to Natural Rubber," *Southern Economic Journal,* v. 22, no. 1 (July 1955), pp. 55-64.

———. "Research and Development in the Synthetic Rubber Industry," *Quarterly Journal of Economics,* v. 68, no. 1 (February 1954), pp. 61-82.

Taylor, Wayne C. *The Firestone Operations in Liberia.* Fifth Case Study in United States Business Performance Abroad. Washington: National Planning Association, 1956. 116 p.

United Nations. Economic Commission for Asia and the Far East. *Economic Survey of Asia and the Far East, 1956.* 1957.II.F.1. Bangkok: Author, 1957. 233 p.

U. S. Bureau of the Census. *United States Rubber Statistics.* Facts for Industry Series. Washington: Author, various years.

U. S. Department of Commerce. *Rubber.* 7th Annual Report by the Secretary of Commerce. Washington: GPO, 1955. 23 p.

U. S. Department of Justice. *First Report of the Attorney General on Competition in the Synthetic Rubber Industry.* Washington: GPO, 1956. 36 p.

———. *Second Report of the Attorney General on Competition in the Synthetic Rubber Industry.* Washington: GPO, 1957. 45 p.

U. S. House. *Report Concerning the Nation's Rubber Requirements and Resources.* 84th Cong., 2d sess., House Doc. no. 391. Washington: GPO, 1956. 52 p.

———. *Synthetic Rubber.* Recommendations of the President together with report on maintenance of synthetic rubber industry in the United States and disposal of government-owned synthetic rubber facilities. 81st Cong., 2d sess., House Doc. no. 448. Washington: GPO, 1950. 121 p.

———. Select Committee on Small Business. *Disposal of Government-owned Synthetic Rubber Facilities.* Staff Report, 84th Cong., 1st sess., pursuant to H. Res. 114. Washington: GPO, 1956. 27 p.

U. S. National Science Foundation. Special Commission for Rubber Research [report on Synthetic Rubber]. In U. S. House, *Report Concerning the Nation's Rubber Requirements and Resources.* 84th Cong., 2d sess., House Doc. no. 391. Washington: GPO, 1956. Pp. 28-51.

U. S. Office of Defense Mobilization. Ad Hoc Rubber Committee. *The*

Rubber Requirements and Resources of the United States. In U. S. House, *Report Concerning the Nation's Rubber Requirements and Resources.* 84th Cong., 2d sess., House Doc. no. 391. Washington: GPO, 1956. Pp. 6-27.

U. S. Office of War Mobilization and Reconversion. *Rubber.* First and Second Reports of the Inter-Agency Policy Committee on Rubber. Washington: GPO, 1946. 95 p.

U. S. President. *Message.* In U. S. House, *Report Concerning the Nation's Rubber Requirements and Resources.* 84th Cong., 2d sess., House Doc. no. 391. Washington: GPO, 1956. Pp. 1-4.

U. S. Reconstruction Finance Corporation. *Report to the Congress on Synthetic Rubber Operations.* Washington: Author, 1954. 19 p.

U. S. Rubber Producing Facilities Disposal Commission. *Report to Congress Recommending Disposal of Government-owned Synthetic Rubber Facilities.* Washington: Author, 1955. 47 p. + appendix; supplement, 241 p.

U. S. Senate. Committee on the Armed Services. Preparedness Subcommittee. *Investigation of the Preparedness Program.* 81st Cong., 2d sess. Washington: GPO, 1950. First Report, *Rubber,* Doc. no. 230, 44 p.; Second Report, *Rubber,* Doc. no. 240, 37 p.

———. ———. ———. *Investigation of the Preparedness Program.* 82d Cong., 1st sess. Washington: GPO, 1951. Twenty-ninth Report, *Rubber,* 48 p.

———. Committee on Banking and Currency. *Disapproval of Proposed Sale of Government-owned Rubber-producing Facilities.* Report no. 117, 84th Cong., 1st sess., to accompany S. Res. 76. Washington: GPO, 1955. 24 p.

———. ———. *Rubber Facilities Disposal.* Hearings before Subcommittee, 84th Cong., 1st sess., on S. 691. Washington: GPO, 1955. 260 + 128A p.

U. S. Tariff Commission. *Rubber.* War Changes in Industry Series, Report no. 6. Washington: Author, 1944. 102 p.

———. *Summaries of Tariff Information.* Washington: GPO, 1950. v. 16, pt. 3, *Free List,* natural rubber, pp. 117-148.

Wool

Benedict, Murray R., and Oscar C. Stine. *The Agricultural Commodity Programs: Two Decades of Experience.* New York: Twentieth Century Fund, 1956. Ch. 8, "Wool," pp. 329-367.

Blinken, Donald M. *Wool Tariffs and American Policy.* Washington: Public Affairs Press, 1948. 168 p.

"Brannan in Sheep's Clothing," *Economist,* v. 182 (January 5, 1957), pp. 33-34.

Evans, James G. "American Wool Import Policy," *Department of State Bulletin,* v. 15 (November 3, 1946), pp. 783-786.

Food and Agriculture Organization. *Natural and Man-made Fibers.* Commodity Series, Bulletin no. 26. Rome: Author, 1954. 83 p.

Great Britain. Commonwealth Economic Committee. *Wool Production and Trade, 1952-56.* London: HMSO, 1956.

Smith, Mark A. *The Tariff on Wool.* New York: Macmillan, 1926. 350 p.

Taussig, Frank W. *Some Aspects of the Tariff Question*. 2d ed. Cambridge: Harvard University Press, 1924. Ch. 19, "Wool," pp. 296-321.

U. S. Bureau of the Census. *Wool Consumption and Stocks*. Facts for Industry Series. Washington: Author, various years.

U. S. Congress. *Public Law* no. 690, 83rd Cong., 2d sess. (August 28, 1954). "Agricultural Act of 1954." Title VII, "National Wool Act of 1954."

U. S. Department of Agriculture. *Achieving a Sound Domestic Wool Industry*. A Report to the President from the Secretary of Agriculture. Washington: Author, 1953. 83 p.

———. *Wool Preparation and Marketing*. A Regional Report by a Technical Committee representing the Agricultural Experiment Stations of nine Western states in cooperation with the Wool Division, Production and Marketing Administration. Bulletin 316. Laramie, Wyoming: Agricultural Experiment Station of the University of Wyoming, 1952. 68 p.

———. Agricultural Marketing Service. *The Wool Situation*. Washington: Author, quarterly.

———. ———. *Wool Statistics and Related Data*. Washington: GPO, various years.

———. Production and Marketing Administration and Bureau of Agricultural Economics. *Domestic Wool Requirements and Sources of Supply*. Washington: Author, 1950. 103 p.

U. S. Department of Commerce. Business and Defense Services Administration. *Wool and Man-made Fibers in the United States*, by Henry A. Thurston. Washington: Author, 1956. 33 p.

U. S. House. Committee on Agriculture. *Agricultural Act of 1954*. Report no. 1927, 83rd Cong., 2d sess. Washington: GPO, 1954. 47 p.

———. ———. *Wool Program*. Hearings, 83rd Cong., 2d sess., on H. R. 7775. Washington: GPO, 1954. 101 p.

———. ———. Subcommittee on Livestock and Agriculture. *Extend National Wool Act of 1954*. Hearings, 85th Cong., 2d sess. Washington: GPO, 1958. 123 p.

U. S. President. "Policy on Wool Imports." Statement of March 4, 1954, in *Department of State Bulletin*, v. 30 (March 15, 1954), pp. 393-394.

U. S. Senate. *Increasing Domestic Wool Production*. 82d Cong., 2d sess., Senate Doc. no. 100. Washington: GPO, 1952. 12 p.

———. Committee on Agriculture and Forestry. *Foreign Trade in Agricultural Products*. Hearings, 83rd Cong., 1st sess. Washington: GPO, 1953. Pt. 3, pp. 367-546.

———. ———. *Wool Program*. Hearing, 83rd Cong., 2d sess., on S. 2911. Washington: GPO, 1954. 79 p.

U. S. Tariff Commission. *Memorandum for the Subcommittee on Customs, Tariffs, and Reciprocal Trade Agreements . . . on H. R. 12227 . . . A Bill "to Suspend for Three Years the Import Duties on Certain Coarse Wool and Hair."* Washington: Author, 1956. 15 p.

———. *Raw Wool*. War Changes in Industry Series, Report no. 1. Washington: Author, 1943. 20 p.

———. *Summaries of Tariff Information*. Washington: GPO, 1948. v. 11, pt. 1, *Raw Wool and Related Hair*. 46 p.

———. *Wool, Wool Tops, and Carbonized Wool*. Report to the President, Investigation no. 8 under Sec. 22 of the Agricultural Adjustment Act. Washington: Author, 1954. 75 p. + appendix.

V. COUNTRIES OR REGIONS

Asia

Allen, G. C., and Audrey G. Donnithorne. *Western Enterprise in Indonesia and Malaya.* London: Allen and Unwin, 1957. 321 p.

Bartlett, Vernon. *Report from Malaya.* New York: Criterion Books, 1955. 128 p.

Boeke, J. H. *Economics and Economic Policy of Dual Societies as Exemplified by Indonesia.* New York: Institute of Pacific Relations, 1953. 324 p.

Crozier, Brian. "The International Situation in Indochina," *Pacific Affairs,* v. 29, no. 4 (December 1956), pp. 309-323.

"The Danger from Djakarta," *Economist,* v. 70 (March 13, 1954), pp. 753-754.

Higgins, Benjamin. "Indonesia's Development Plans and Problems," *Pacific Affairs,* v. 29, no. 2 (June 1956), pp. 107-125.

———. *Indonesia's Economic Stabilization and Development.* New York: Institute of Pacific Relations, 1957. 179 p.

International Bank for Reconstruction and Development. *The Economic Development of Malaya.* Baltimore: Johns Hopkins Press, 1955. 707 p.

Purcell, Victor. *Malaya: Communist or Free?* Stanford: Stanford University Press, 1954. 288 p.

Robinson, J. B. Perry. *Transformation in Malaya.* London: Secker & Warburg, 1956. 232 p.

United Nations. Technical Assistance Administration. *Industrial Development in Indonesia,* prepared for the Government of Indonesia by J. E. Stepanek. New York: Author, 1955. 161 p.

U. S. Bureau of Foreign Commerce. *Investment in Indonesia.* Washington: GPO, 1956. 155 p.

U. S. Congress. *Report of a Special Study Mission to Southeast Asia and the Pacific.* 83rd Cong. Washington: GPO, 1954. 107 p.

U. S. Department of Commerce. *Investment in India.* Washington: GPO, 1953. 166 p.

U. S. Senate. Committee on Foreign Relations. Subcommittee on Technical Assistance Programs. *Economic Development in India and Communist China.* Staff Study no. 6. 84th Cong., 2d sess. Washington: GPO, 1956. 51 p.

Wertheim, W. F. *Indonesian Society in Transition.* The Hague: van Hoeve, 1956. 360 p.

Australia

Australia. Commonwealth Bureau of Census and Statistics. *Yearbook of the Commonwealth of Australia.* Canberra: Commonwealth Government Printer, various years.

Horsfall, J. C. *Australia.* New York: Praeger, 1955. 223 p.

U. S. Bureau of Foreign Commerce. *Investment in Australia.* Washington: GPO, 1956. 126 p.

Canada

Canada. Dominion Bureau of Statistics. *Canada 1957: Official Handbook of Present Conditions and Recent Progress.* Ottawa: Queen's Printer, 1957. Pp. 69-83.

———. ———. Mineral Statistics Section. *Canadian Mineral Statistics.* Ottawa: Queen's Printer, 1957. 120 p.

———. Royal Commission on Canada's Economic Prospects. *Canada-United States Economic Relations,* by Irving Brecher and S. S. Reisman. Ottawa: Queen's Printer, 1957. 344 p.

———. ———. *Preliminary Report.* Ottawa: Queen's Printer, 1956. 142 p.

Ferguson, G. V. "Likely Trends in Canadian-American Political Relations," *Canadian Journal of Economics and Political Science,* v. 22, no. 4 (November 1956), pp. 437-448.

Gibson, J. Douglas. "The Changing Influence of the United States on the Canadian Economy," *Canadian Journal of Economics and Political Science,* v. 22, no. 4 (November 1956), pp. 421-436.

———. "Economic Development and Policy in Canada," *Canadian Journal of Economics and Political Science,* v. 20, no. 2 (May 1954), pp. 439-455.

Kent, T. W. "The American Boom in Canada," *Conference Board Business Record,* v. 14, no. 3 (March 1957), pp. 135-142.

Scott, Anthony. "National Wealth and Natural Wealth," *Canadian Journal of Economics and Political Science,* v. 22, no. 3 (August 1956), pp. 373-378.

Latin America

International Bank for Reconstruction and Development. *The Economic Development of Mexico.* Report of the Combined Mexican Working Party. Baltimore: Johns Hopkins Press, 1953. 392 p.

Mikesell, Raymond F. *Foreign Investments in Latin America.* Economic Research Series, Inter-American Economic and Social Council, Organization of American States. Washington: Pan American Union, 1955. 141 p.

United Nations. Department of Economic and Social Affairs. *Foreign Capital in Latin America.* 1954.II.G.4. New York: Author, 1955. 164 p.

U. S. Bureau of Foreign Commerce. *Investment in Mexico.* Washington: GPO, 1955. 179 p.

———. *Investment in Peru.* Washington: GPO, 1957. 157 p.

U. S. Department of Commerce. *Investment in Venezuela.* Washington: GPO, 1953. 158 p.

———. *U. S. Investments in the Latin American Economy,* by Samuel Pizer and Frederick Cutler. Washington: GPO, 1957. 194 p.

U. S. Senate. Committee on Banking and Currency. *Study of Latin American Countries.* Report no. 1082, 83rd Cong., 2d sess. Washington: GPO, 1954. 648 p.

VI. RAW MATERIALS—GENERAL

Adams, Walter, and Horace M. Gray. *Monopoly in America: The Government as Promoter.* New York: Macmillan, 1956. 221 p.

American Metal Market. Daily newspaper.

American Metal Market. *Metal Statistics*. New York: Author, annual.

Aubrey, Henry G. *United States Imports and World Trade*. Oxford: Clarendon Press, 1957. 169 p.

Backman, Jules, and others. *War and Defense Economics*. New York: Rinehart, 1952. 458 p.

Bateman, Alan M. *Economic Mineral Deposits*. 2d ed. New York: Wiley, 1950. 916 p.

Bauer, Peter T., and Basil S. Yamey. *The Economics of Underdeveloped Countries*. Chicago: University of Chicago Press, 1957. 271 p.

Burgess, Eric. *Guided Missiles*. New York: Macmillan, 1957. 255 p.

Campbell, Robert F. *The History of Basic Metals: Price Control in World War II*. New York: Columbia University Press, 1948. 263 p.

Ciriacy-Wantrup, S. V. *Resource Conservation: Economics and Policies*. Berkeley and Los Angeles: University of California Press, 1952. 395 p.

Committee for Economic Development. *Problems of United States Economic Development*. New York: Author, 1958. 2 v.

Commodity Research Bureau, Inc. *Commodity Year Book*. New York: Author, annual.

Dennis, W. H. *Metallurgy of the Non-ferrous Metals*. London: Pitman, 1954. 647 p.

De Voto, Bernard A. *The Easy Chair*. New York: Houghton, 1955. 356 p.

Dewhurst, J. Frederic, and Associates. *America's Needs and Resources: A New Survey*. New York: Twentieth Century Fund, 1955. 1148 p.

Economist. Weekly journal.

Elliott, William Y., and others. *International Control in the Non-ferrous Metals*. New York: Macmillan, 1937. 801 p.

Emeny, Brooks. *The Strategy of Raw Materials*. New York: Macmillan, 1934. 202 p.

Engineering and Mining Journal. Monthly journal.

Engineering and Mining Journal Metal and Mineral Markets. Weekly journal.

Fleischmann, Manly. "An International Materials Policy," *Annals of the American Academy of Political and Social Science*, v. 282 (July 1952), pp. 31-35.

———. "An International Materials Policy for a Free World," *Department of State Bulletin*, v. 26 (February 25, 1952), pp. 297-302.

Gardner, Richard N. "Organizing World Trade — A Challenge for American Lawyers," *The Record* (of the Association of the Bar of the City of New York), v. 12, no. 4 (April 1957), pp. 202-226.

Gottmann, J. *Les Marchés des Matières Premières*. Paris: Armand Colin, 1957. 435 p.

Gray, Gordon. *Report to the President on Foreign Economic Policies*. Washington: GPO, 1950. 131 p.

Hall, H. Duncan. *North American Supply*. London: HMSO, 1955. 559 p.

———, and C. C. Wrigley. *Studies of Overseas Supply*. London: HMSO, 1956. 537 p.

Harris, Seymour E. *The Economics of Mobilization and Inflation*. New York: Norton, 1951. 308 p.

Hickey, John. "The Economics of Self-Pity," *Inter-American Economic Affairs*, v. 10, no. 1 (Summer 1956), pp. 26-46.

Humphrey, Don D. *American Imports.* New York: Twentieth Century Fund, 1955. 546 p.

Hurstfield, J. *The Control of Raw Materials: History of the Second World War.* London: HMSO and Longmans, 1953. 530 p.

International Commodity Position. Monthly review, prepared by H. Heymann for the Bank for International Settlements.

International Materials Conference. *Report on Operations.* Washington: Author. First report (1952), 91 p.; second report (1953), 54 p.; final report (1953), 16 p.

Leith, C. K. "Exploitation and World Progress," *Foreign Affairs,* v. 6, no. 1 (October 1927), pp. 128-139.

———. "The Political Control of Mineral Resources," *Foreign Affairs,* v. 3, no. 4 (July 1925), pp. 541-555.

———, H. Foster Bain and S. M. Marshall. *Elements of a National Mineral Policy.* New York: Mineral Inquiry, 1933. 162 p.

Liebhafsky, H. H. "The International Materials Conference in Retrospect," *Quarterly Journal of Economics,* v. 71, no. 2 (May 1957), pp. 267-288.

Livermore, Shaw. "International Control of Raw Materials," *Annals of the American Academy of Political and Social Science,* v. 278 (November 1951), pp. 157-165.

Lovasy, Gertrud. "Prices of Raw Materials in the 1953-54 U. S. Recession," *Staff Papers* (of the International Monetary Fund), v. 5, no. 1 (February 1956), pp. 47-73.

Mason, Edward S. "American Security and Access to Raw Materials," *World Politics,* v. 1, no. 2 (January 1949), pp. 147-160.

———. *Economic Concentration and the Monopoly Problem.* Cambridge: Harvard University Press, 1957. 411 p.

———. "Raw Materials, Rearmament, and Economic Development," *Quarterly Journal of Economics,* v. 66, no. 3 (August 1952), pp. 327-341.

Meyerhoff, Howard A. "What Is Involved in Metals Conservation Today?" *Annals of the American Academy of Political and Social Science,* v. 281 (May 1952), pp. 33-41.

Mid-Century Conference on Resources for the Future. *The Nation Looks at Its Resources.* Washington: Author, 1953. 418 p.

Millikan, Max F., and W. W. Rostow. *A Proposal: Key to An Effective Foreign Policy.* New York: Harper, 1957. 170 p.

Mineral Trade Notes. Monthly journal, by the U. S. Bureau of Mines.

Model, Roland & Stone. "The Paley Report: Four Years Later," *Quarterly Review and Investment Survey,* v. 10, no. 2 (2d Quarter 1956), pp. 1-9.

Myrdal, Gunnar. *Rich Lands and Poor: The Road to World Prosperity.* New York: Harper, 1957. 168 p.

Orchard, John E. "Strategic Materials: Procurement and Allocation." In *Mobilizing American Power for Defense,* Proceedings of the Academy of Political Science, v. 24, no. 3 (May 1951), pp. 19-40.

Pehrson, Elmer W. "Our Mineral Resources and Security," *Foreign Affairs,* v. 23, no. 4 (July 1945), pp. 644-657.

Rosen, S. McKee. *The Combined Boards of the Second World War: An Experiment in International Administration.* New York: Columbia University Press, 1951. 288 p.

Schurr, Sam H., and Jacob Marshak. *Economic Aspects of Atomic Power.* Princeton: Princeton University Press, 1950. 289 p.

Shimkin, Demitri B. *Minerals: A Key to Soviet Power.* Cambridge: Harvard University Press, 1953. 452 p.

Staley, Eugene. *The Future of Underdeveloped Countries.* New York: Harper, for the Council on Foreign Relations, 1954. Ch. 15, "Raw Materials and Industrialization," pp. 286-311.

Thorp, Willard L. "The New International Economic Challenge," *Department of State Bulletin,* v. 25 (August 13, 1951), pp. 245-250.

United Nations. Department of Economic Affairs. *Development of Mineral Resources in Asia and the Far East.* 1953.II.F.5. Bangkok: Author, 1953. 366 p.

———. ———. *Instability in Export Markets of Under-developed Countries, in Relation to Their Ability to Obtain Foreign Exchange from Exports of Primary Commodities, 1901-1950.* 1952.II.A.1. New York: Columbia University Press, 1952. 94 p.

U. S. Bureau of the Census. *Raw Materials in the United States Economy,* by Vivian E. Spencer and Charles A. R. Wardwell. Bureau of the Census Working Paper no. 1. Washington: Author, 1954.

———. *United States Exports of Domestic and Foreign Merchandise.* Report no. FT 410. Washington: GPO, annual.

———. *United States Imports of Merchandise for Consumption.* Report no. FT 110. Washington: GPO, annual.

U. S. Bureau of Foreign Commerce. *Contribution of Imports to U. S. Raw Material Supplies, 1955,* by Muriel S. Moore. World Trade Information Service, Pt. 3, no. 57-1. Washington: GPO, 1957. 8 p.

———. *Foreign Trade of . . .* [various countries]. World Trade Information Service, Pt. 3. Washington: GPO, various years.

U. S. Bureau of Mines. *Mineral Facts and Problems.* Bulletin 556. Washington: GPO, 1956. 1042 p.

———. "Mineral Market Reports," *Mineral Industry Surveys.* Washington: Author, various years.

———. *Minerals Yearbook.* Washington: GPO, annual.

U. S. Civilian Production Administration. *Industrial Mobilization for War.* Washington: GPO, 1947. v. 1, *Program and Administration,* 1010 p.

U. S. Commission on Foreign Economic Policy. *Report to the President and the Congress.* Washington: GPO, 1954. 94 p.

———. *Staff Papers.* Washington: GPO, 1954. 531 p.

U. S. Congress. Joint Committee on Defense Production. *Annual Report.* Washington: GPO, various years.

———. Joint Committee on Foreign Economic Cooperation. *ECA and Strategic Materials.* Senate Report no. 140, 81st Cong., 1st sess. Washington: GPO, 1949. 56 p.

U. S. Defense Production Administration. *Raw Materials Imports: Area of Growing Dependency.* Washington: Author, 1953. 2 pts., 15 p.

U. S. Department of Commerce. *Factors Limiting U. S. Investment Abroad.* Washington: GPO, 1953, 1954. Pt. 1, 132 p.; pt. 2, 59 p.

U. S. Department of the Interior. *Long-range Minerals Program,* presented by Secretary of the Interior Fred A. Seaton. Washington: Author, 1957. 28 p.

U. S. Export-Import Bank of Washington. *Report to the Congress.* Washington: GPO, semiannual.

U. S. House. Committee on Banking and Currency. *Defense Production Act of 1950.* Hearings, 81st Cong., 2d sess., on H. R. 9176. Washington: GPO, 1950. 130 p.

———. ———. *Defense Production Act—1956.* Hearings, 84th Cong., 2d sess., on H. R. 9852. Washington: GPO, 1956. 196 p.

———. Committee on Ways and Means. *Trade Agreements Extension.* Hearings, 84th Cong., 1st sess., on H. R. 1. Washington: GPO, 1955. 2 pts., 2601 p.

———. ———. Subcommittee on Foreign Trade Policy. *Foreign Trade Policy.* Compendium of papers collected by the staff. Washington: GPO, 1957. 1157 p.

———. ———. ———. *Foreign Trade Policy.* Hearings, 85th Cong., 1st sess., pursuant to H. Res. 104. Washington: GPO, 1958. 865 p.

U. S. International Development Advisory Board. *Partners in Progress.* Washington: GPO, 1951. 120 p.

U. S. Office of Defense Mobilization. *Defense Mobilization in a Full Economy.* Report to the Joint Committee on Defense Production. Washington: Author, 1957. 32 p.

U. S. President's Cabinet Committee on Minerals Policy. *Report.* Washington: Author, 1954. 18 p.

U. S. President's Materials Policy Commission. *Resources for Freedom.* Washington: GPO, 1952. v. 1, *Foundations for Growth and Security,* 184 p.; v. 2, *The Outlook for Key Commodities,* 210 p.; v. 3, *The Outlook for Energy Sources,* 43 p.; v. 4, *The Promise of Technology,* 228 p.; v. 5, *Selected Reports to the Commission,* 154 p.

U. S. Senate. Committee on Agriculture and Forestry. *Disposal of Agricultural Surpluses—General.* Hearings before Subcommittee, 84th Cong., 1st sess. Washington: GPO, 1955. 844 p.

———. Committee on Banking and Currency. *Defense Production Act of 1950.* Hearings, 81st Cong., 2d sess., on S. 3936. Washington: GPO, 1950. 329 p.

———. ———. *Defense Production Act Amendments of 1956.* Hearings before Subcommittee, 84th Cong., 2d sess., on S. 3407. Washington: GPO, 1956. 293 p.

———. ———. *Defense Production Act Amendments of 1956.* Report no. 2237, 84th Cong., 2d sess. Washington: GPO, 1956. 28 p.

———. Committee on Finance. *Trade Agreements Extension.* Hearings, 84th Cong., 1st sess., on H. R. 1. Washington: GPO, 1955. 4 pts., 2352 p.

———. Committee on Interior and Insular Affairs. *National Resources Policy.* Hearings, 81st Cong., 1st sess. Washington: GPO, 1949. 470 p.

———. ———. Subcommittee on Minerals, Materials and Fuels. *Long-range Minerals Program.* Hearings, 85th Cong., 1st sess. Washington: GPO, 1957. 2 pts., 258 p.

———. ———. Subcommittee on Minerals, Materials and Fuels Economics. *Critical Materials: Factors Affecting Self-sufficiency within Nations of the Western Hemisphere.* Senate Doc. no. 83, 84th Cong., 1st sess., pursuant to S. Res. 271 (83rd Cong.), Supplement to Senate Report 1627 (83rd Cong.). Washington: GPO, 1955. 619 p.

U. S. Senate. Committee on Public Lands. *Investigation of National Resources.* Hearings before Subcommittee, 80th Cong., 1st sess. Washington: GPO, 1947. 338 p.

————. Special Committee to Study the Foreign Aid Program. *Foreign Aid Program.* 85th Cong., 1st sess. Washington: GPO, 1957.

American Enterprise Association, Inc. *American Private Enterprise, Foreign Economic Development, and the Aid Programs.* Study no. 7, 68 p.

Massachusetts Institute of Technology Center for International Studies. *The Objectives of United States Economic Assistance Programs.* Study no. 1, 73 p.

National Planning Association. *Agricultural Surplus Disposal and Foreign Aid.* Study no. 5, 41 p.

Voskuil, Walter H. *Minerals in World Industry.* New York: McGraw-Hill, 1955. 324 p.

Wallace, Donald H. *Economic Controls and Defense.* New York: Twentieth Century Fund, 1953. 260 p.

Watkins, Myron W. "Scarce Raw Materials: An Analysis and a Proposal," *American Economic Review,* v. 34, no. 2 (June 1944), pp. 227-260.

Wilcox, Clair. *Public Policies toward Business.* Chicago: Irwin, 1955. 898 p.

INDEX